High School Prodigies Have It Easy Even in Another World!

10

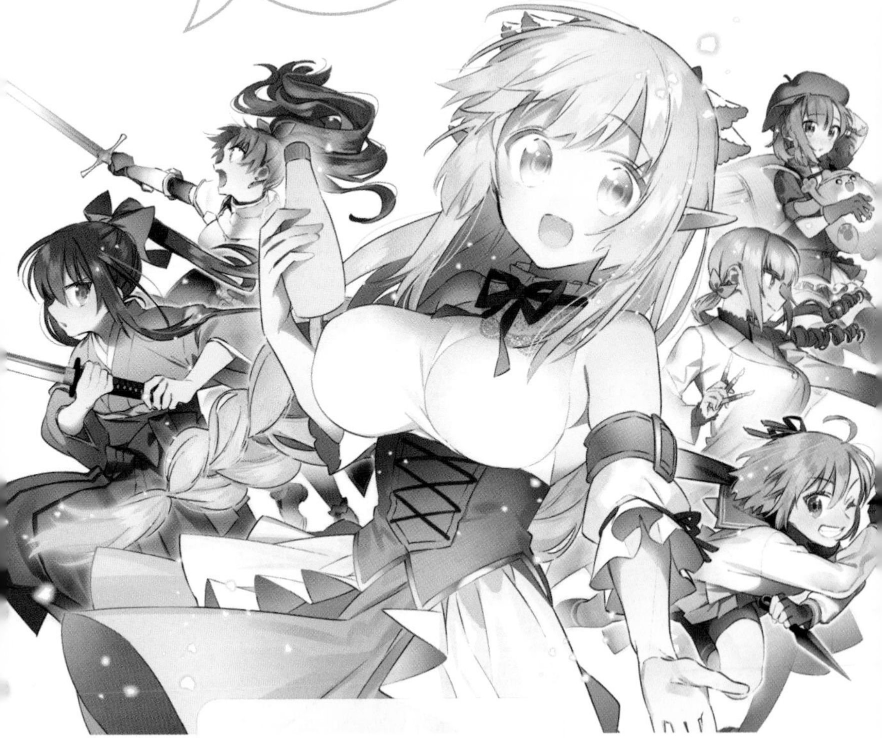

STORY BY
Riku Mis

ART BY
Kotaro Ya

CHARACTER DESIGN BY
Sacraneco

contents

HIGH SCHOOL
PRODIGIES HAVE
IT EASY EVEN IN
ANOTHER WORLD!

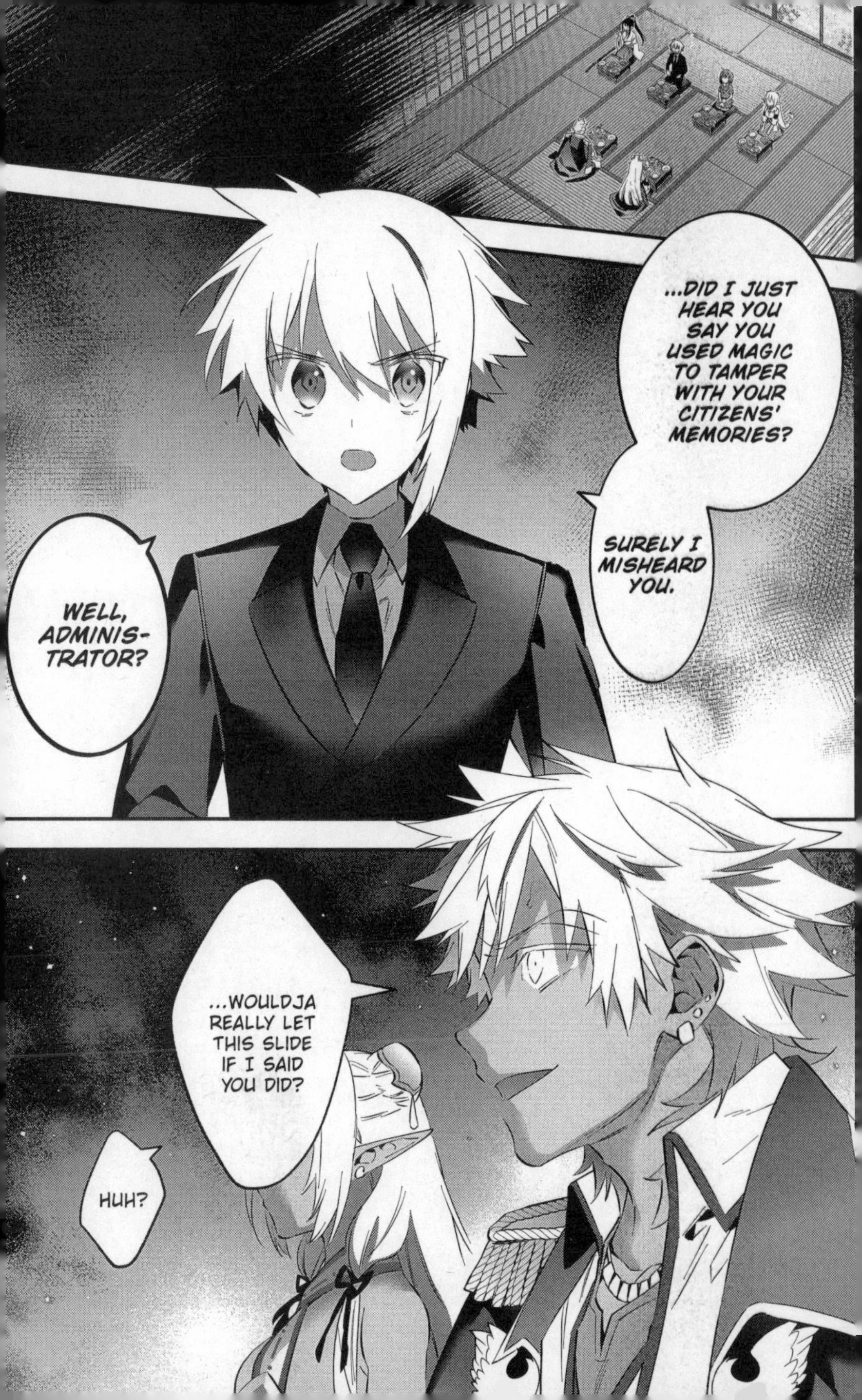
...DID I JUST HEAR YOU SAY YOU USED MAGIC TO TAMPER WITH YOUR CITIZENS' MEMORIES?
SURELY I MISHEARD YOU.
WELL, ADMINISTRATOR?
...WOULDJA REALLY LET THIS SLIDE IF I SAID YOU DID?
HUH?

CHAPTER 70: MECHANISM BEHIND THE MIRACLE

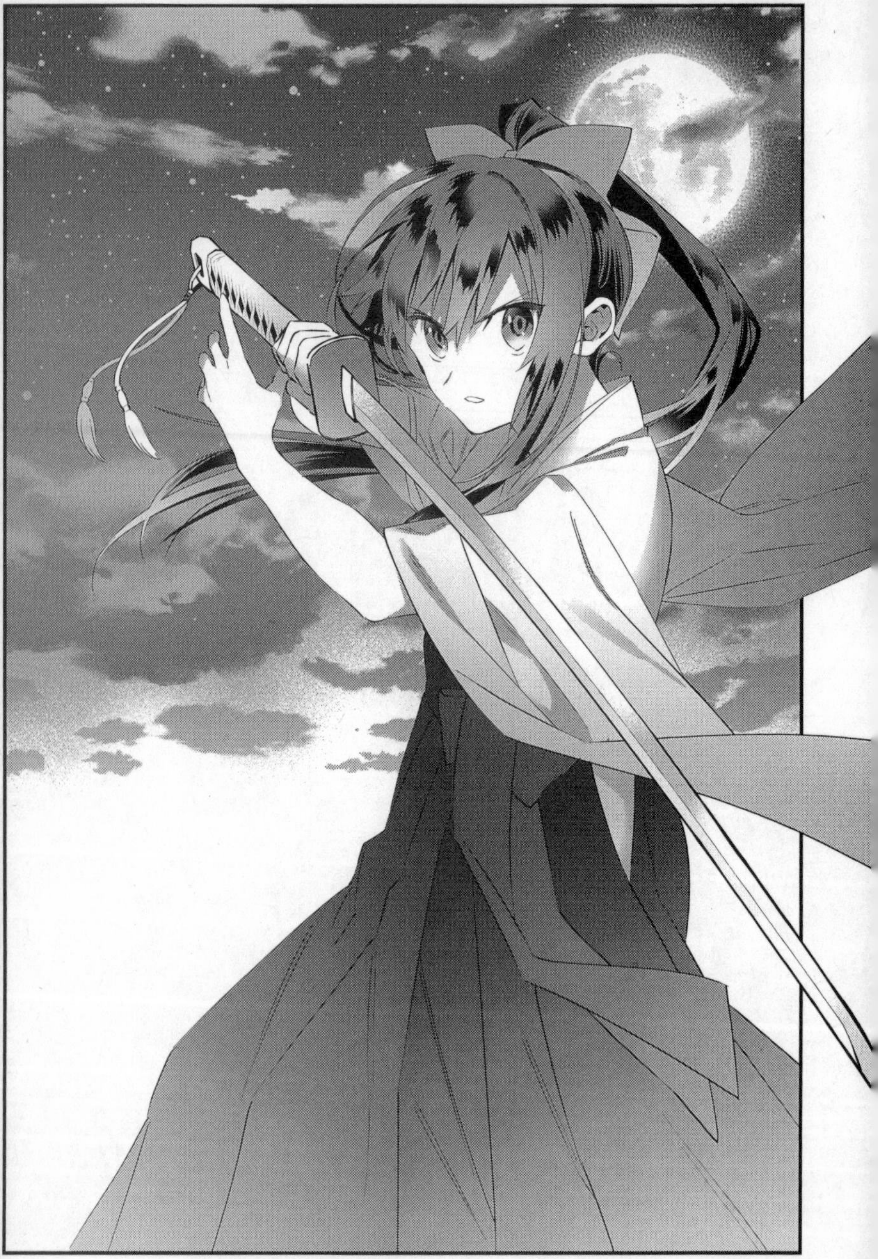

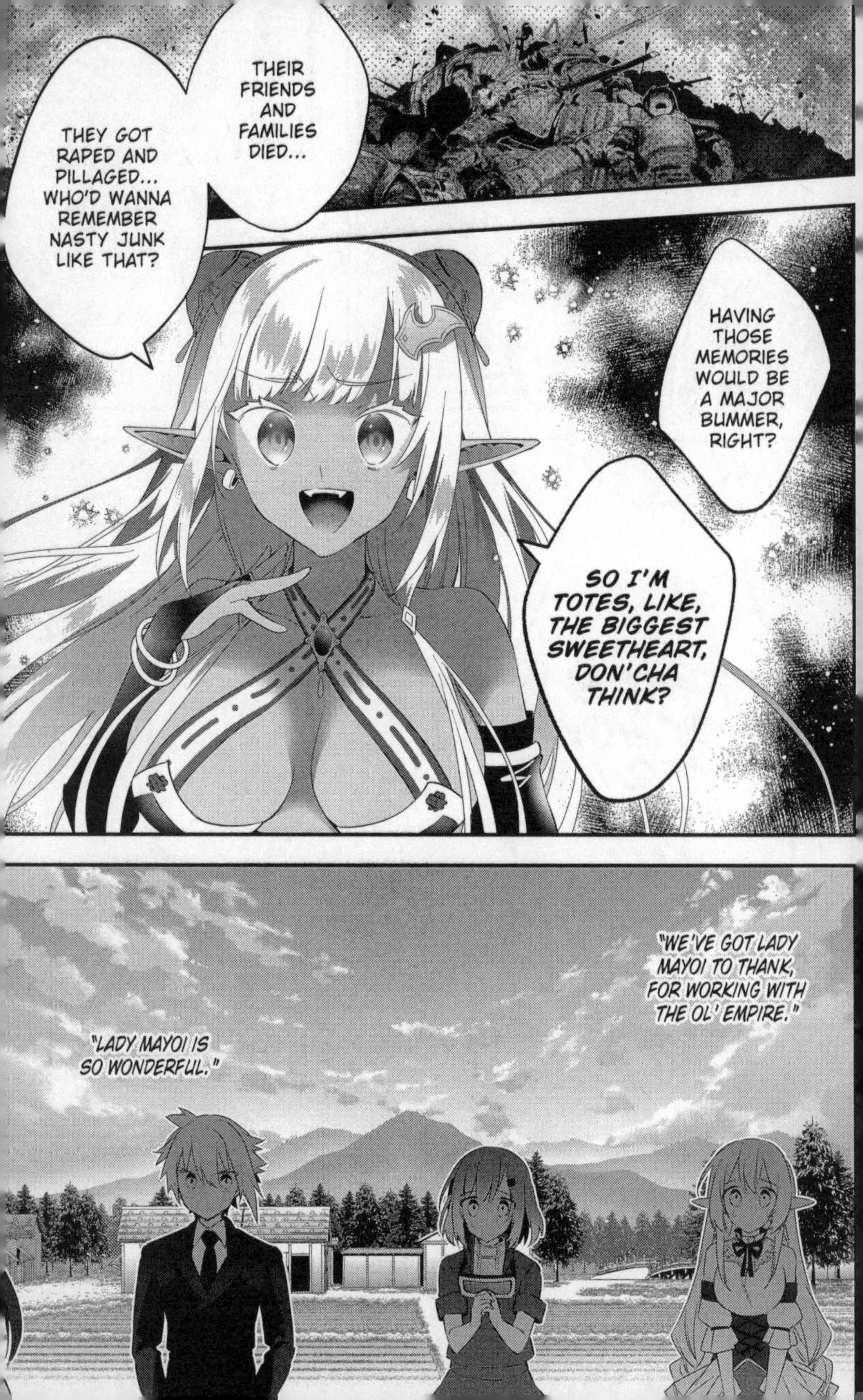
THEIR FRIENDS AND FAMILIES DIED...
THEY GOT RAPED AND PILLAGED... WHO'D WANNA REMEMBER NASTY JUNK LIKE THAT?
HAVING THOSE MEMORIES WOULD BE A MAJOR BUMMER, RIGHT?
SO I'M TOTES, LIKE, THE BIGGEST SWEETHEART, DON'CHA THINK?
"WE'VE GOT LADY MAYOI TO THANK, FOR WORKING WITH THE OL' EMPIRE."
"LADY MAYOI IS SO WONDERFUL."

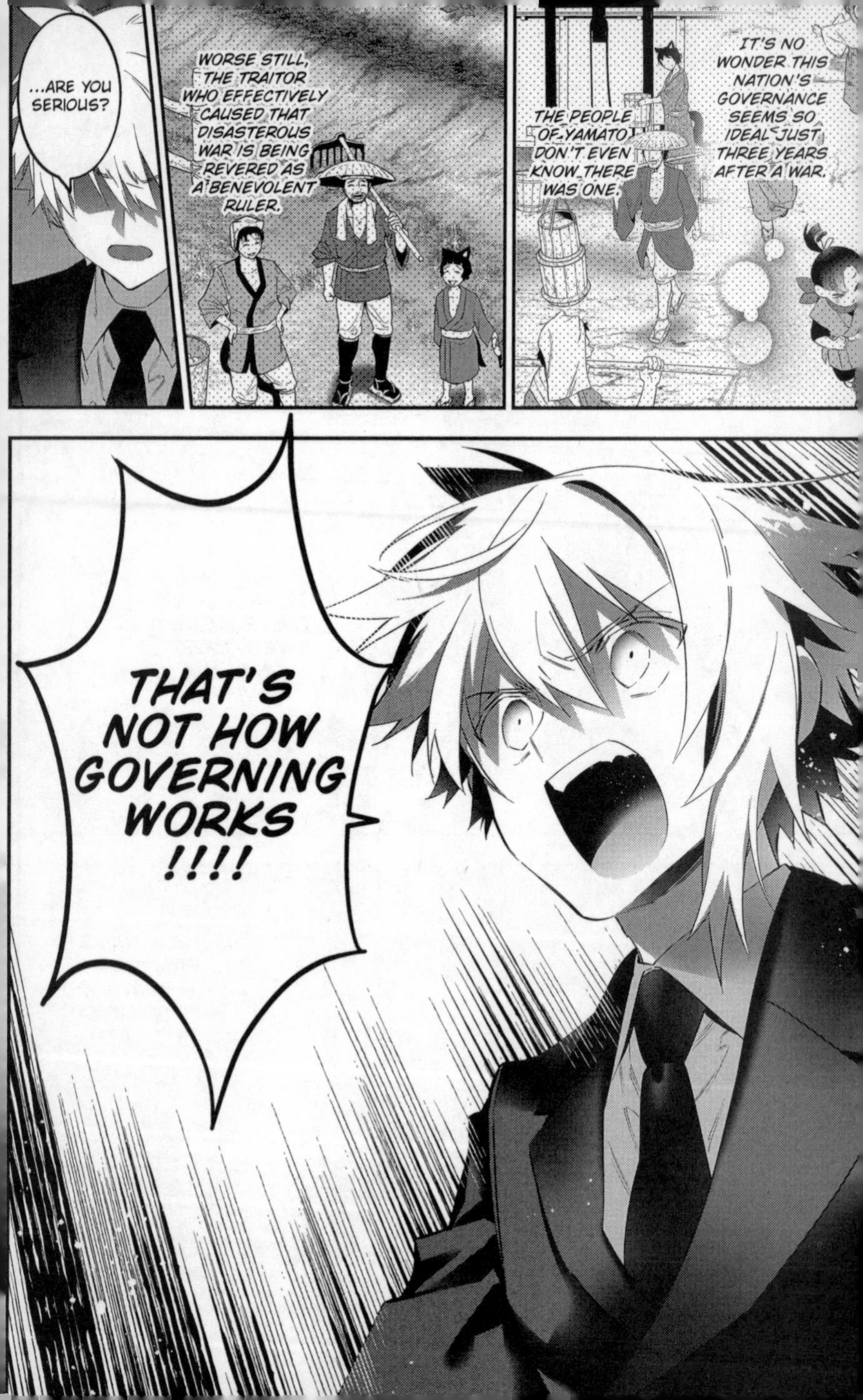
IT'S NO WONDER THIS NATION'S GOVERNANCE SEEMS SO IDEAL JUST THREE YEARS AFTER A WAR.
THE PEOPLE OF YAMATO DON'T EVEN KNOW THERE WAS ONE.
WORSE STILL, THE TRAITOR WHO EFFECTIVELY CAUSED THAT DISASTEROUS WAR IS BEING REVERED AS A BENEVOLENT RULER.
...ARE YOU SERIOUS?
THAT'S NOT HOW GOVERNING WORKS !!!!

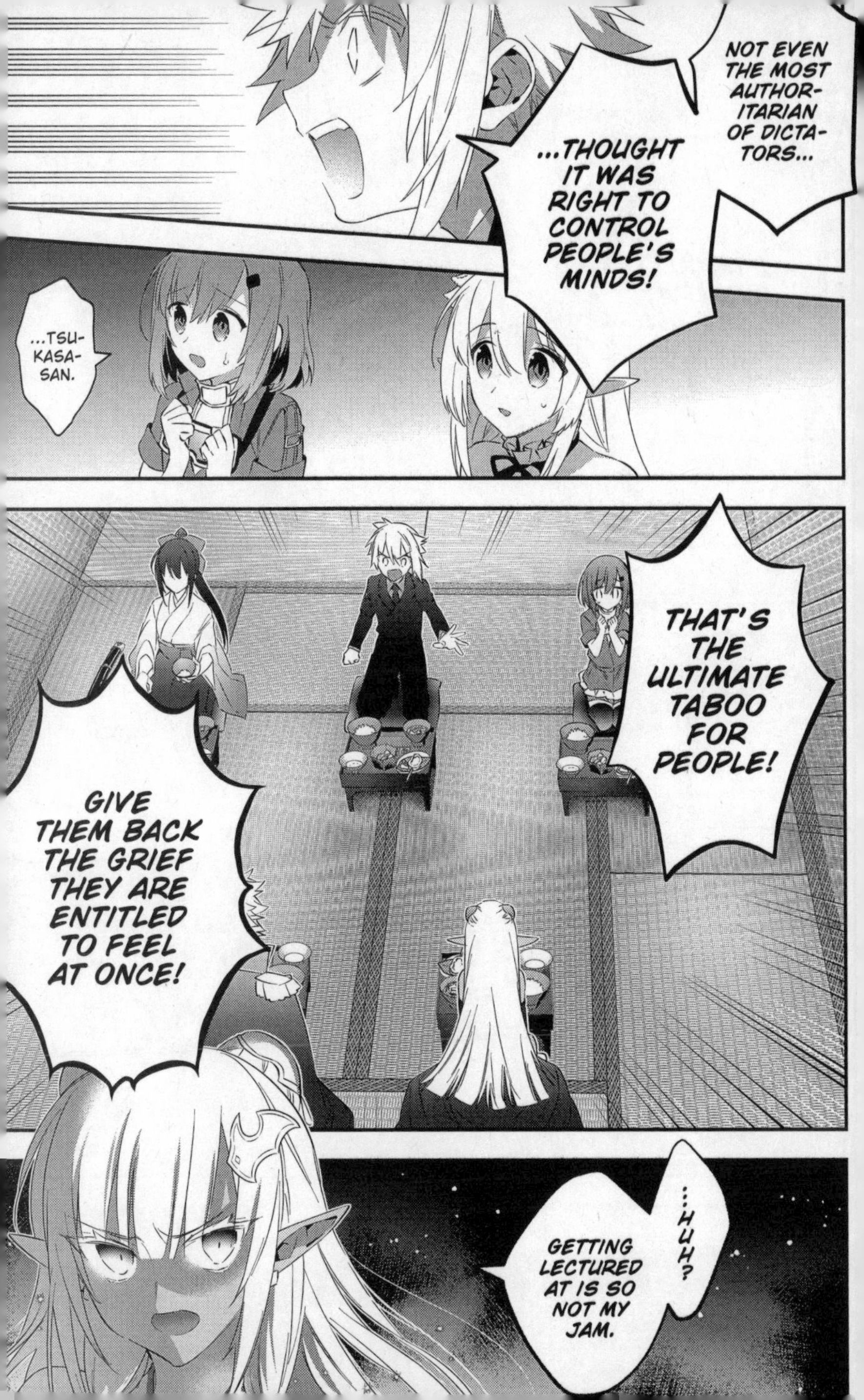
NOT EVEN THE MOST AUTHOR-ITARIAN OF DICTA-TORS...
...THOUGHT IT WAS RIGHT TO CONTROL PEOPLE'S MINDS!
...TSU-KASA-SAN.
THAT'S THE ULTIMATE TABOO FOR PEOPLE!
GIVE THEM BACK THE GRIEF THEY ARE ENTITLED TO FEEL AT ONCE!
...HUH?
GETTING LECTURED AT IS SO NOT MY JAM.

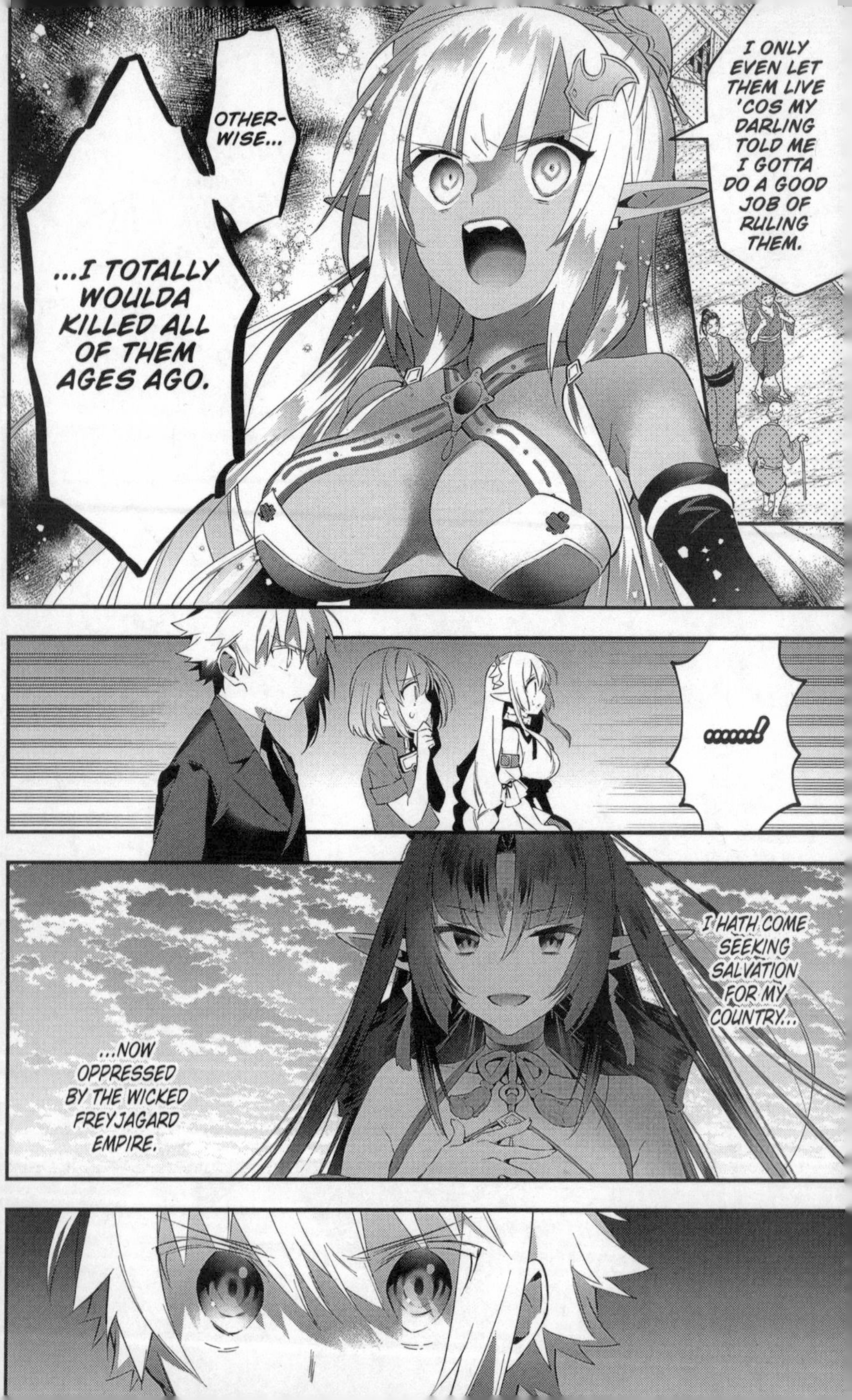
I ONLY EVEN LET THEM LIVE 'COS MY DARLING TOLD ME I GOTTA DO A GOOD JOB OF RULING THEM.
OTHER-WISE...
...I TOTALLY WOULDA KILLED ALL OF THEM AGES AGO.
......!
I HATH COME SEEKING SALVATION FOR MY COUNTRY...
...NOW OPPRESSED BY THE WICKED FREYJAGARD EMPIRE.

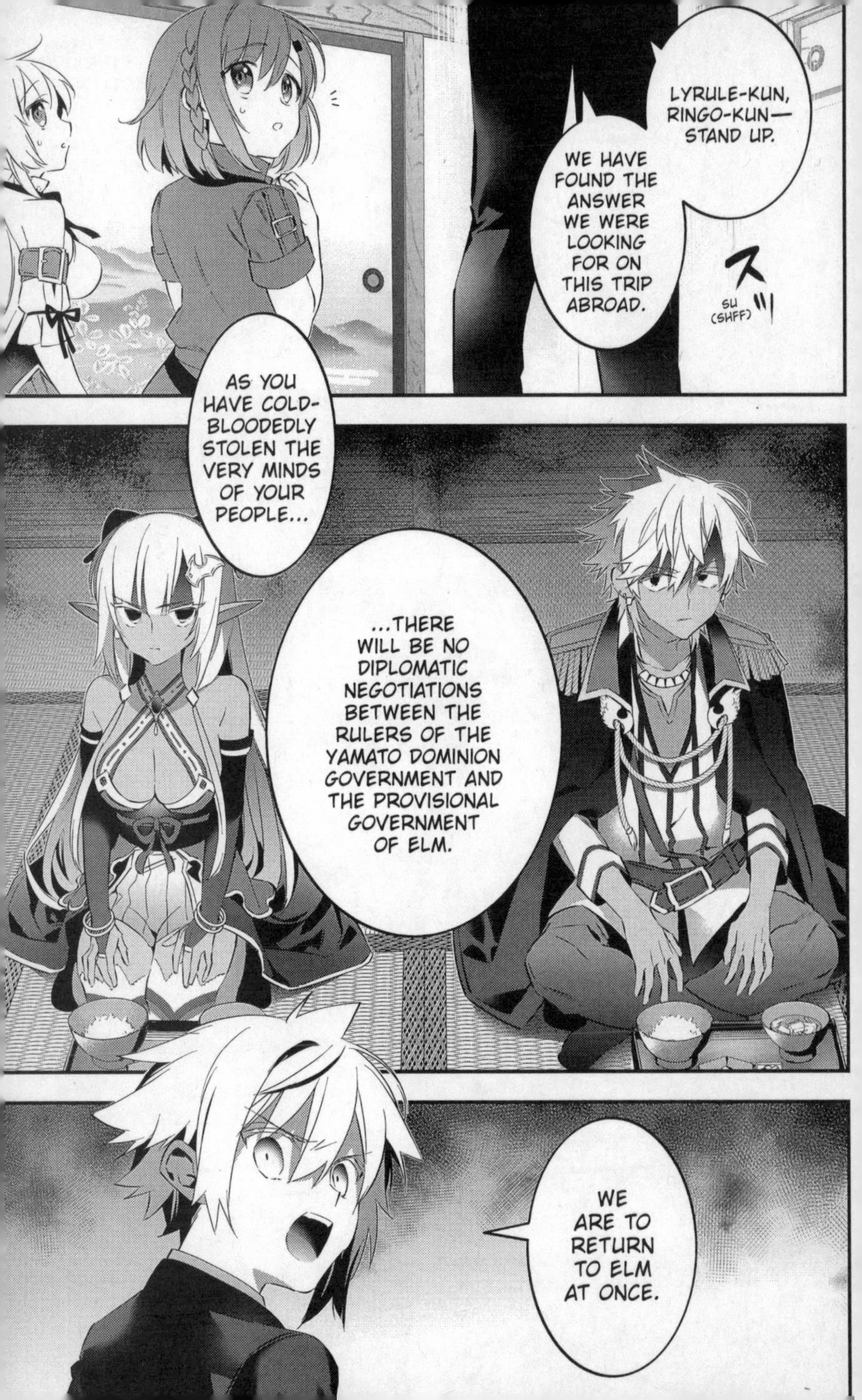
LYRULE-KUN, RINGO-KUN— STAND UP.
WE HAVE FOUND THE ANSWER WE WERE LOOKING FOR ON THIS TRIP ABROAD.
ス
SU (SHFF)
AS YOU HAVE COLD-BLOODEDLY STOLEN THE VERY MINDS OF YOUR PEOPLE...
...THERE WILL BE NO DIPLOMATIC NEGOTIATIONS BETWEEN THE RULERS OF THE YAMATO DOMINION GOVERNMENT AND THE PROVISIONAL GOVERNMENT OF ELM.
WE ARE TO RETURN TO ELM AT ONCE.

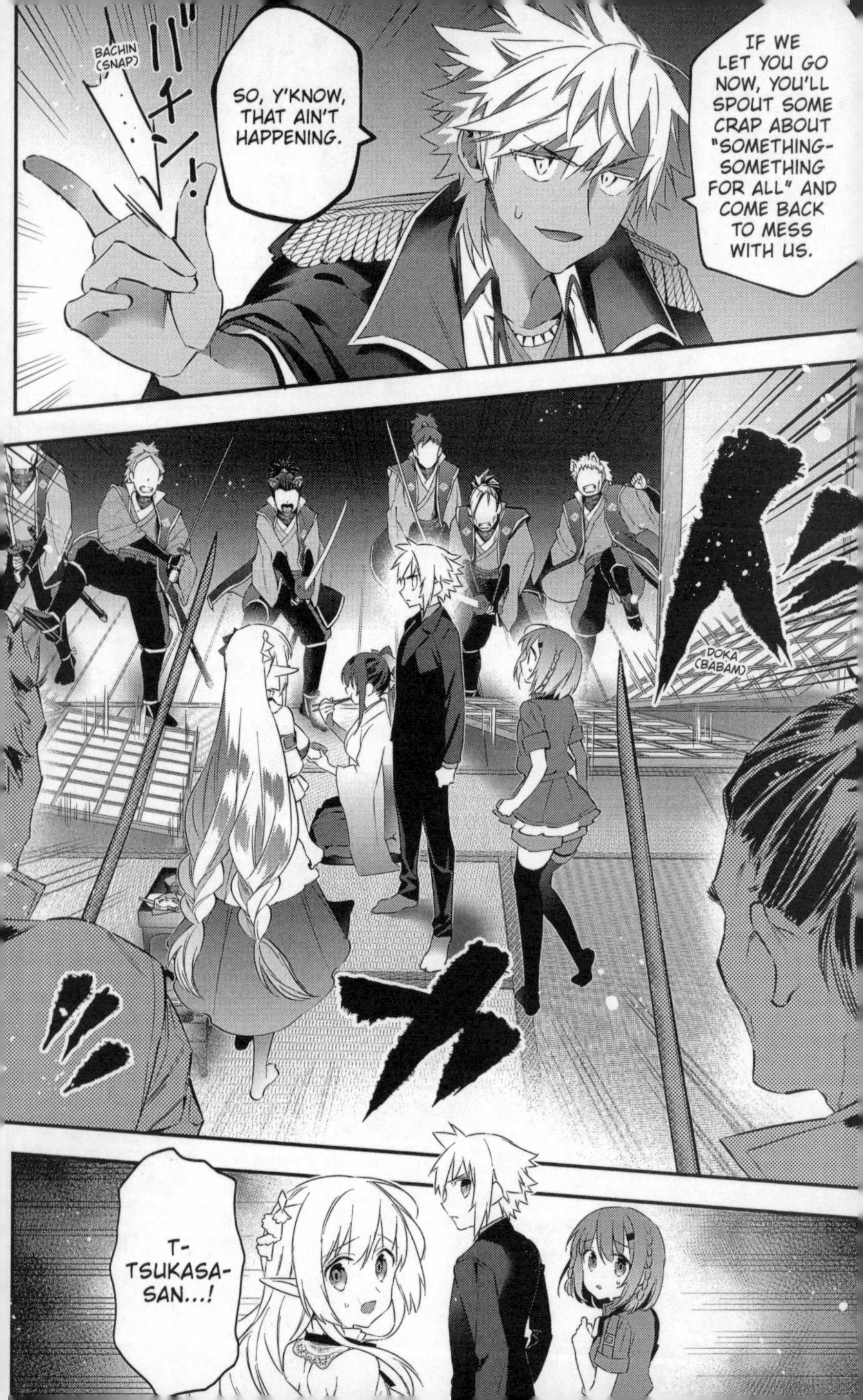
IF WE LET YOU GO NOW, YOU'LL SPOUT SOME CRAP ABOUT "SOMETHING-SOMETHING FOR ALL" AND COME BACK TO MESS WITH US.
SO, Y'KNOW, THAT AIN'T HAPPENING.
BACHIN (SNAP)
DOKA (BABAM)
T-TSUKASA-SAN...!

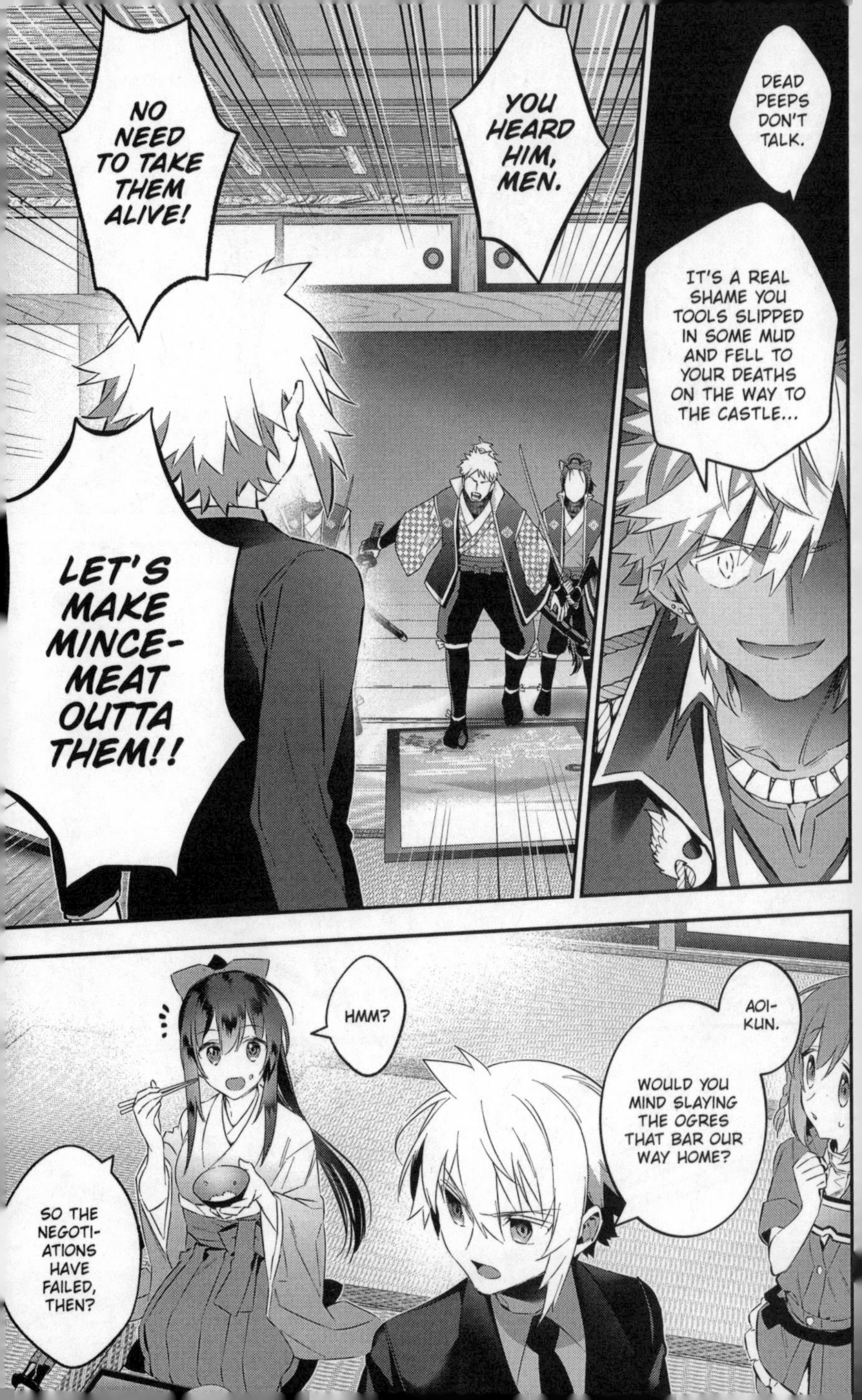
DEAD PEEPS DON'T TALK.
IT'S A REAL SHAME YOU TOOLS SLIPPED IN SOME MUD AND FELL TO YOUR DEATHS ON THE WAY TO THE CASTLE...
YOU HEARD HIM, MEN.
NO NEED TO TAKE THEM ALIVE!
LET'S MAKE MINCE-MEAT OUTTA THEM!!
AOI-KUN.
WOULD YOU MIND SLAYING THE OGRES THAT BAR OUR WAY HOME?
HMM?
SO THE NEGOTI-ATIONS HAVE FAILED, THEN?

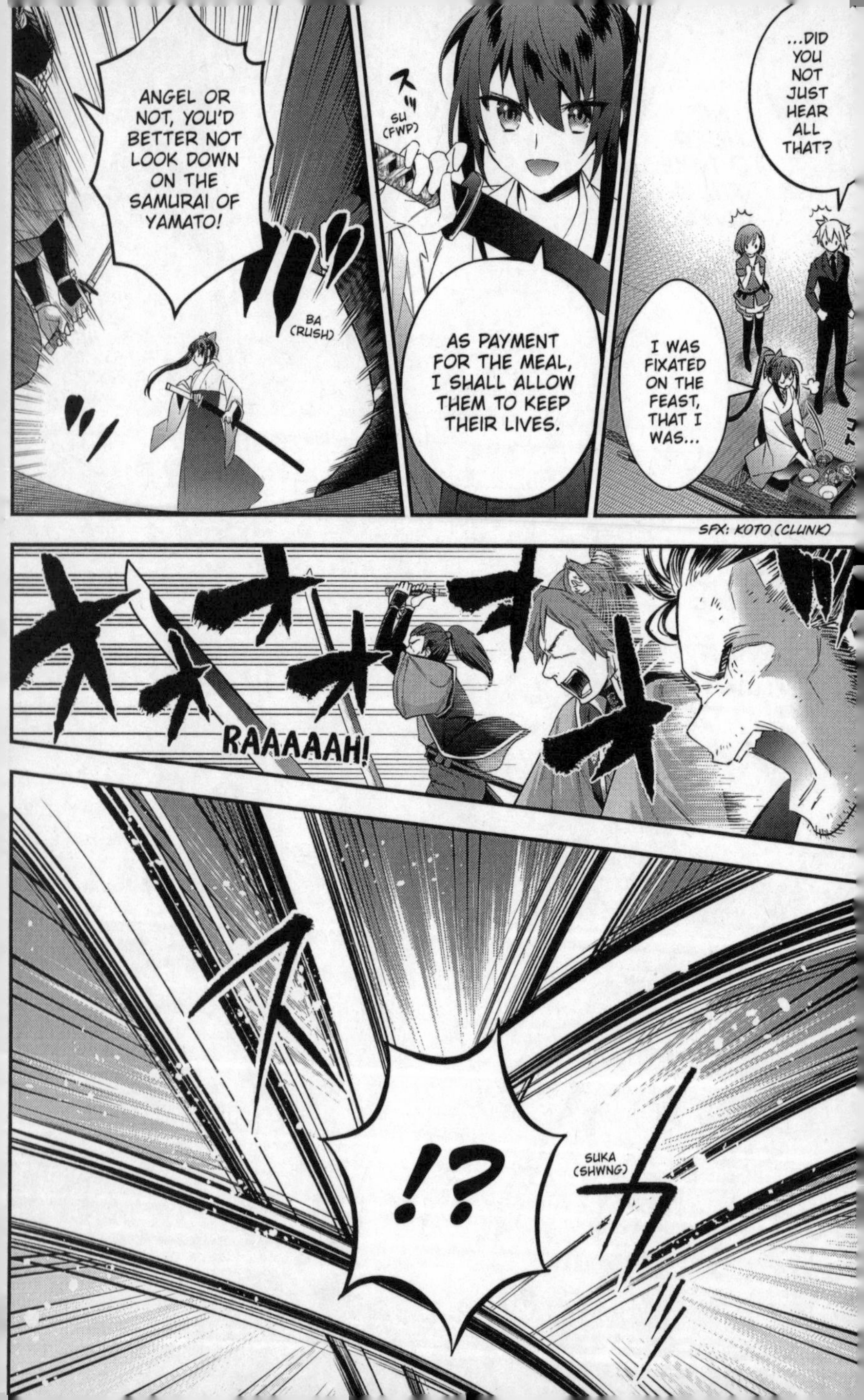
...DID YOU NOT JUST HEAR ALL THAT?
I WAS FIXATED ON THE FEAST, THAT I WAS...
SFX: KOTO (CLUNK)
SU (FWP)
AS PAYMENT FOR THE MEAL, I SHALL ALLOW THEM TO KEEP THEIR LIVES.
ANGEL OR NOT, YOU'D BETTER NOT LOOK DOWN ON THE SAMURAI OF YAMATO!
BA (RUSH)
RAAAAAH!
SUKA (SHWNG)
!?

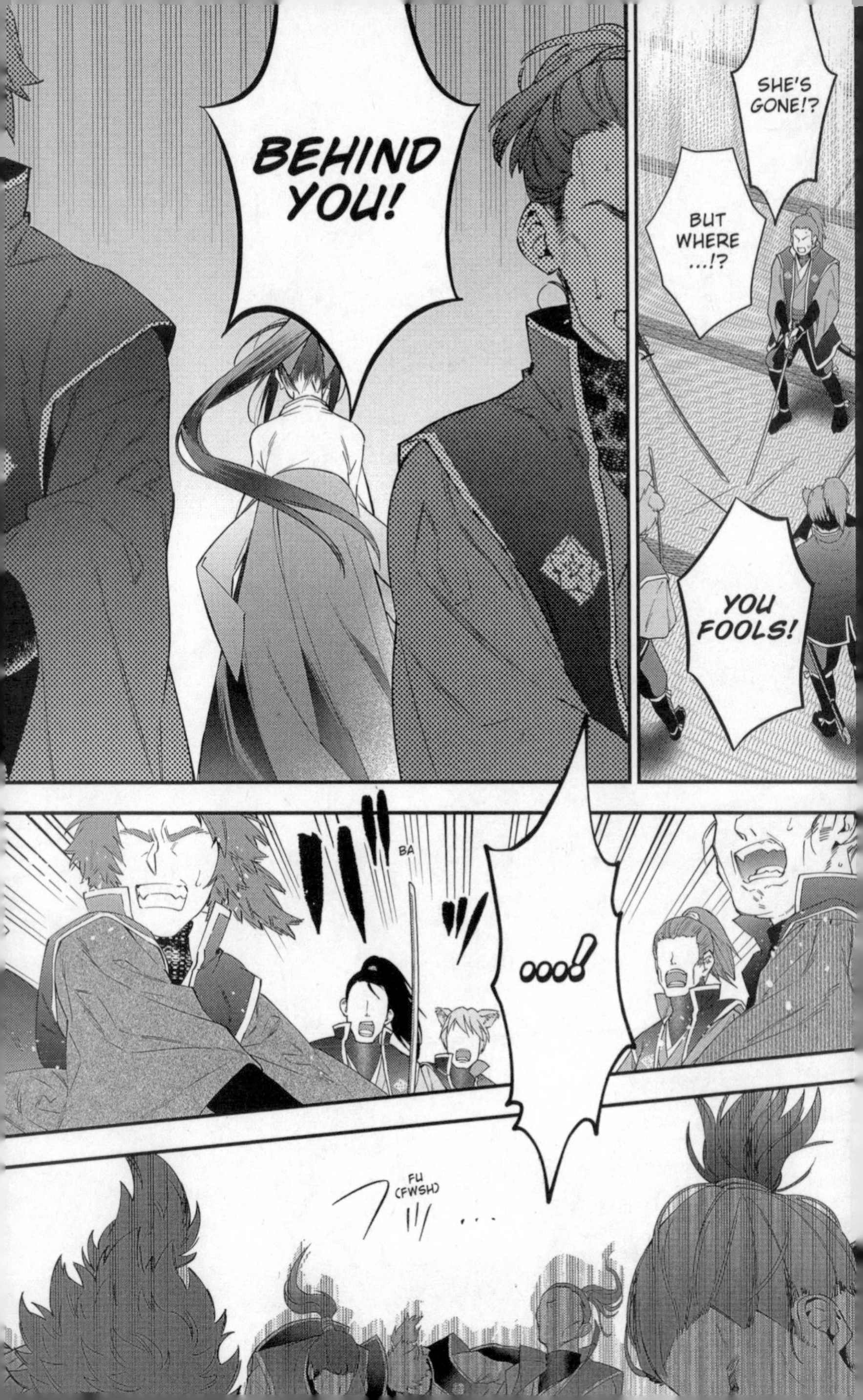
SHE'S GONE!?
BUT WHERE ...!?
YOU FOOLS!
BEHIND YOU!
ooo!
BA
FU (FWSH)
...

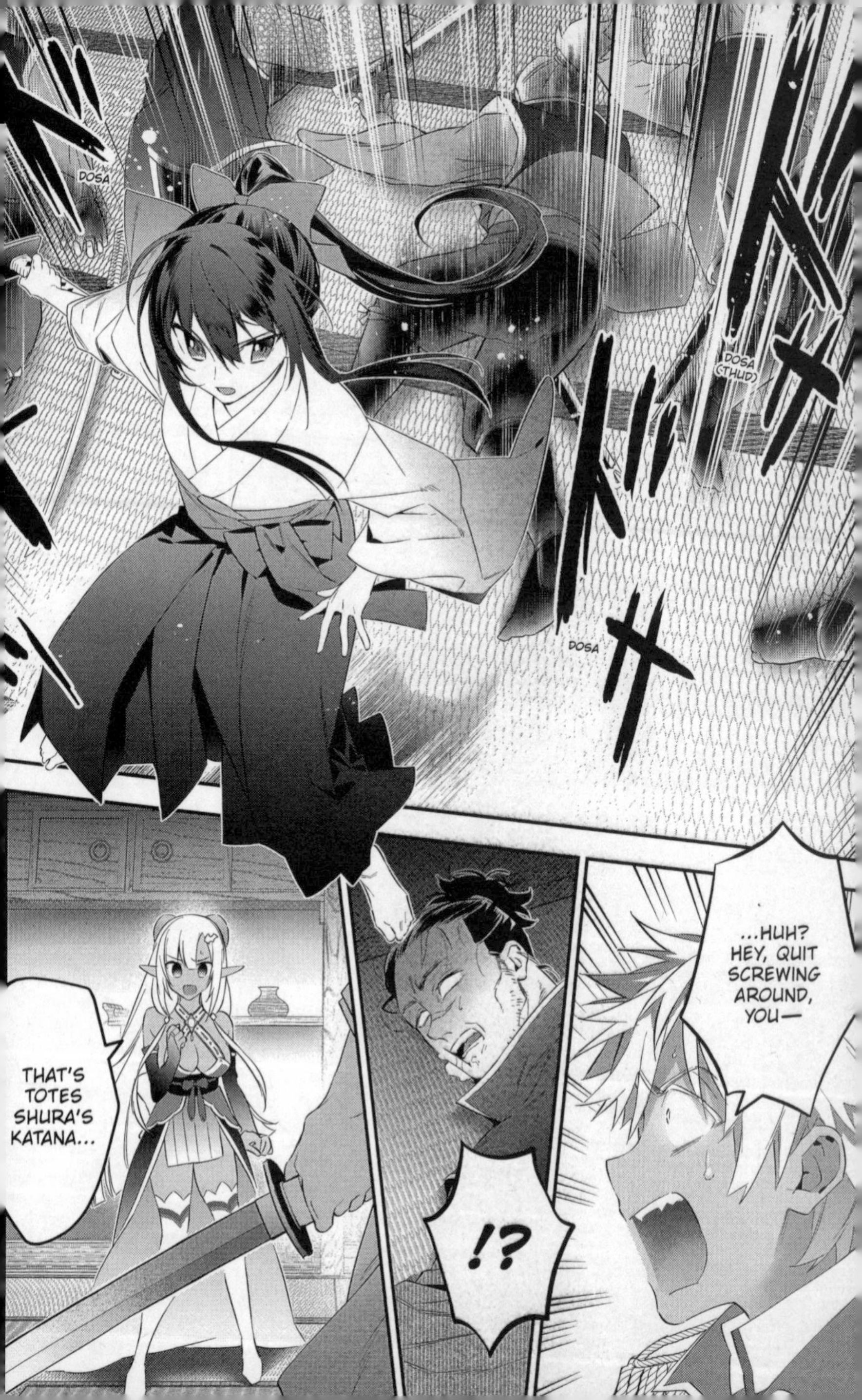
DOSA
(THUD)
DOSA
DOSA
...HUH? HEY, QUIT SCREWING AROUND, YOU—
!?
THAT'S TOTES SHURA'S KATANA...

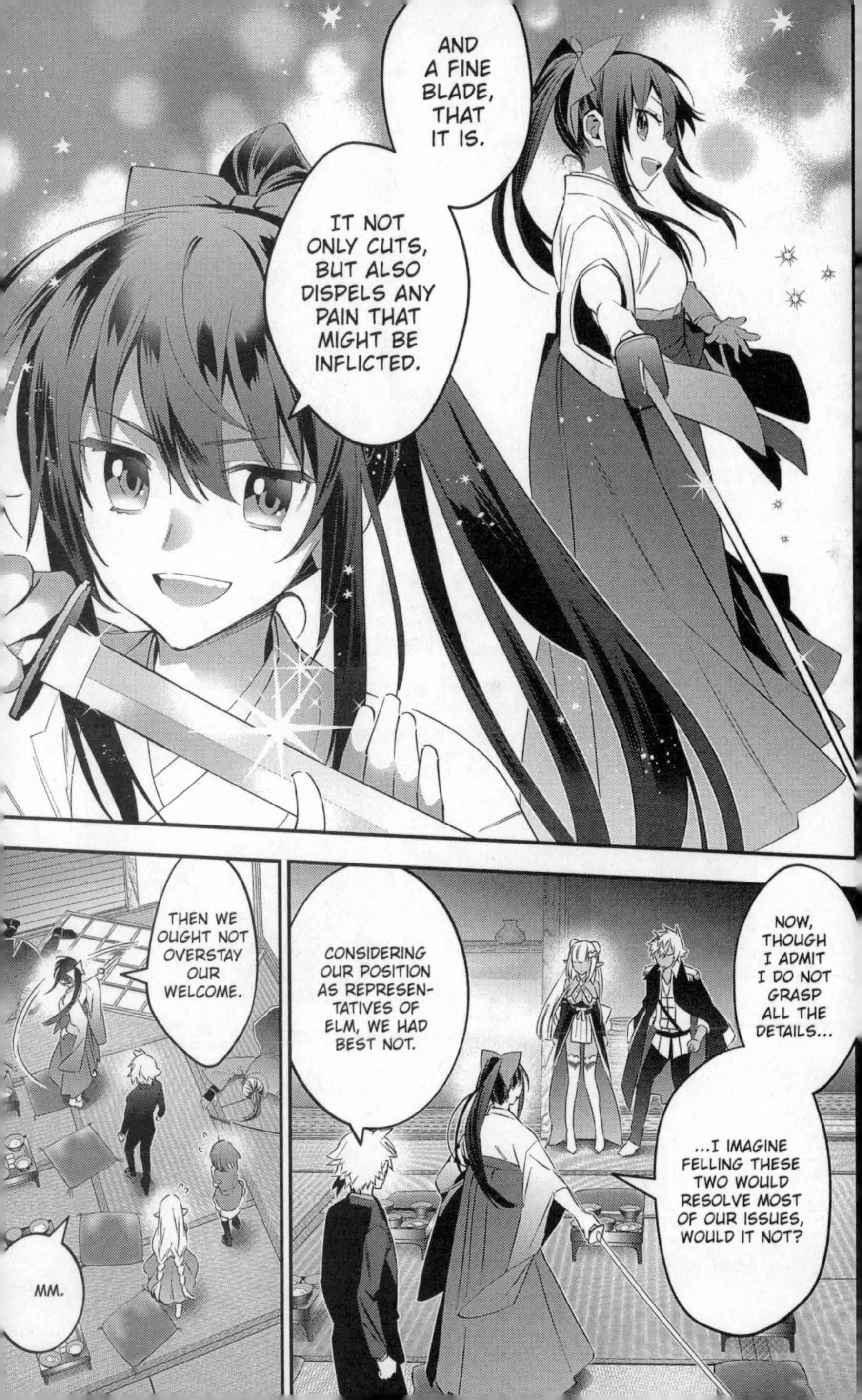
AND A FINE BLADE, THAT IT IS.
IT NOT ONLY CUTS, BUT ALSO DISPELS ANY PAIN THAT MIGHT BE INFLICTED.
NOW, THOUGH I ADMIT I DO NOT GRASP ALL THE DETAILS...
...I IMAGINE FELLING THESE TWO WOULD RESOLVE MOST OF OUR ISSUES, WOULD IT NOT?
CONSIDERING OUR POSITION AS REPRESEN-TATIVES OF ELM, WE HAD BEST NOT.
THEN WE OUGHT NOT OVERSTAY OUR WELCOME.
MM.

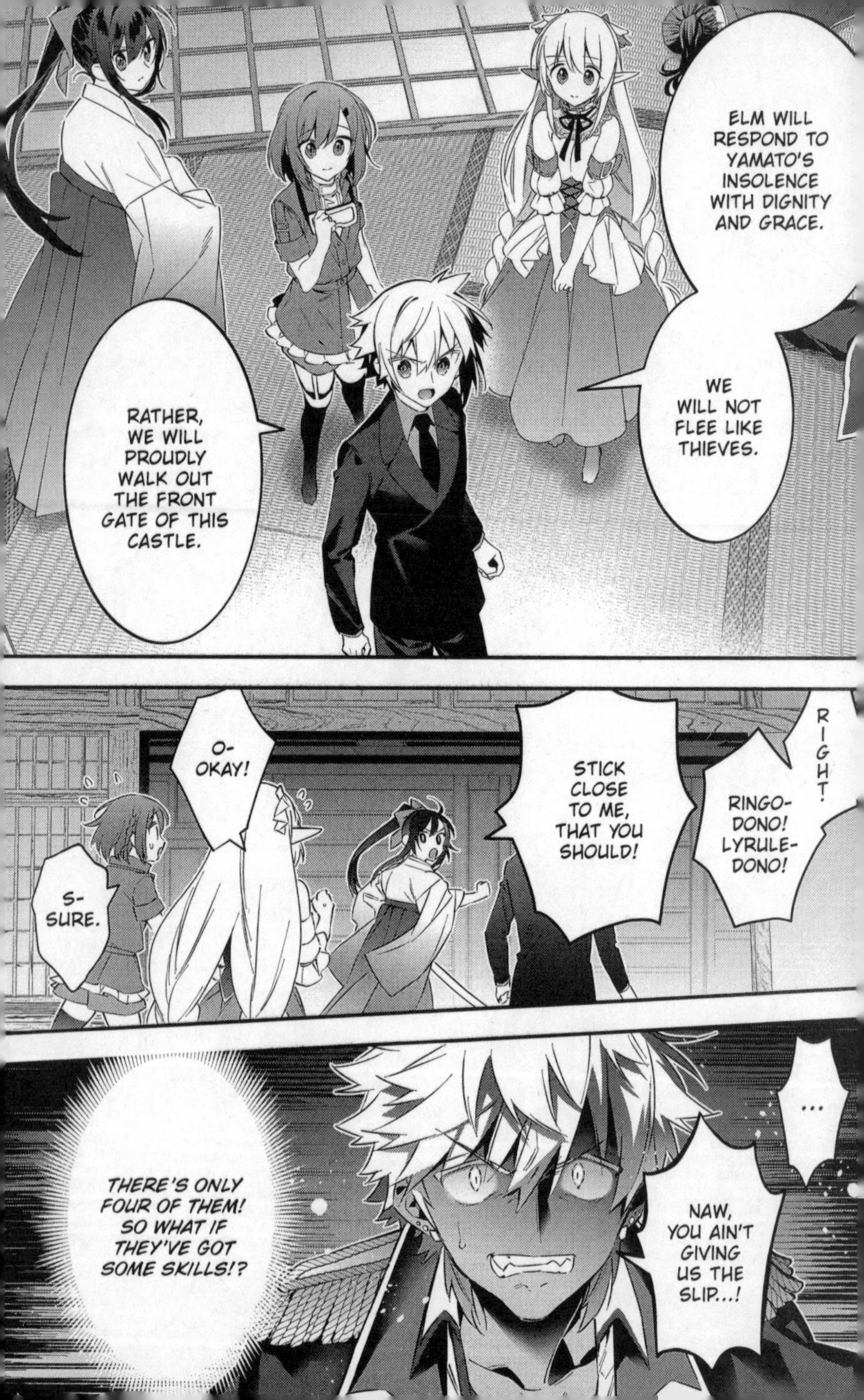
ELM WILL RESPOND TO YAMATO'S INSOLENCE WITH DIGNITY AND GRACE.
WE WILL NOT FLEE LIKE THIEVES.
RATHER, WE WILL PROUDLY WALK OUT THE FRONT GATE OF THIS CASTLE.
RIGHT!
RINGO-DONO! LYRULE-DONO!
STICK CLOSE TO ME, THAT YOU SHOULD!
O-OKAY!
S-SURE.
...
NAW, YOU AIN'T GIVING US THE SLIP...!
THERE'S ONLY FOUR OF THEM! SO WHAT IF THEY'VE GOT SOME SKILLS!?

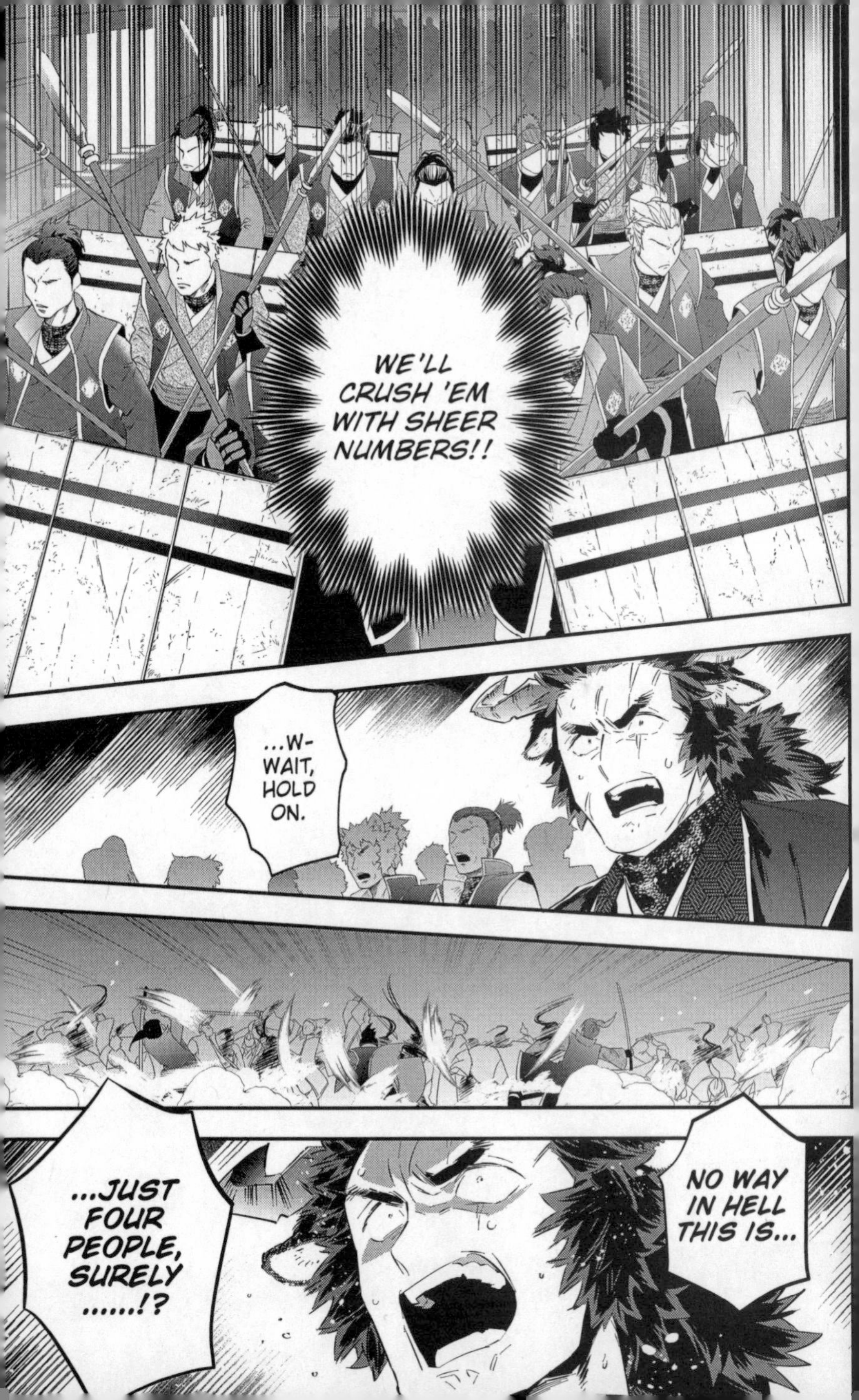
WE'LL CRUSH 'EM WITH SHEER NUMBERS!!
...W-WAIT, HOLD ON.
NO WAY IN HELL THIS IS...
...JUST FOUR PEOPLE, SURELY ......!?

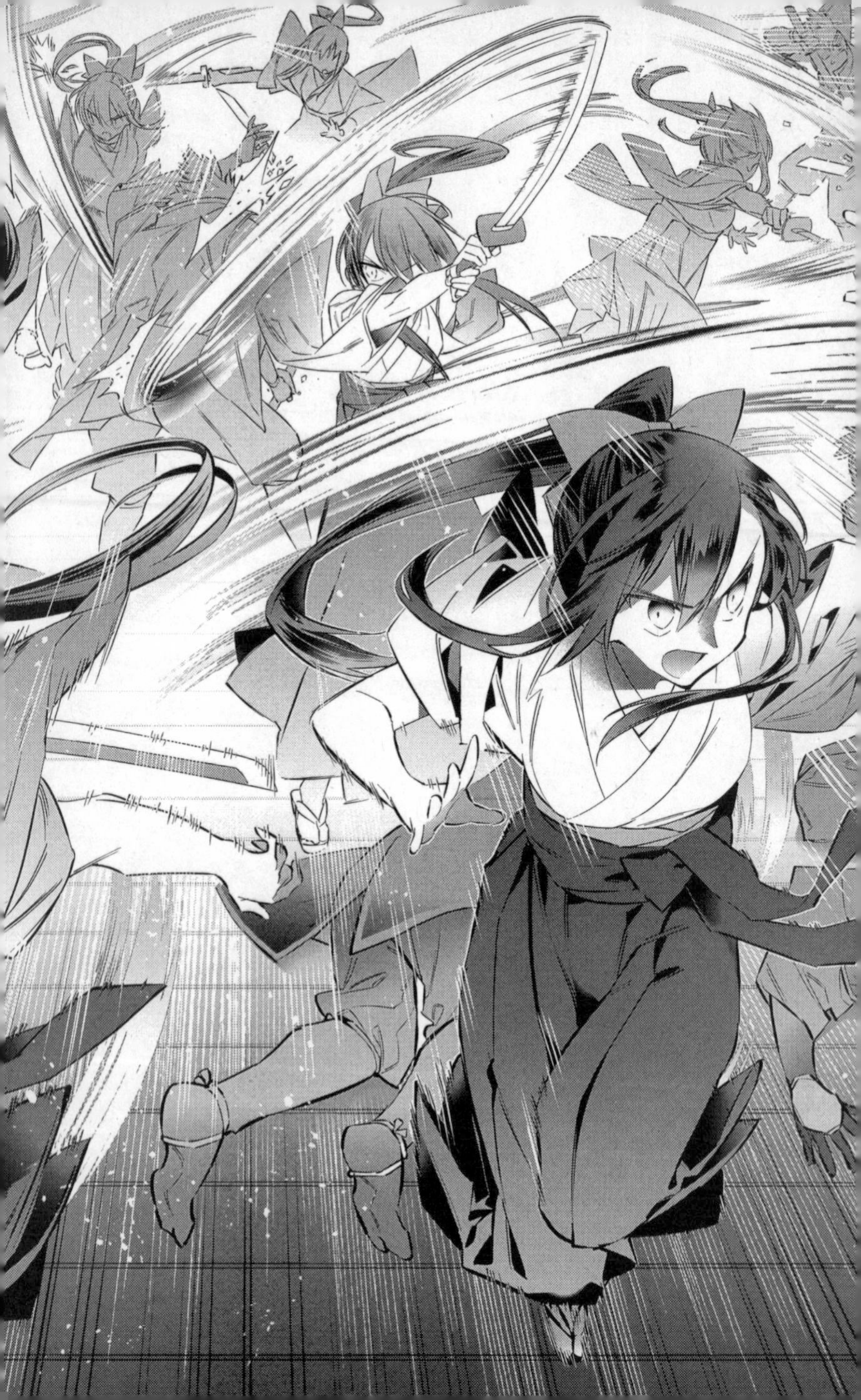

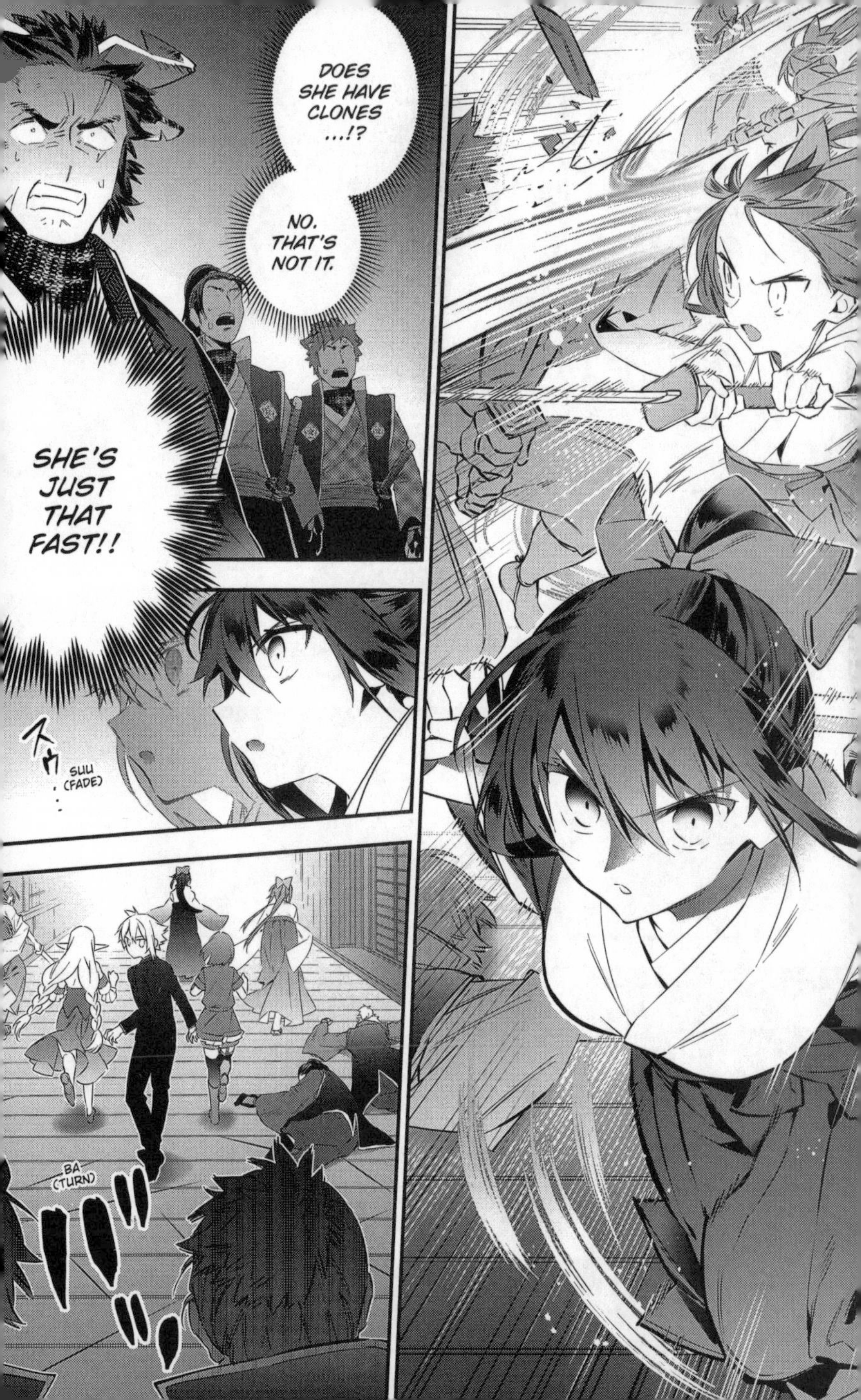
DOES SHE HAVE CLONES ...!?
NO. THAT'S NOT IT.
SHE'S JUST THAT FAST!!
スゥ
SUU (FADE)
BA (TURN)

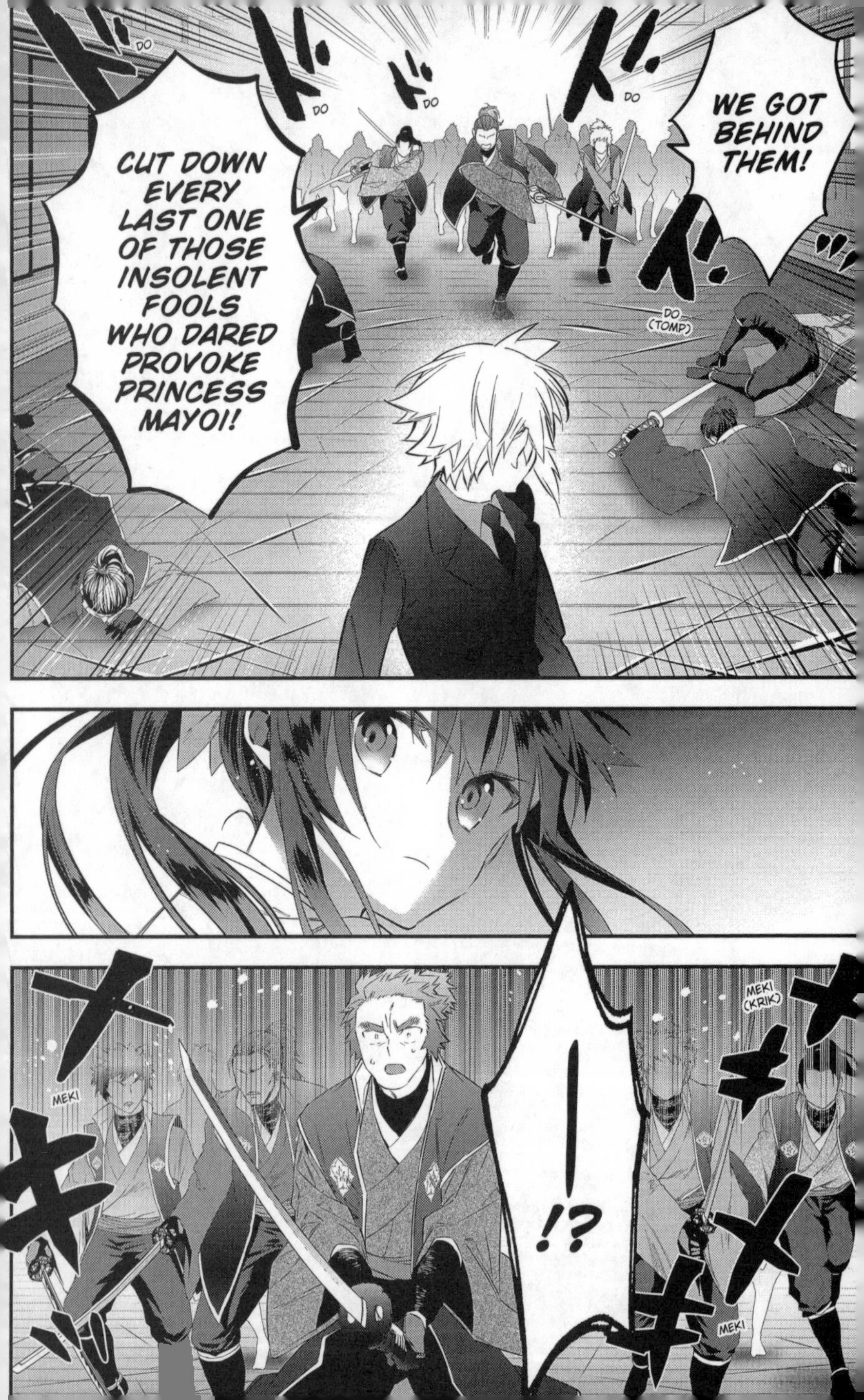
DO
WE GOT BEHIND THEM!
DO
DO
DO
DO
CUT DOWN EVERY LAST ONE OF THOSE INSOLENT FOOLS WHO DARED PROVOKE PRINCESS MAYOI!
DO (TOMP)
MEKI (KRIK)
!?
MEKI
MEKI

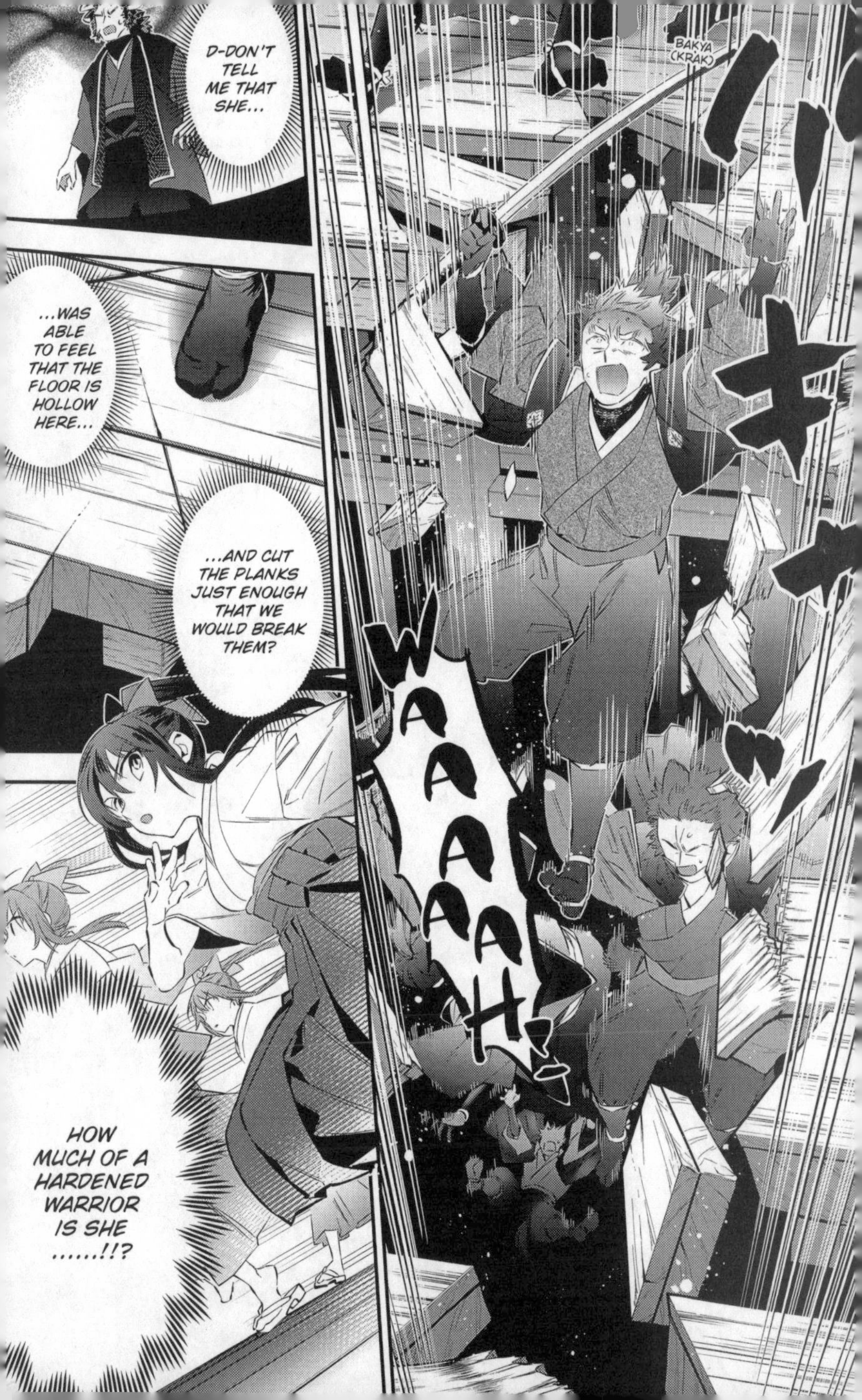
BAKYA (KRAK)
WAAAAAAH!
D-DON'T TELL ME THAT SHE...
...WAS ABLE TO FEEL THAT THE FLOOR IS HOLLOW HERE...
...AND CUT THE PLANKS JUST ENOUGH THAT WE WOULD BREAK THEM?
HOW MUCH OF A HARDENED WARRIOR IS SHE ......!!?

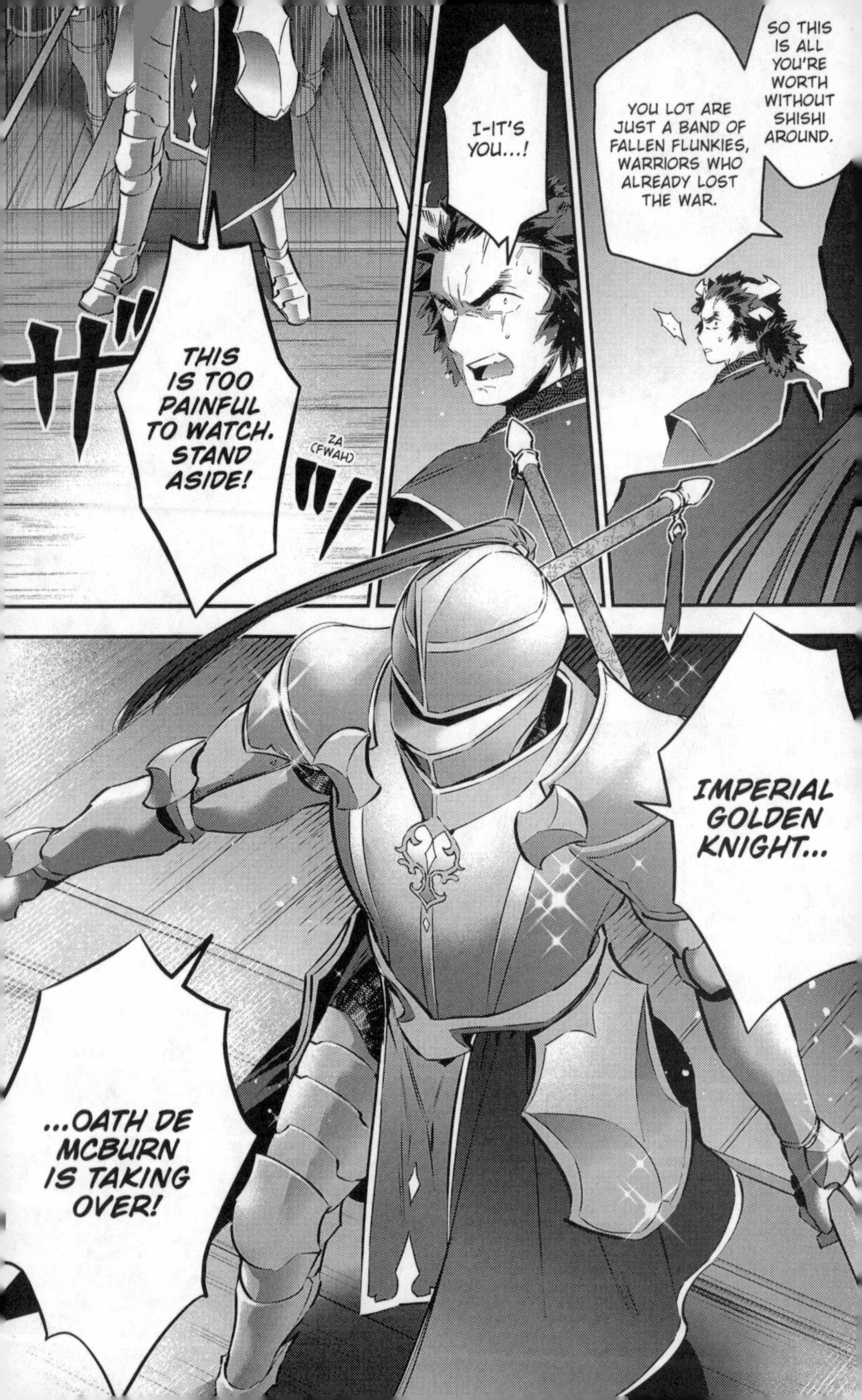
SO THIS IS ALL YOU'RE WORTH WITHOUT SHISHI AROUND.
YOU LOT ARE JUST A BAND OF FALLEN FLUNKIES, WARRIORS WHO ALREADY LOST THE WAR.
I-IT'S YOU...!
THIS IS TOO PAINFUL TO WATCH. STAND ASIDE!
ZA (FWAH)
IMPERIAL GOLDEN KNIGHT...
...OATH DE MCBURN IS TAKING OVER!

HIGH SCHOOL PRODIGIES HAVE IT EASY EVEN IN ANOTHER WORLD!

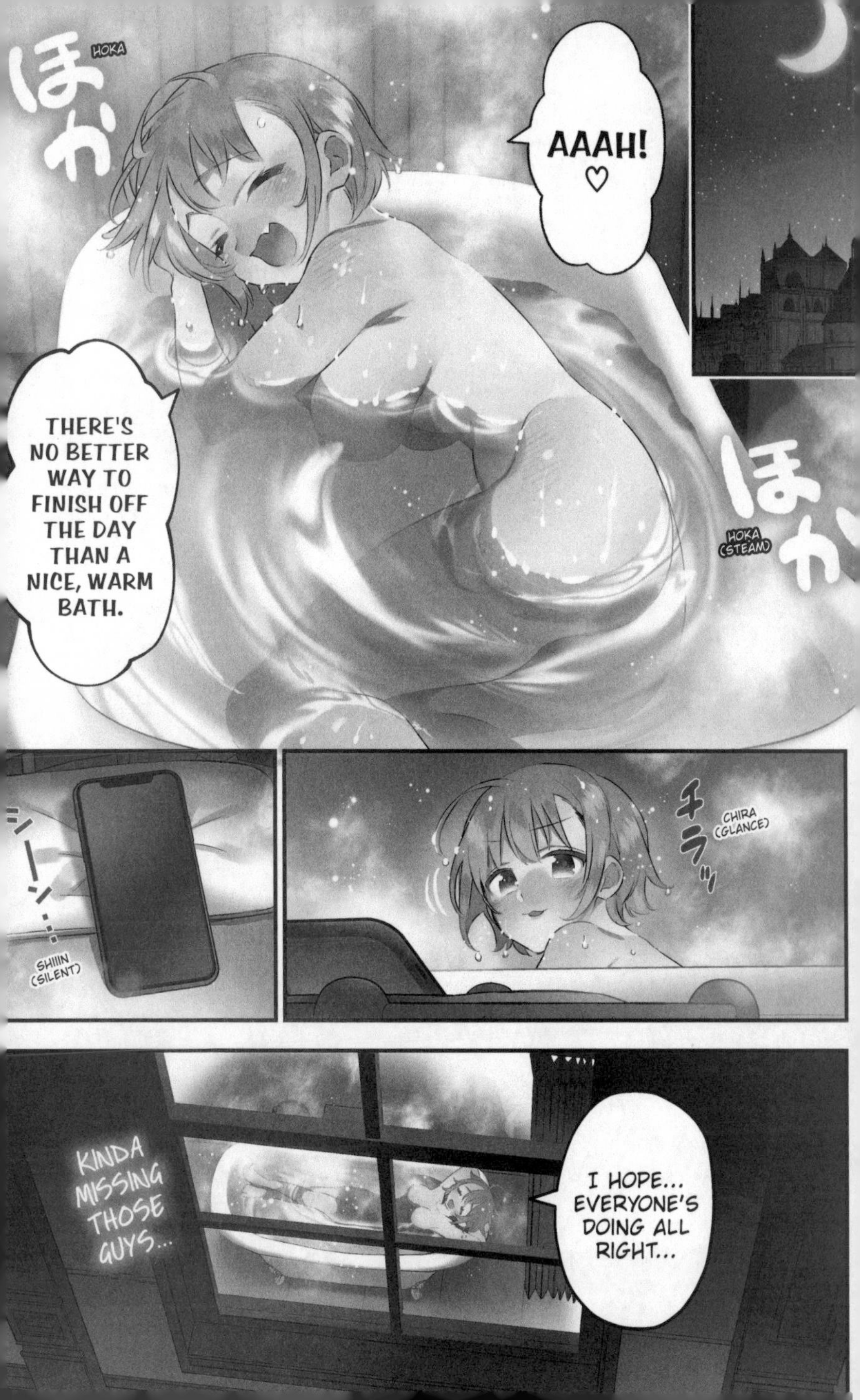

AAAH! ♡
ほか
HOKA
THERE'S NO BETTER WAY TO FINISH OFF THE DAY THAN A NICE, WARM BATH.
ほか
HOKA (STEAM)
チラッ
CHIRA (GLANCE)
シーン…
SHIIIN (SILENT)
I HOPE... EVERYONE'S DOING ALL RIGHT...
KINDA MISSING THOSE GUYS...

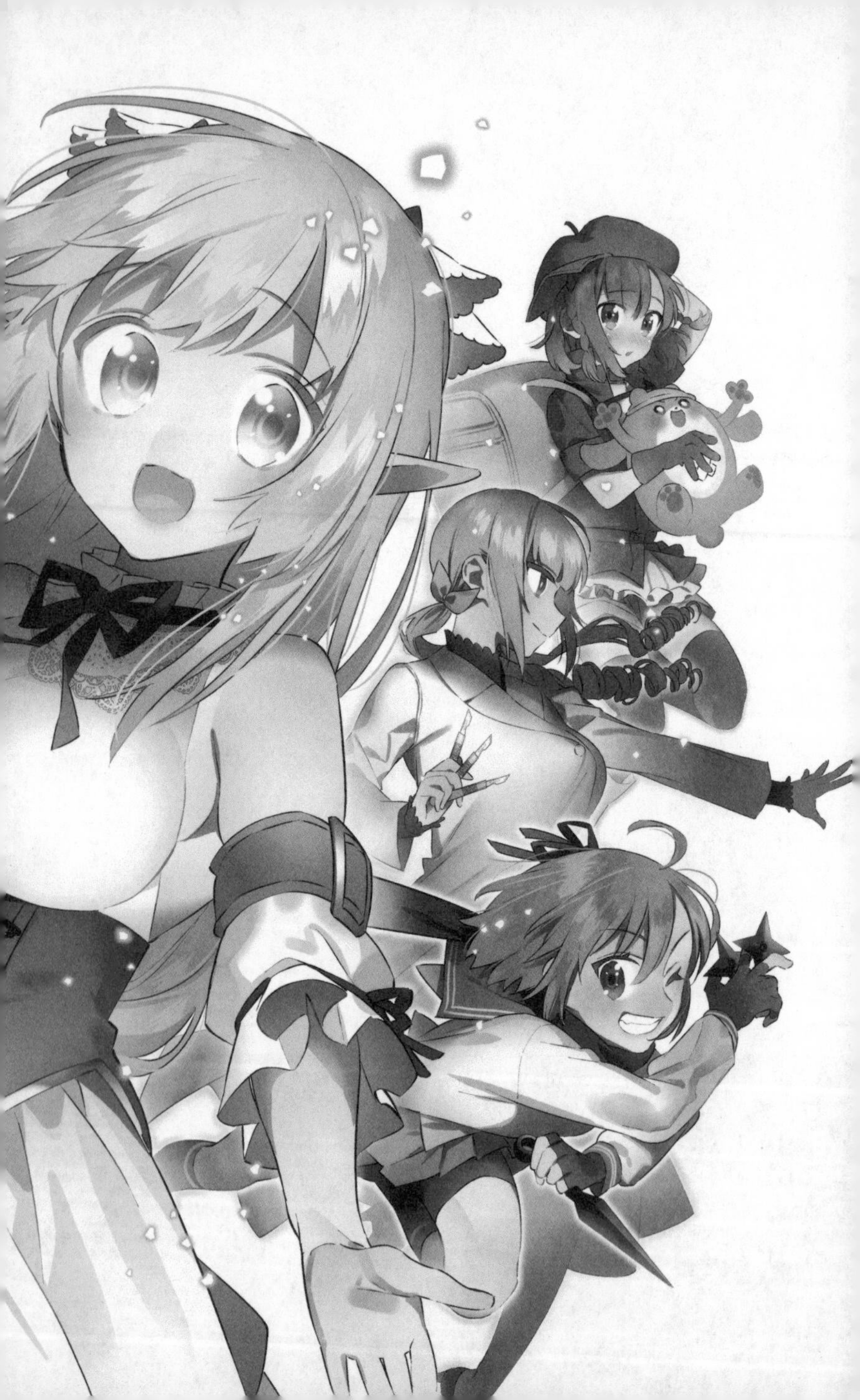

CHAPTER 71: THE TRUTH ABOUT YAMATO

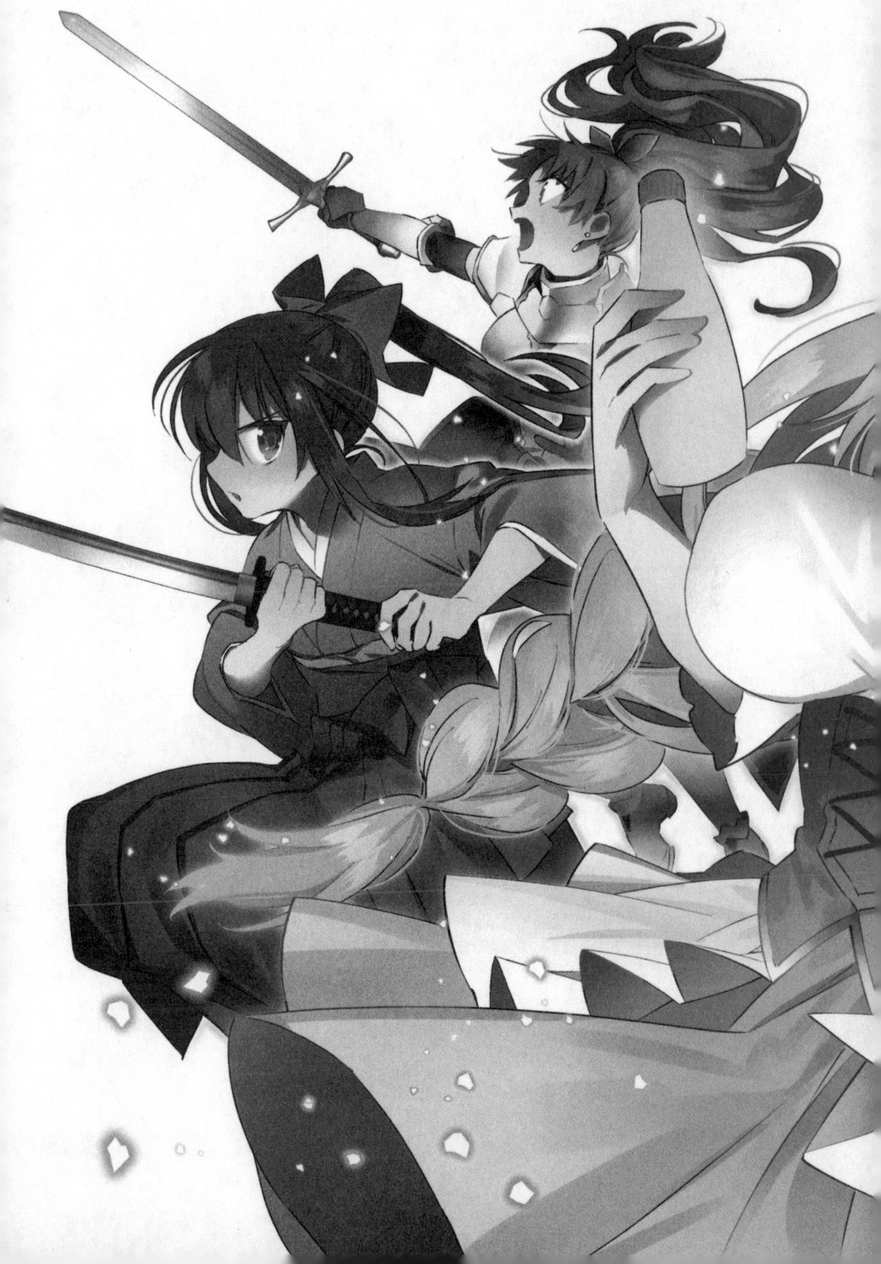

HIGH SCHOOL
PRODIGIES HAVE
IT EASY EVEN IN
ANOTHER
WORLD!

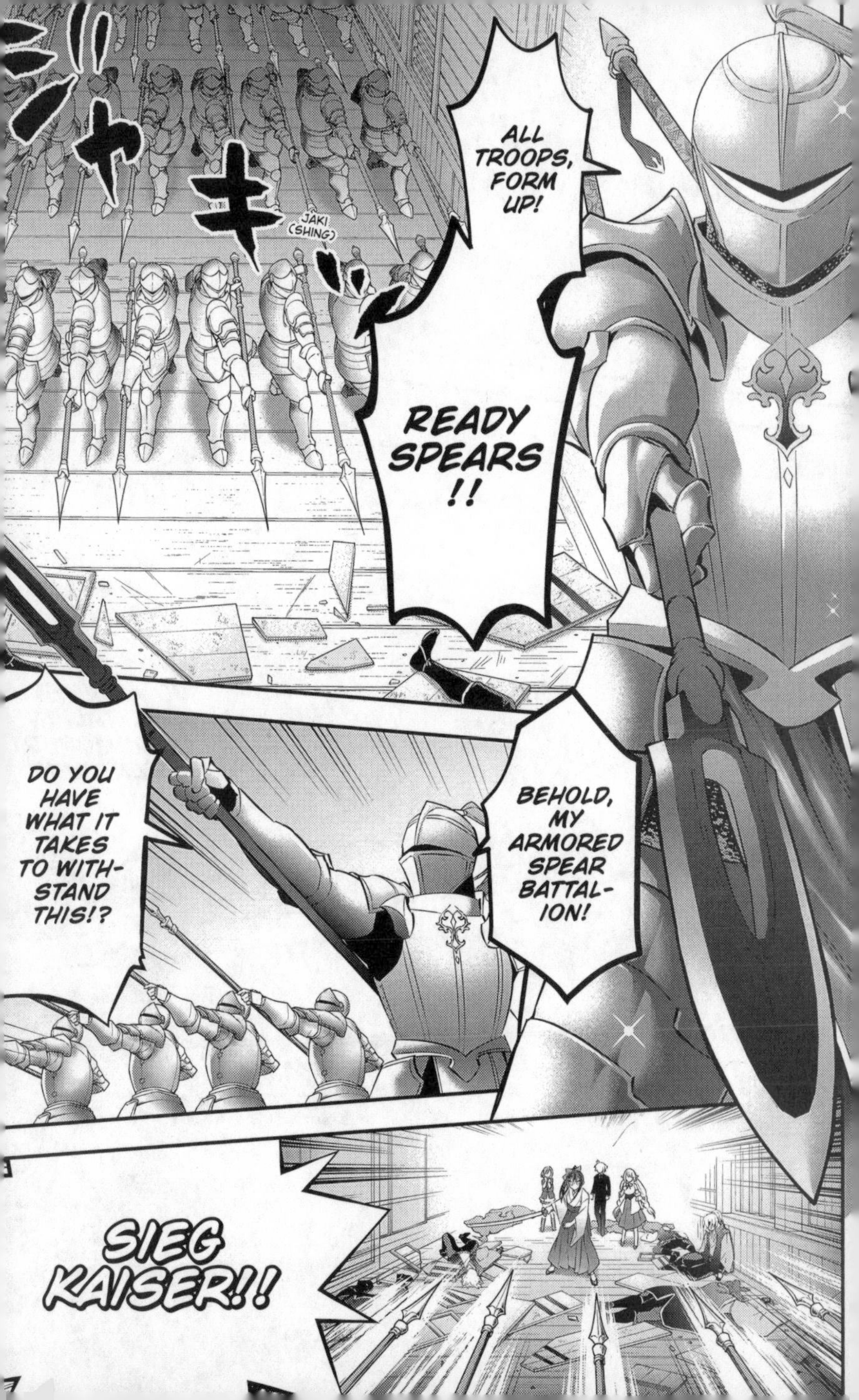

ALL TROOPS, FORM UP!
READY SPEARS!!
JAKI (SHING)
BEHOLD, MY ARMORED SPEAR BATTAL-ION!
DO YOU HAVE WHAT IT TAKES TO WITH-STAND THIS!?
SIEG KAISER!!

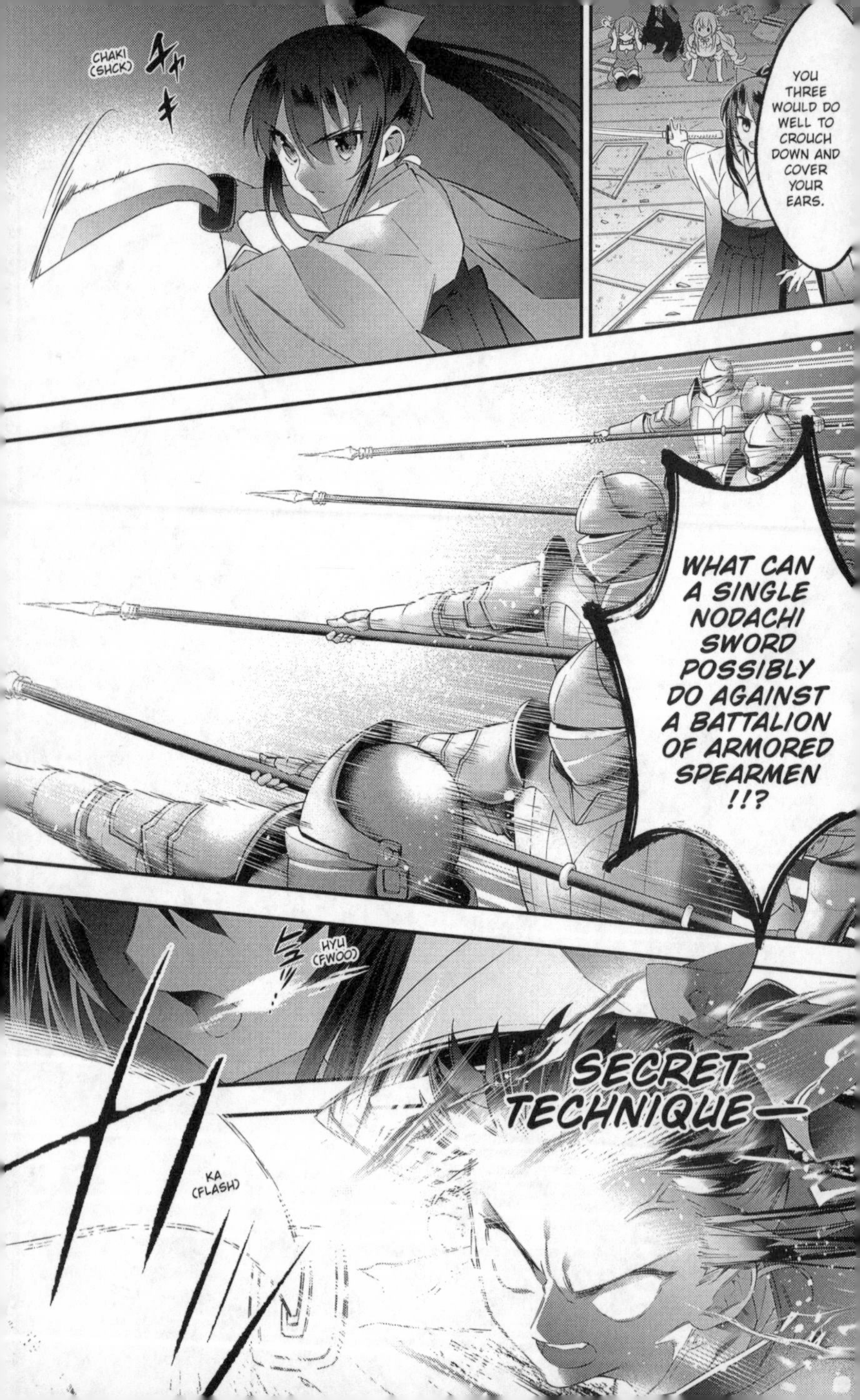
YOU THREE WOULD DO WELL TO CROUCH DOWN AND COVER YOUR EARS.
CHAKI (SHCK)
WHAT CAN A SINGLE NODACHI SWORD POSSIBLY DO AGAINST A BATTALION OF ARMORED SPEARMEN !!?
HYU (FWOO)
SECRET TECHNIQUE—
KA (FLASH)

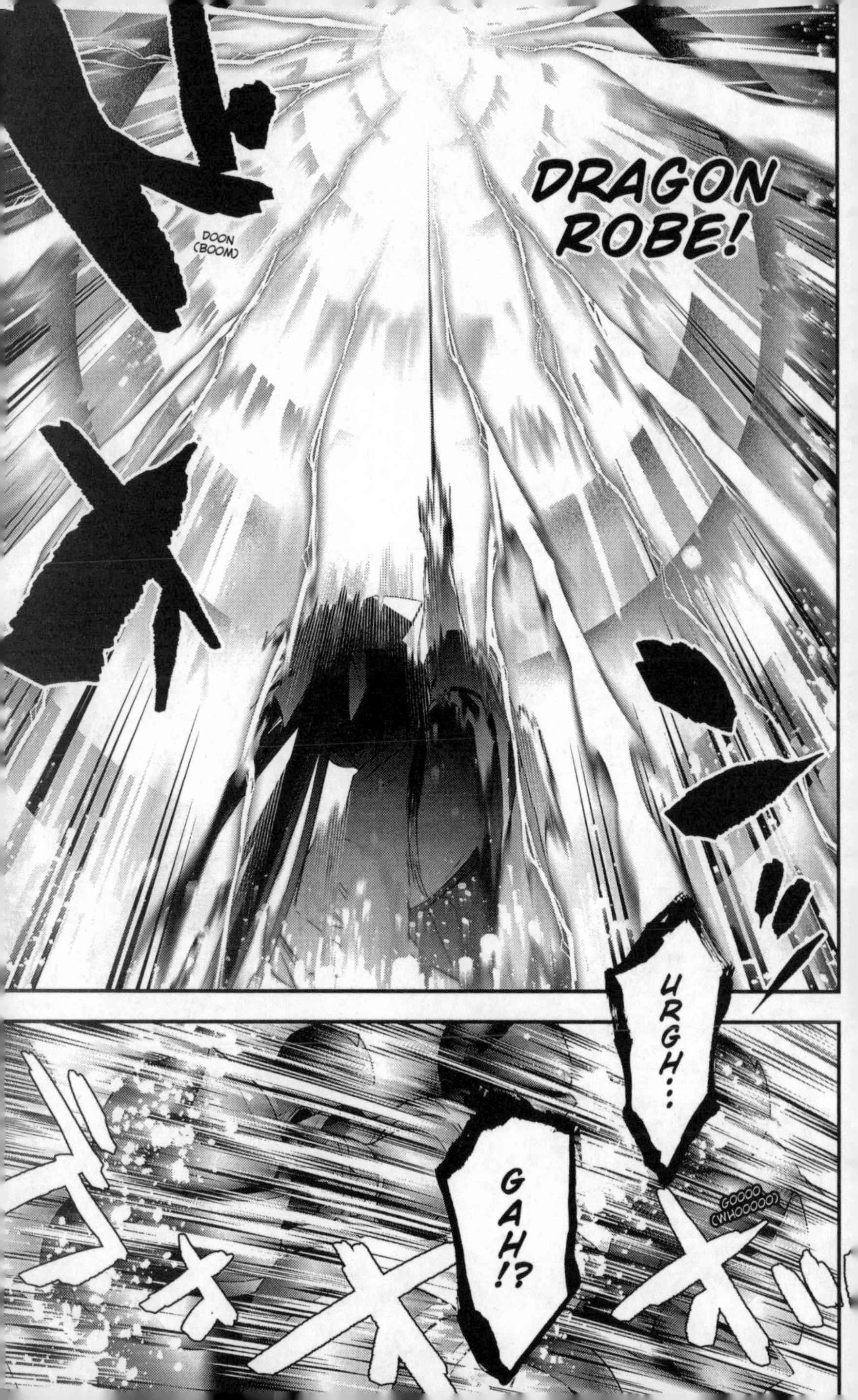
DRAGON ROBE!
DOON (BOOM)
URGH...
GOOOO (WHOOOOO)
GAH!?

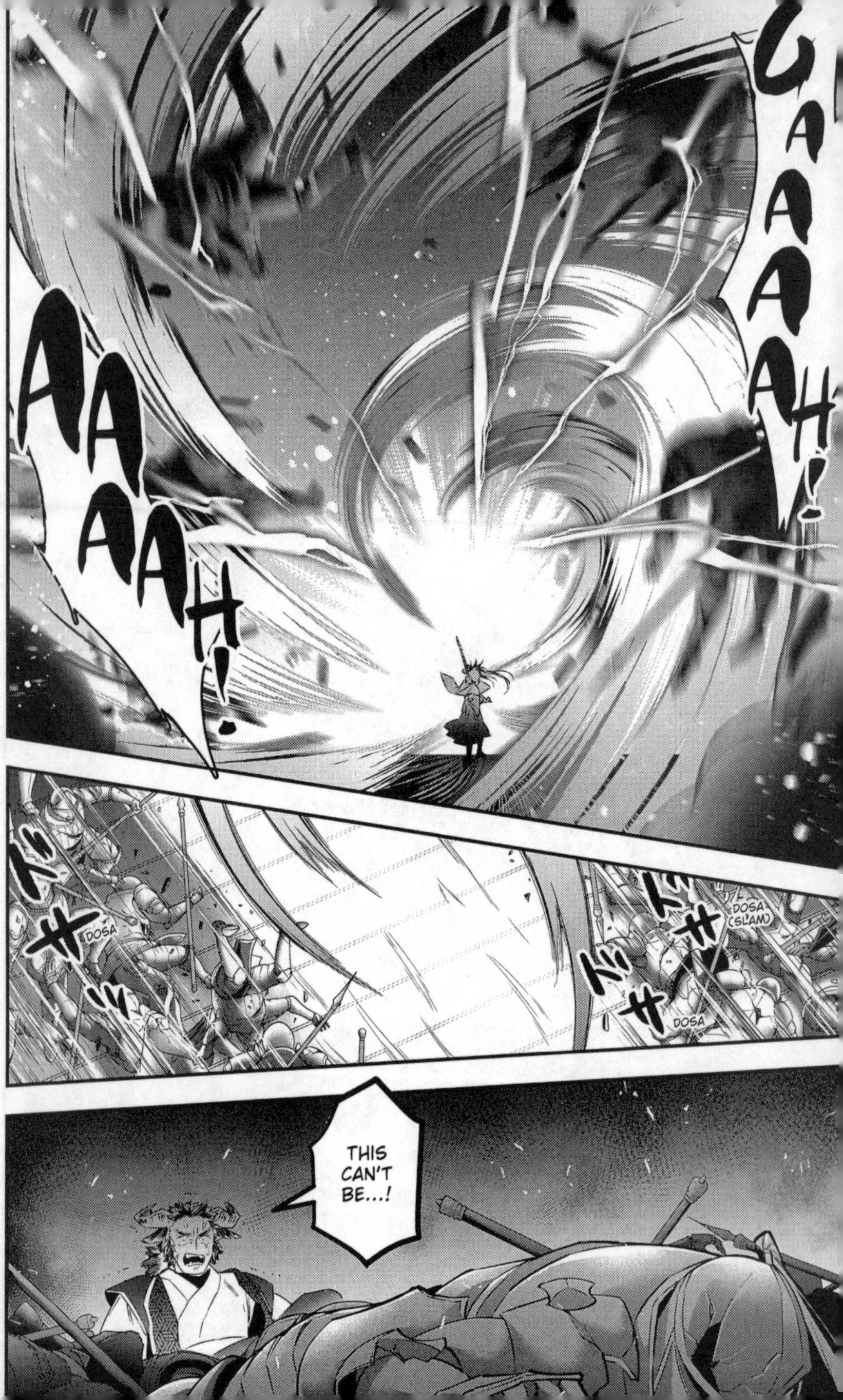
GAAAAAH!
AAAAH!
DOSA (SLAM)
DOSA
DOSA
THIS CAN'T BE...!

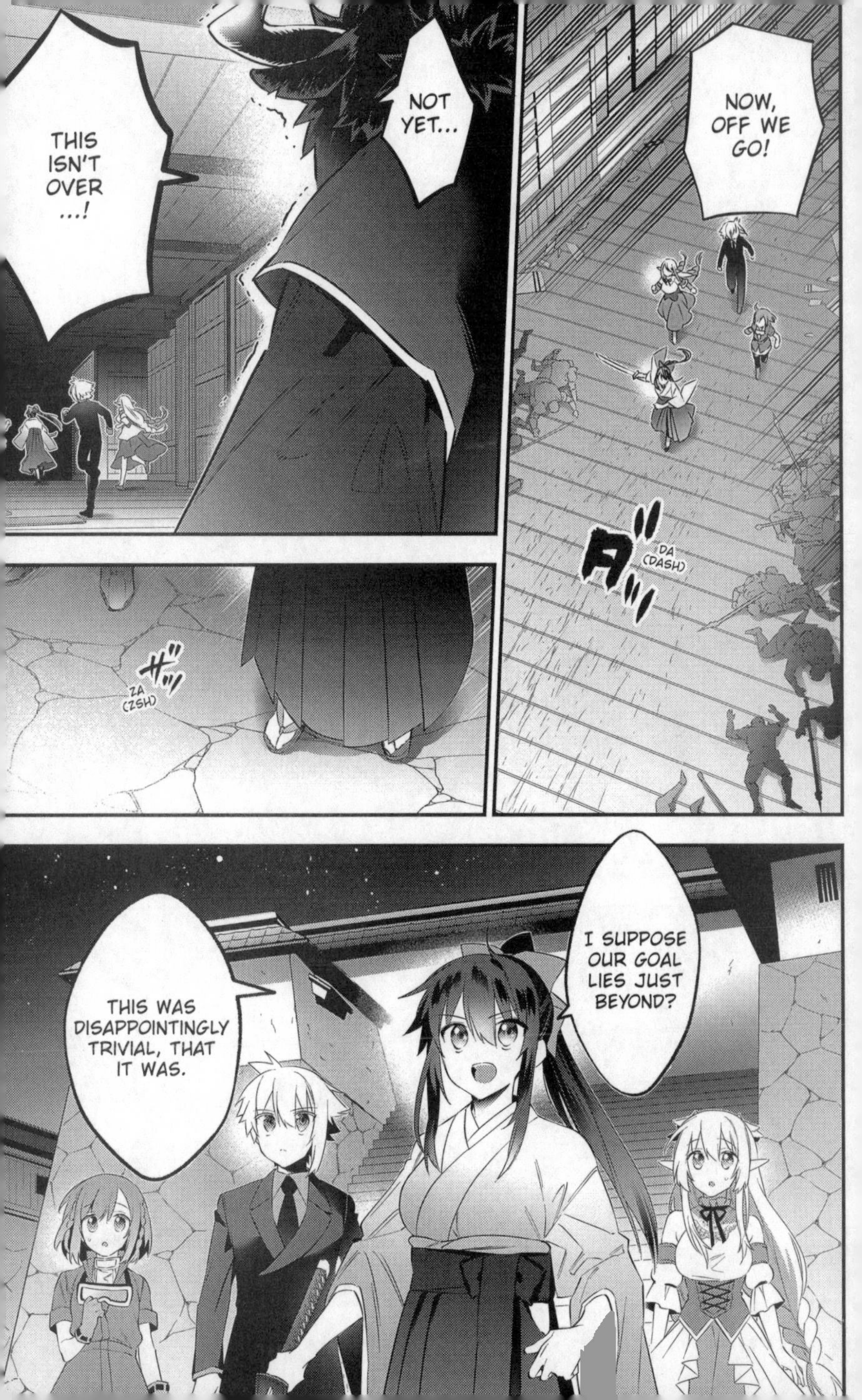
NOW, OFF WE GO!
ダッ
DA (DASH)
NOT YET...
THIS ISN'T OVER ...!
ザッ
ZA (ZSH)
I SUPPOSE OUR GOAL LIES JUST BEYOND?
THIS WAS DISAPPOINTINGLY TRIVIAL, THAT IT WAS.

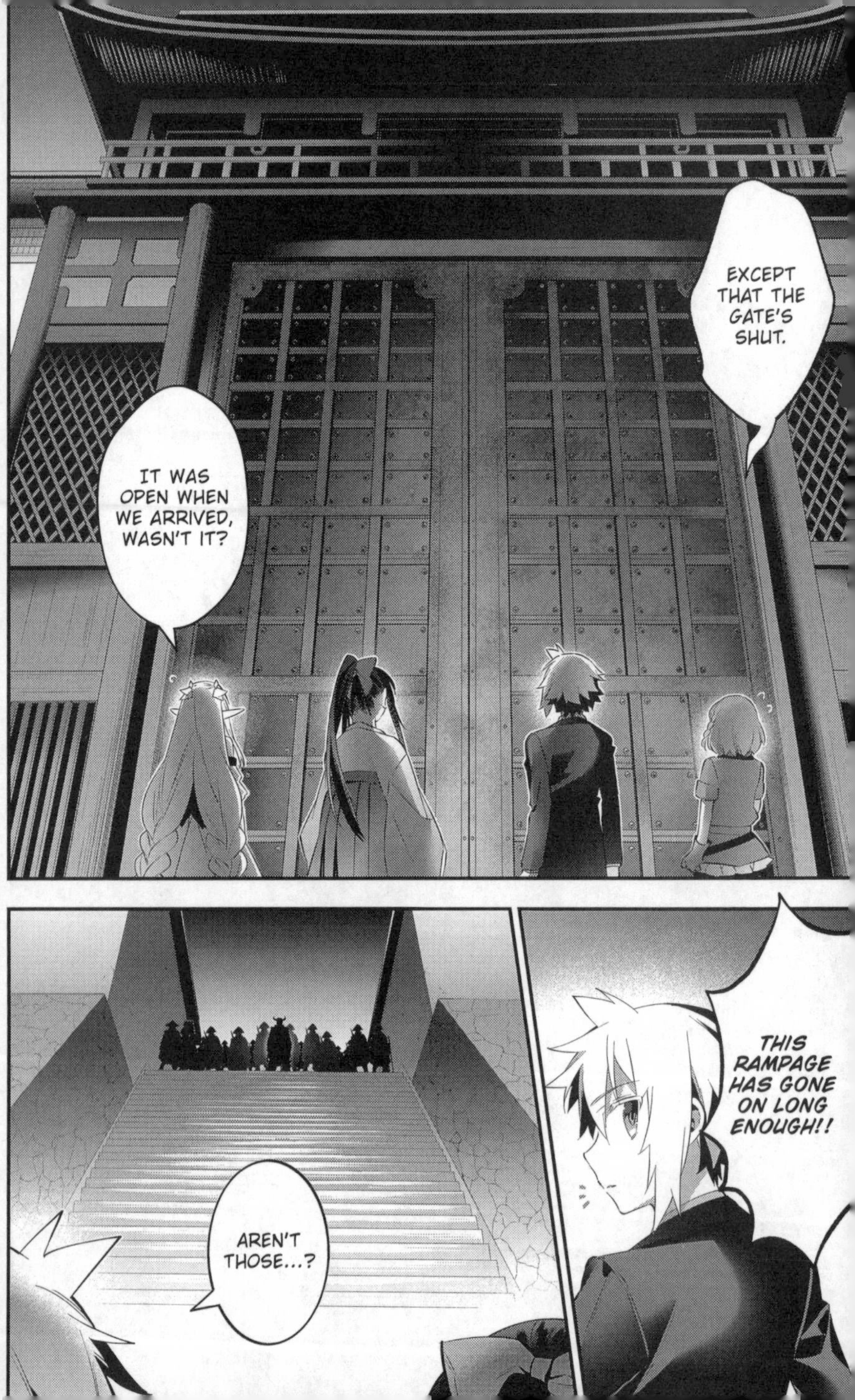
EXCEPT THAT THE GATE'S SHUT.
IT WAS OPEN WHEN WE ARRIVED, WASN'T IT?
THIS RAMPAGE HAS GONE ON LONG ENOUGH!!
AREN'T THOSE...?

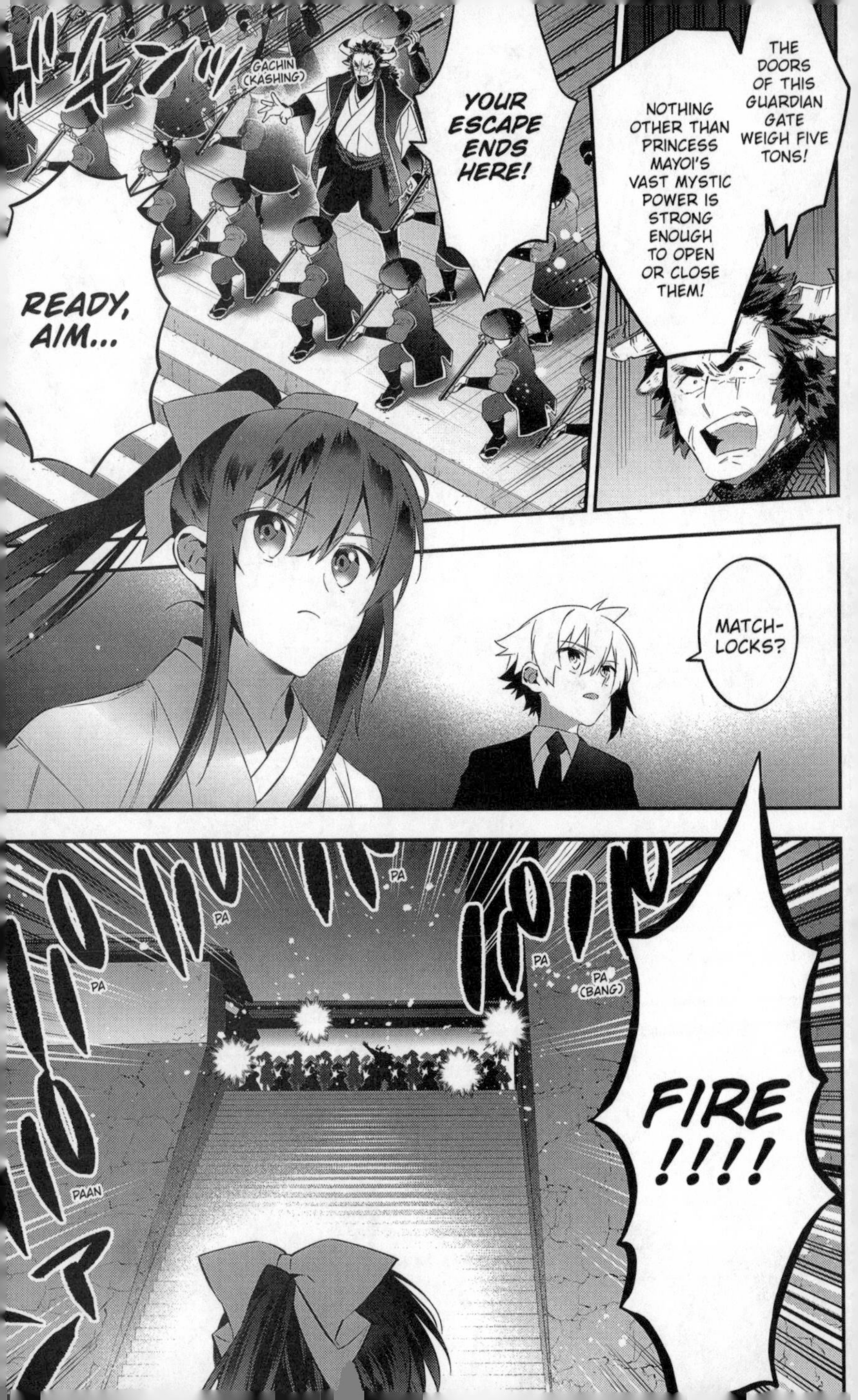
THE DOORS OF THIS GUARDIAN GATE WEIGH FIVE TONS!
NOTHING OTHER THAN PRINCESS MAYOI'S VAST MYSTIC POWER IS STRONG ENOUGH TO OPEN OR CLOSE THEM!
YOUR ESCAPE ENDS HERE!
GACHIN (KASHING)
READY, AIM...
MATCH-LOCKS?
FIRE!!!!
PA (BANG)
PA
PA
PA
PA
PAAN

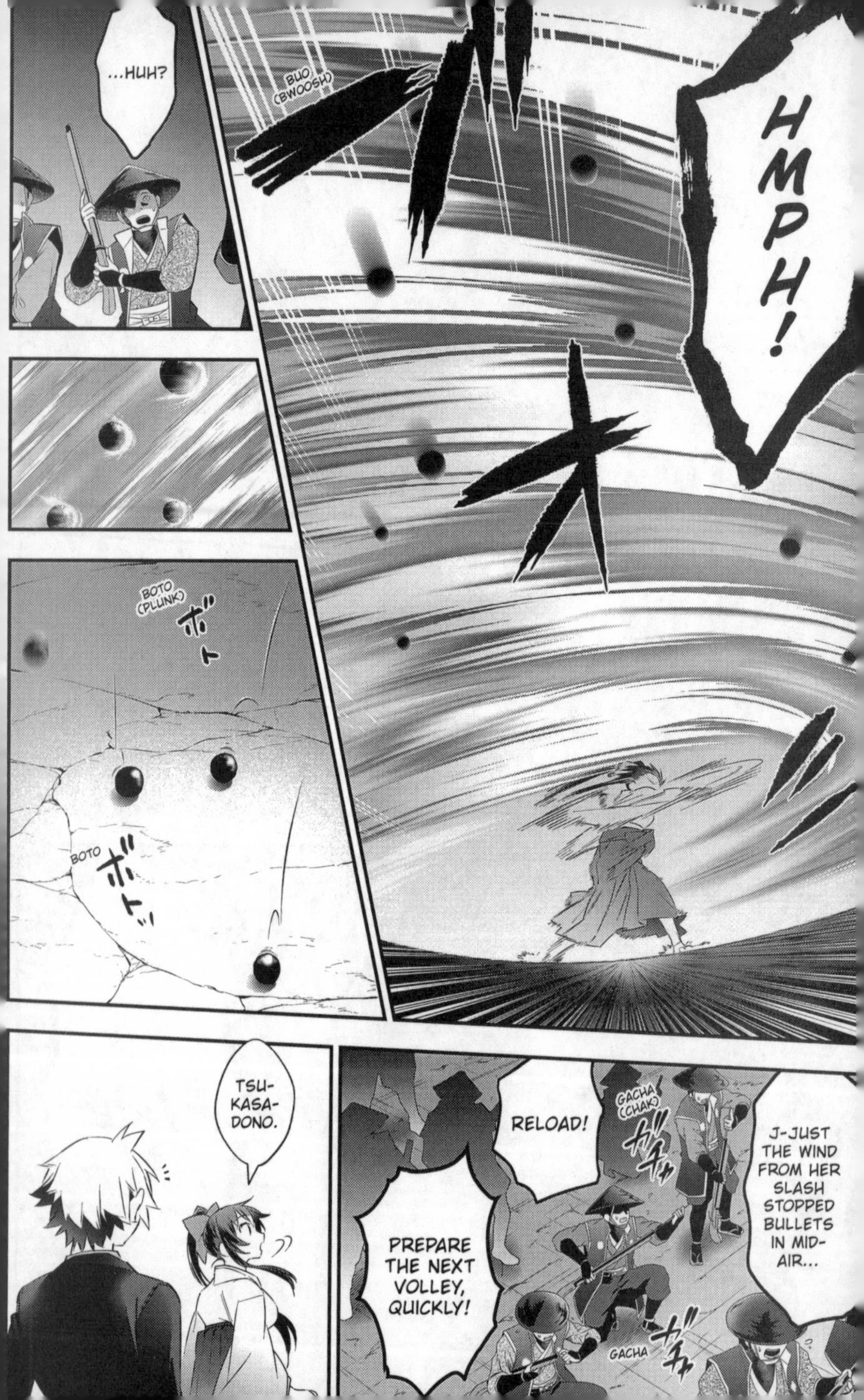
HMPH!
BUO (BWOOSH)
...HUH?
BOTO (PLUNK)
ボト
BOTO
ボトッ
J-JUST THE WIND FROM HER SLASH STOPPED BULLETS IN MID-AIR...
GACHA (CHAK)
ガチャ
RELOAD!
PREPARE THE NEXT VOLLEY, QUICKLY!
GACHA
ガチャ
TSU-KASA-DONO.

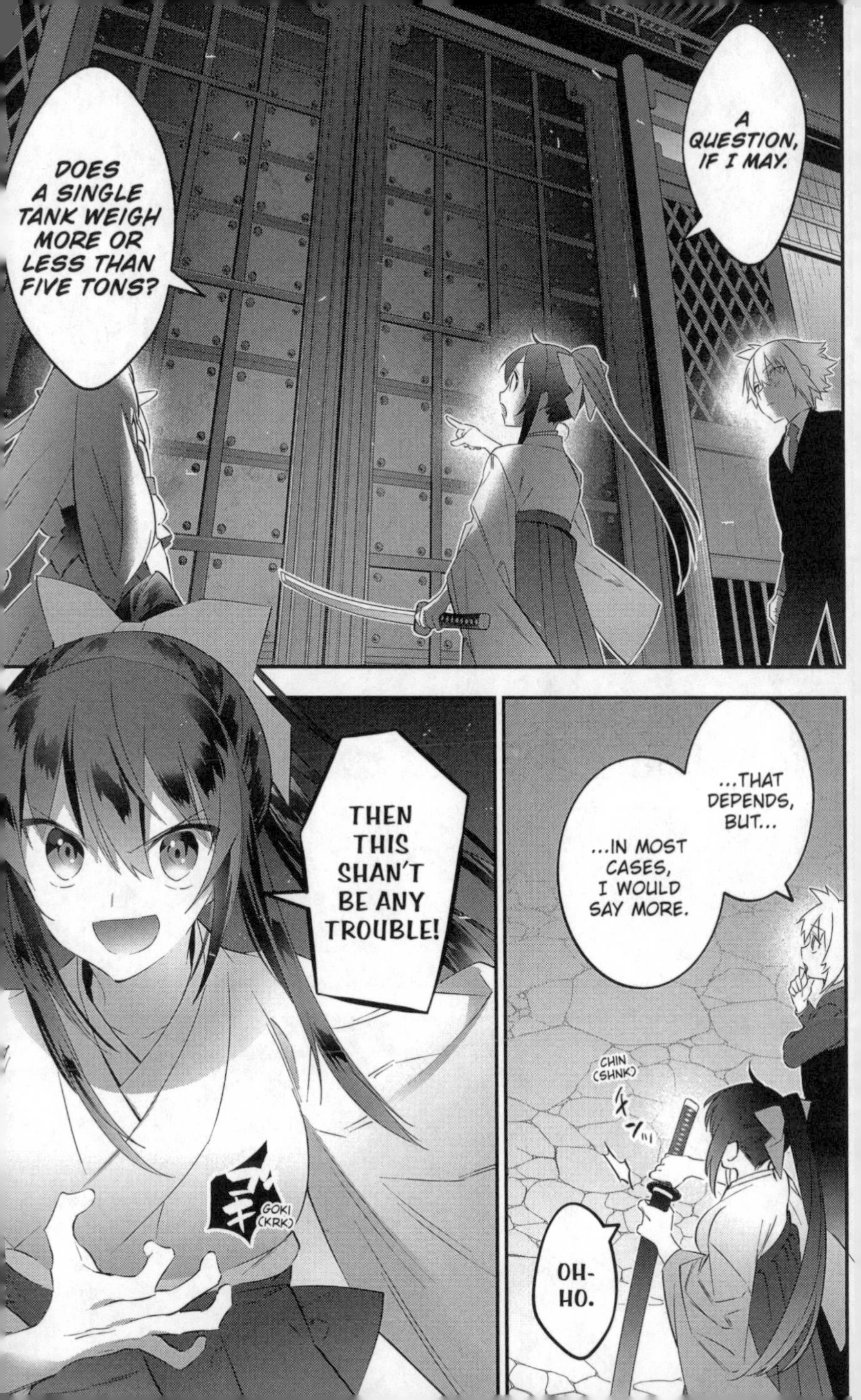
A QUESTION, IF I MAY.
DOES A SINGLE TANK WEIGH MORE OR LESS THAN FIVE TONS?
...THAT DEPENDS, BUT...
...IN MOST CASES, I WOULD SAY MORE.
CHIN (SHNK)
OH-HO.
THEN THIS SHAN'T BE ANY TROUBLE!
GOKI (KRK)

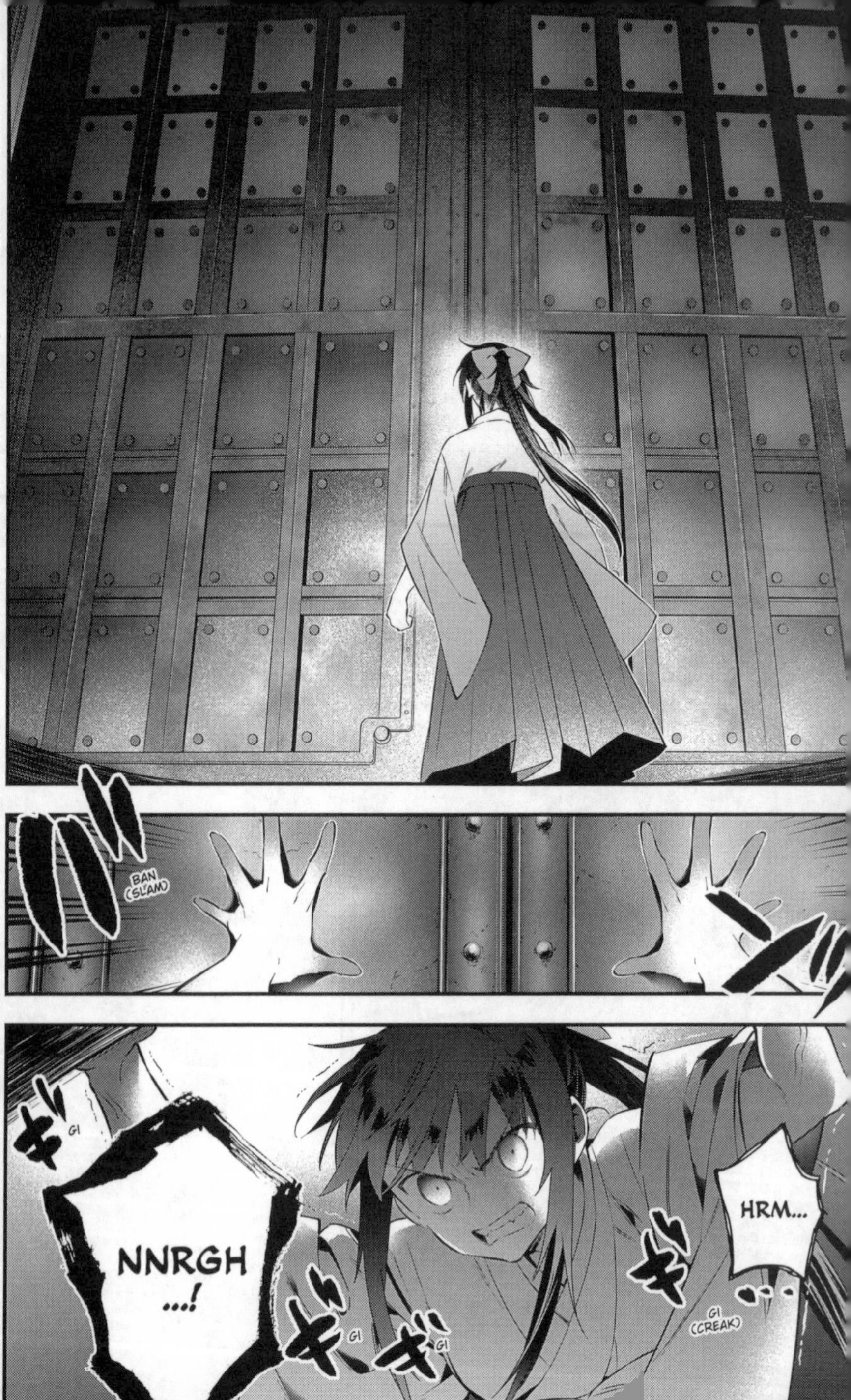
BAN (SLAM)
HRM...
GI (CREAK)
GI
GI
NNRGH ...!
GI

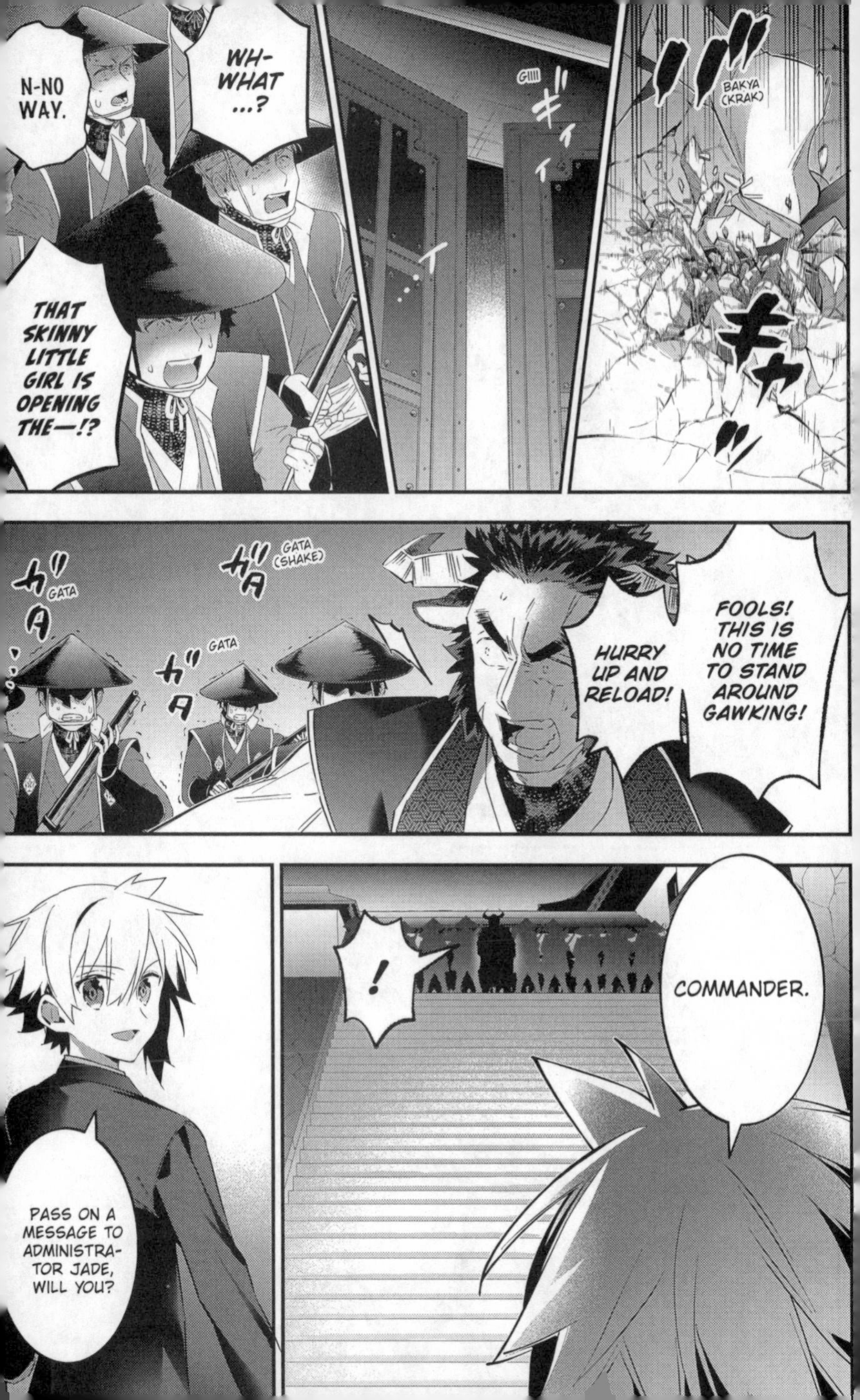
BAKYA (KRAK)
GIIII
WH-WHAT ...?
N-NO WAY.
THAT SKINNY LITTLE GIRL IS OPENING THE—!?
FOOLS! THIS IS NO TIME TO STAND AROUND GAWKING!
HURRY UP AND RELOAD!
GATA (SHAKE)
GATA
GATA
COMMANDER.
!
PASS ON A MESSAGE TO ADMINISTRATOR JADE, WILL YOU?

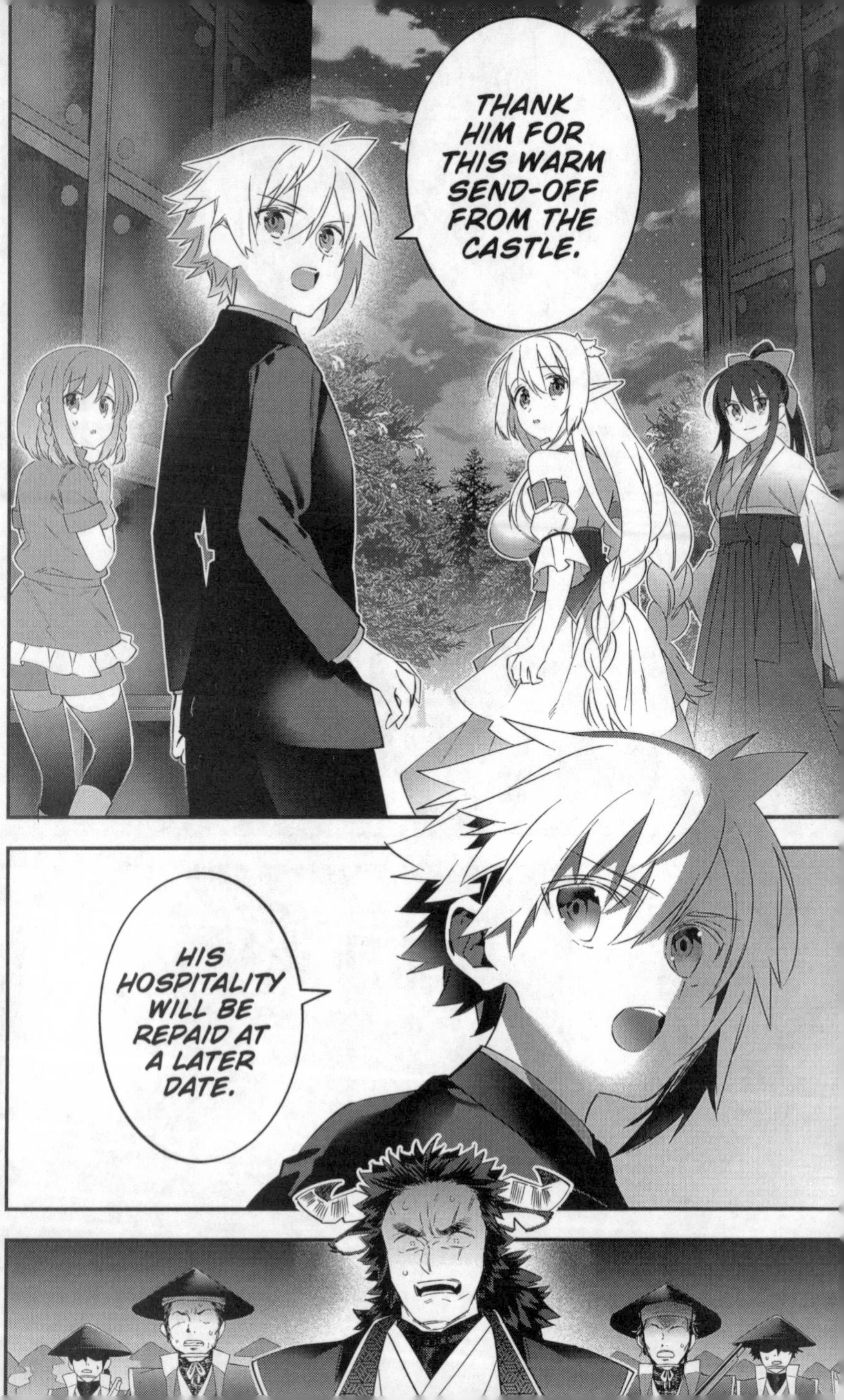
THANK HIM FOR THIS WARM SEND-OFF FROM THE CASTLE.
HIS HOSPITALITY WILL BE REPAID AT A LATER DATE.

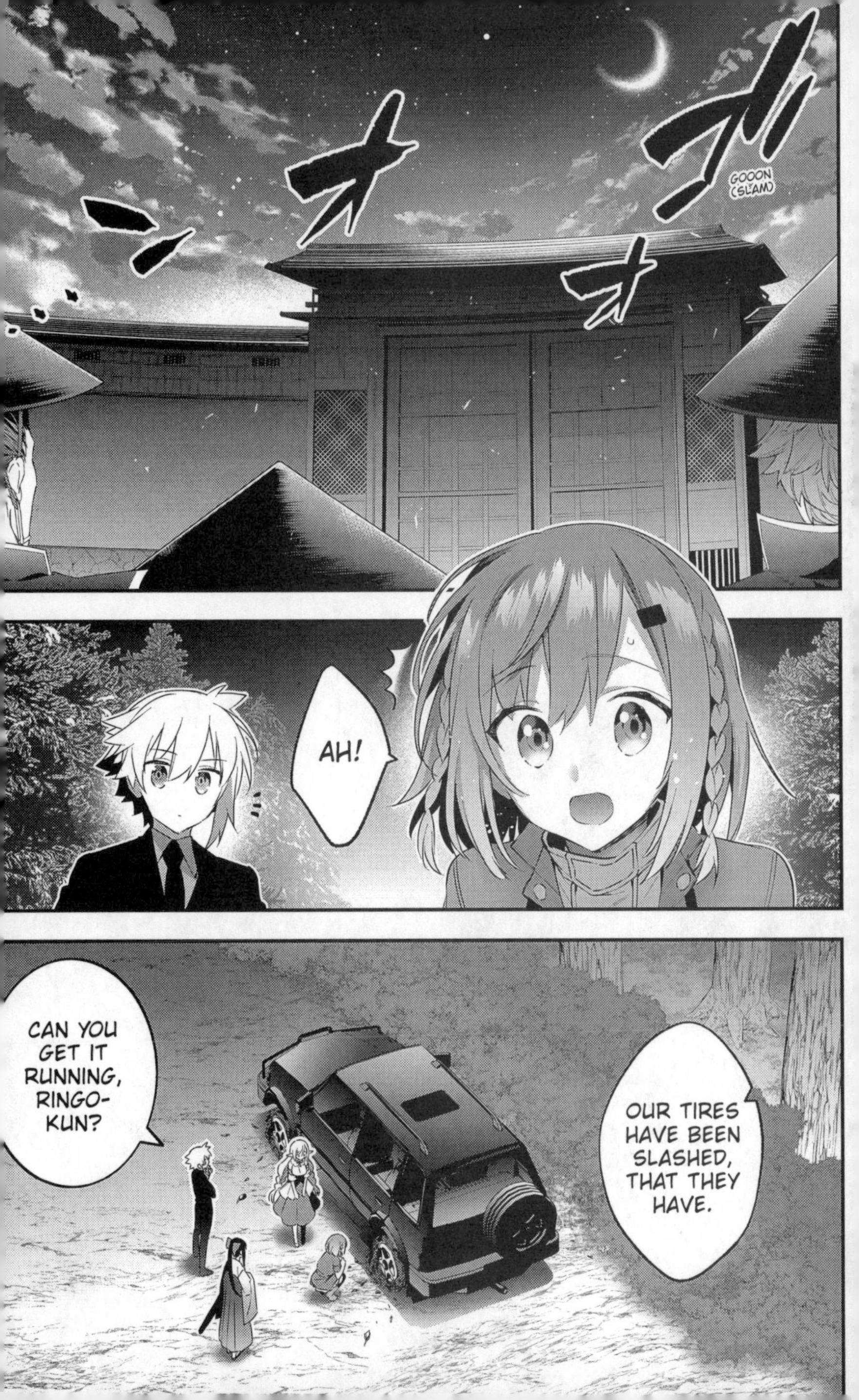
GOOON (SLAM)
AH!
OUR TIRES HAVE BEEN SLASHED, THAT THEY HAVE.
CAN YOU GET IT RUNNING, RINGO-KUN?

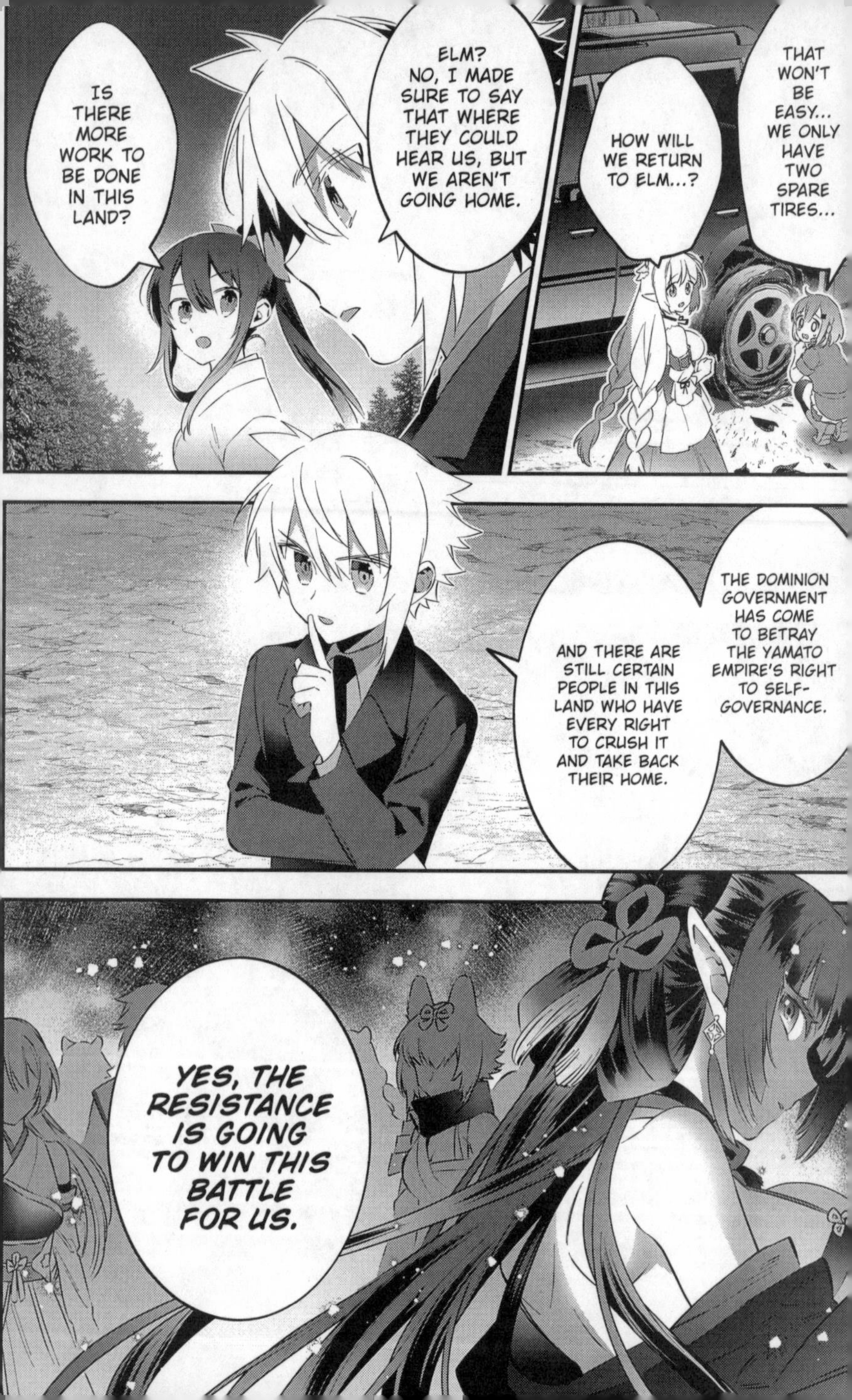
THAT WON'T BE EASY... WE ONLY HAVE TWO SPARE TIRES...
HOW WILL WE RETURN TO ELM...?
ELM? NO, I MADE SURE TO SAY THAT WHERE THEY COULD HEAR US, BUT WE AREN'T GOING HOME.
IS THERE MORE WORK TO BE DONE IN THIS LAND?
THE DOMINION GOVERNMENT HAS COME TO BETRAY THE YAMATO EMPIRE'S RIGHT TO SELF-GOVERNANCE.
AND THERE ARE STILL CERTAIN PEOPLE IN THIS LAND WHO HAVE EVERY RIGHT TO CRUSH IT AND TAKE BACK THEIR HOME.
YES, THE RESISTANCE IS GOING TO WIN THIS BATTLE FOR US.

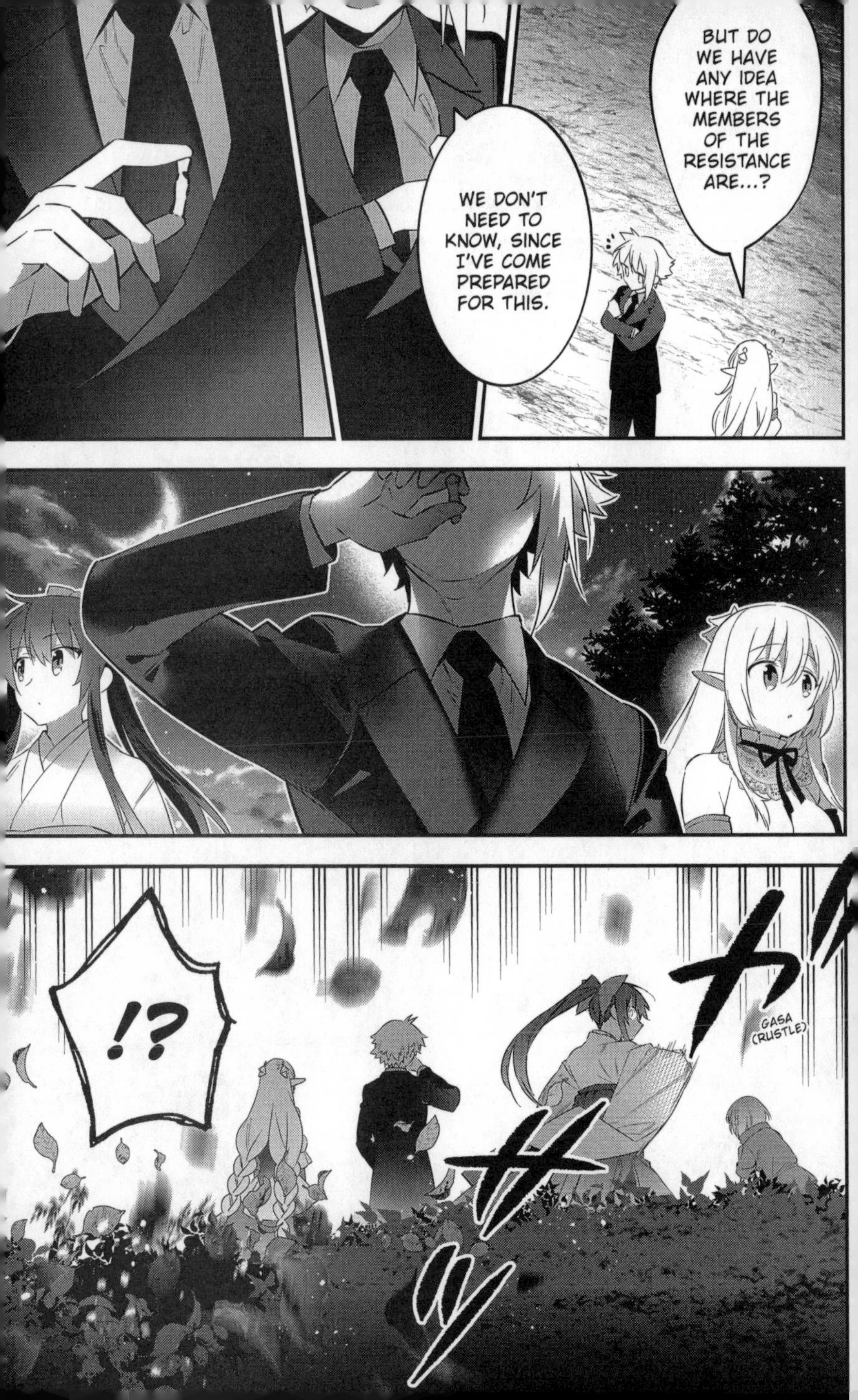
BUT DO WE HAVE ANY IDEA WHERE THE MEMBERS OF THE RESISTANCE ARE...?
WE DON'T NEED TO KNOW, SINCE I'VE COME PREPARED FOR THIS.
GASA (RUSTLE)
!?

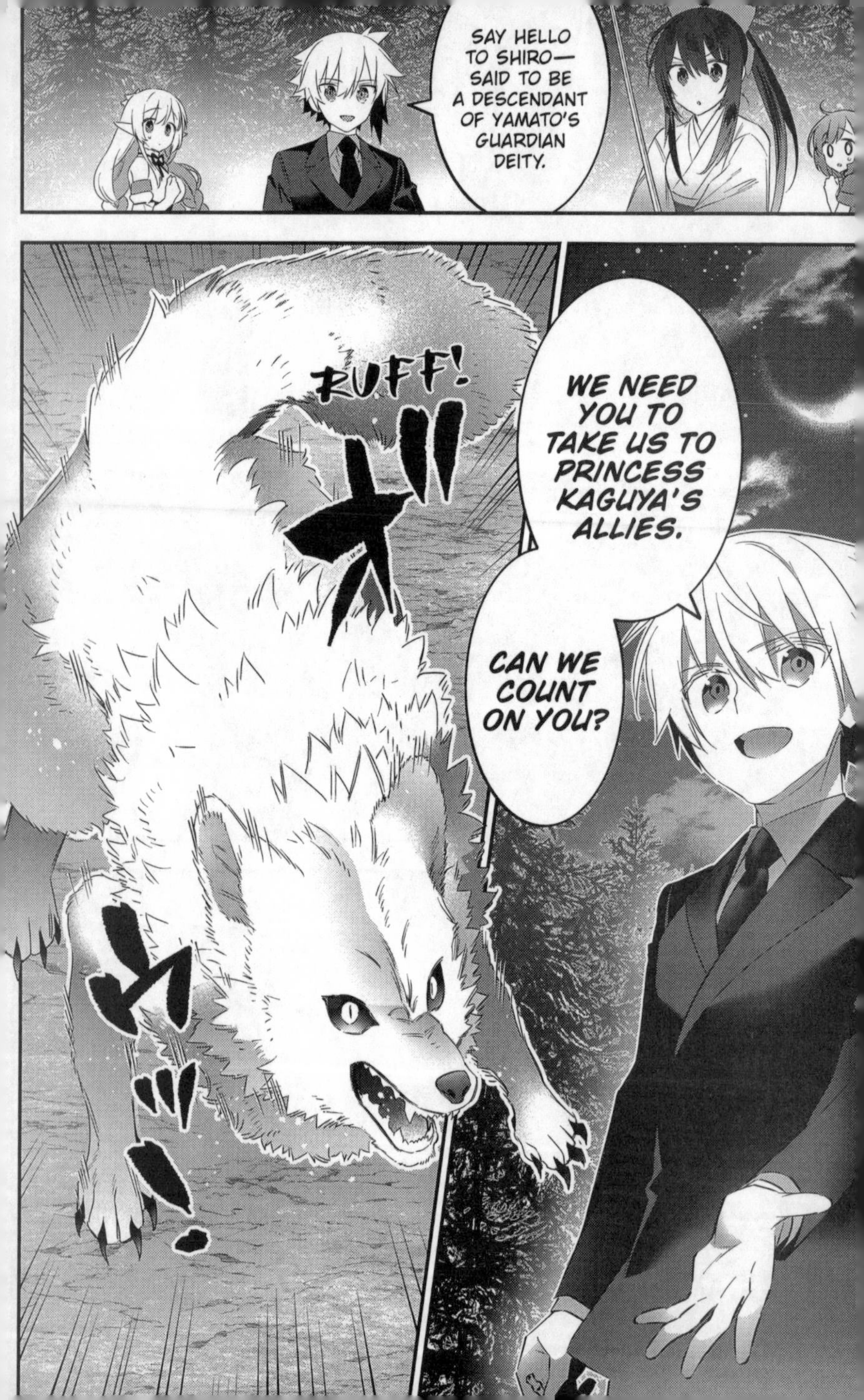
SAY HELLO TO SHIRO— SAID TO BE A DESCENDANT OF YAMATO'S GUARDIAN DEITY.
WE NEED YOU TO TAKE US TO PRINCESS KAGUYA'S ALLIES.
CAN WE COUNT ON YOU?
RUFF!

HIGH SCHOOL PRODIGIES HAVE IT EASY EVEN IN ANOTHER WORLD!

CHAPTER 72: FALSE LOVE

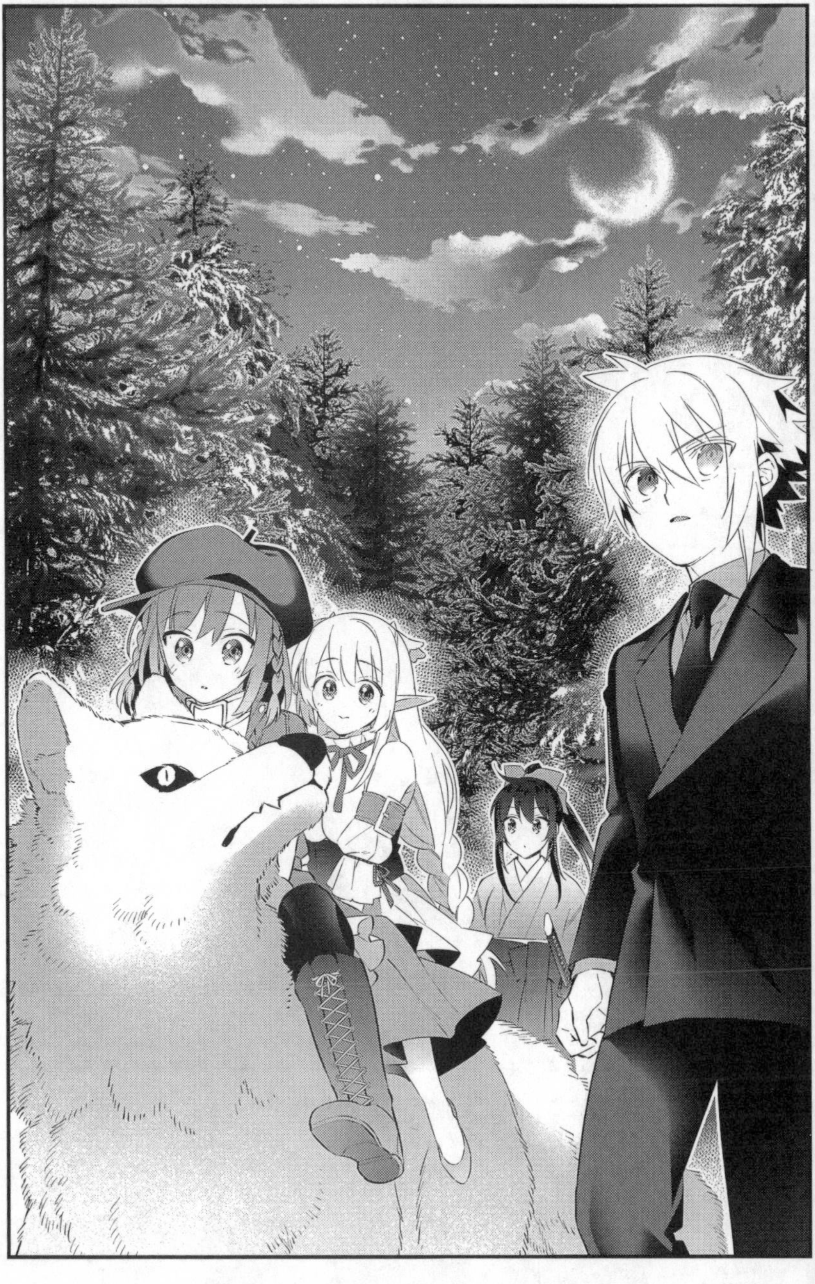

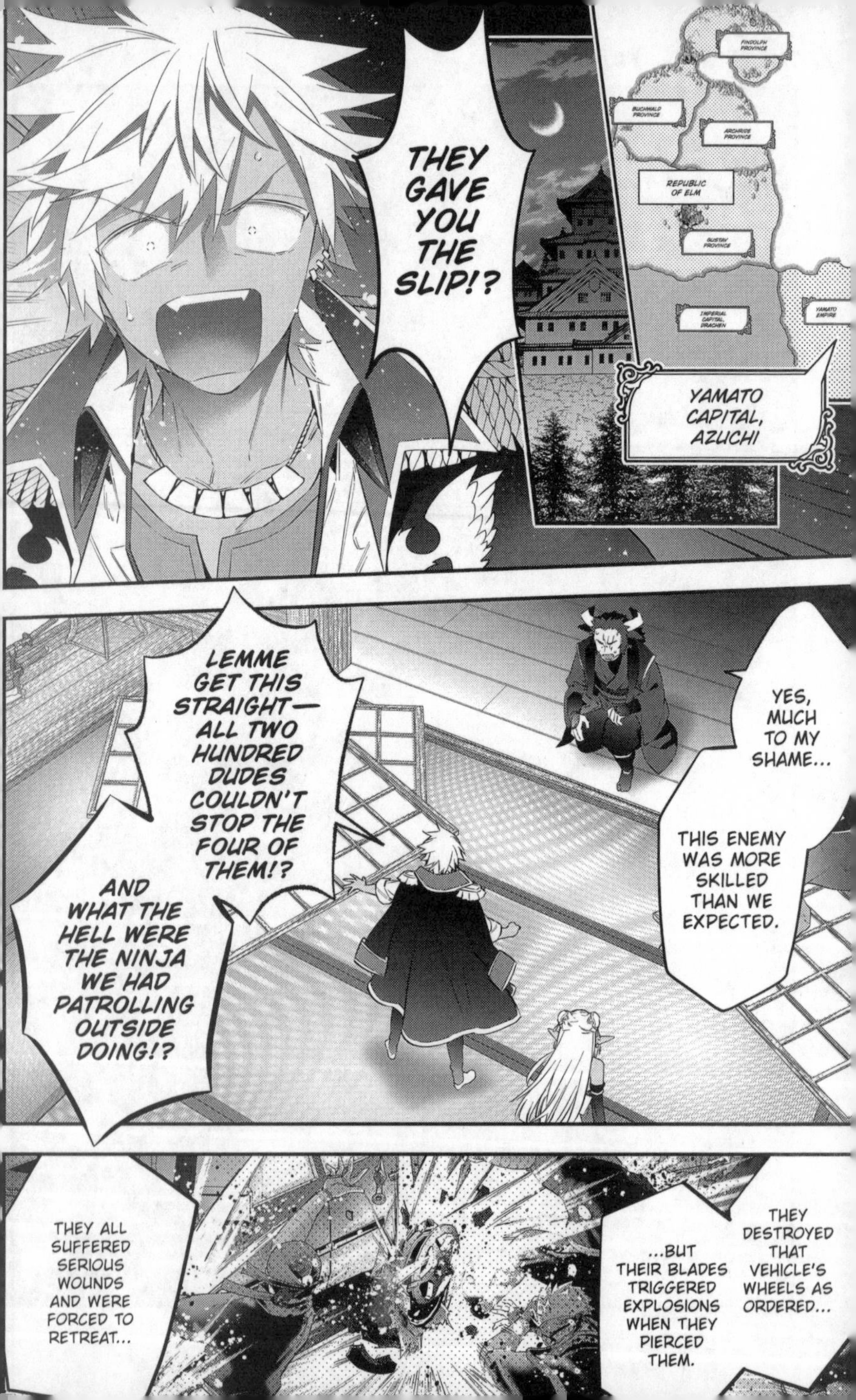
FINDOLPH PROVINCE
BUCHWALD PROVINCE
ARCHRIDE PROVINCE
REPUBLIC OF ELM
GUSTAV PROVINCE
YAMATO EMPIRE
IMPERIAL CAPITAL, DRACHEN
YAMATO CAPITAL, AZUCHI
THEY GAVE YOU THE SLIP!?
YES, MUCH TO MY SHAME...
THIS ENEMY WAS MORE SKILLED THAN WE EXPECTED.
LEMME GET THIS STRAIGHT—ALL TWO HUNDRED DUDES COULDN'T STOP THE FOUR OF THEM!?
AND WHAT THE HELL WERE THE NINJA WE HAD PATROLLING OUTSIDE DOING!?
THEY DESTROYED THAT VEHICLE'S WHEELS AS ORDERED...
...BUT THEIR BLADES TRIGGERED EXPLOSIONS WHEN THEY PIERCED THEM.
THEY ALL SUFFERED SERIOUS WOUNDS AND WERE FORCED TO RETREAT...

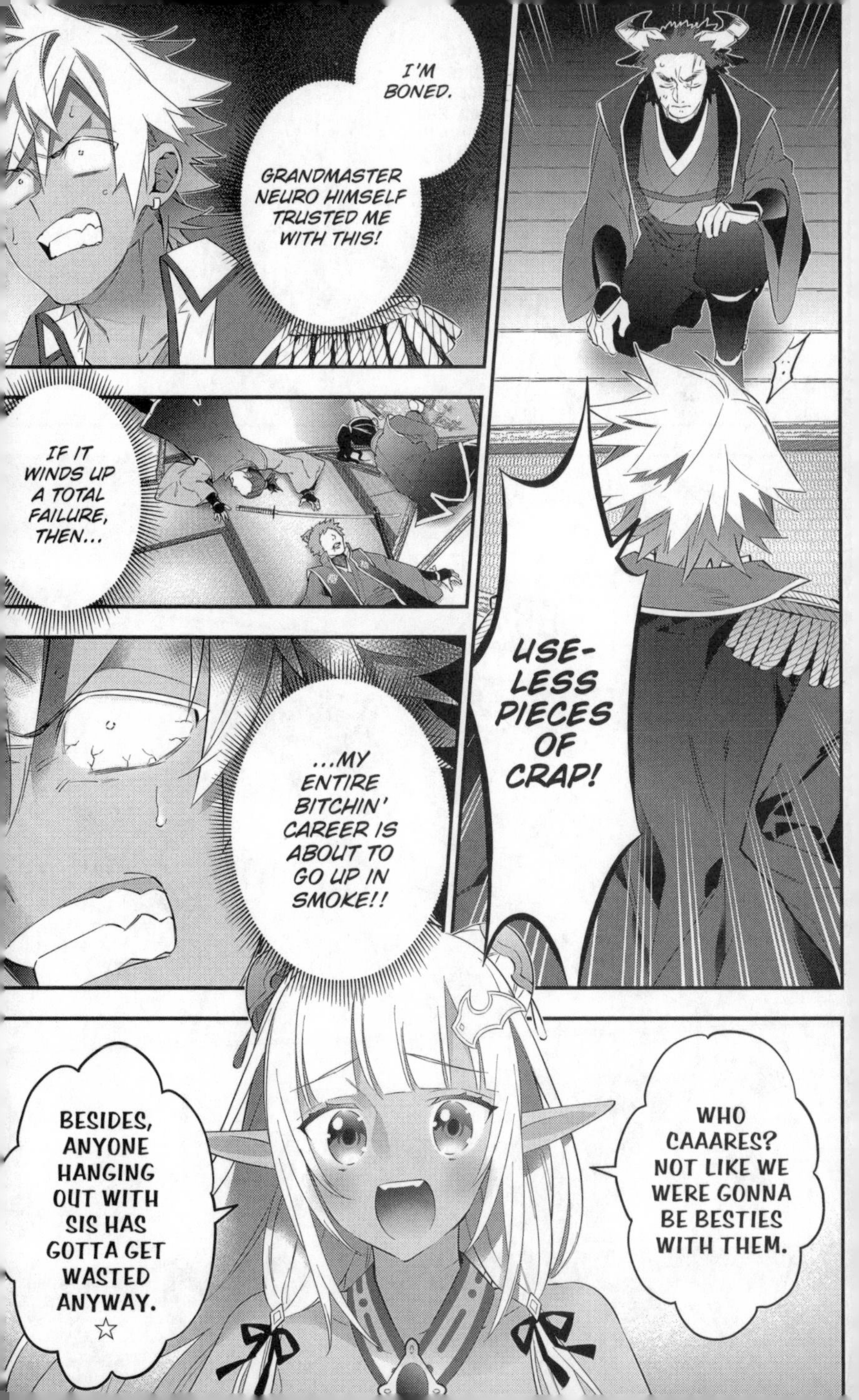
USE-LESS PIECES OF CRAP!
I'M BONED.
GRANDMASTER NEURO HIMSELF TRUSTED ME WITH THIS!
IF IT WINDS UP A TOTAL FAILURE, THEN...
...MY ENTIRE BITCHIN' CAREER IS ABOUT TO GO UP IN SMOKE!!
WHO CAAARES? NOT LIKE WE WERE GONNA BE BESTIES WITH THEM.
BESIDES, ANYONE HANGING OUT WITH SIS HAS GOTTA GET WASTED ANYWAY. ☆

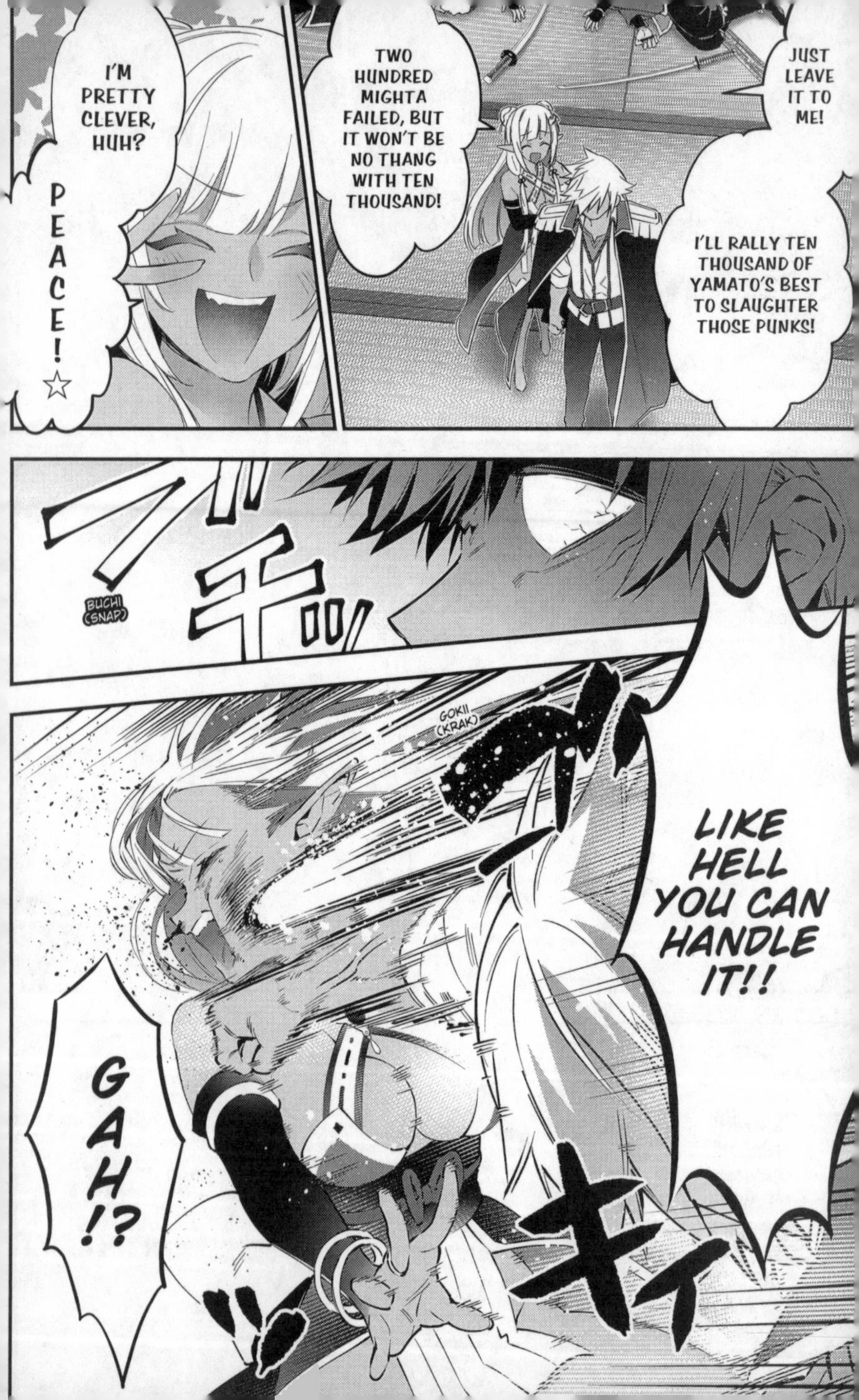
JUST LEAVE IT TO ME!
I'LL RALLY TEN THOUSAND OF YAMATO'S BEST TO SLAUGHTER THOSE PUNKS!
TWO HUNDRED MIGHTA FAILED, BUT IT WON'T BE NO THANG WITH TEN THOUSAND!
I'M PRETTY CLEVER, HUH?
PEACE!☆
BUCHI (SNAP)
GOKI (KRAK)
LIKE HELL YOU CAN HANDLE IT!!
GAH!?

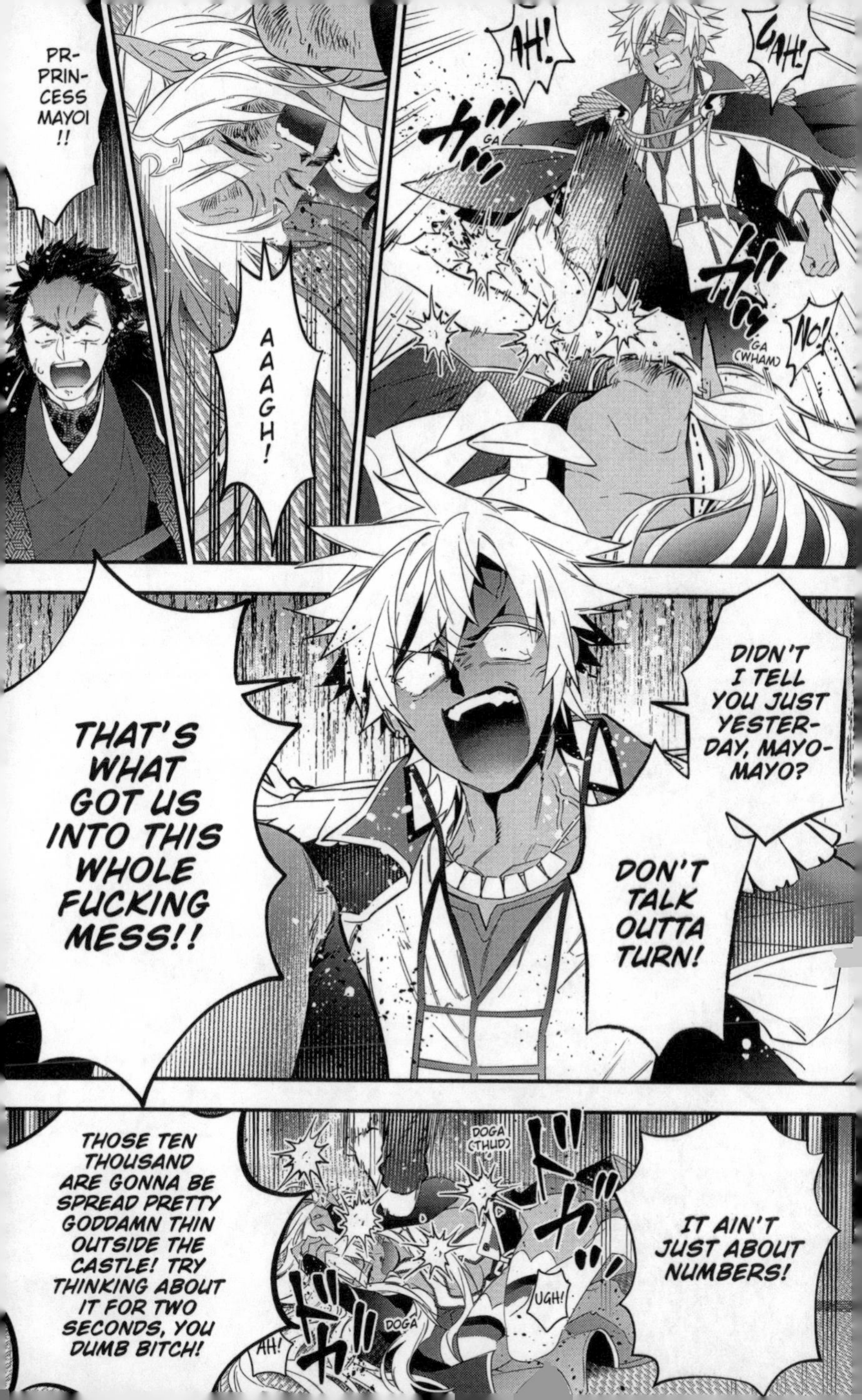
UAH!
AH!
GA
NO!
GA (WHAM)
AAAAGH!
PR-PRINCESS MAYOI!!
DIDN'T I TELL YOU JUST YESTERDAY, MAYO-MAYO?
DON'T TALK OUTTA TURN!
THAT'S WHAT GOT US INTO THIS WHOLE FUCKING MESS!!
IT AIN'T JUST ABOUT NUMBERS!
DOGA (THUD)
UGH!
THOSE TEN THOUSAND ARE GONNA BE SPREAD PRETTY GODDAMN THIN OUTSIDE THE CASTLE! TRY THINKING ABOUT IT FOR TWO SECONDS, YOU DUMB BITCH!
DOGA
AH!

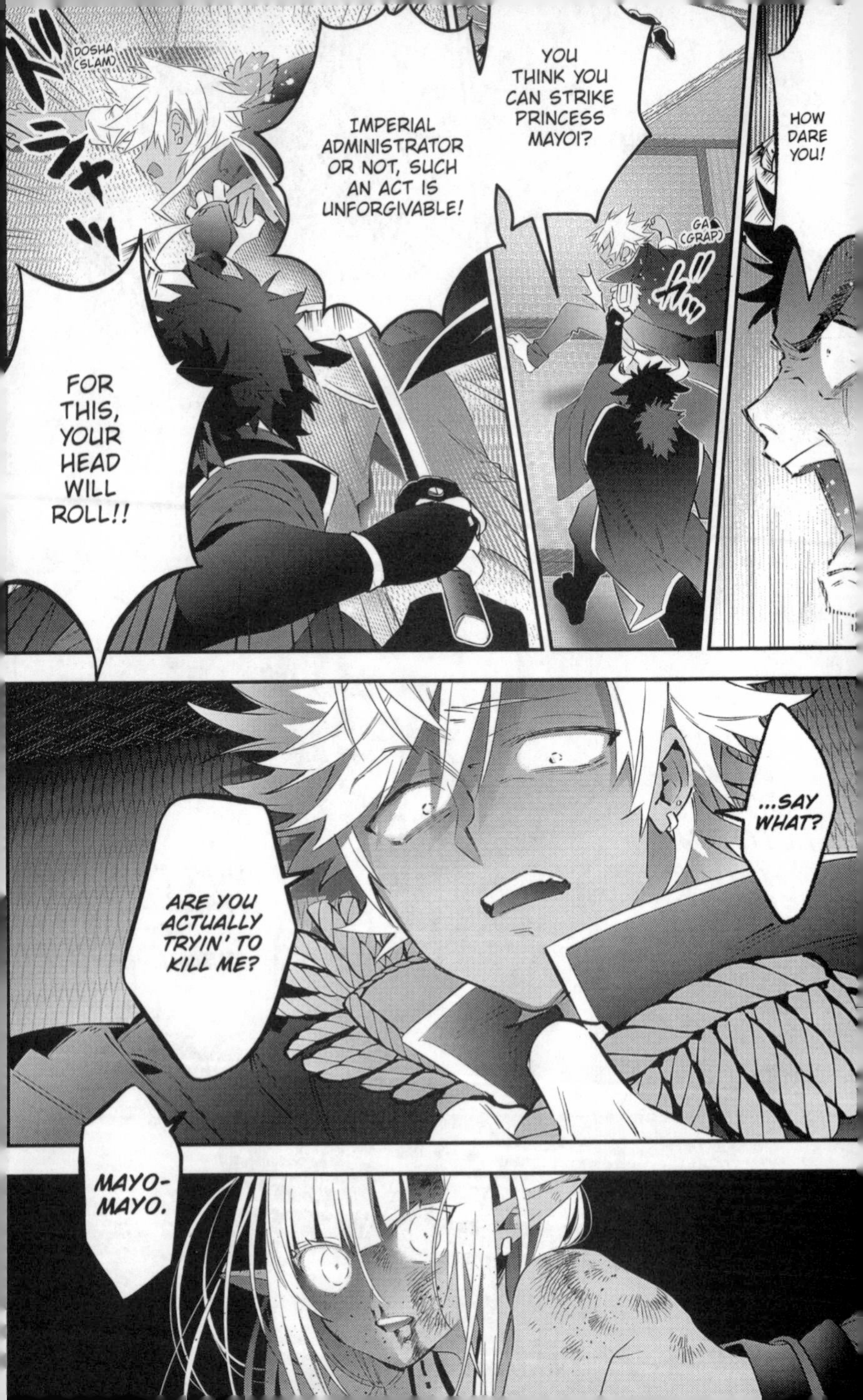
HOW DARE YOU!
YOU THINK YOU CAN STRIKE PRINCESS MAYOI?
GA (GRAP)
DOSHA (SLAM)
IMPERIAL ADMINISTRATOR OR NOT, SUCH AN ACT IS UNFORGIVABLE!
FOR THIS, YOUR HEAD WILL ROLL!!
...SAY WHAT?
ARE YOU ACTUALLY TRYIN' TO KILL ME?
MAYO-MAYO.

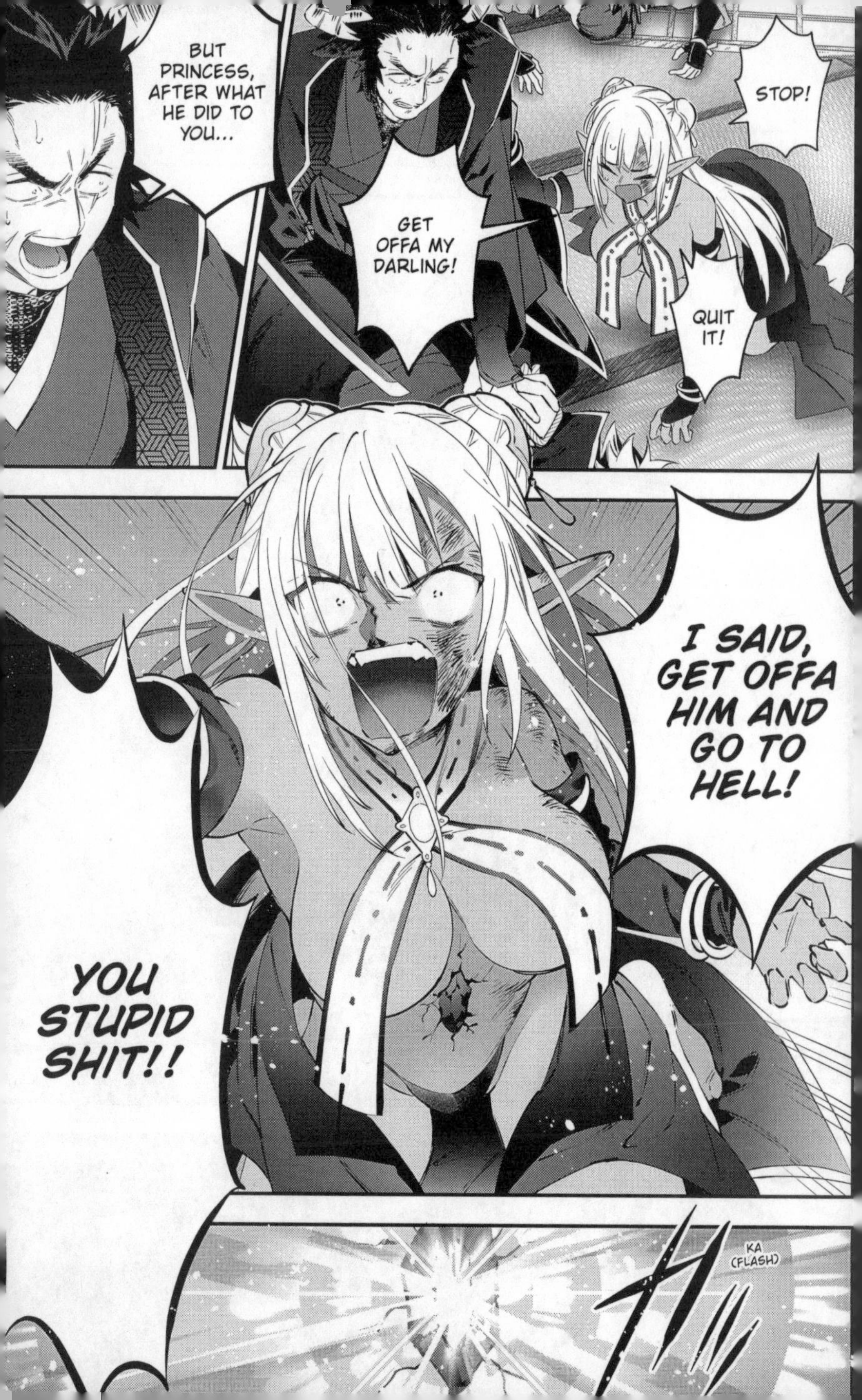
STOP!
BUT PRINCESS, AFTER WHAT HE DID TO YOU...
GET OFFA MY DARLING!
QUIT IT!
I SAID, GET OFFA HIM AND GO TO HELL!
YOU STUPID SHIT!!
KA (FLASH)

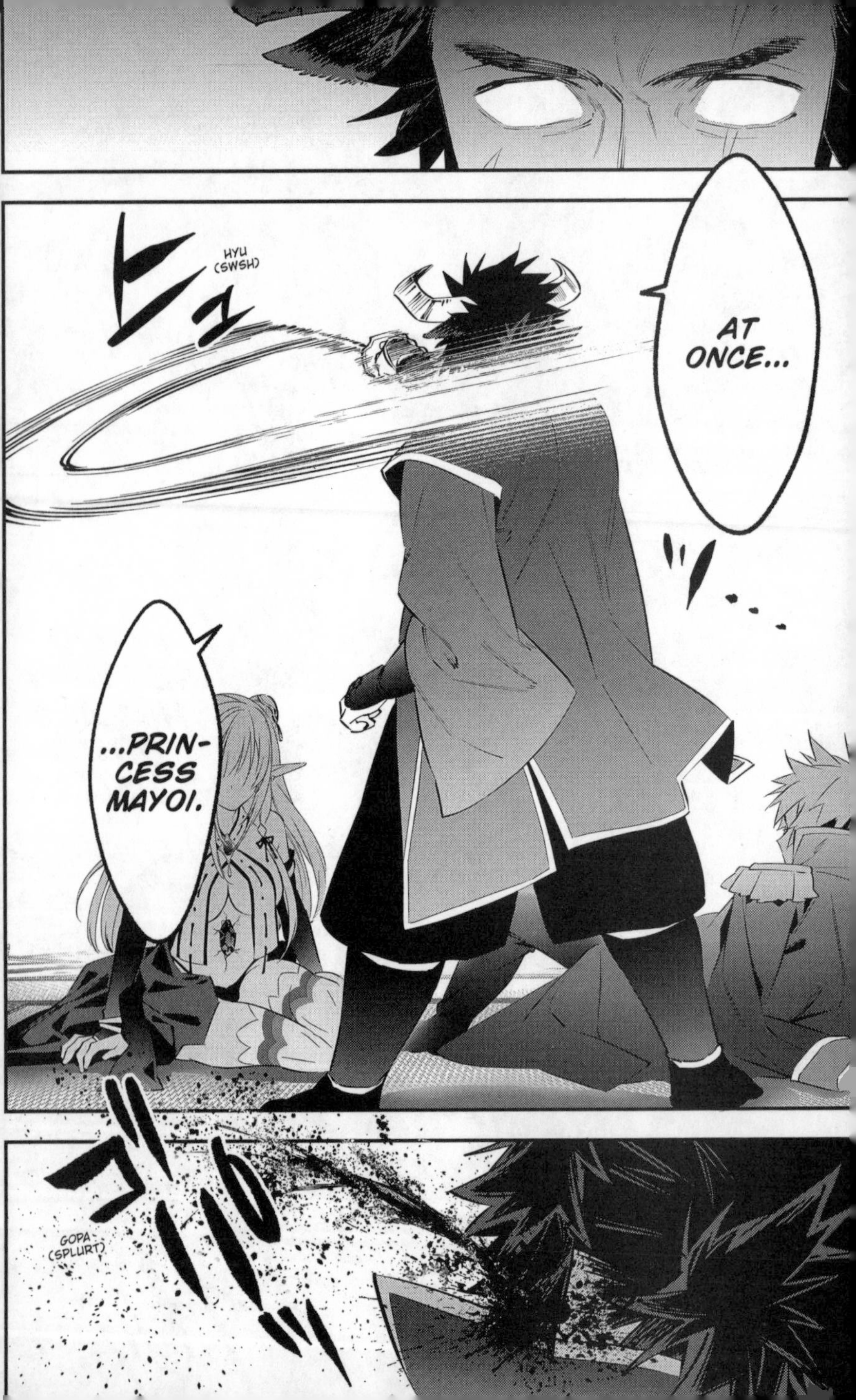
AT ONCE...
HYU (SWSH)
...PRIN-CESS MAYOI.
GOPA (SPLURT)

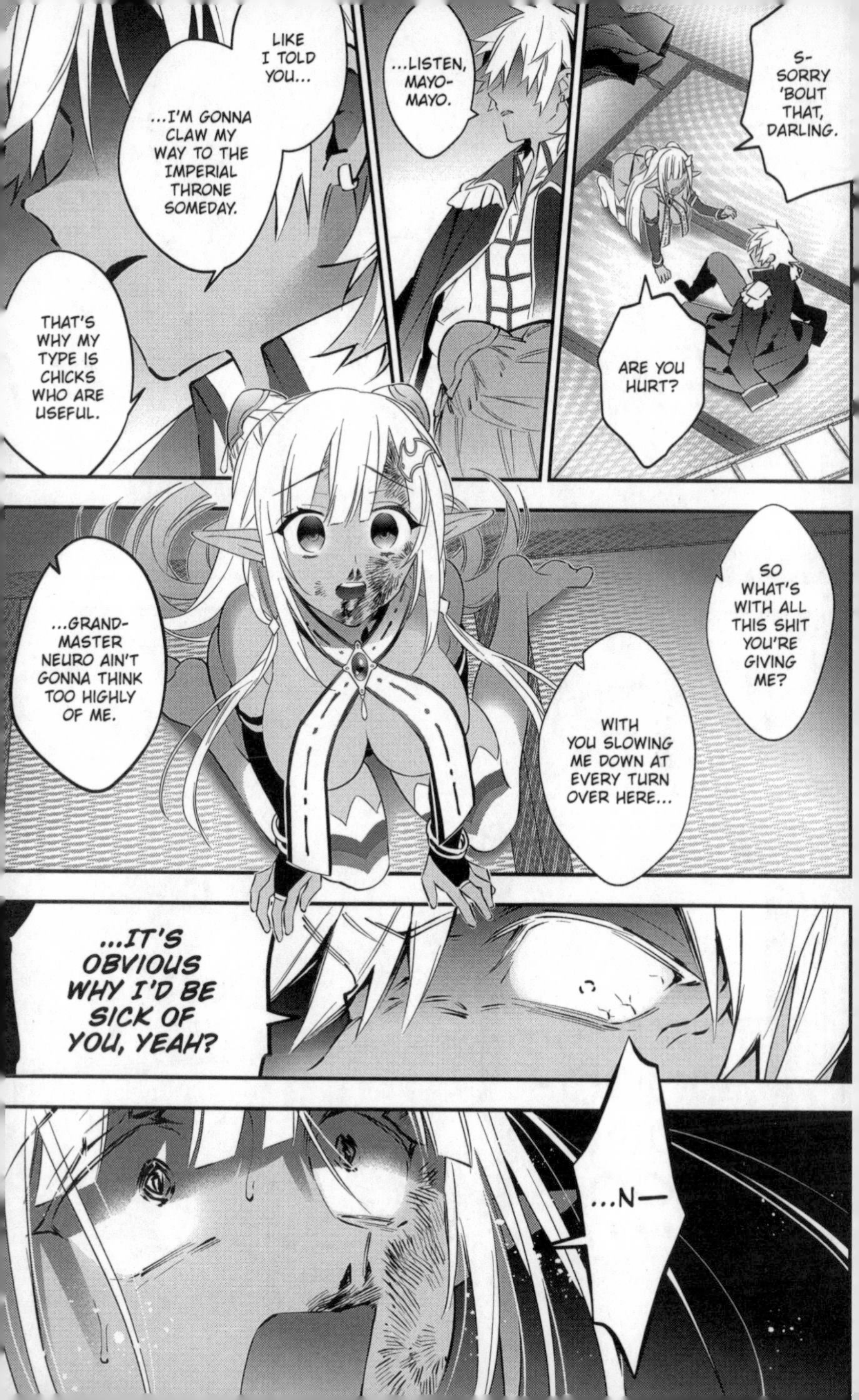
S-SORRY 'BOUT THAT, DARLING.
ARE YOU HURT?
...LISTEN, MAYO-MAYO.
LIKE I TOLD YOU...
...I'M GONNA CLAW MY WAY TO THE IMPERIAL THRONE SOMEDAY.
THAT'S WHY MY TYPE IS CHICKS WHO ARE USEFUL.
SO WHAT'S WITH ALL THIS SHIT YOU'RE GIVING ME?
WITH YOU SLOWING ME DOWN AT EVERY TURN OVER HERE...
...GRAND-MASTER NEURO AIN'T GONNA THINK TOO HIGHLY OF ME.
...IT'S OBVIOUS WHY I'D BE SICK OF YOU, YEAH?
...N—

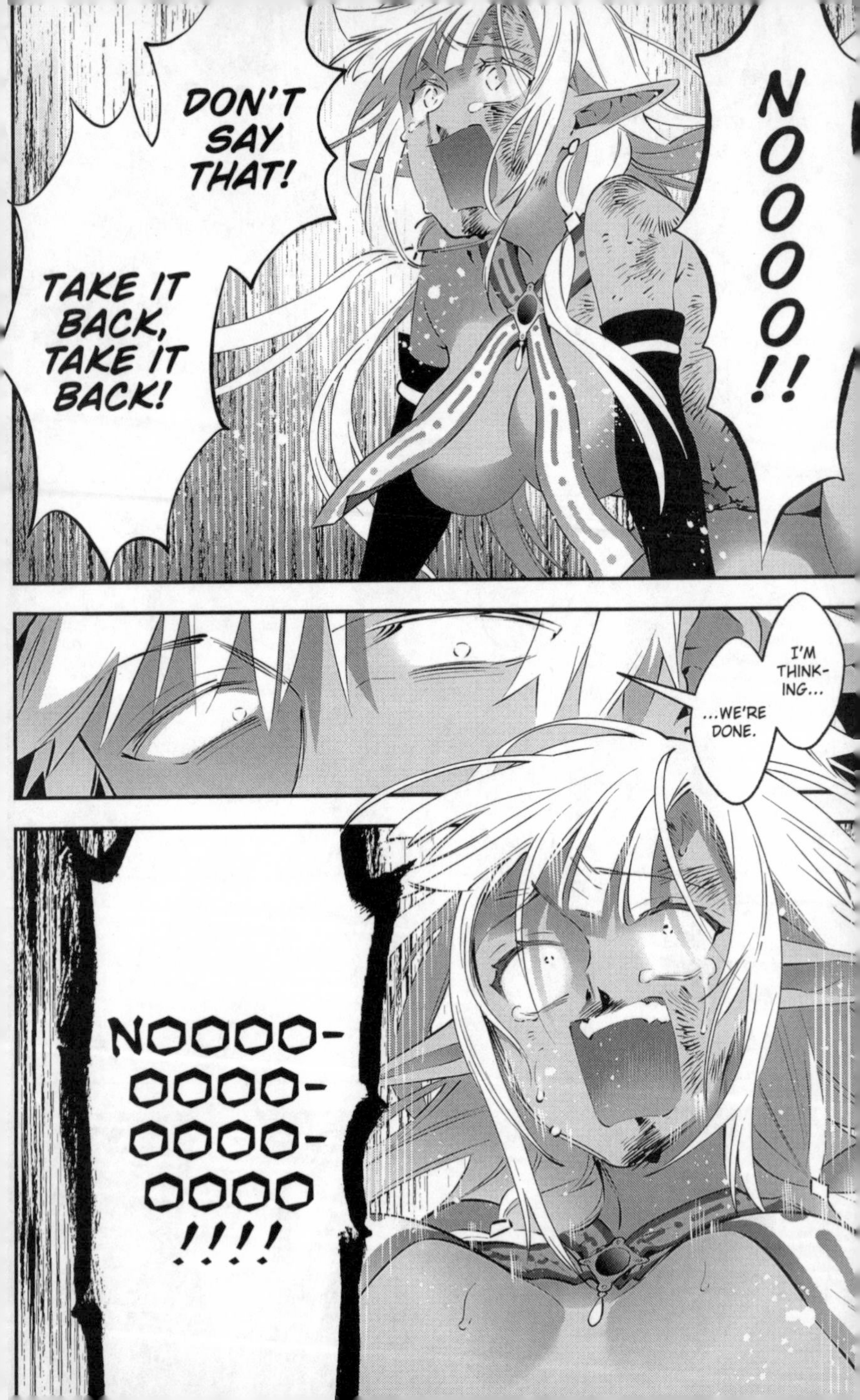
NOOOO!!
DON'T SAY THAT!
TAKE IT BACK, TAKE IT BACK!
I'M THINK-ING...
...WE'RE DONE.
NOOOO-OOOO-OOOO-OOOO!!!!

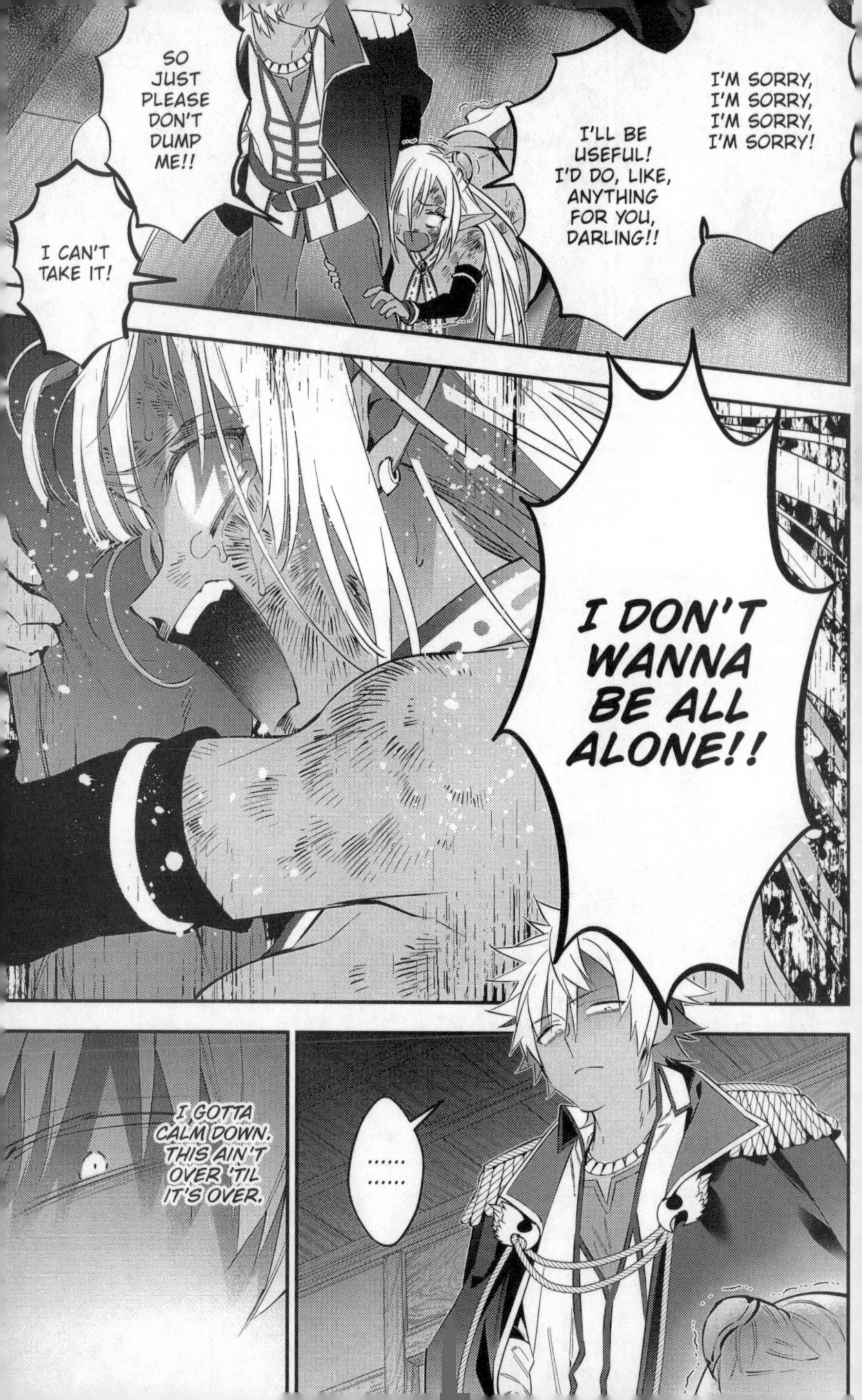
I'M SORRY, I'M SORRY, I'M SORRY, I'M SORRY!
I'LL BE USEFUL! I'D DO, LIKE, ANYTHING FOR YOU, DARLING!!
SO JUST PLEASE DON'T DUMP ME!!
I CAN'T TAKE IT!
I DON'T WANNA BE ALL ALONE!!
......
......
I GOTTA CALM DOWN. THIS AIN'T OVER 'TIL IT'S OVER.

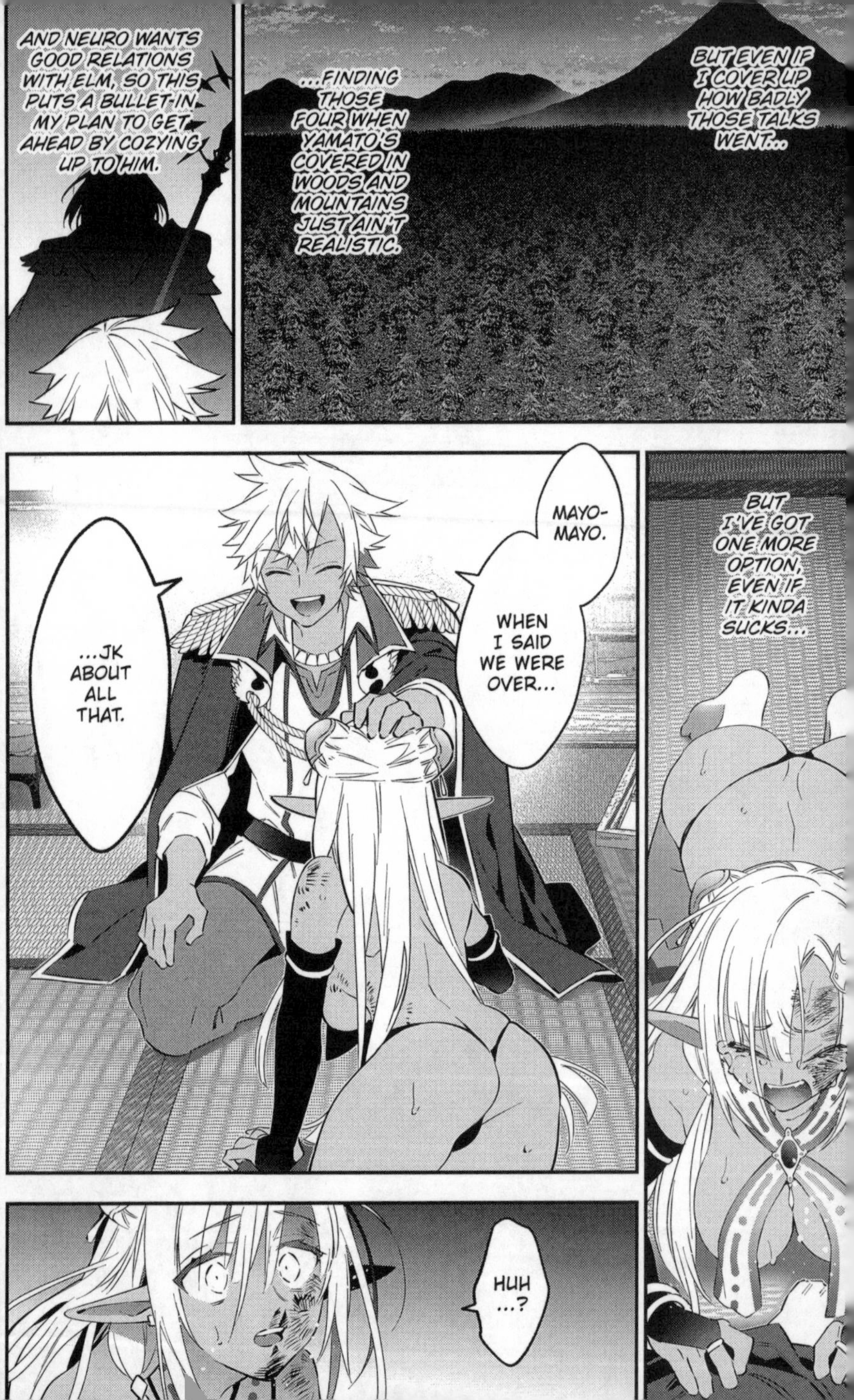
BUT EVEN IF I COVER UP HOW BADLY THOSE TALKS WENT...
...FINDING THOSE FOUR WHEN YAMATO'S COVERED IN WOODS AND MOUNTAINS JUST AIN'T REALISTIC.
AND NEURO WANTS GOOD RELATIONS WITH ELM, SO THIS PUTS A BULLET IN MY PLAN TO GET AHEAD BY COZYING UP TO HIM.
BUT I'VE GOT ONE MORE OPTION, EVEN IF IT KINDA SUCKS...
MAYO-MAYO.
WHEN I SAID WE WERE OVER...
...JK ABOUT ALL THAT.
HUH ...?

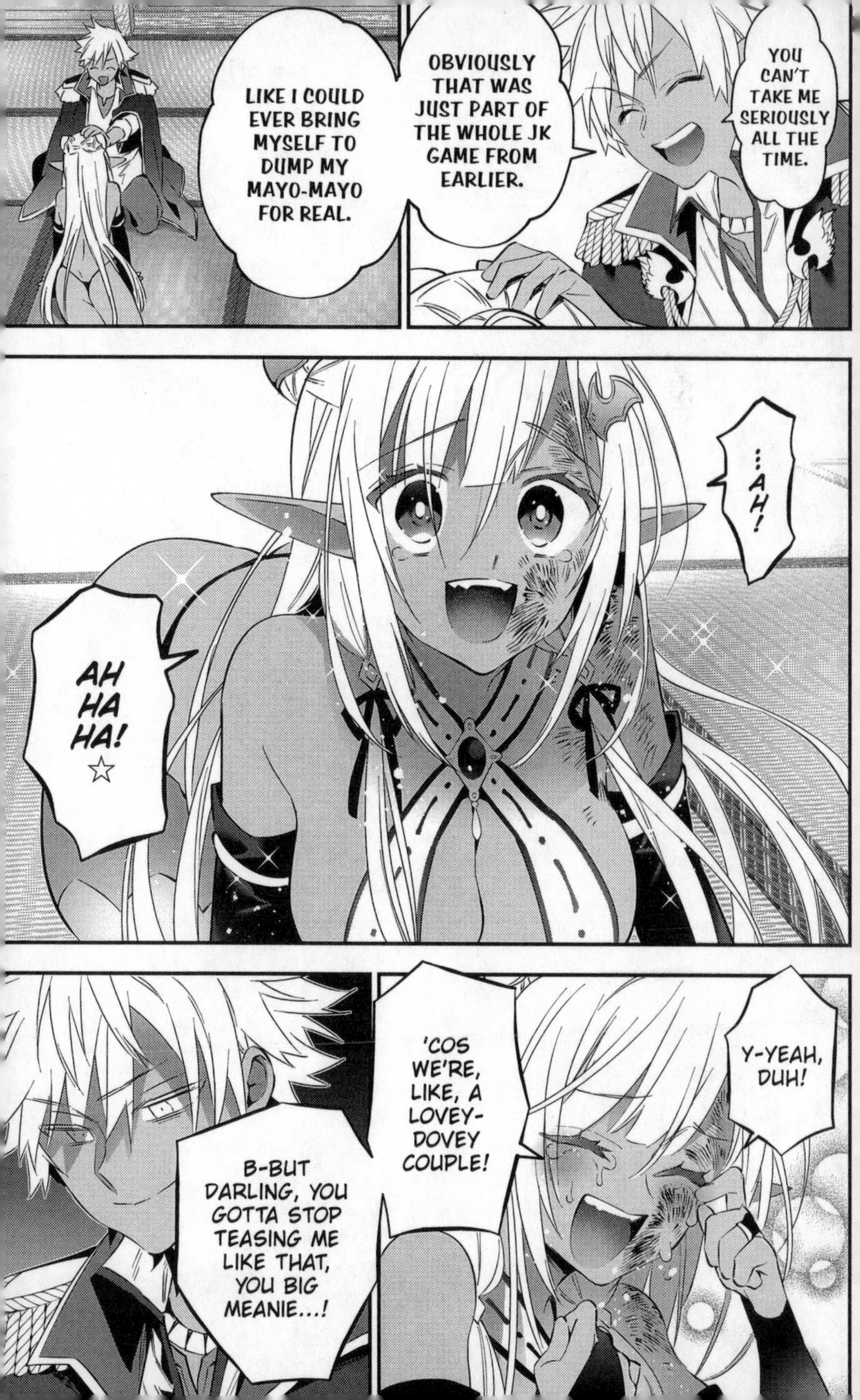
YOU CAN'T TAKE ME SERIOUSLY ALL THE TIME.
OBVIOUSLY THAT WAS JUST PART OF THE WHOLE JK GAME FROM EARLIER.
LIKE I COULD EVER BRING MYSELF TO DUMP MY MAYO-MAYO FOR REAL.
...AH!
AH HA HA! ☆
Y-YEAH, DUH!
'COS WE'RE, LIKE, A LOVEY-DOVEY COUPLE!
B-BUT DARLING, YOU GOTTA STOP TEASING ME LIKE THAT, YOU BIG MEANIE...!

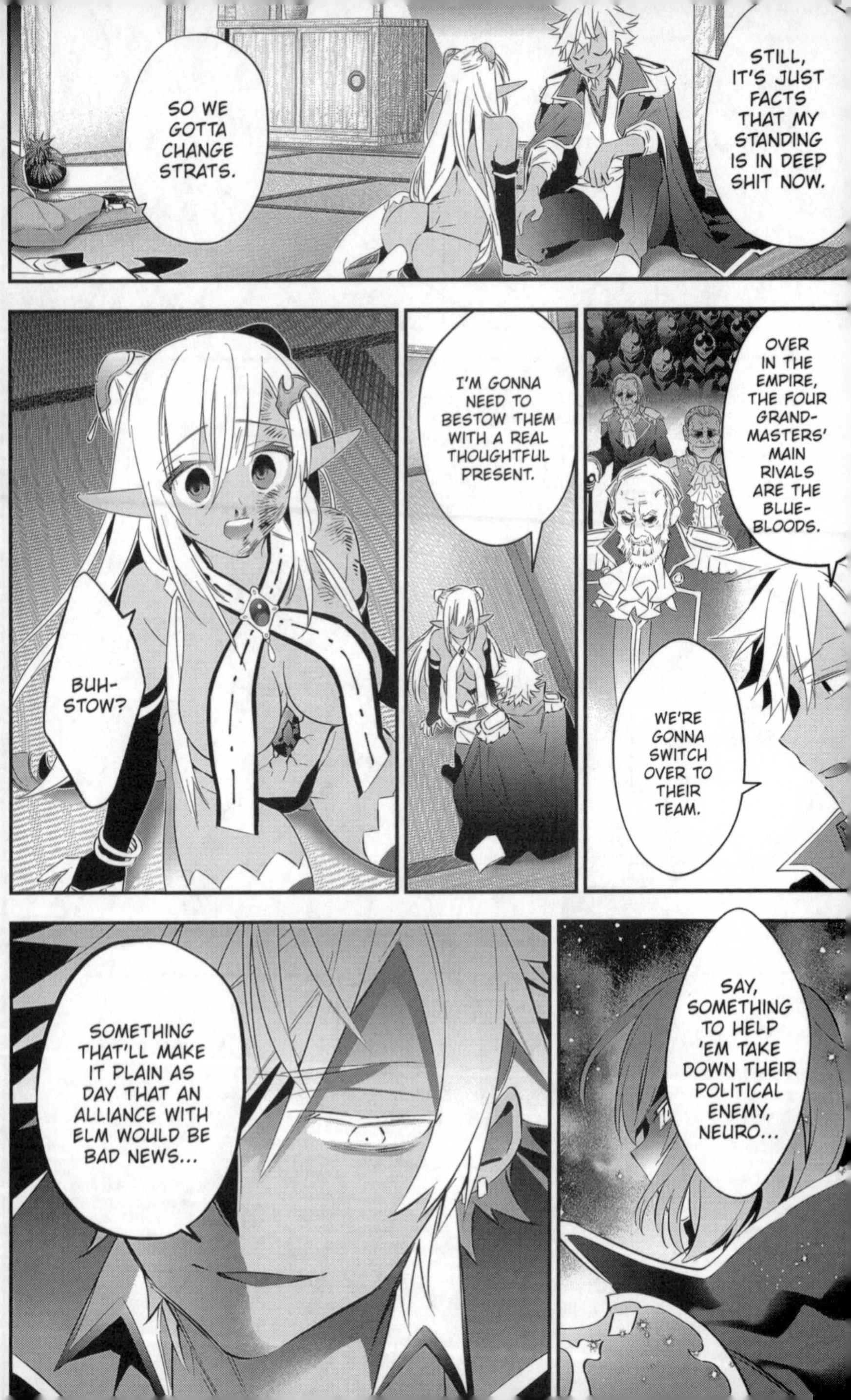
STILL, IT'S JUST FACTS THAT MY STANDING IS IN DEEP SHIT NOW.
SO WE GOTTA CHANGE STRATS.
OVER IN THE EMPIRE, THE FOUR GRAND-MASTERS' MAIN RIVALS ARE THE BLUE-BLOODS.
WE'RE GONNA SWITCH OVER TO THEIR TEAM.
I'M GONNA NEED TO BESTOW THEM WITH A REAL THOUGHTFUL PRESENT.
BUH-STOW?
SAY, SOMETHING TO HELP 'EM TAKE DOWN THEIR POLITICAL ENEMY, NEURO...
SOMETHING THAT'LL MAKE IT PLAIN AS DAY THAT AN ALLIANCE WITH ELM WOULD BE BAD NEWS...

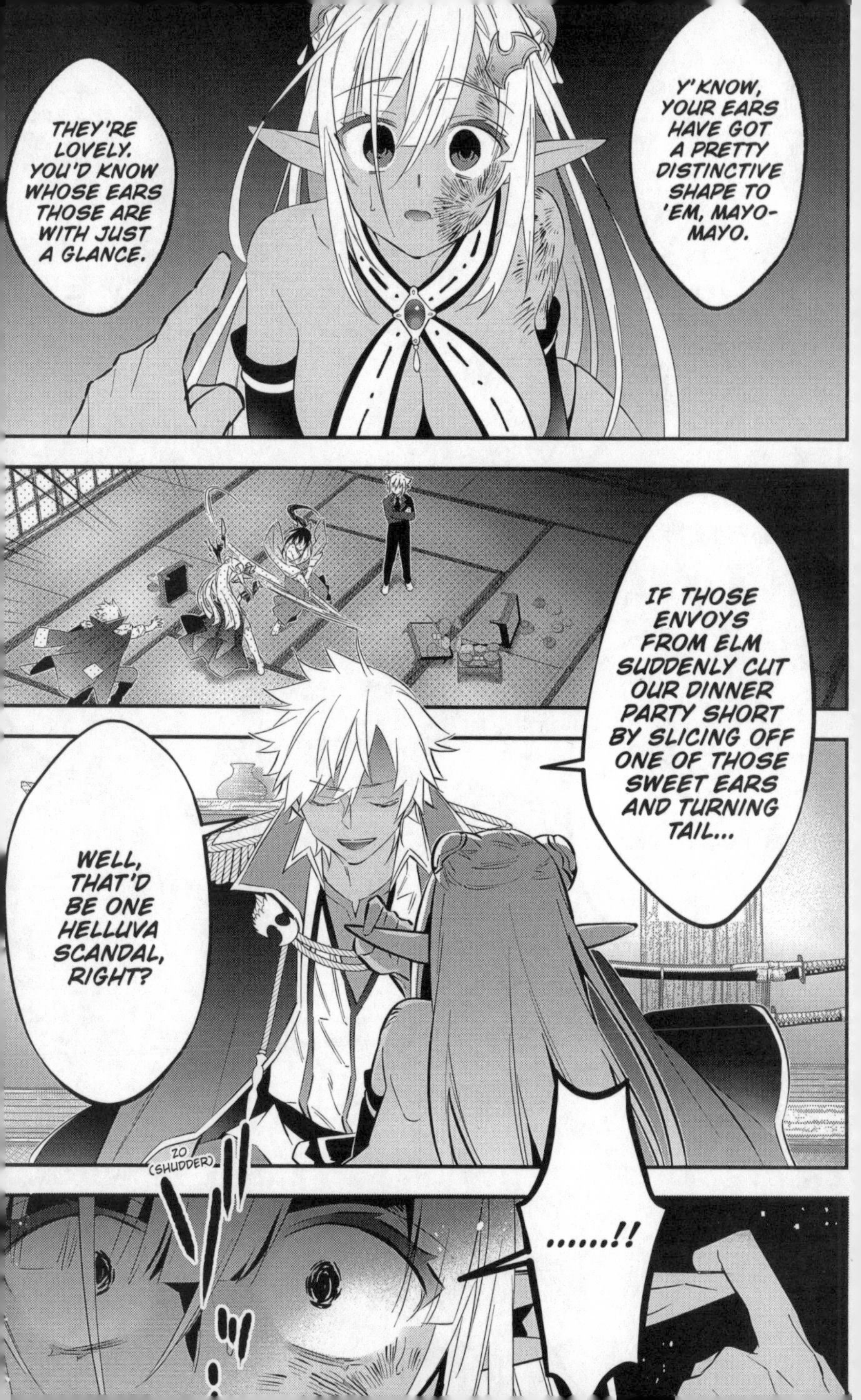
Y'KNOW, YOUR EARS HAVE GOT A PRETTY DISTINCTIVE SHAPE TO 'EM, MAYO-MAYO.
THEY'RE LOVELY. YOU'D KNOW WHOSE EARS THOSE ARE WITH JUST A GLANCE.
IF THOSE ENVOYS FROM ELM SUDDENLY CUT OUR DINNER PARTY SHORT BY SLICING OFF ONE OF THOSE SWEET EARS AND TURNING TAIL...
WELL, THAT'D BE ONE HELLUVA SCANDAL, RIGHT?
ZO (SHUDDER)
......!!

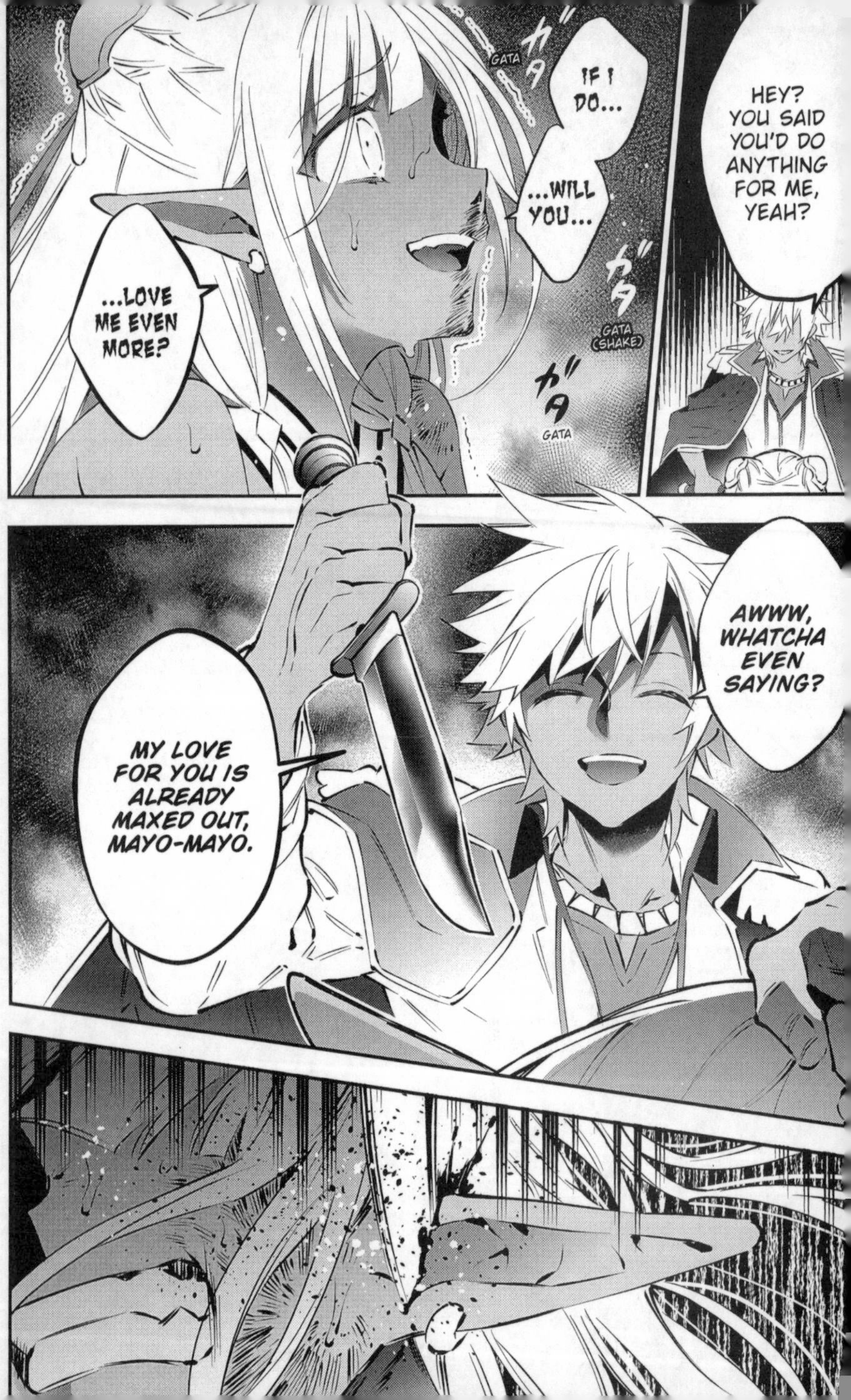
HEY? YOU SAID YOU'D DO ANYTHING FOR ME, YEAH?
GATA
IF I DO...
...WILL YOU...
GATA (SHAKE)
GATA
...LOVE ME EVEN MORE?
AWWW, WHATCHA EVEN SAYING?
MY LOVE FOR YOU IS ALREADY MAXED OUT, MAYO-MAYO.

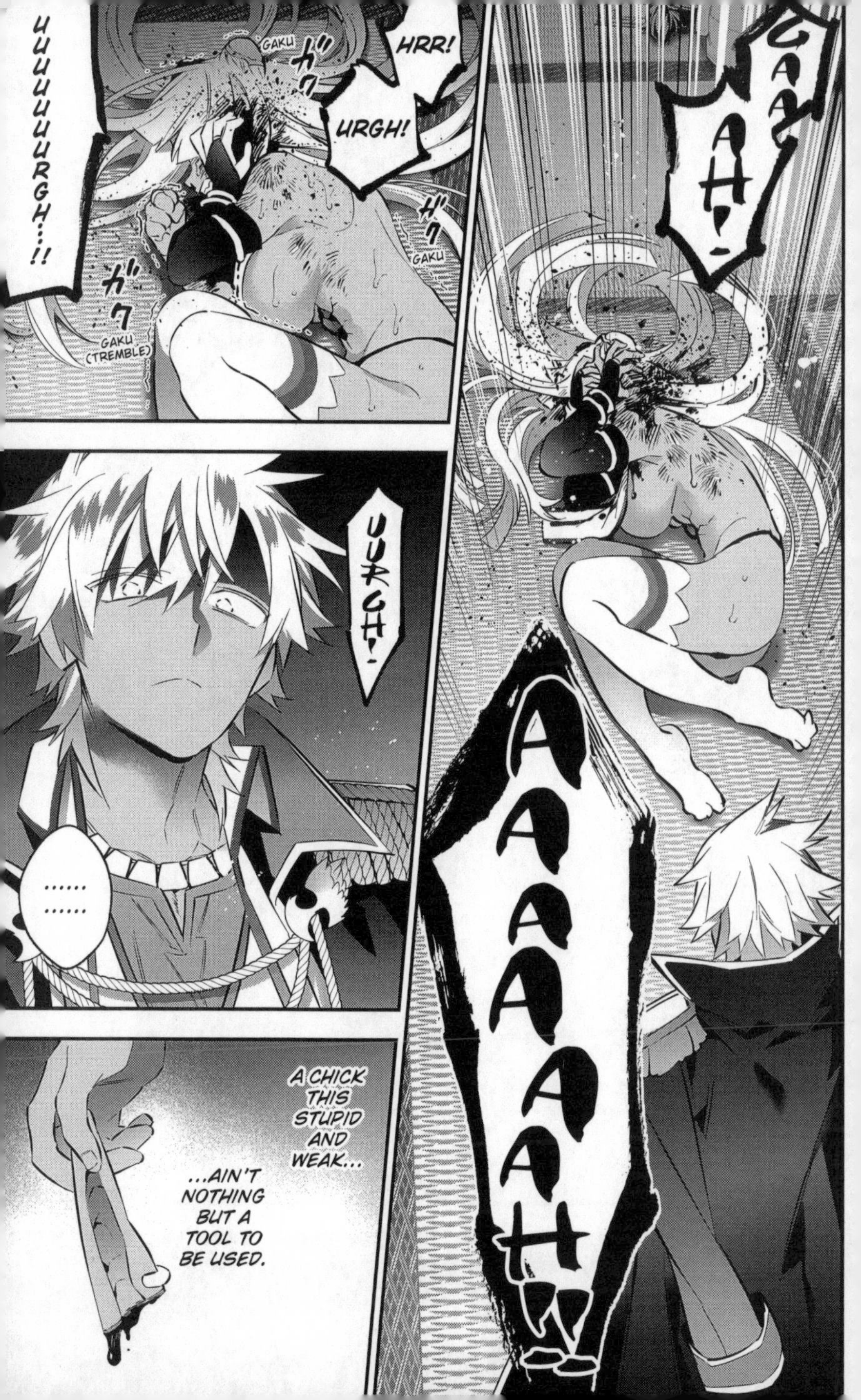
GAAAH!
AAAAAAH!!
HRR!
URGH!
ガク GAKU
ガク GAKU
UUUUUUURGH...!!
ガク GAKU (TREMBLE)
UURGH!
......
......
A CHICK THIS STUPID AND WEAK...
...AIN'T NOTHING BUT A TOOL TO BE USED.

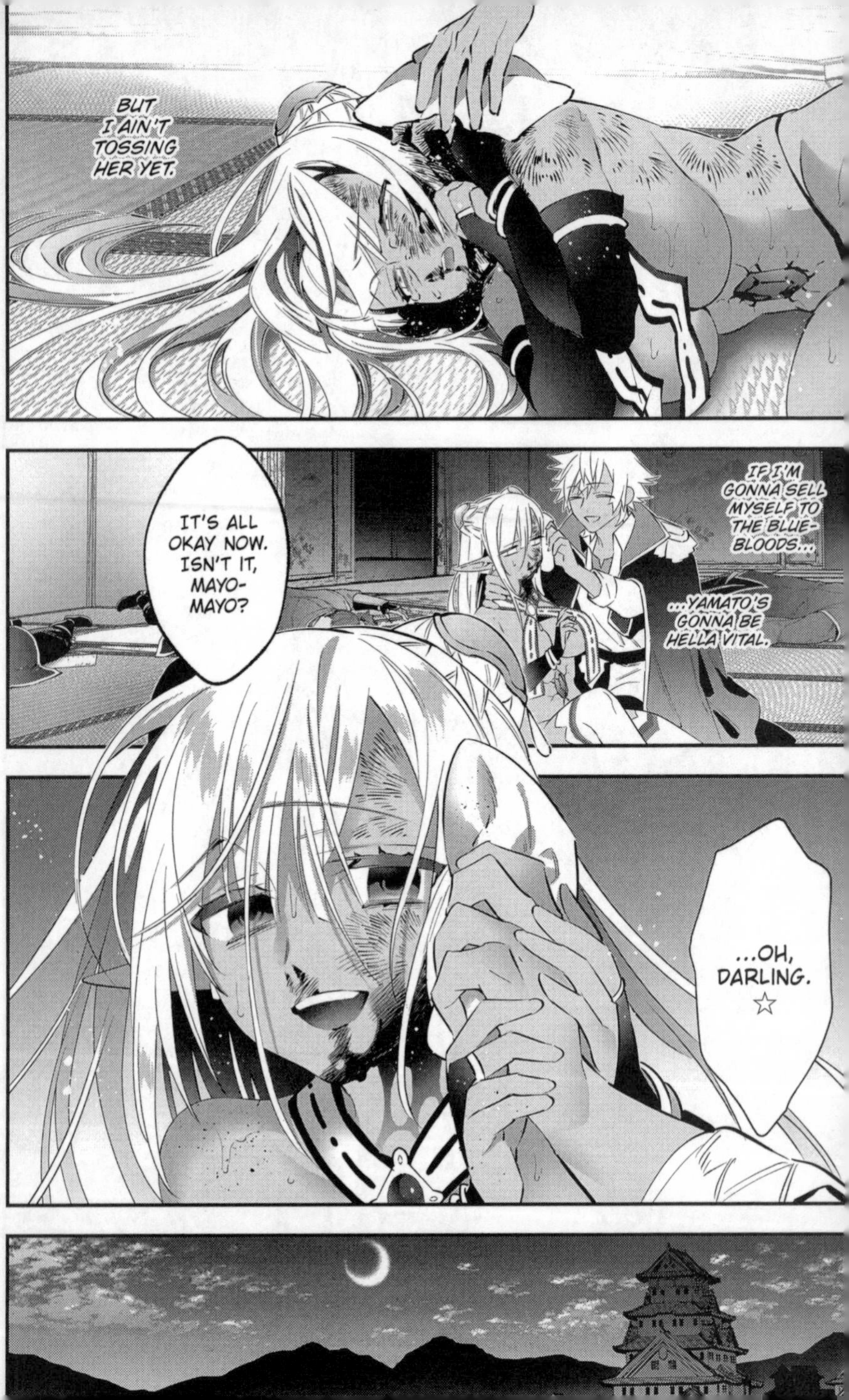
BUT I AIN'T TOSSING HER YET.
IF I'M GONNA SELL MYSELF TO THE BLUE-BLOODS...
...YAMATO'S GONNA BE HELLA VITAL.
IT'S ALL OKAY NOW. ISN'T IT, MAYO-MAYO?
...OH, DARLING. ☆

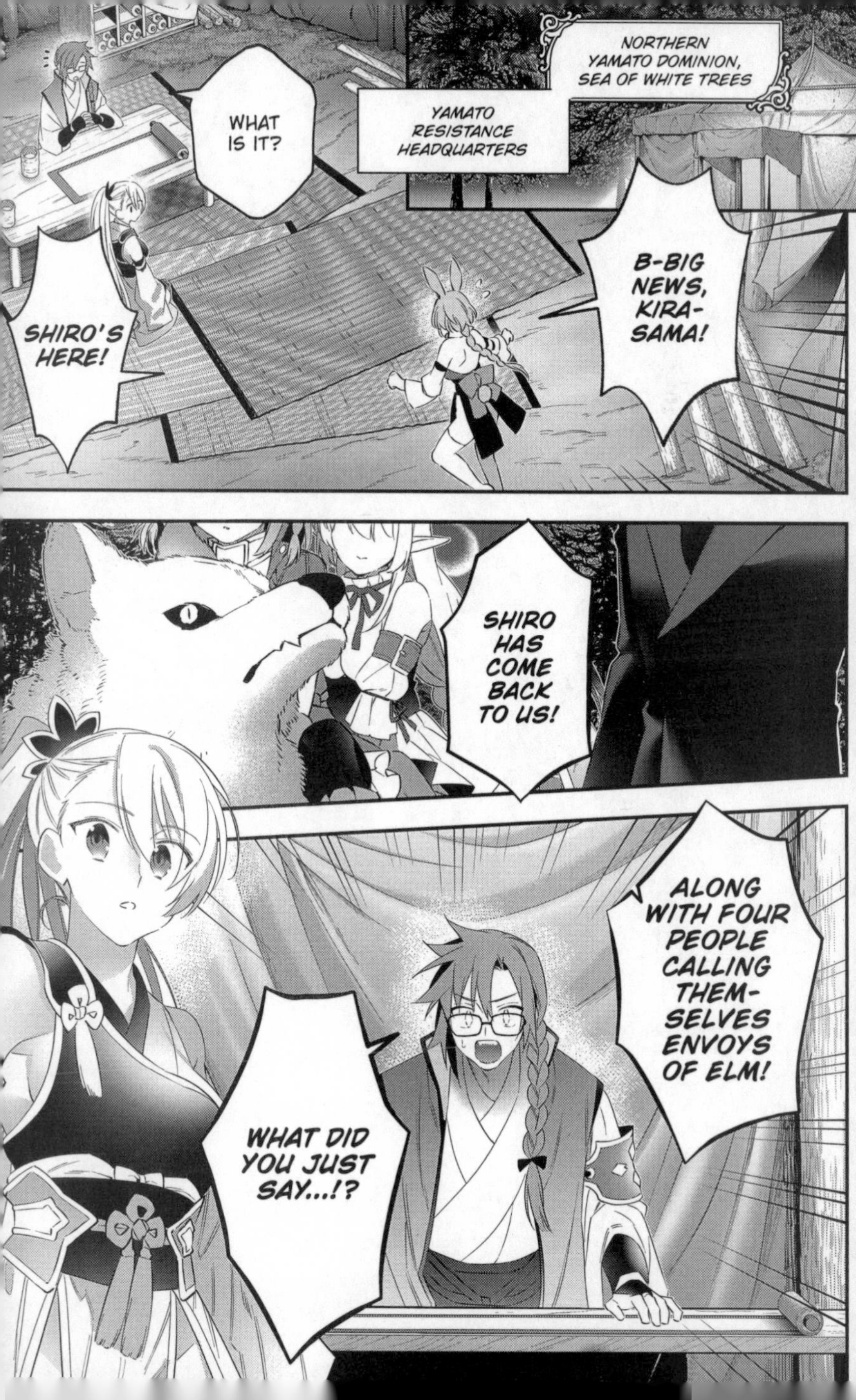
NORTHERN YAMATO DOMINION, SEA OF WHITE TREES
YAMATO RESISTANCE HEADQUARTERS
B-BIG NEWS, KIRA-SAMA!
WHAT IS IT?
SHIRO'S HERE!
SHIRO HAS COME BACK TO US!
ALONG WITH FOUR PEOPLE CALLING THEM-SELVES ENVOYS OF ELM!
WHAT DID YOU JUST SAY...!?

HIGH SCHOOL PRODIGIES HAVE IT EASY EVEN IN ANOTHER WORLD!

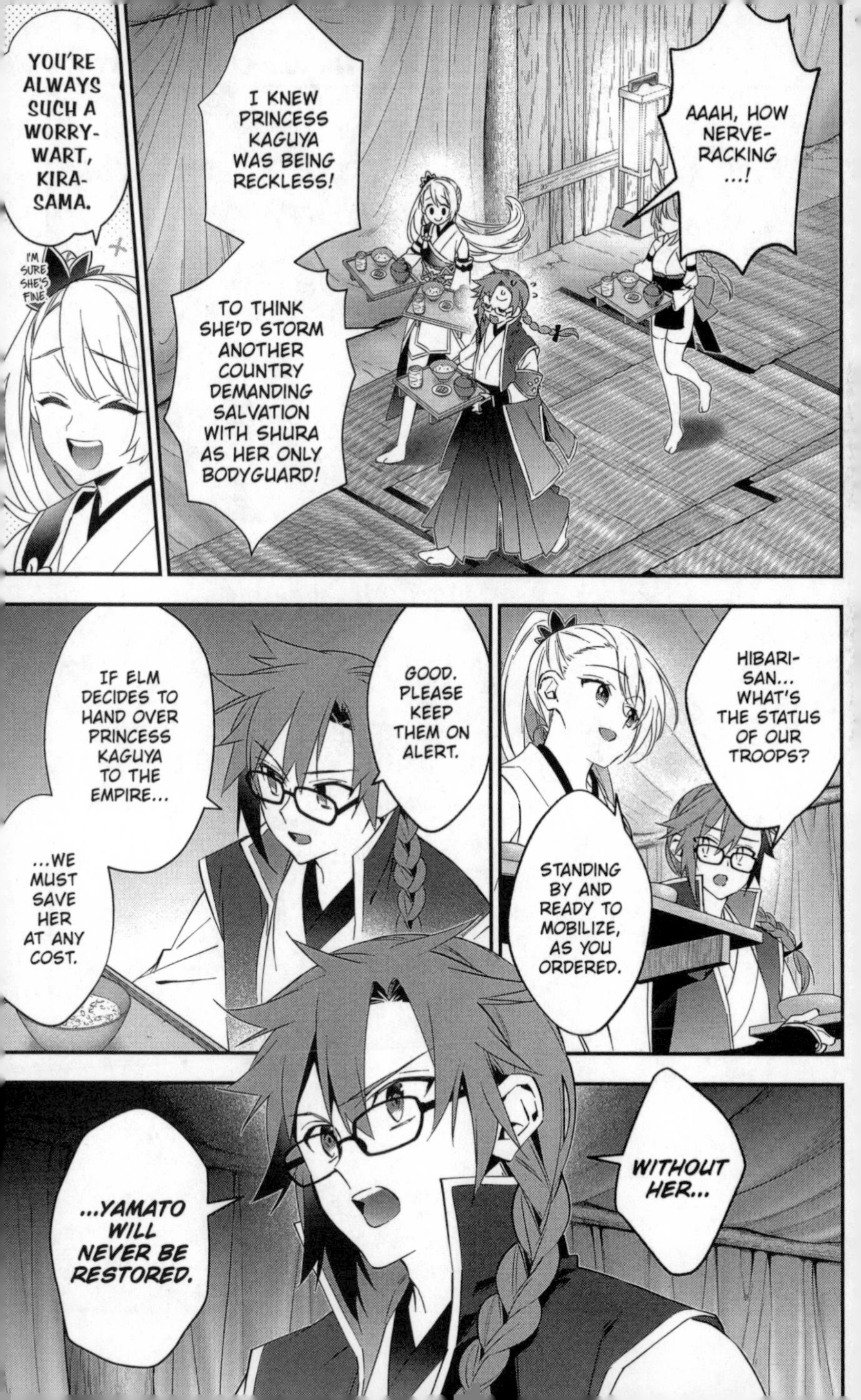

AAAH, HOW NERVE-RACKING ...!
I KNEW PRINCESS KAGUYA WAS BEING RECKLESS!
TO THINK SHE'D STORM ANOTHER COUNTRY DEMANDING SALVATION WITH SHURA AS HER ONLY BODYGUARD!
YOU'RE ALWAYS SUCH A WORRY-WART, KIRA-SAMA.
I'M SURE SHE'S FINE.
HIBARI-SAN... WHAT'S THE STATUS OF OUR TROOPS?
STANDING BY AND READY TO MOBILIZE, AS YOU ORDERED.
GOOD. PLEASE KEEP THEM ON ALERT.
IF ELM DECIDES TO HAND OVER PRINCESS KAGUYA TO THE EMPIRE...
...WE MUST SAVE HER AT ANY COST.
WITHOUT HER...
...YAMATO WILL NEVER BE RESTORED.

CHAPTER 73: ONE STEP TOWARD A COUNTERATTACK

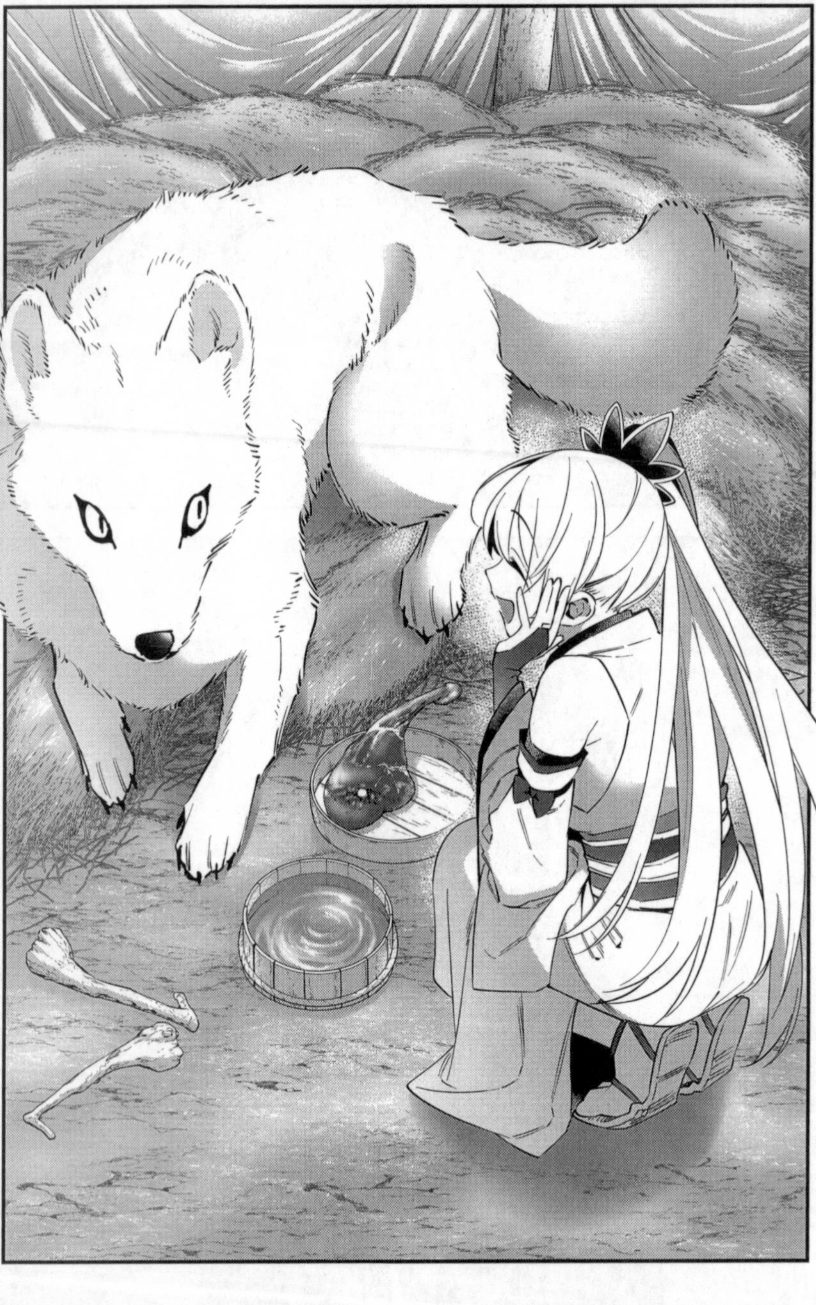

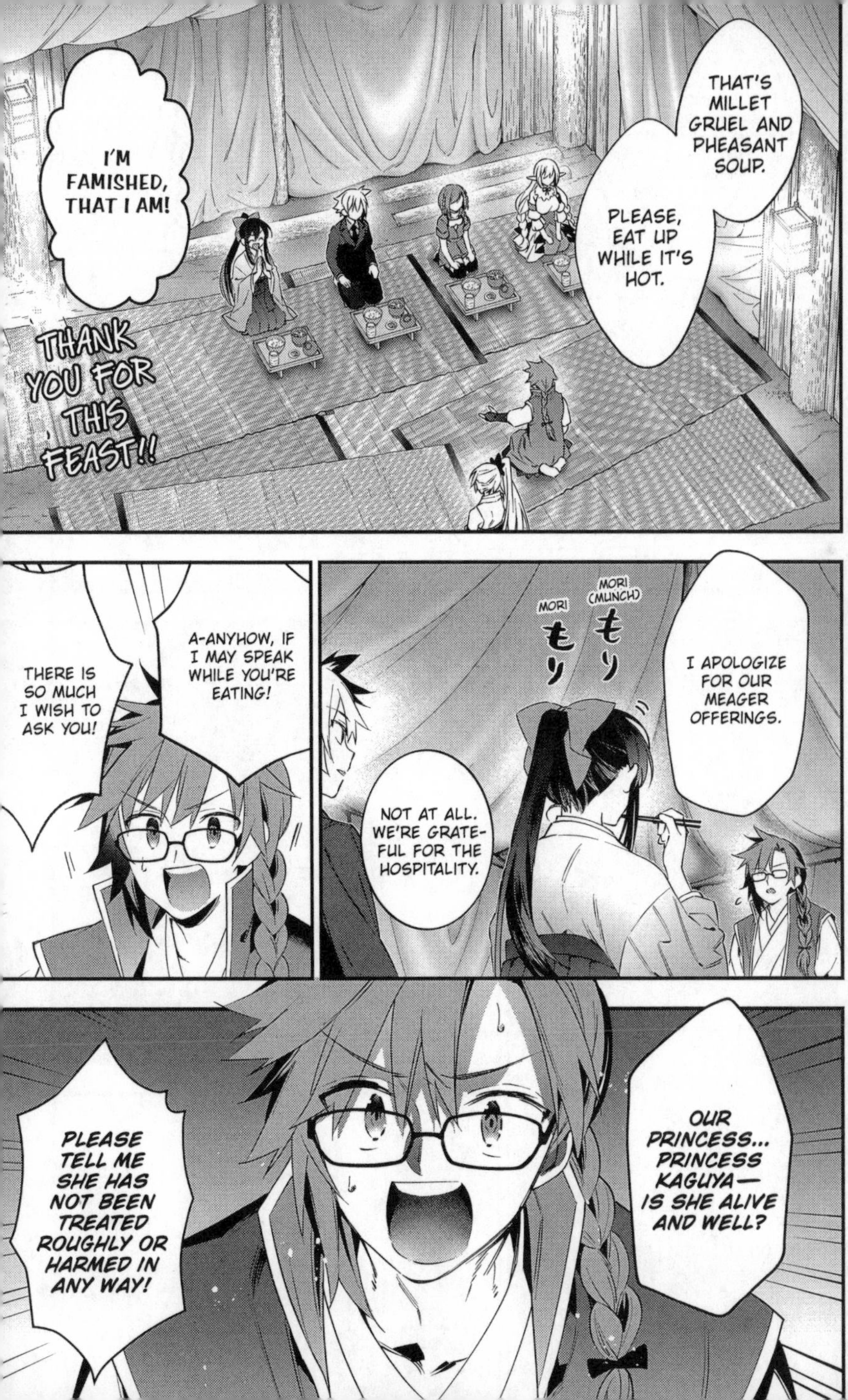
THAT'S MILLET GRUEL AND PHEASANT SOUP.
PLEASE, EAT UP WHILE IT'S HOT.
I'M FAMISHED, THAT I AM!
THANK YOU FOR THIS FEAST!!
I APOLOGIZE FOR OUR MEAGER OFFERINGS.
MORI (MUNCH)
もり
MORI
もり
NOT AT ALL. WE'RE GRATEFUL FOR THE HOSPITALITY.
A-ANYHOW, IF I MAY SPEAK WHILE YOU'RE EATING!
THERE IS SO MUCH I WISH TO ASK YOU!
OUR PRINCESS... PRINCESS KAGUYA— IS SHE ALIVE AND WELL?
PLEASE TELL ME SHE HAS NOT BEEN TREATED ROUGHLY OR HARMED IN ANY WAY!

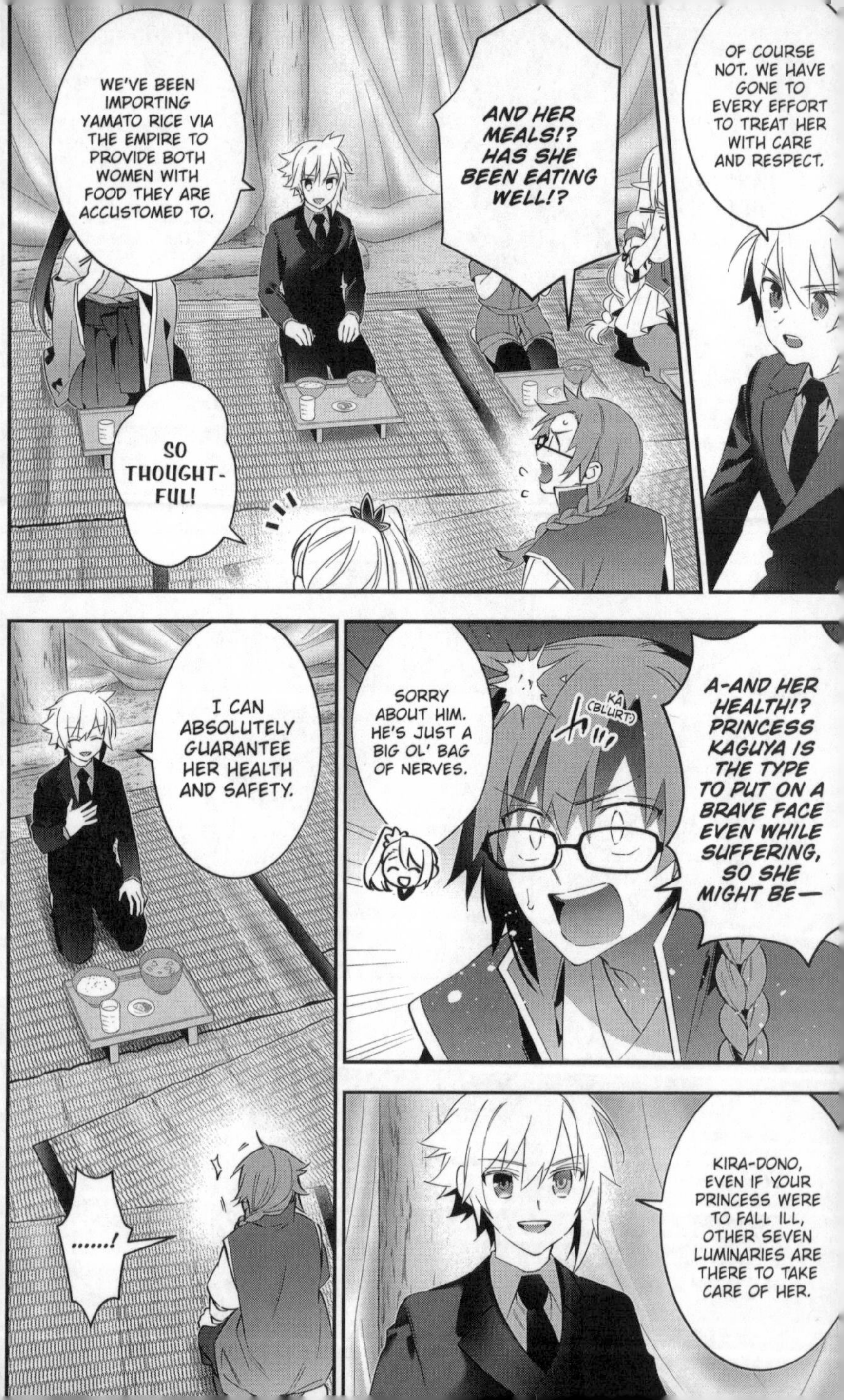
OF COURSE NOT. WE HAVE GONE TO EVERY EFFORT TO TREAT HER WITH CARE AND RESPECT.
AND HER MEALS!? HAS SHE BEEN EATING WELL!?
WE'VE BEEN IMPORTING YAMATO RICE VIA THE EMPIRE TO PROVIDE BOTH WOMEN WITH FOOD THEY ARE ACCUSTOMED TO.
SO THOUGHT-FUL!
A-AND HER HEALTH!? PRINCESS KAGUYA IS THE TYPE TO PUT ON A BRAVE FACE EVEN WHILE SUFFERING, SO SHE MIGHT BE—
KA (BLURT)
SORRY ABOUT HIM. HE'S JUST A BIG OL' BAG OF NERVES.
KIRA-DONO, EVEN IF YOUR PRINCESS WERE TO FALL ILL, OTHER SEVEN LUMINARIES ARE THERE TO TAKE CARE OF HER.
I CAN ABSOLUTELY GUARANTEE HER HEALTH AND SAFETY.
......!

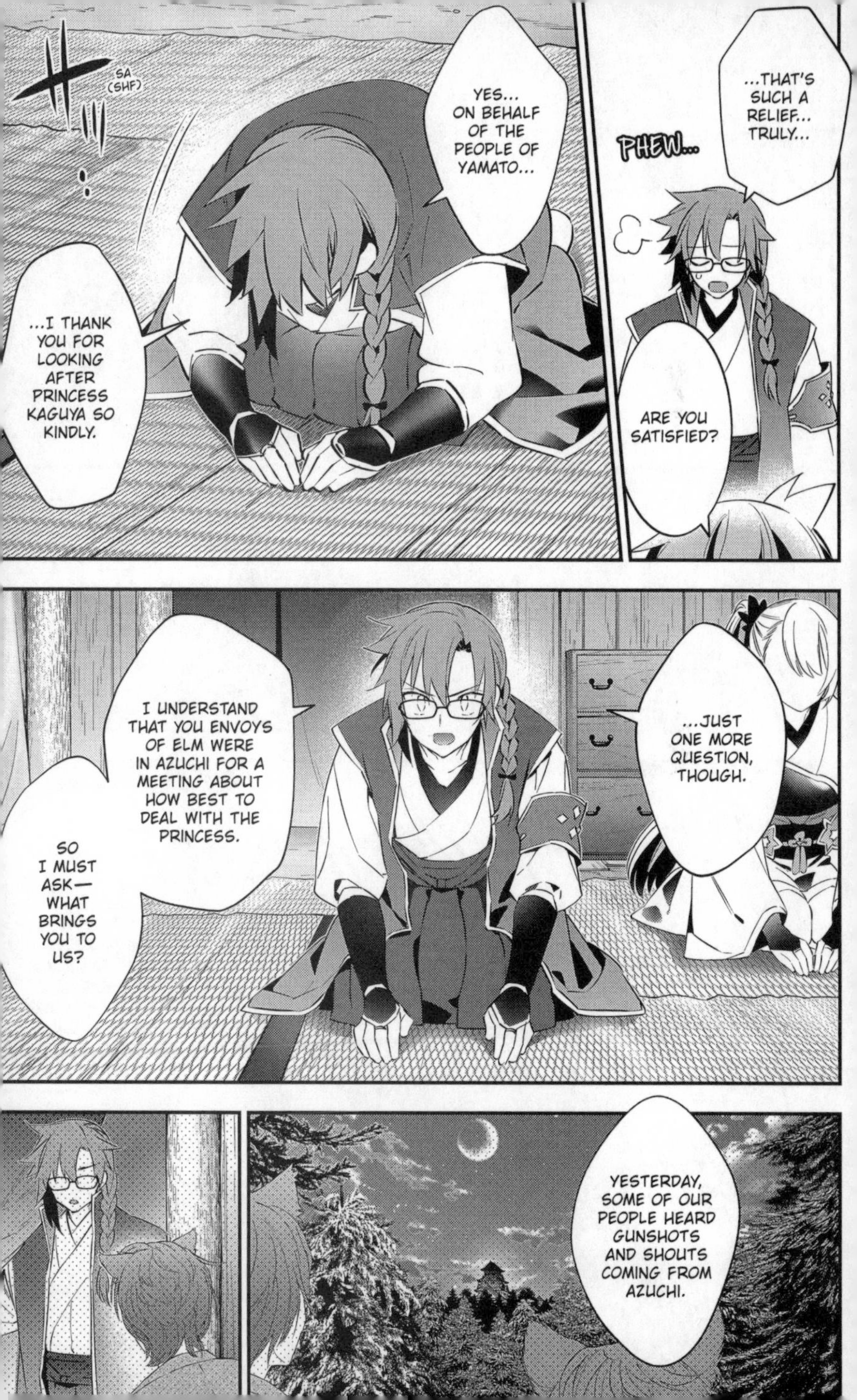

...THAT'S SUCH A RELIEF... TRULY...
PHEW...
ARE YOU SATISFIED?
SA (SHF)
YES... ON BEHALF OF THE PEOPLE OF YAMATO...
...I THANK YOU FOR LOOKING AFTER PRINCESS KAGUYA SO KINDLY.
...JUST ONE MORE QUESTION, THOUGH.
I UNDERSTAND THAT YOU ENVOYS OF ELM WERE IN AZUCHI FOR A MEETING ABOUT HOW BEST TO DEAL WITH THE PRINCESS.
SO I MUST ASK—WHAT BRINGS YOU TO US?
YESTERDAY, SOME OF OUR PEOPLE HEARD GUNSHOTS AND SHOUTS COMING FROM AZUCHI.

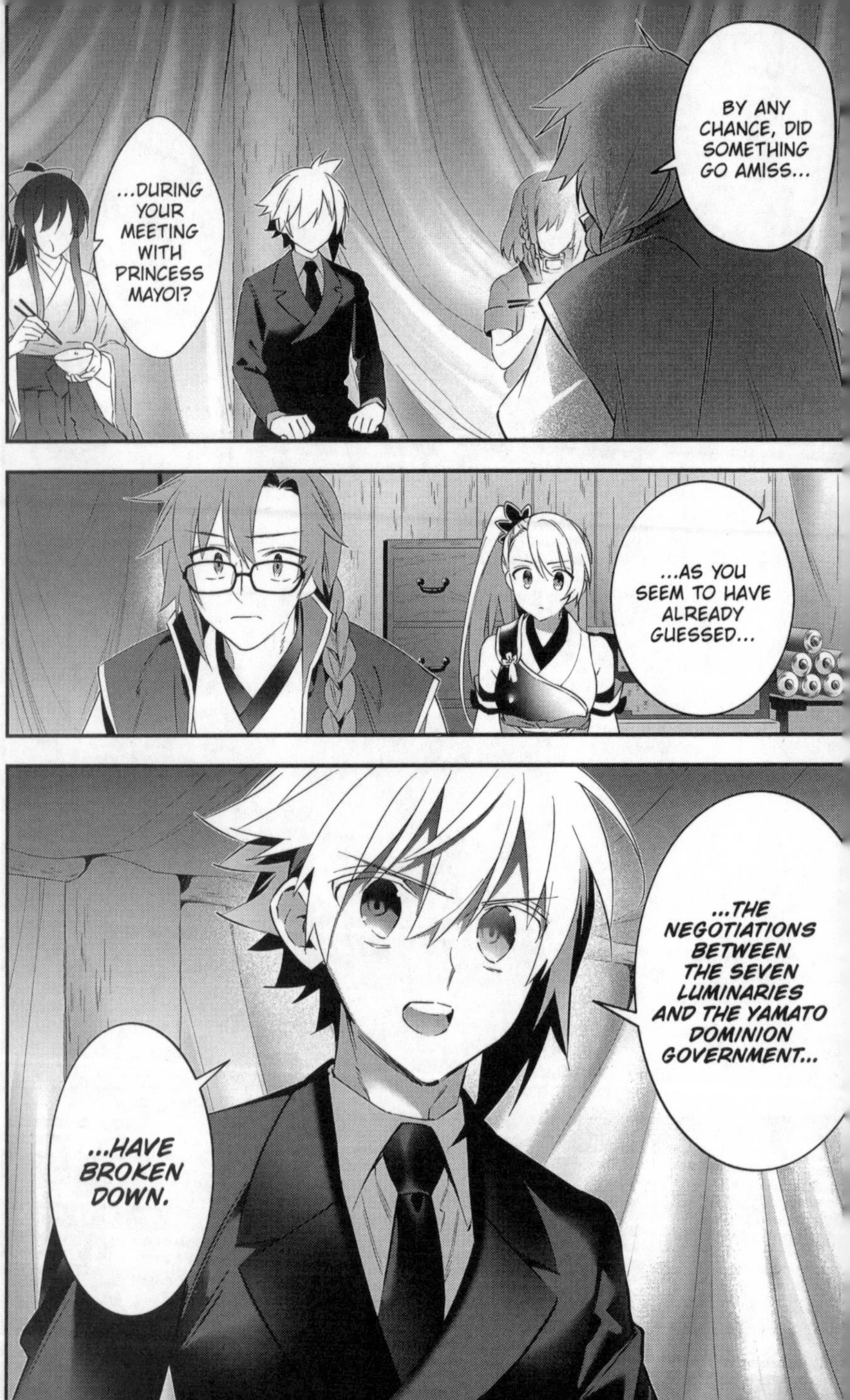
BY ANY CHANCE, DID SOMETHING GO AMISS...
...DURING YOUR MEETING WITH PRINCESS MAYOI?
...AS YOU SEEM TO HAVE ALREADY GUESSED...
...THE NEGOTIATIONS BETWEEN THE SEVEN LUMINARIES AND THE YAMATO DOMINION GOVERNMENT...
...HAVE BROKEN DOWN.

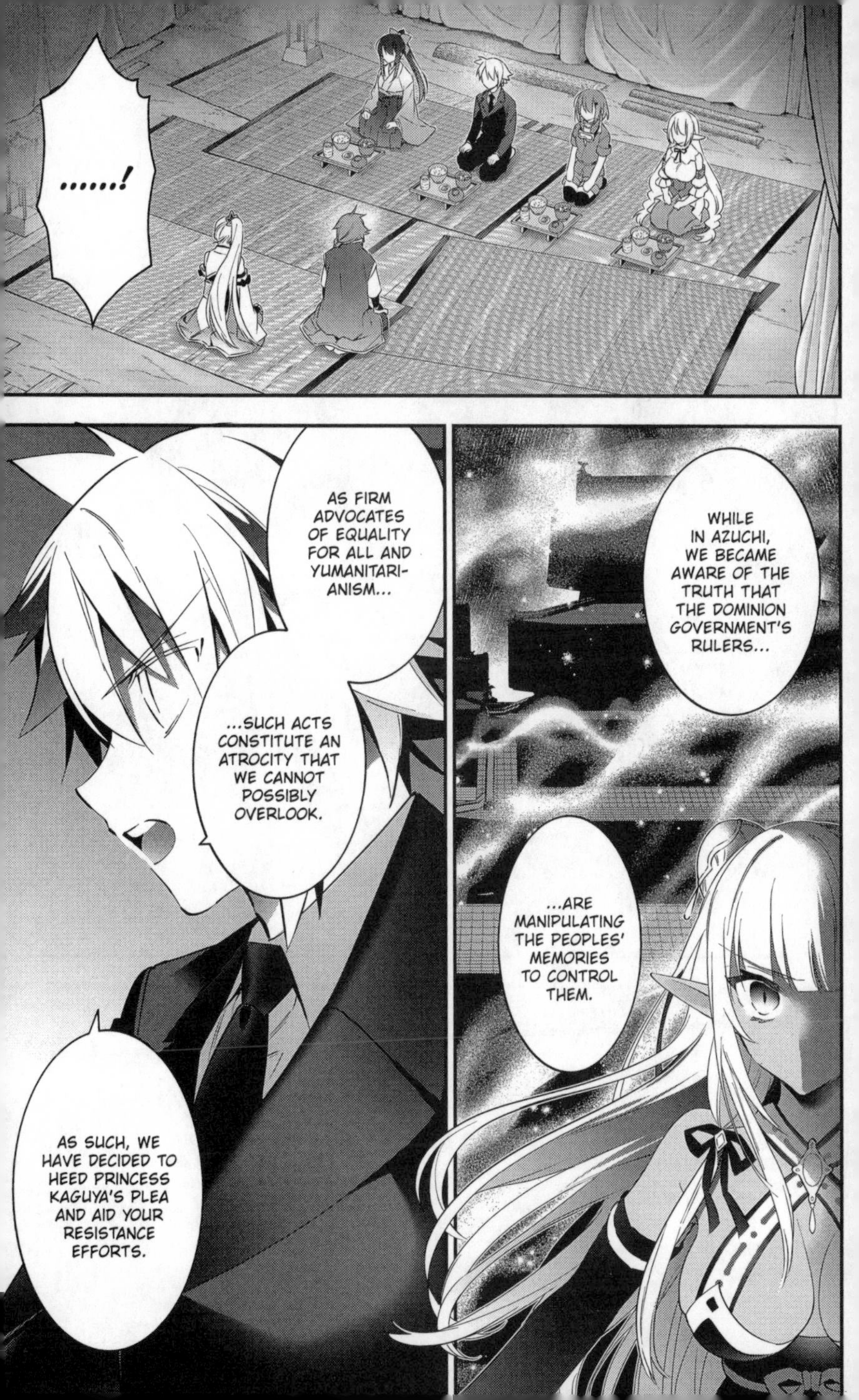
......!
WHILE IN AZUCHI, WE BECAME AWARE OF THE TRUTH THAT THE DOMINION GOVERNMENT'S RULERS...
...ARE MANIPULATING THE PEOPLES' MEMORIES TO CONTROL THEM.
AS FIRM ADVOCATES OF EQUALITY FOR ALL AND YUMANITARI-ANISM...
...SUCH ACTS CONSTITUTE AN ATROCITY THAT WE CANNOT POSSIBLY OVERLOOK.
AS SUCH, WE HAVE DECIDED TO HEED PRINCESS KAGUYA'S PLEA AND AID YOUR RESISTANCE EFFORTS.

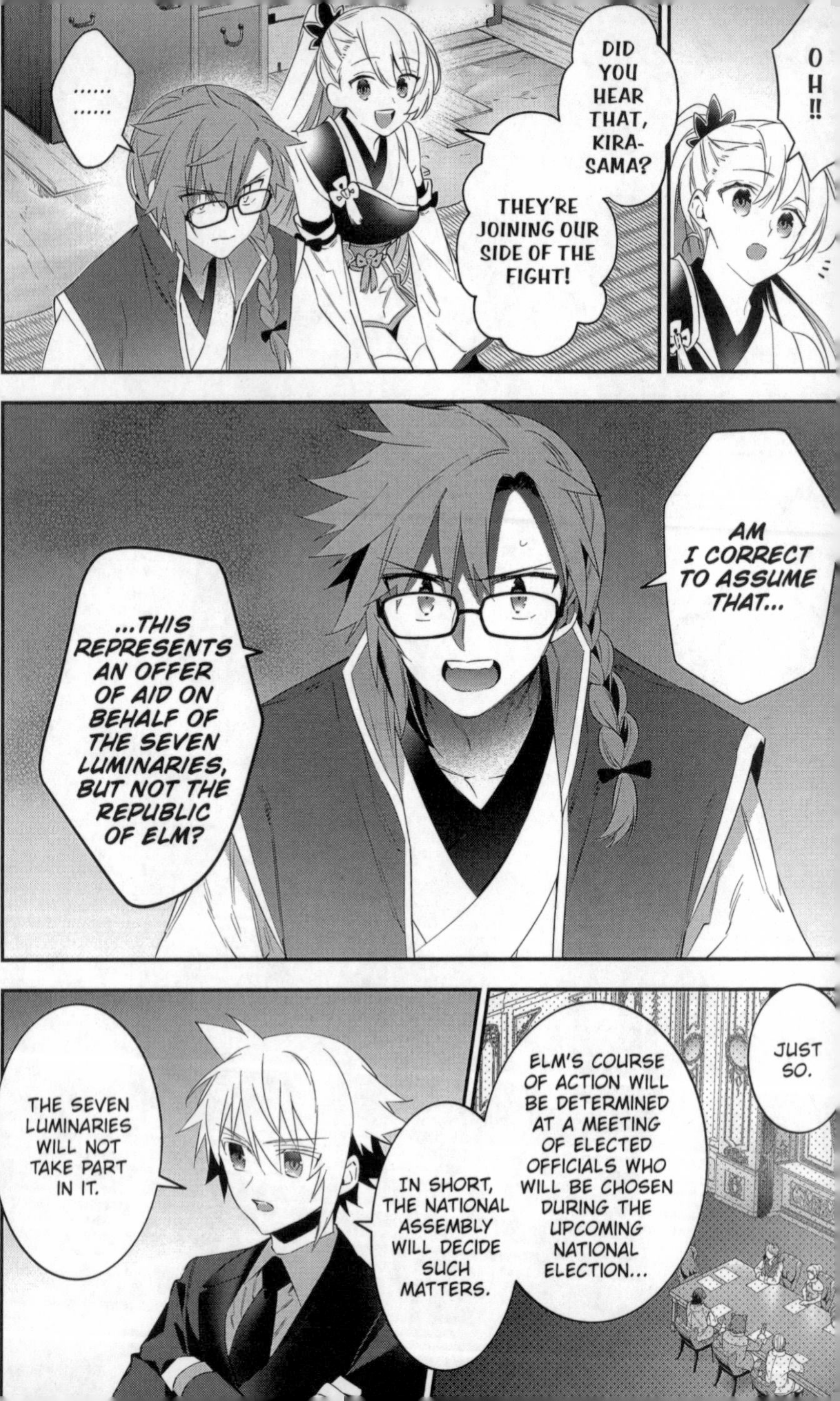
OH!!
DID YOU HEAR THAT, KIRA-SAMA?
THEY'RE JOINING OUR SIDE OF THE FIGHT!
......
......
AM I CORRECT TO ASSUME THAT...
...THIS REPRESENTS AN OFFER OF AID ON BEHALF OF THE SEVEN LUMINARIES, BUT NOT THE REPUBLIC OF ELM?
JUST SO.
ELM'S COURSE OF ACTION WILL BE DETERMINED AT A MEETING OF ELECTED OFFICIALS WHO WILL BE CHOSEN DURING THE UPCOMING NATIONAL ELECTION...
IN SHORT, THE NATIONAL ASSEMBLY WILL DECIDE SUCH MATTERS.
THE SEVEN LUMINARIES WILL NOT TAKE PART IN IT.

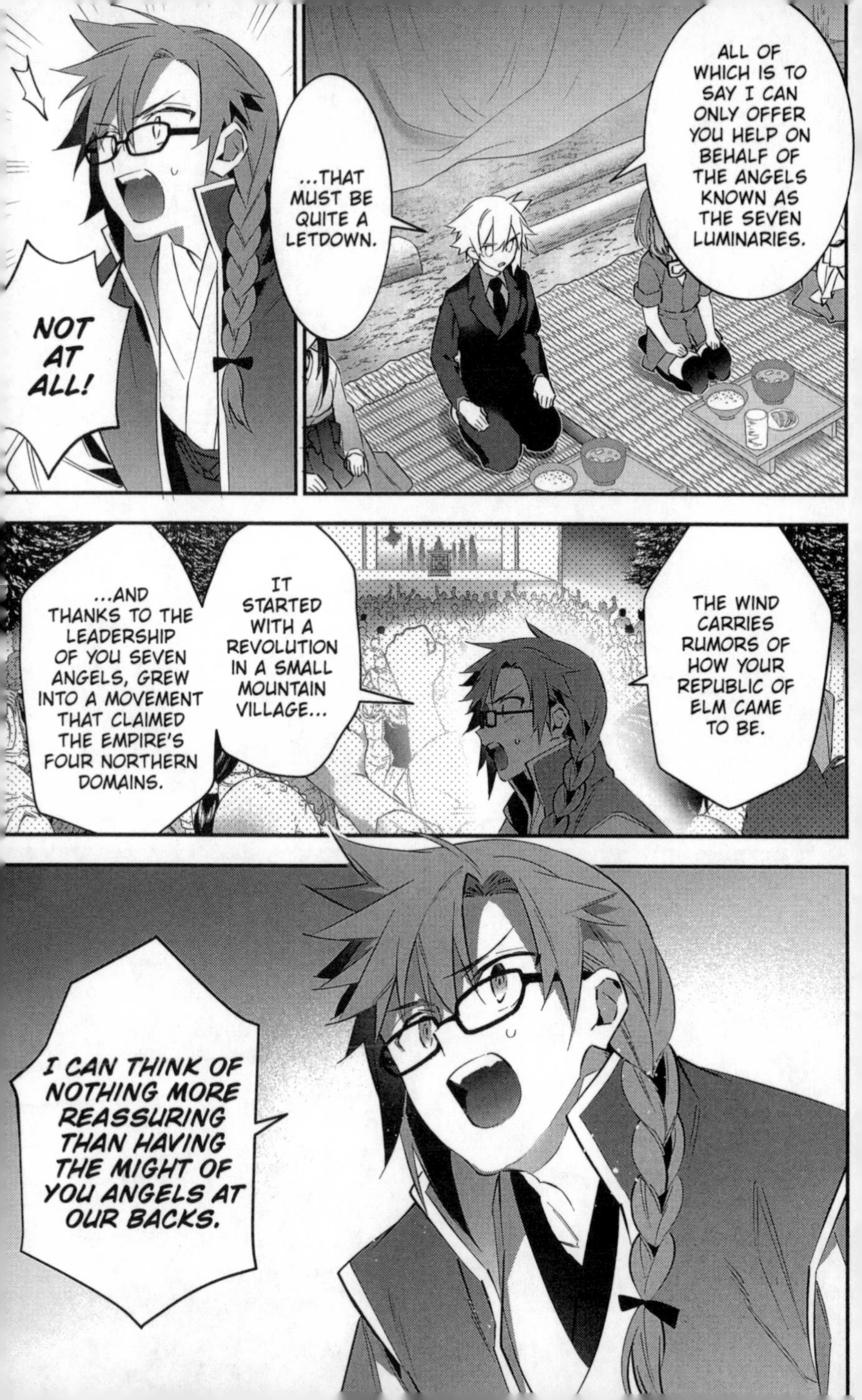
ALL OF WHICH IS TO SAY I CAN ONLY OFFER YOU HELP ON BEHALF OF THE ANGELS KNOWN AS THE SEVEN LUMINARIES.
...THAT MUST BE QUITE A LETDOWN.
NOT AT ALL!
THE WIND CARRIES RUMORS OF HOW YOUR REPUBLIC OF ELM CAME TO BE.
IT STARTED WITH A REVOLUTION IN A SMALL MOUNTAIN VILLAGE...
...AND THANKS TO THE LEADERSHIP OF YOU SEVEN ANGELS, GREW INTO A MOVEMENT THAT CLAIMED THE EMPIRE'S FOUR NORTHERN DOMAINS.
I CAN THINK OF NOTHING MORE REASSURING THAN HAVING THE MIGHT OF YOU ANGELS AT OUR BACKS.

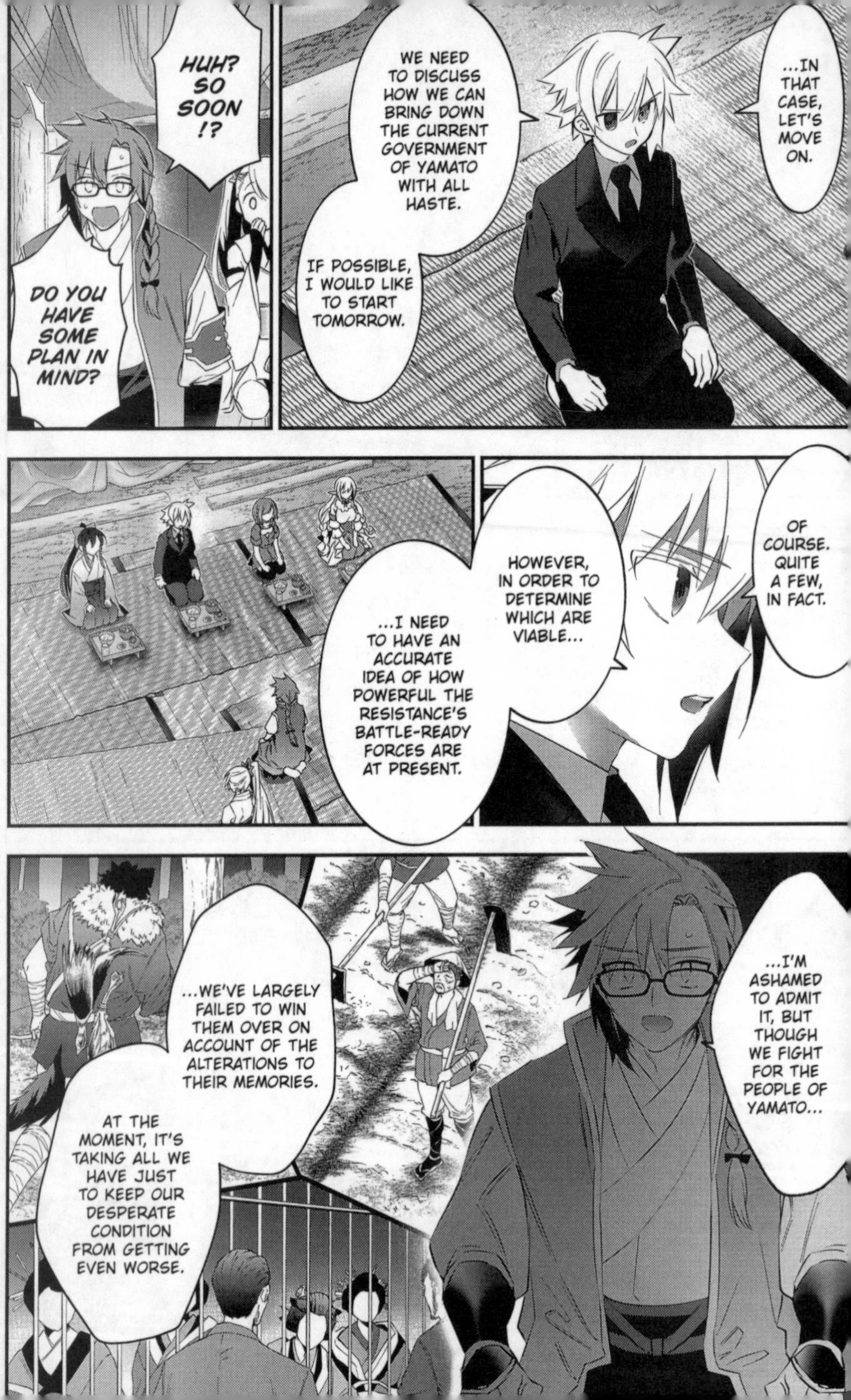
...IN THAT CASE, LET'S MOVE ON.
WE NEED TO DISCUSS HOW WE CAN BRING DOWN THE CURRENT GOVERNMENT OF YAMATO WITH ALL HASTE.
IF POSSIBLE, I WOULD LIKE TO START TOMORROW.
HUH? SO SOON!?
DO YOU HAVE SOME PLAN IN MIND?
OF COURSE. QUITE A FEW, IN FACT.
HOWEVER, IN ORDER TO DETERMINE WHICH ARE VIABLE...
...I NEED TO HAVE AN ACCURATE IDEA OF HOW POWERFUL THE RESISTANCE'S BATTLE-READY FORCES ARE AT PRESENT.
...I'M ASHAMED TO ADMIT IT, BUT THOUGH WE FIGHT FOR THE PEOPLE OF YAMATO...
...WE'VE LARGELY FAILED TO WIN THEM OVER ON ACCOUNT OF THE ALTERATIONS TO THEIR MEMORIES.
AT THE MOMENT, IT'S TAKING ALL WE HAVE JUST TO KEEP OUR DESPERATE CONDITION FROM GETTING EVEN WORSE.

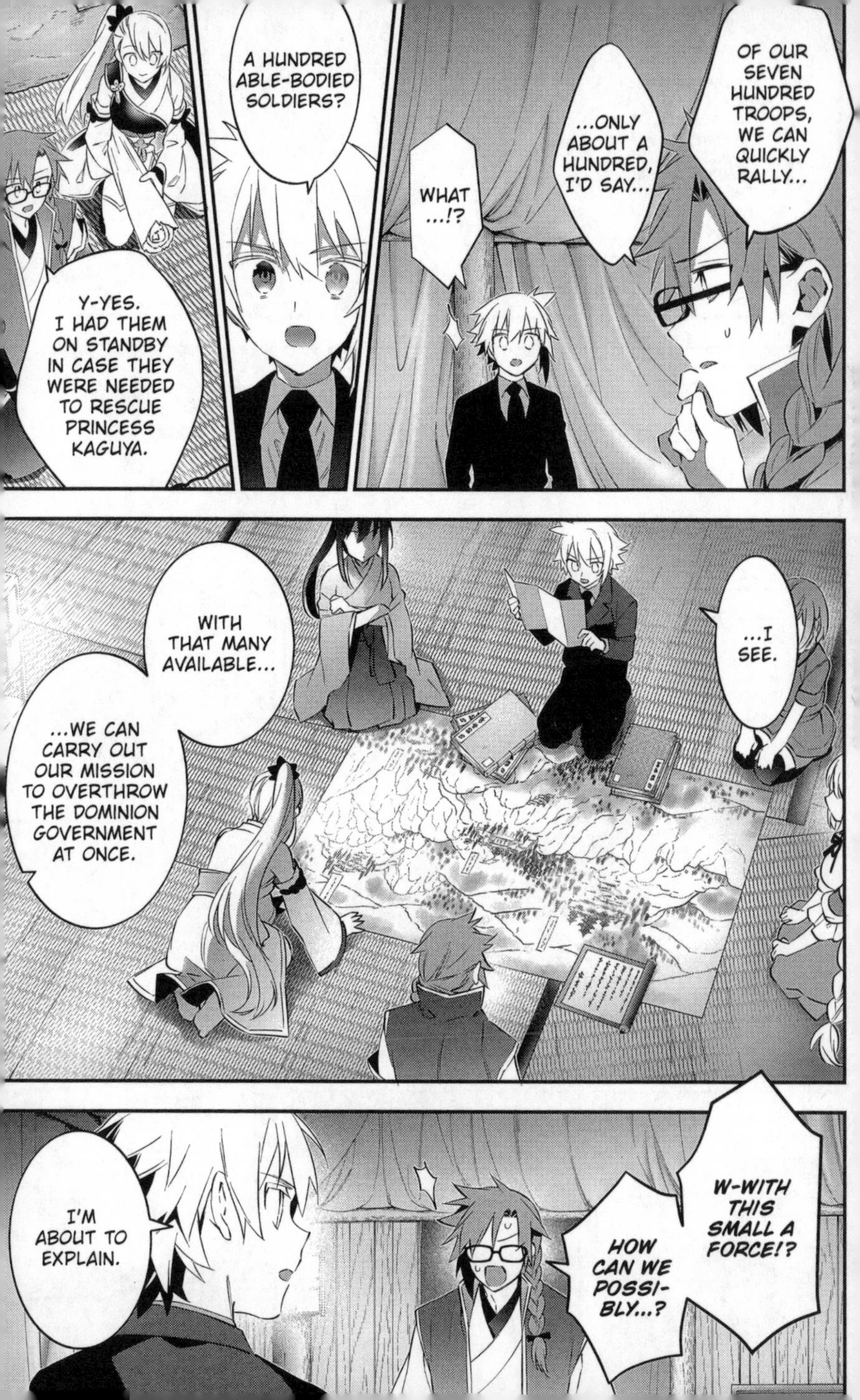
OF OUR SEVEN HUNDRED TROOPS, WE CAN QUICKLY RALLY...
...ONLY ABOUT A HUNDRED, I'D SAY...
WHAT ...!?
A HUNDRED ABLE-BODIED SOLDIERS?
Y-YES. I HAD THEM ON STANDBY IN CASE THEY WERE NEEDED TO RESCUE PRINCESS KAGUYA.
...I SEE.
WITH THAT MANY AVAILABLE...
...WE CAN CARRY OUT OUR MISSION TO OVERTHROW THE DOMINION GOVERNMENT AT ONCE.
W-WITH THIS SMALL A FORCE!?
HOW CAN WE POSSI-BLY...?
I'M ABOUT TO EXPLAIN.

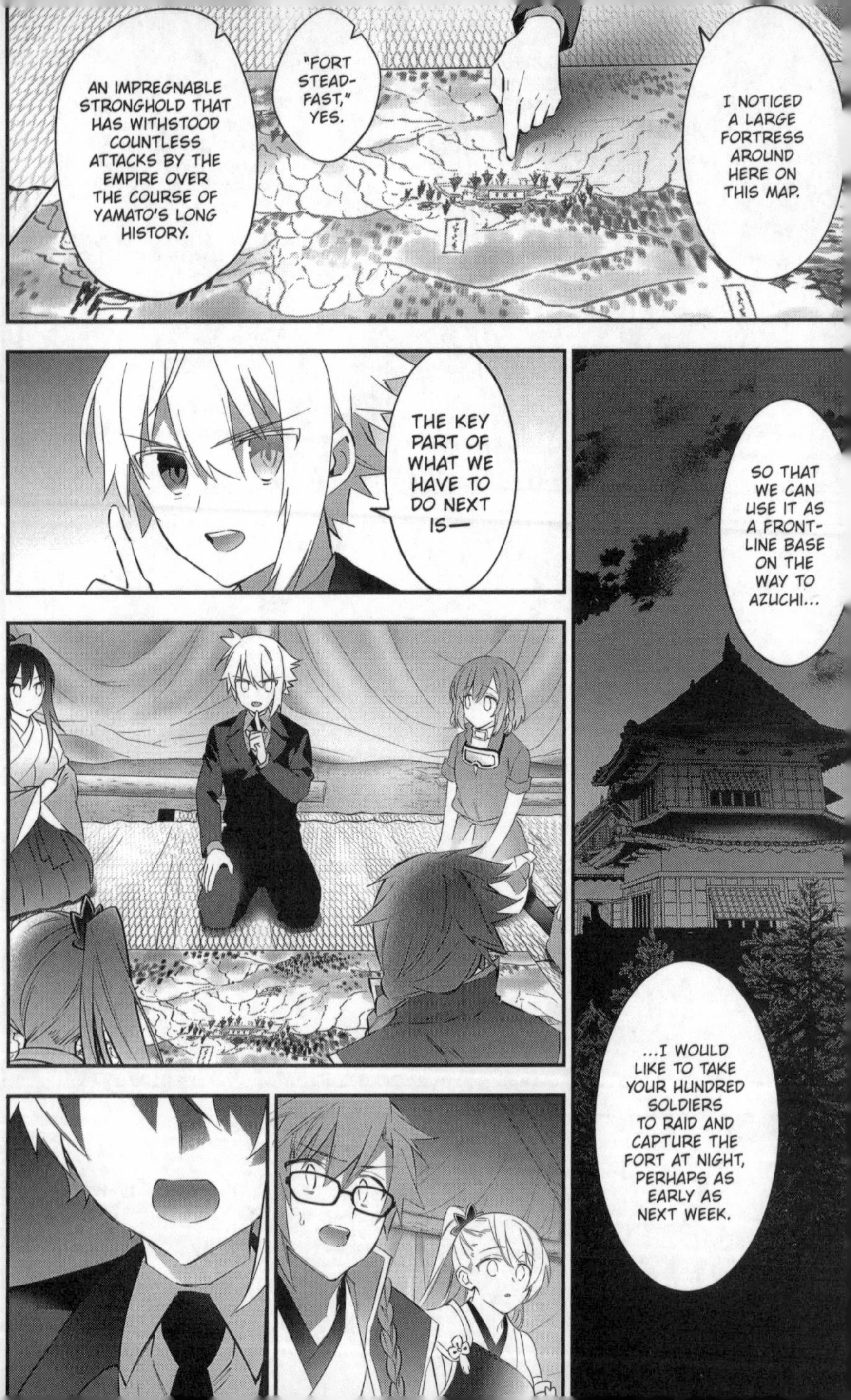
I NOTICED A LARGE FORTRESS AROUND HERE ON THIS MAP.
"FORT STEAD-FAST," YES.
AN IMPREGNABLE STRONGHOLD THAT HAS WITHSTOOD COUNTLESS ATTACKS BY THE EMPIRE OVER THE COURSE OF YAMATO'S LONG HISTORY.
THE KEY PART OF WHAT WE HAVE TO DO NEXT IS—
SO THAT WE CAN USE IT AS A FRONT-LINE BASE ON THE WAY TO AZUCHI...
...I WOULD LIKE TO TAKE YOUR HUNDRED SOLDIERS TO RAID AND CAPTURE THE FORT AT NIGHT, PERHAPS AS EARLY AS NEXT WEEK.

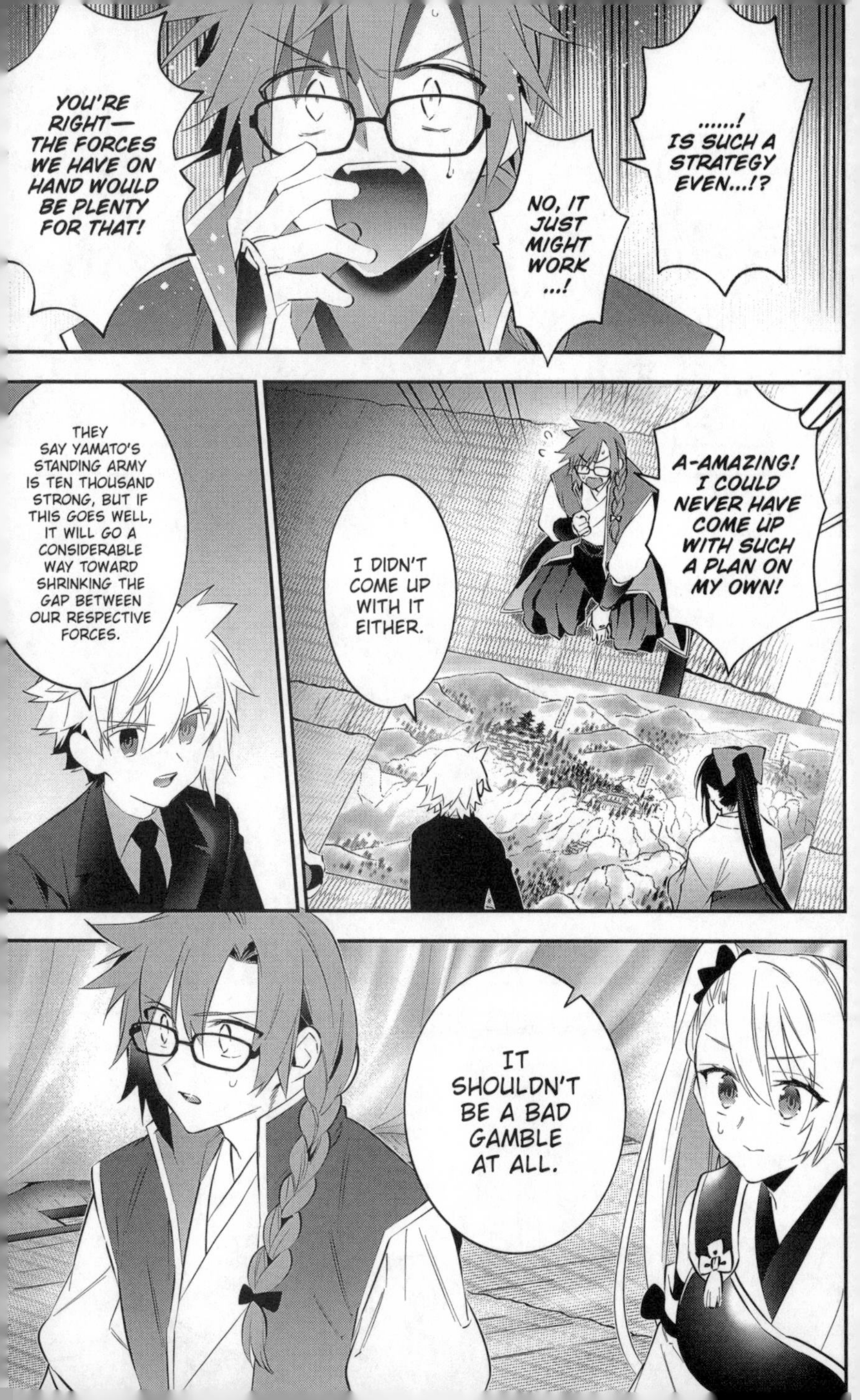
......! IS SUCH A STRATEGY EVEN...!?
NO, IT JUST MIGHT WORK...!
YOU'RE RIGHT— THE FORCES WE HAVE ON HAND WOULD BE PLENTY FOR THAT!
A-AMAZING! I COULD NEVER HAVE COME UP WITH SUCH A PLAN ON MY OWN!
I DIDN'T COME UP WITH IT EITHER.
THEY SAY YAMATO'S STANDING ARMY IS TEN THOUSAND STRONG, BUT IF THIS GOES WELL, IT WILL GO A CONSIDERABLE WAY TOWARD SHRINKING THE GAP BETWEEN OUR RESPECTIVE FORCES.
IT SHOULDN'T BE A BAD GAMBLE AT ALL.

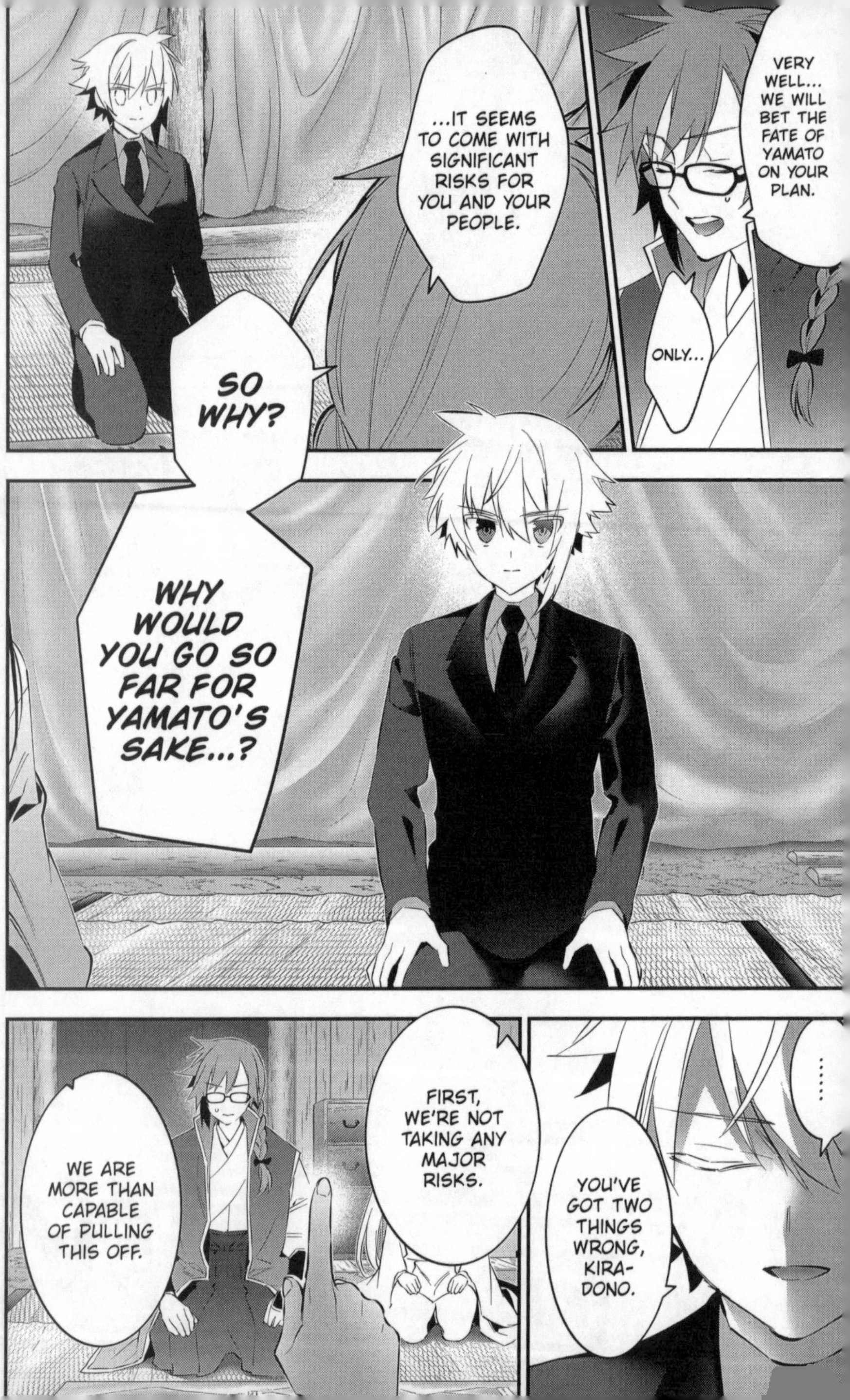
VERY WELL... WE WILL BET THE FATE OF YAMATO ON YOUR PLAN.
ONLY...
...IT SEEMS TO COME WITH SIGNIFICANT RISKS FOR YOU AND YOUR PEOPLE.
SO WHY?
WHY WOULD YOU GO SO FAR FOR YAMATO'S SAKE...?
......
YOU'VE GOT TWO THINGS WRONG, KIRA-DONO.
FIRST, WE'RE NOT TAKING ANY MAJOR RISKS.
WE ARE MORE THAN CAPABLE OF PULLING THIS OFF.

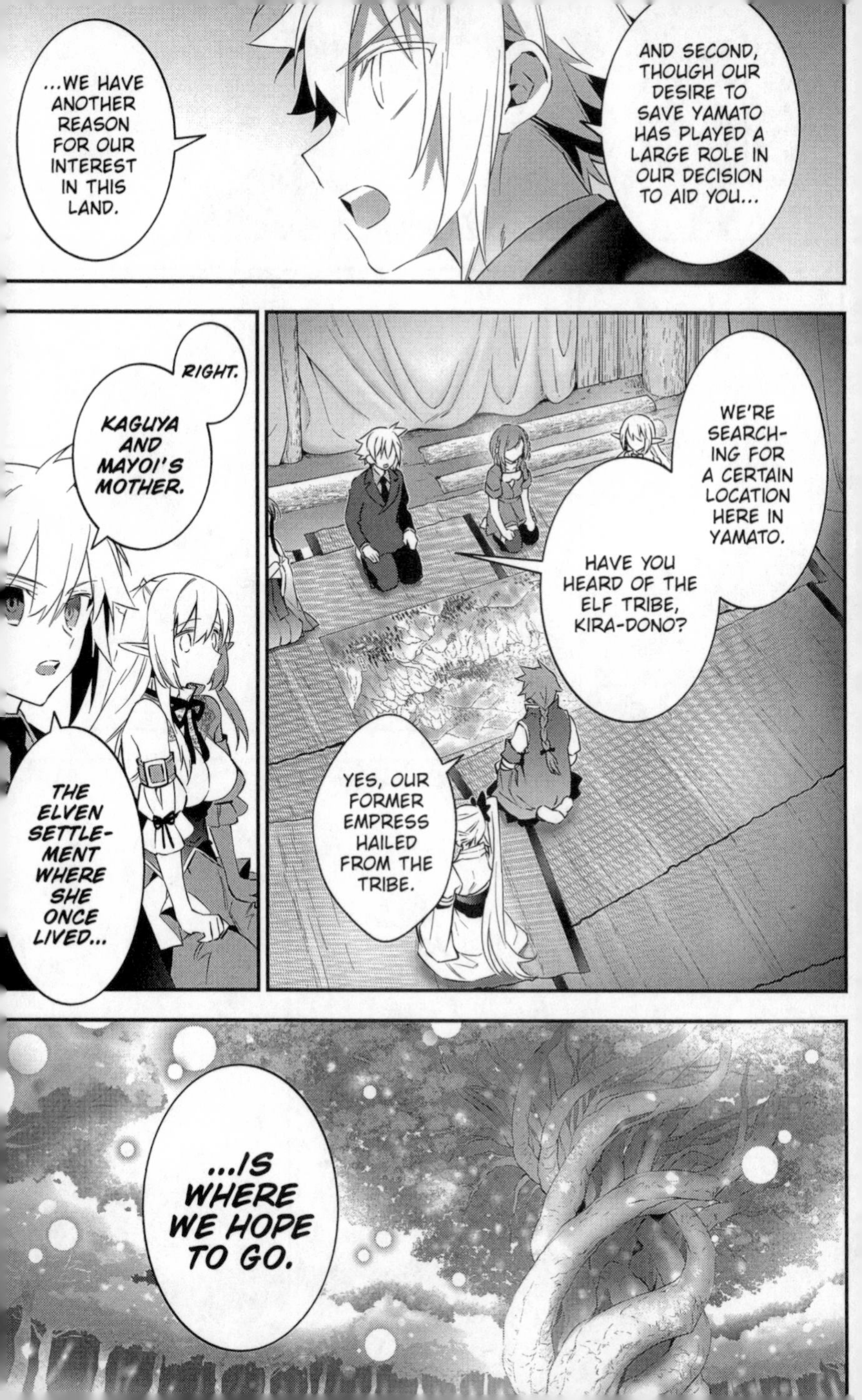
AND SECOND, THOUGH OUR DESIRE TO SAVE YAMATO HAS PLAYED A LARGE ROLE IN OUR DECISION TO AID YOU...
...WE HAVE ANOTHER REASON FOR OUR INTEREST IN THIS LAND.
WE'RE SEARCH-ING FOR A CERTAIN LOCATION HERE IN YAMATO.
HAVE YOU HEARD OF THE ELF TRIBE, KIRA-DONO?
YES, OUR FORMER EMPRESS HAILED FROM THE TRIBE.
RIGHT.
KAGUYA AND MAYOI'S MOTHER.
THE ELVEN SETTLE-MENT WHERE SHE ONCE LIVED...
...IS WHERE WE HOPE TO GO.

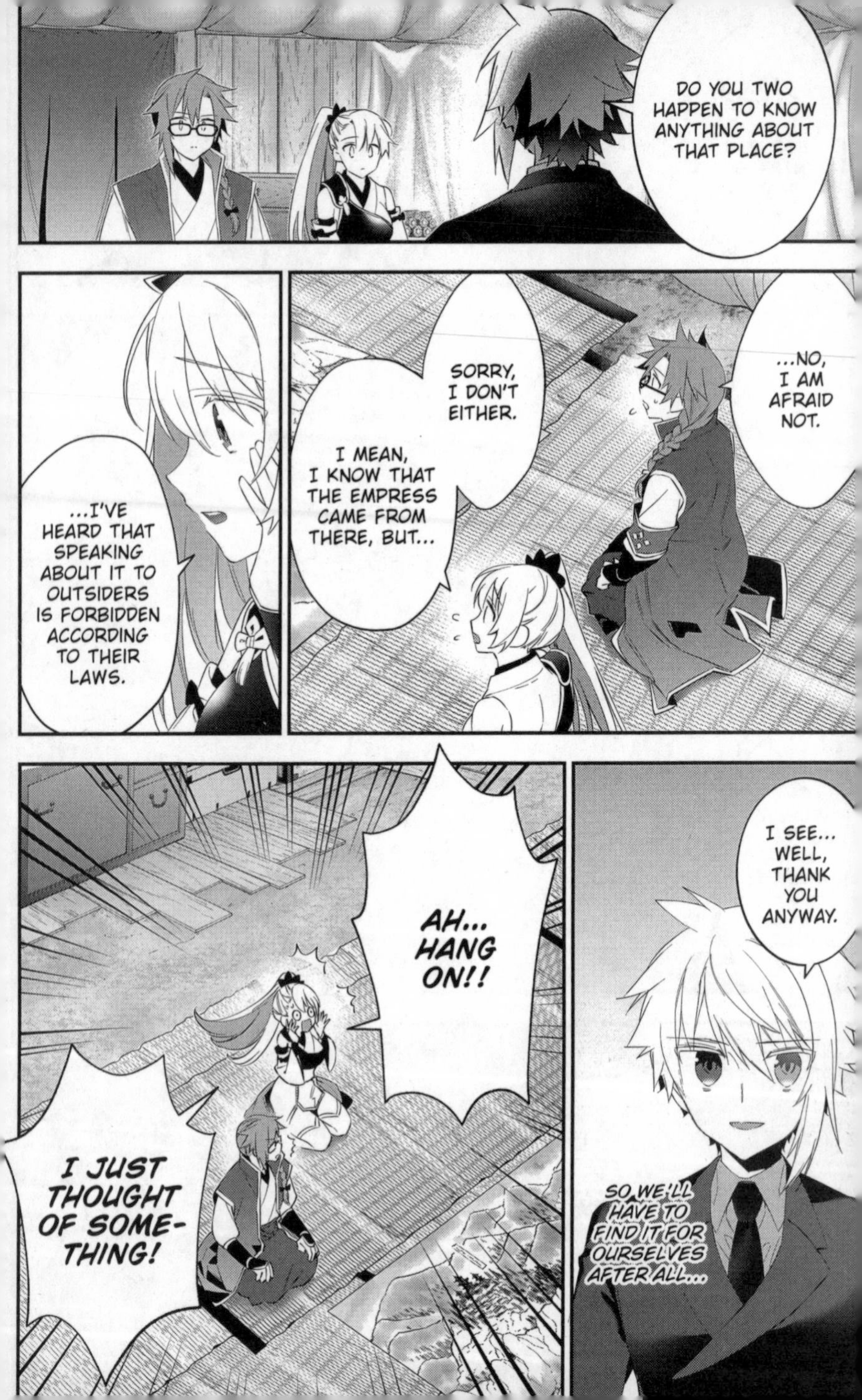
DO YOU TWO HAPPEN TO KNOW ANYTHING ABOUT THAT PLACE?
...NO, I AM AFRAID NOT.
SORRY, I DON'T EITHER.
I MEAN, I KNOW THAT THE EMPRESS CAME FROM THERE, BUT...
...I'VE HEARD THAT SPEAKING ABOUT IT TO OUTSIDERS IS FORBIDDEN ACCORDING TO THEIR LAWS.
I SEE... WELL, THANK YOU ANYWAY.
SO WE'LL HAVE TO FIND IT FOR OURSELVES AFTER ALL...
AH... HANG ON!!
I JUST THOUGHT OF SOME-THING!

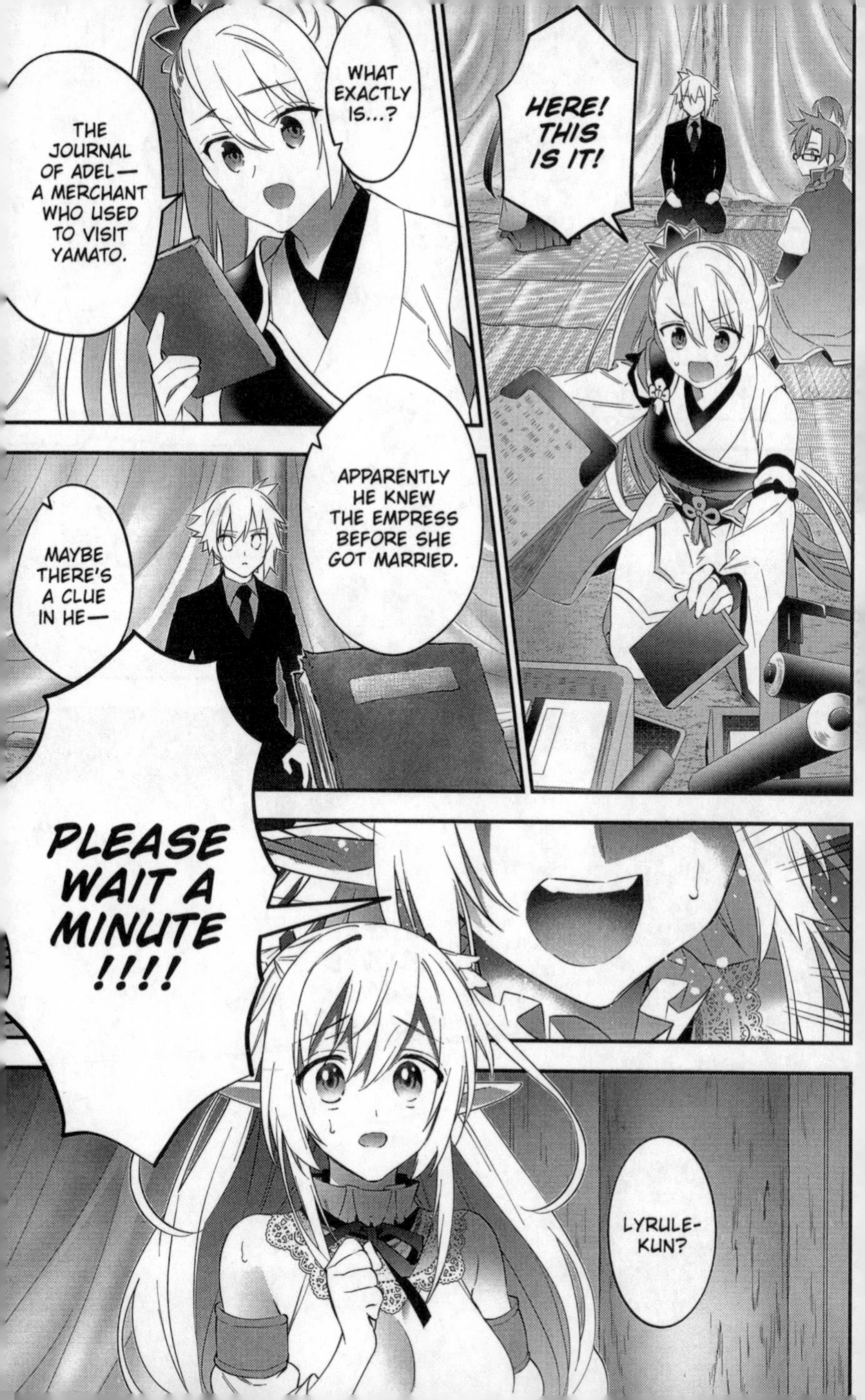
HERE! THIS IS IT!
WHAT EXACTLY IS...?
THE JOURNAL OF ADEL—A MERCHANT WHO USED TO VISIT YAMATO.
APPARENTLY HE KNEW THE EMPRESS BEFORE SHE GOT MARRIED.
MAYBE THERE'S A CLUE IN HE—
PLEASE WAIT A MINUTE !!!!
LYRULE-KUN?

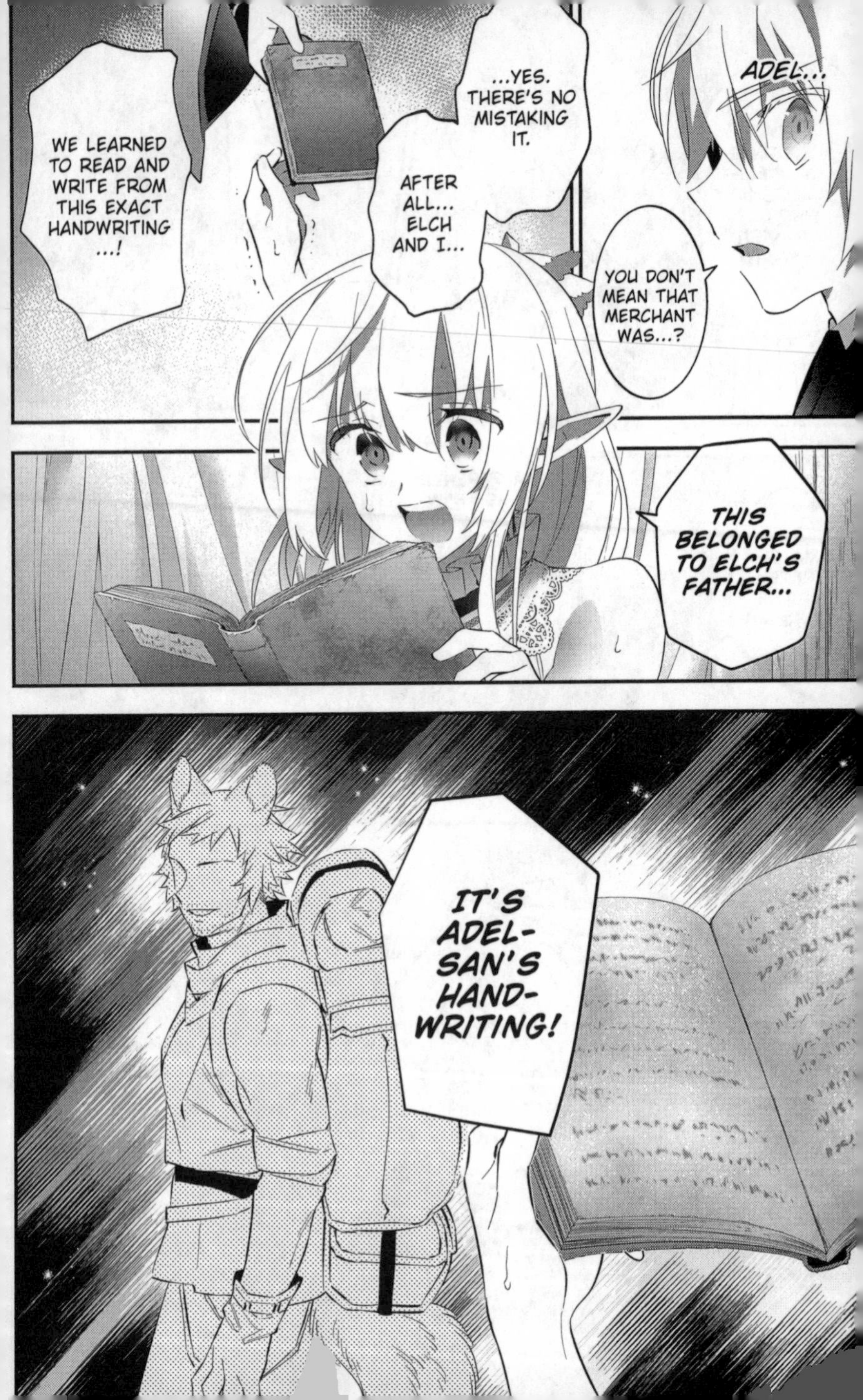
ADEL...
YOU DON'T MEAN THAT MERCHANT WAS...?
...YES. THERE'S NO MISTAKING IT.
AFTER ALL... ELCH AND I...
WE LEARNED TO READ AND WRITE FROM THIS EXACT HANDWRITING...!
THIS BELONGED TO ELCH'S FATHER...
IT'S ADEL-SAN'S HAND-WRITING!

HIGH SCHOOL
PRODIGIES HAVE
IT EASY EVEN IN
ANOTHER
WORLD!

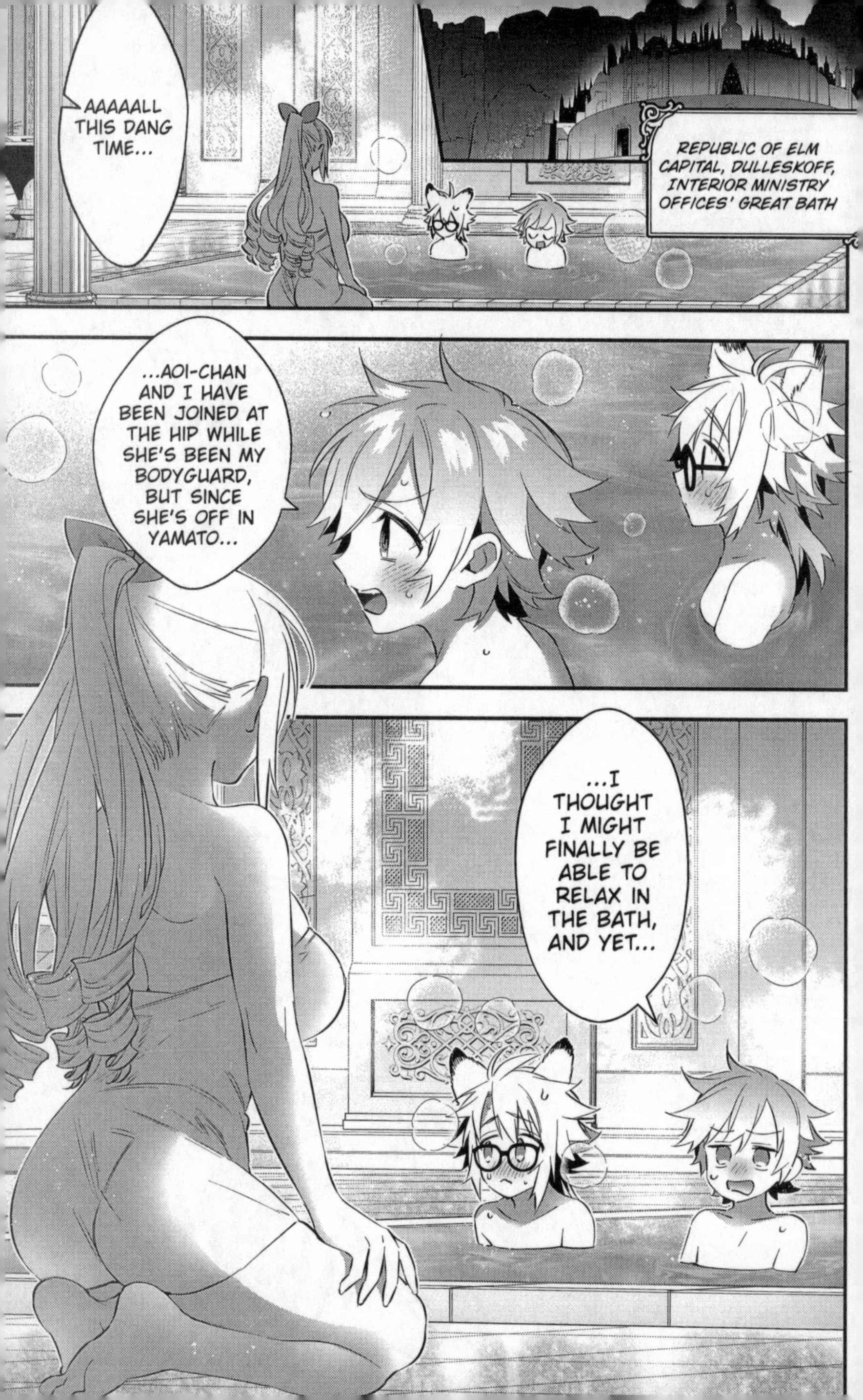
REPUBLIC OF ELM CAPITAL, DULLESKOFF, INTERIOR MINISTRY OFFICES' GREAT BATH
AAAAALL THIS DANG TIME...
...AOI-CHAN AND I HAVE BEEN JOINED AT THE HIP WHILE SHE'S BEEN MY BODYGUARD, BUT SINCE SHE'S OFF IN YAMATO...
...I THOUGHT I MIGHT FINALLY BE ABLE TO RELAX IN THE BATH, AND YET...

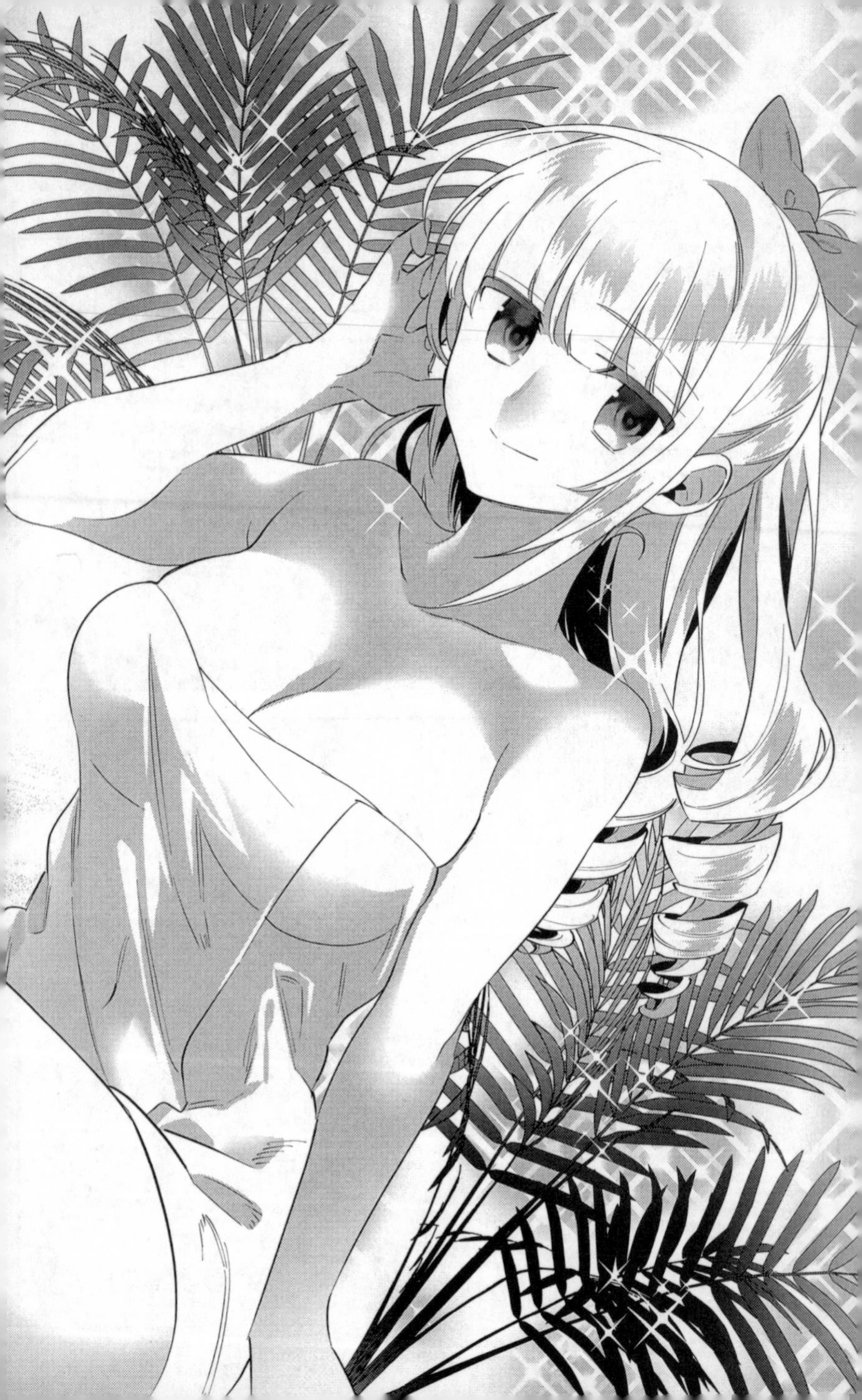

CHAPTER 74: BEFORE THE BIG DEBATE

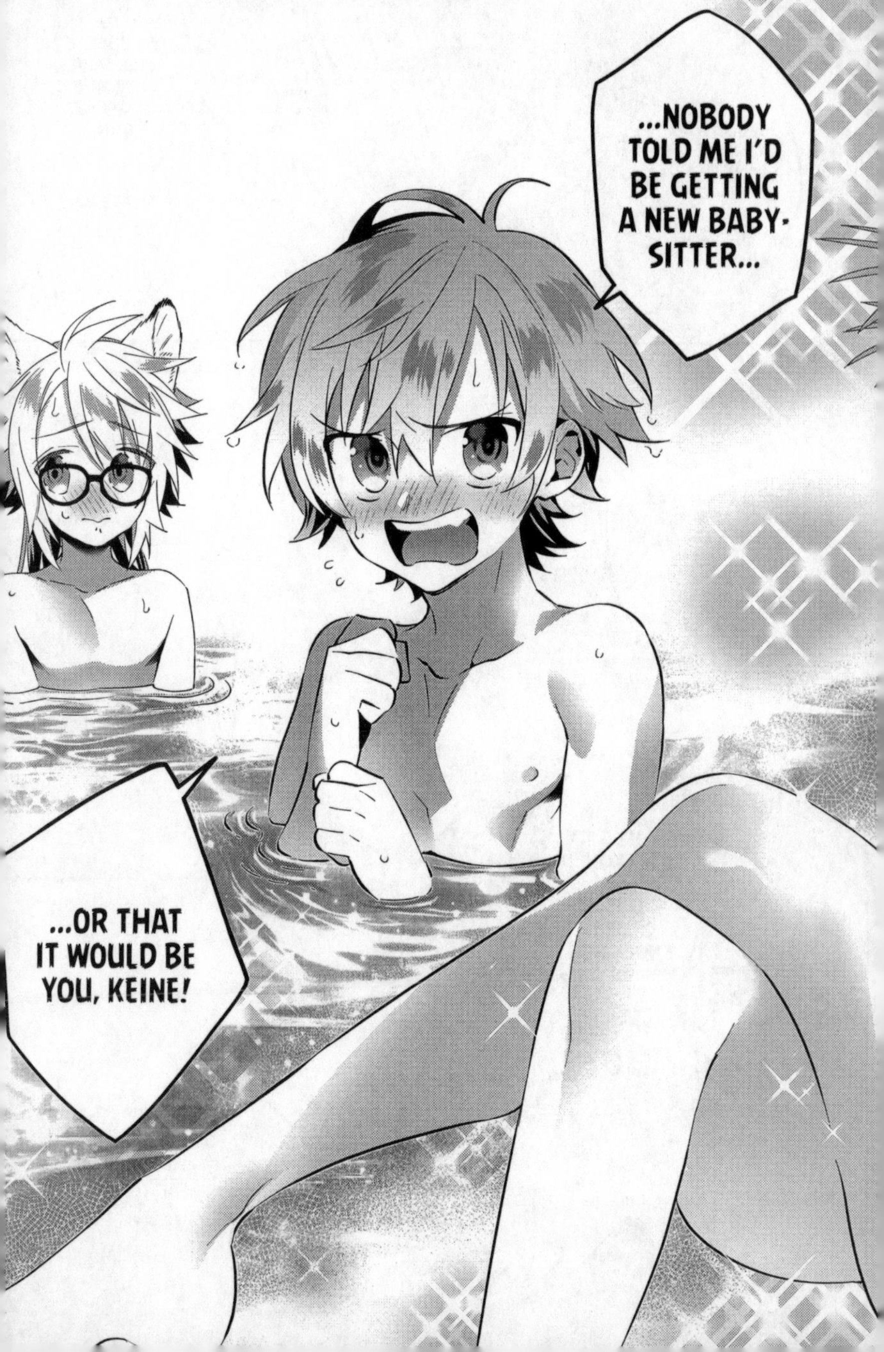
...NOBODY TOLD ME I'D BE GETTING A NEW BABY-SITTER...
...OR THAT IT WOULD BE YOU, KEINE!

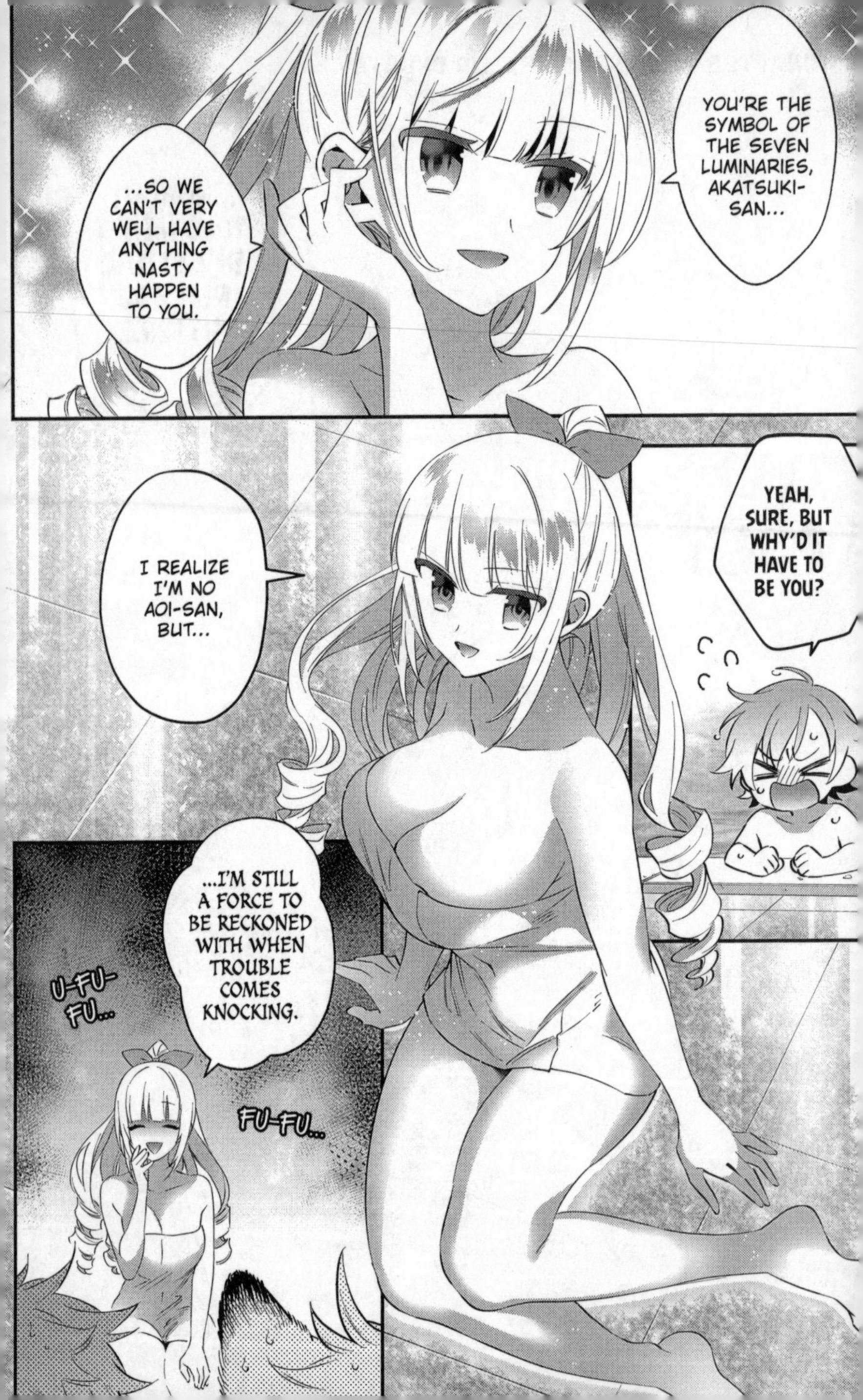
YOU'RE THE SYMBOL OF THE SEVEN LUMINARIES, AKATSUKI-SAN...
...SO WE CAN'T VERY WELL HAVE ANYTHING NASTY HAPPEN TO YOU.
YEAH, SURE, BUT WHY'D IT HAVE TO BE YOU?
I REALIZE I'M NO AOI-SAN, BUT...
...I'M STILL A FORCE TO BE RECKONED WITH WHEN TROUBLE COMES KNOCKING.
FU-FU...
U-FU-FU...

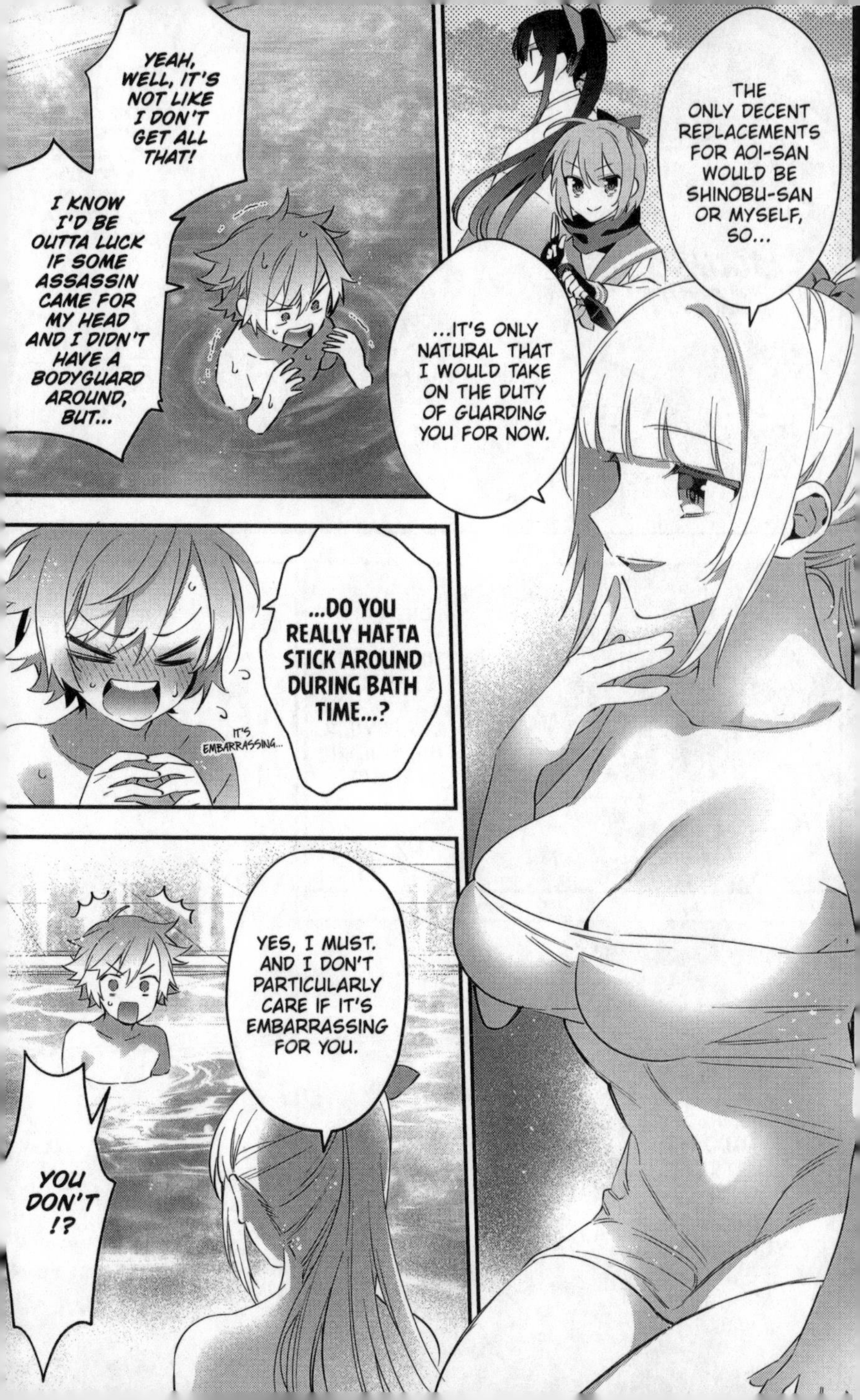
THE ONLY DECENT REPLACEMENTS FOR AOI-SAN WOULD BE SHINOBU-SAN OR MYSELF, SO...
...IT'S ONLY NATURAL THAT I WOULD TAKE ON THE DUTY OF GUARDING YOU FOR NOW.
YEAH, WELL, IT'S NOT LIKE I DON'T GET ALL THAT!
I KNOW I'D BE OUTTA LUCK IF SOME ASSASSIN CAME FOR MY HEAD AND I DIDN'T HAVE A BODYGUARD AROUND, BUT...
...DO YOU REALLY HAFTA STICK AROUND DURING BATH TIME...?
IT'S EMBARRASSING...
YES, I MUST. AND I DON'T PARTICULARLY CARE IF IT'S EMBARRASSING FOR YOU.
YOU DON'T!?

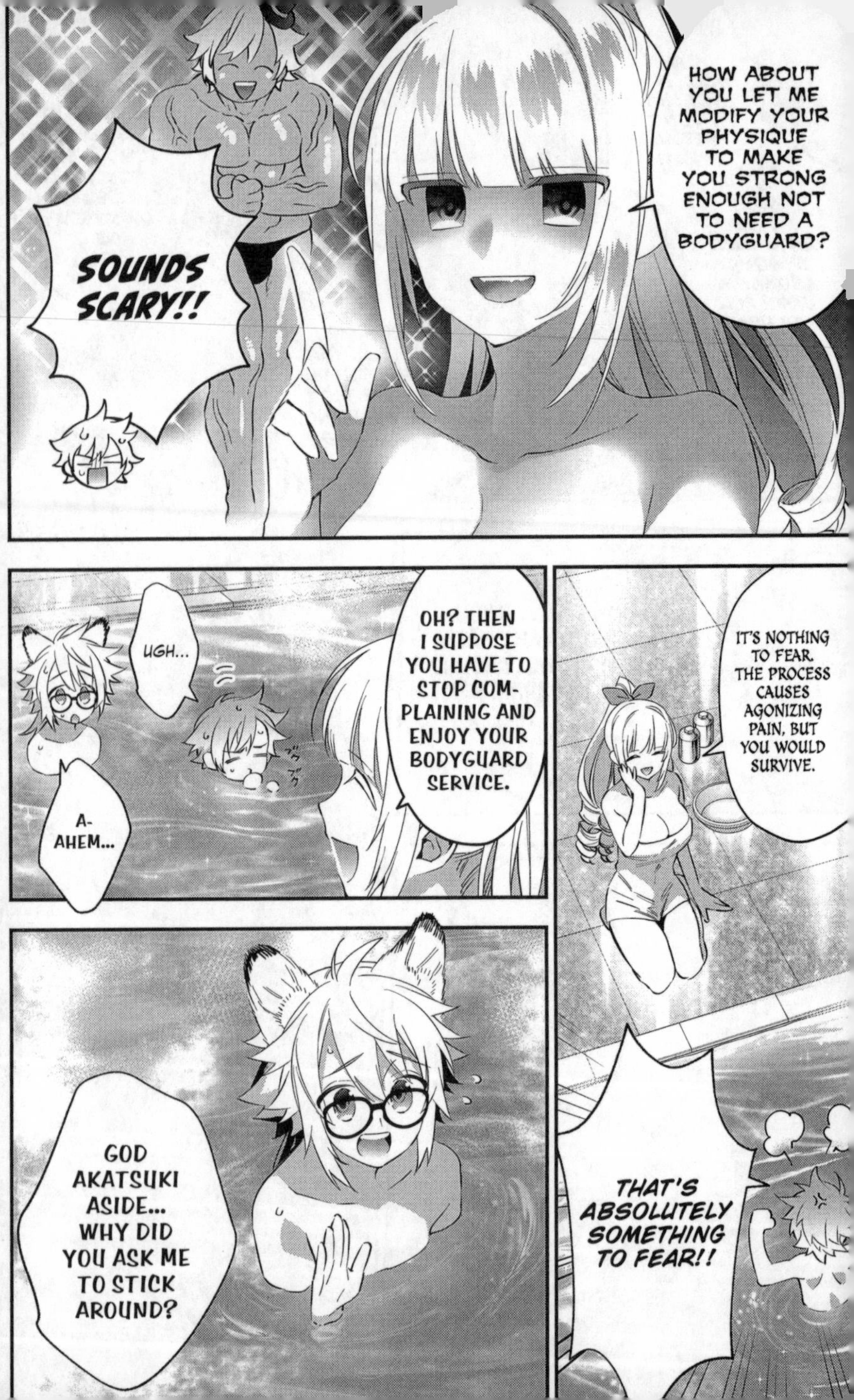
HOW ABOUT YOU LET ME MODIFY YOUR PHYSIQUE TO MAKE YOU STRONG ENOUGH NOT TO NEED A BODYGUARD?
SOUNDS SCARY!!
IT'S NOTHING TO FEAR. THE PROCESS CAUSES AGONIZING PAIN, BUT YOU WOULD SURVIVE.
THAT'S ABSOLUTELY SOMETHING TO FEAR!!
OH? THEN I SUPPOSE YOU HAVE TO STOP COM-PLAINING AND ENJOY YOUR BODYGUARD SERVICE.
UGH...
A-AHEM...
GOD AKATSUKI ASIDE... WHY DID YOU ASK ME TO STICK AROUND?

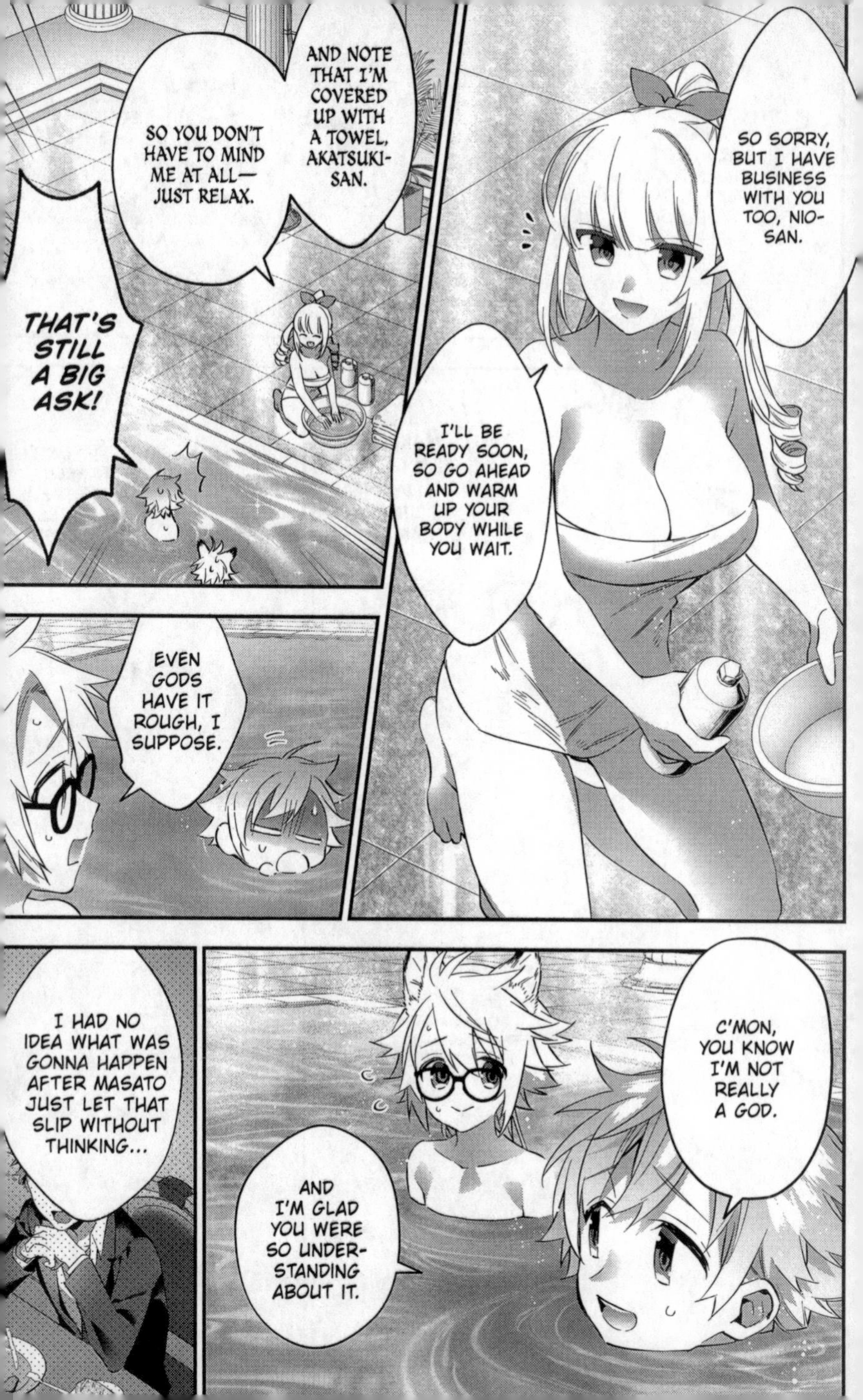
SO SORRY, BUT I HAVE BUSINESS WITH YOU TOO, NIO-SAN.
I'LL BE READY SOON, SO GO AHEAD AND WARM UP YOUR BODY WHILE YOU WAIT.
AND NOTE THAT I'M COVERED UP WITH A TOWEL, AKATSUKI-SAN.
SO YOU DON'T HAVE TO MIND ME AT ALL—JUST RELAX.
THAT'S STILL A BIG ASK!
EVEN GODS HAVE IT ROUGH, I SUPPOSE.
C'MON, YOU KNOW I'M NOT REALLY A GOD.
AND I'M GLAD YOU WERE SO UNDER-STANDING ABOUT IT.
I HAD NO IDEA WHAT WAS GONNA HAPPEN AFTER MASATO JUST LET THAT SLIP WITHOUT THINKING...

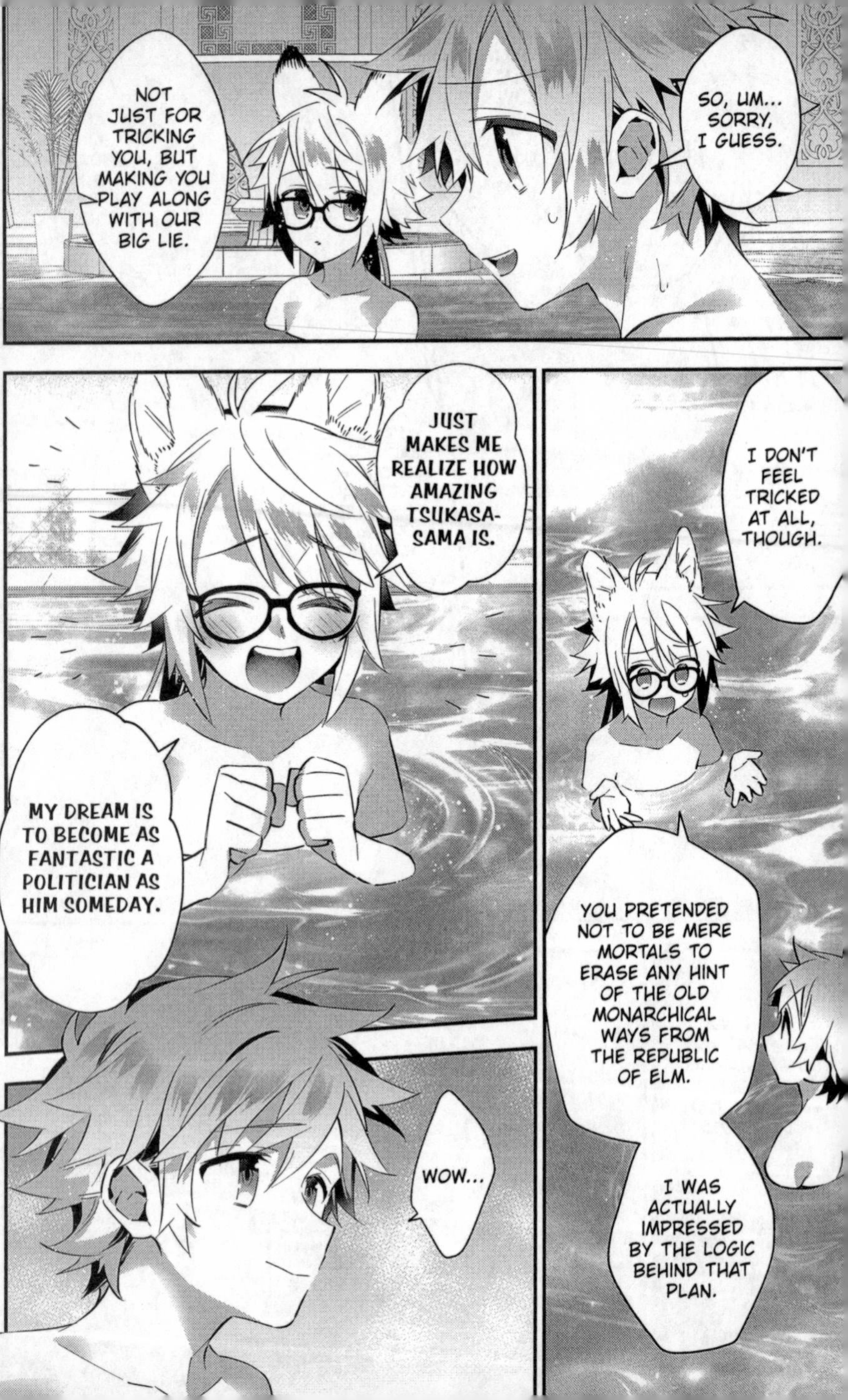
SO, UM... SORRY, I GUESS.
NOT JUST FOR TRICKING YOU, BUT MAKING YOU PLAY ALONG WITH OUR BIG LIE.
I DON'T FEEL TRICKED AT ALL, THOUGH.
YOU PRETENDED NOT TO BE MERE MORTALS TO ERASE ANY HINT OF THE OLD MONARCHICAL WAYS FROM THE REPUBLIC OF ELM.
I WAS ACTUALLY IMPRESSED BY THE LOGIC BEHIND THAT PLAN.
JUST MAKES ME REALIZE HOW AMAZING TSUKASA-SAMA IS.
MY DREAM IS TO BECOME AS FANTASTIC A POLITICIAN AS HIM SOMEDAY.
WOW...

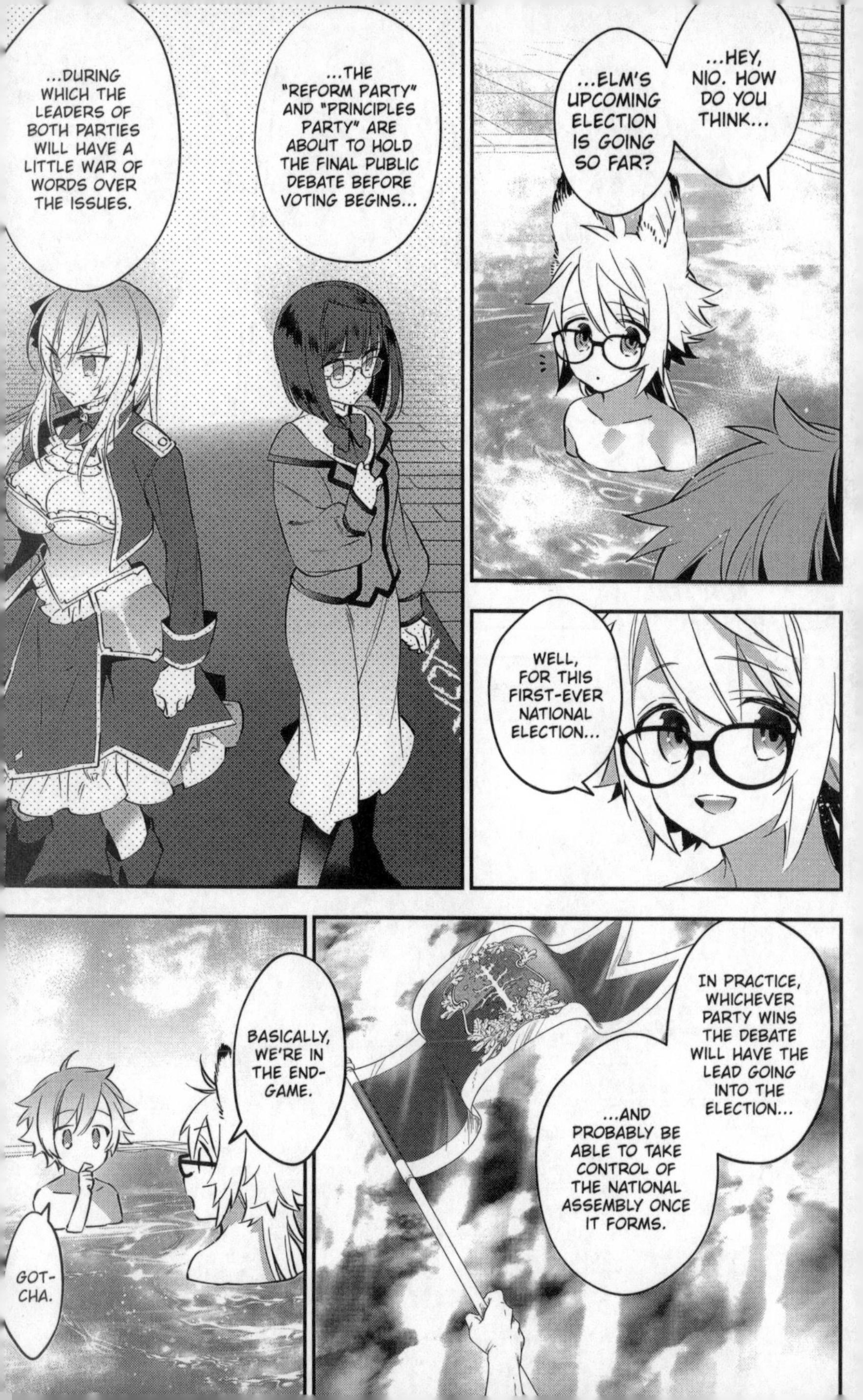
...HEY, NIO. HOW DO YOU THINK...
...ELM'S UPCOMING ELECTION IS GOING SO FAR?
WELL, FOR THIS FIRST-EVER NATIONAL ELECTION...
...THE "REFORM PARTY" AND "PRINCIPLES PARTY" ARE ABOUT TO HOLD THE FINAL PUBLIC DEBATE BEFORE VOTING BEGINS...
...DURING WHICH THE LEADERS OF BOTH PARTIES WILL HAVE A LITTLE WAR OF WORDS OVER THE ISSUES.
IN PRACTICE, WHICHEVER PARTY WINS THE DEBATE WILL HAVE THE LEAD GOING INTO THE ELECTION...
...AND PROBABLY BE ABLE TO TAKE CONTROL OF THE NATIONAL ASSEMBLY ONCE IT FORMS.
BASICALLY, WE'RE IN THE END-GAME.
GOT-CHA.

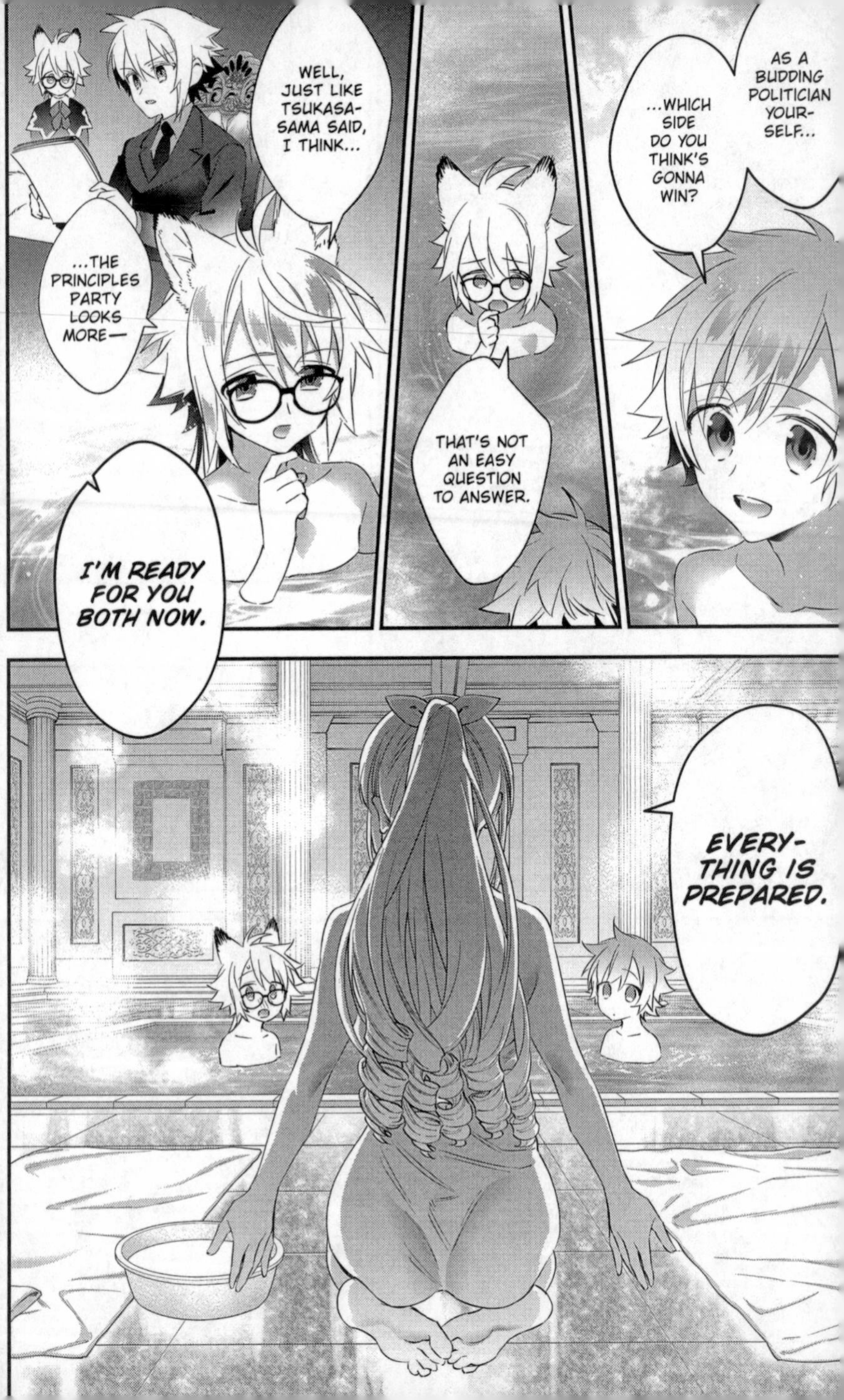
AS A BUDDING POLITICIAN YOUR-SELF...
...WHICH SIDE DO YOU THINK'S GONNA WIN?
THAT'S NOT AN EASY QUESTION TO ANSWER.
WELL, JUST LIKE TSUKASA-SAMA SAID, I THINK...
...THE PRINCIPLES PARTY LOOKS MORE—
I'M READY FOR YOU BOTH NOW.
EVERY-THING IS PREPARED.

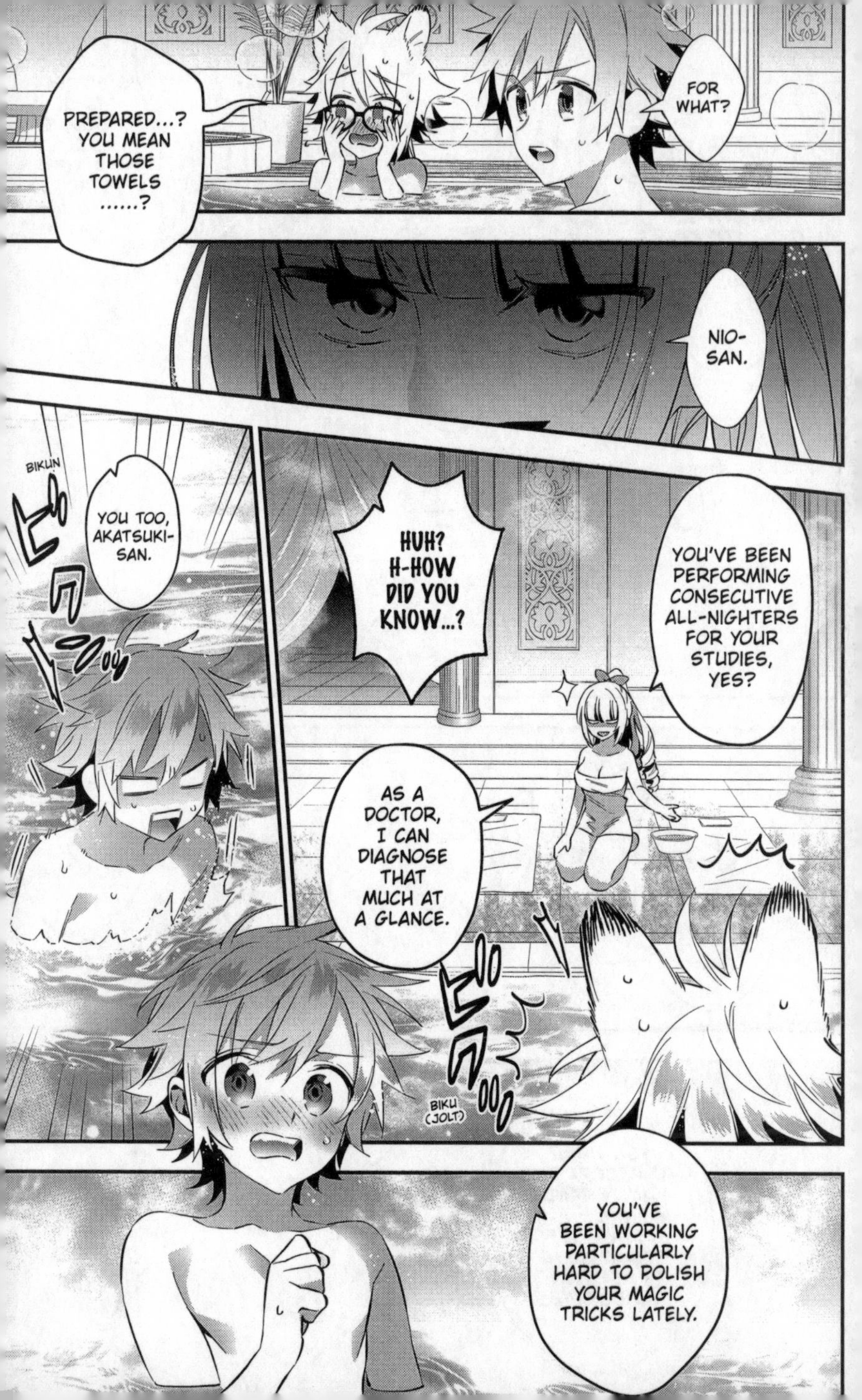
FOR WHAT?
PREPARED...? YOU MEAN THOSE TOWELS ......?
NIO-SAN.
YOU'VE BEEN PERFORMING CONSECUTIVE ALL-NIGHTERS FOR YOUR STUDIES, YES?
HUH? H-HOW DID YOU KNOW...?
AS A DOCTOR, I CAN DIAGNOSE THAT MUCH AT A GLANCE.
BIKU (JOLT)
BIKUN
YOU TOO, AKATSUKI-SAN.
YOU'VE BEEN WORKING PARTICULARLY HARD TO POLISH YOUR MAGIC TRICKS LATELY.

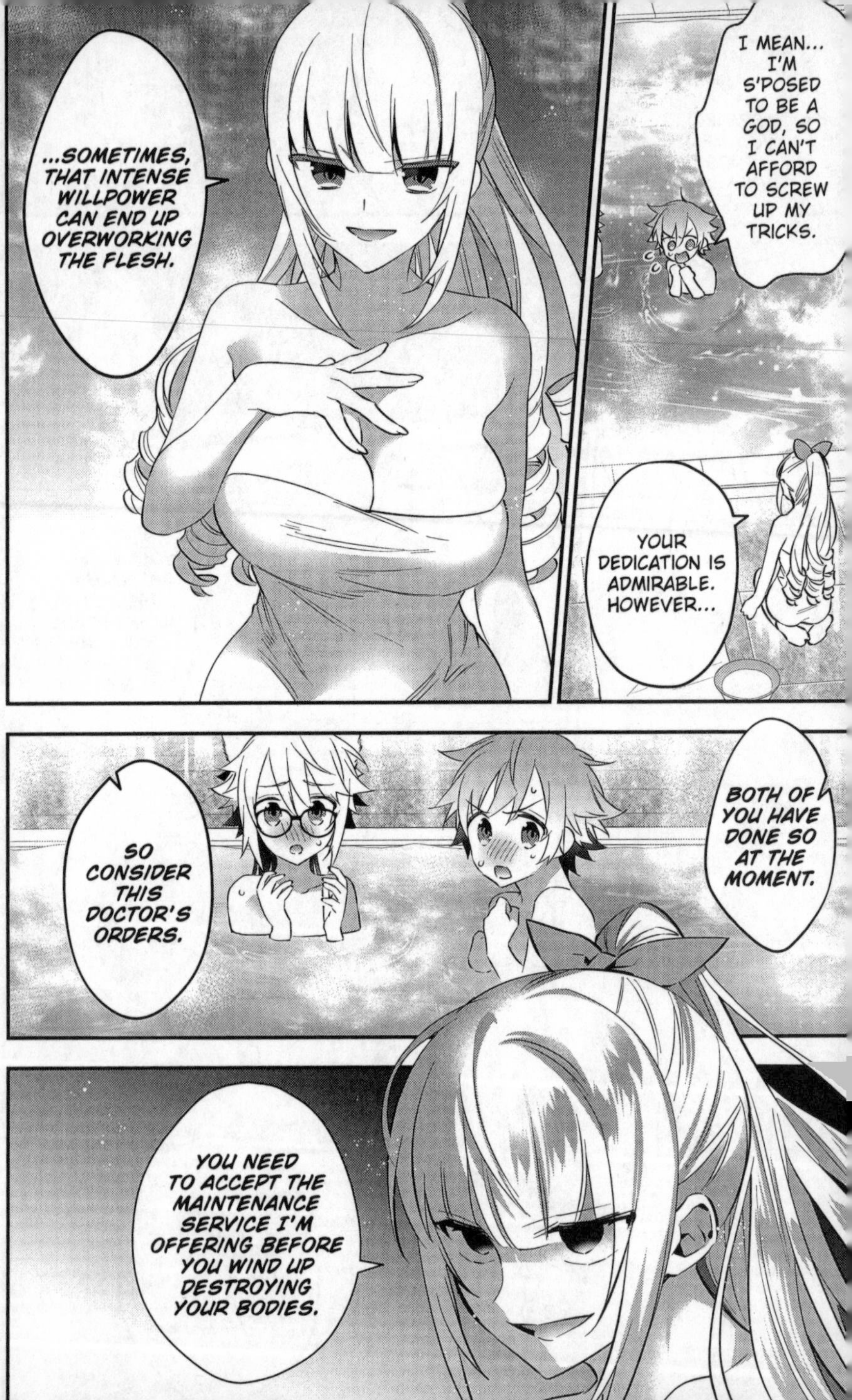
I MEAN... I'M S'POSED TO BE A GOD, SO I CAN'T AFFORD TO SCREW UP MY TRICKS.
YOUR DEDICATION IS ADMIRABLE. HOWEVER...
...SOMETIMES, THAT INTENSE WILLPOWER CAN END UP OVERWORKING THE FLESH.
BOTH OF YOU HAVE DONE SO AT THE MOMENT.
SO CONSIDER THIS DOCTOR'S ORDERS.
YOU NEED TO ACCEPT THE MAINTENANCE SERVICE I'M OFFERING BEFORE YOU WIND UP DESTROYING YOUR BODIES.

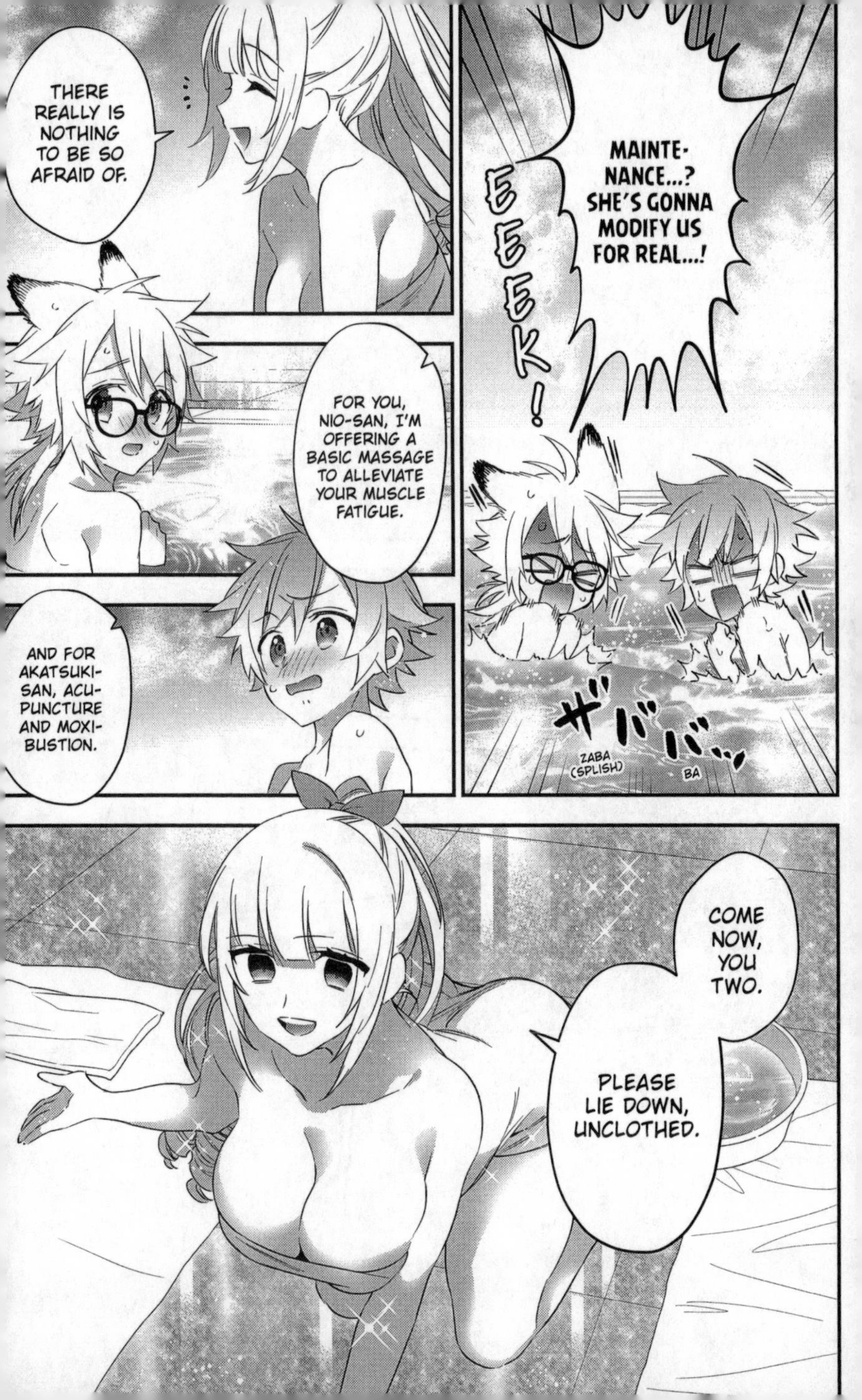
MAINTE-NANCE...? SHE'S GONNA MODIFY US FOR REAL...!
EEEEK!
ザババッ
ZABA (SPLISH)
BA
THERE REALLY IS NOTHING TO BE SO AFRAID OF.
FOR YOU, NIO-SAN, I'M OFFERING A BASIC MASSAGE TO ALLEVIATE YOUR MUSCLE FATIGUE.
AND FOR AKATSUKI-SAN, ACUPUNCTURE AND MOXI-BUSTION.
COME NOW, YOU TWO.
PLEASE LIE DOWN, UNCLOTHED.

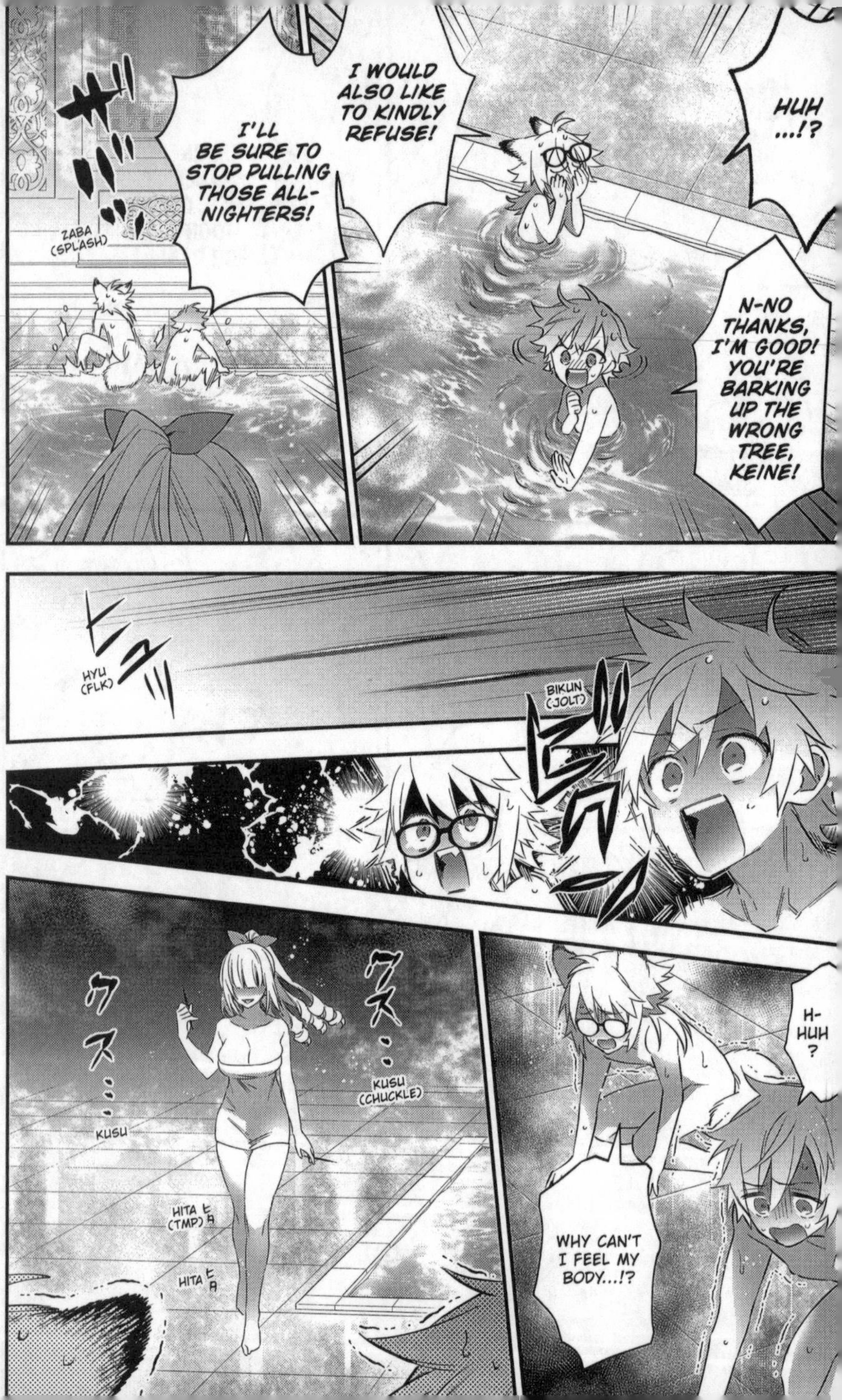
HUH ...!?
I WOULD ALSO LIKE TO KINDLY REFUSE!
N-NO THANKS, I'M GOOD! YOU'RE BARKING UP THE WRONG TREE, KEINE!
I'LL BE SURE TO STOP PULLING THOSE ALL-NIGHTERS!
ZABA (SPLASH)
HYU (FLK)
BIKUN (JOLT)
H-HUH?
WHY CAN'T I FEEL MY BODY...!?
KUSU (CHUCKLE)
KUSU
HITA (TMP) ヒタ
HITA ヒタ

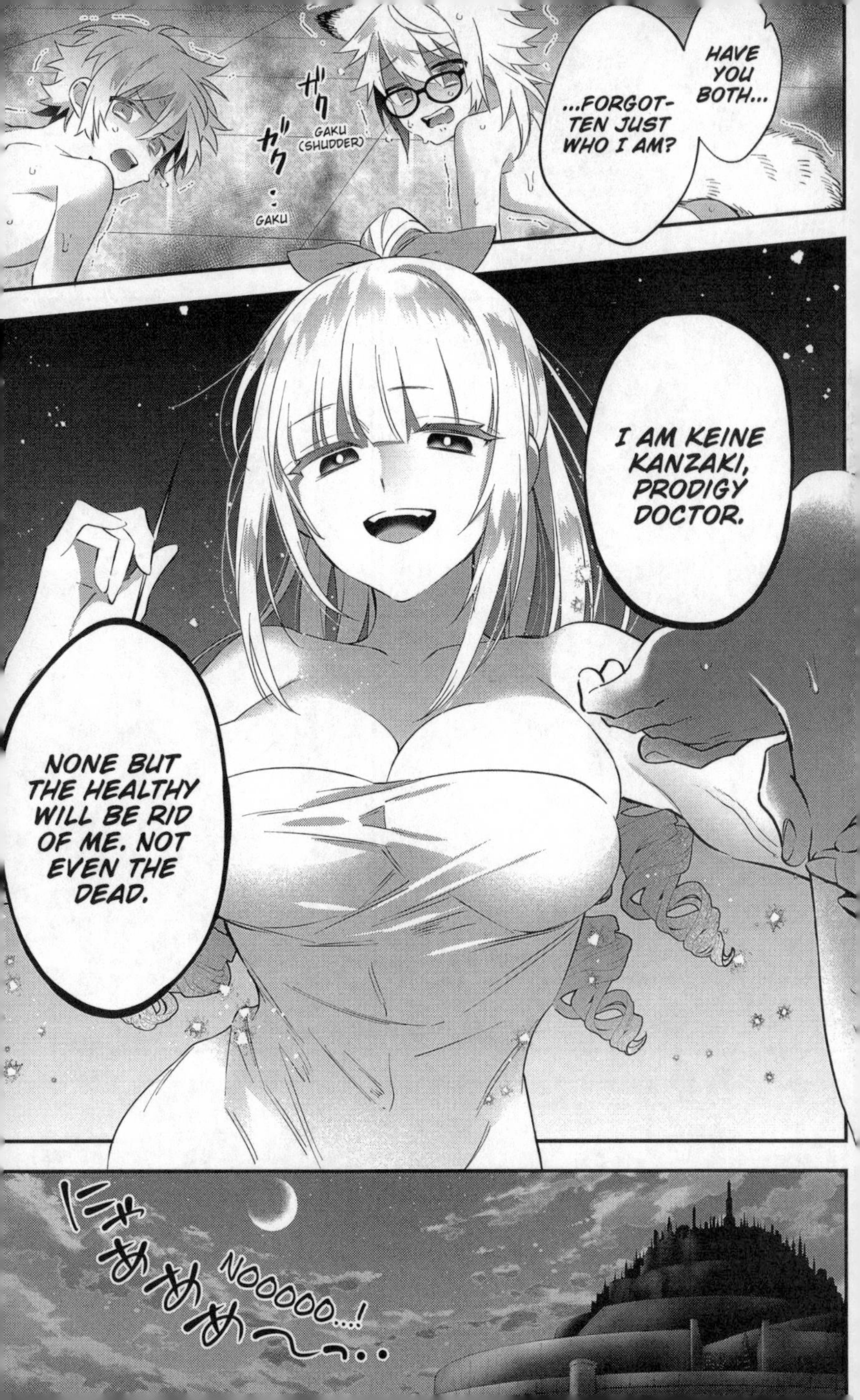
HAVE YOU BOTH...
...FORGOT-TEN JUST WHO I AM?
ガク
GAKU (SHUDDER)
ガク...
GAKU
I AM KEINE KANZAKI, PRODIGY DOCTOR.
NONE BUT THE HEALTHY WILL BE RID OF ME. NOT EVEN THE DEAD.
にゃあああ〜っ..
NOOOOOO...!

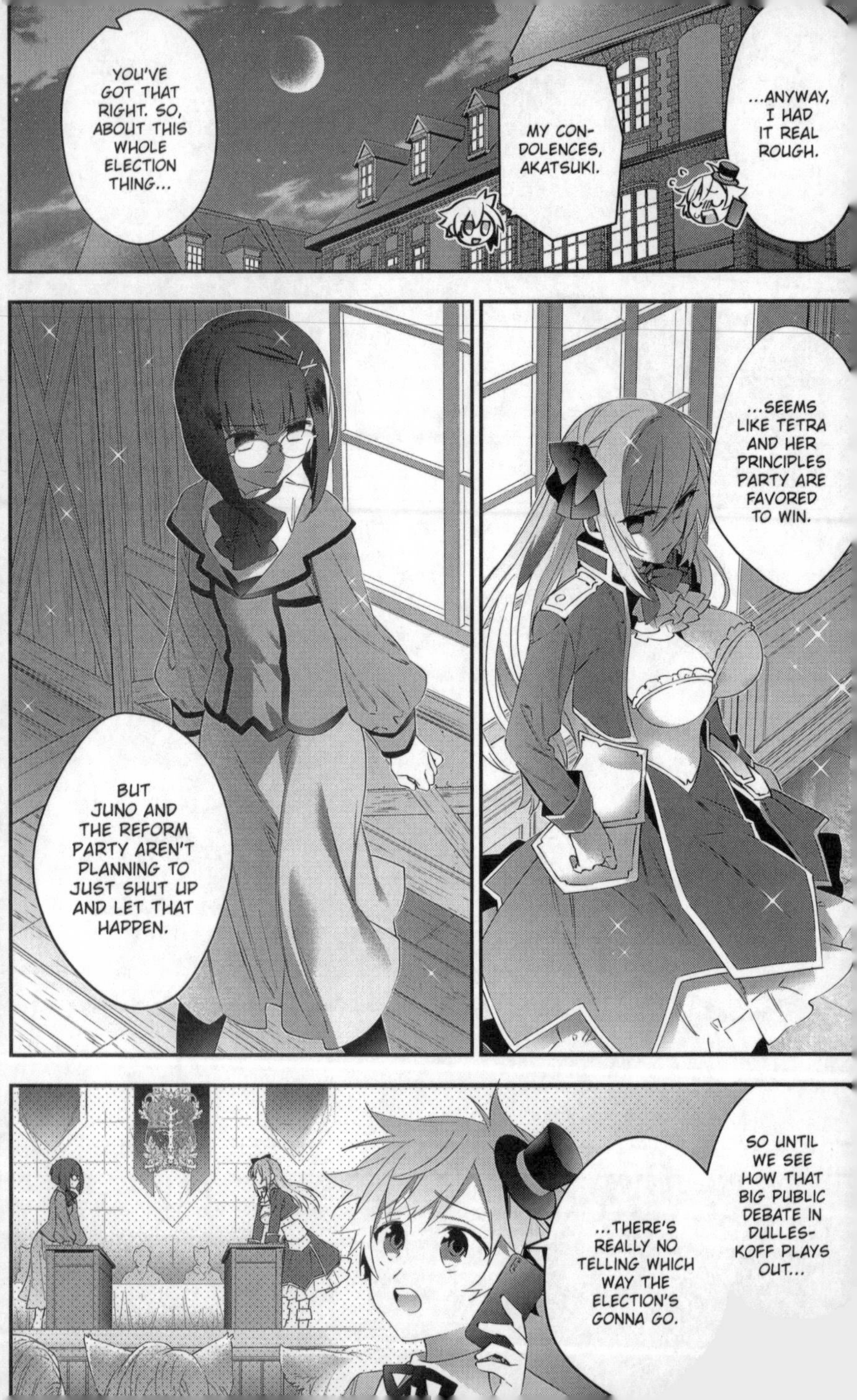
...ANYWAY, I HAD IT REAL ROUGH.
MY CON-DOLENCES, AKATSUKI.
YOU'VE GOT THAT RIGHT. SO, ABOUT THIS WHOLE ELECTION THING...
...SEEMS LIKE TETRA AND HER PRINCIPLES PARTY ARE FAVORED TO WIN.
BUT JUNO AND THE REFORM PARTY AREN'T PLANNING TO JUST SHUT UP AND LET THAT HAPPEN.
SO UNTIL WE SEE HOW THAT BIG PUBLIC DEBATE IN DULLES-KOFF PLAYS OUT...
...THERE'S REALLY NO TELLING WHICH WAY THE ELECTION'S GONNA GO.

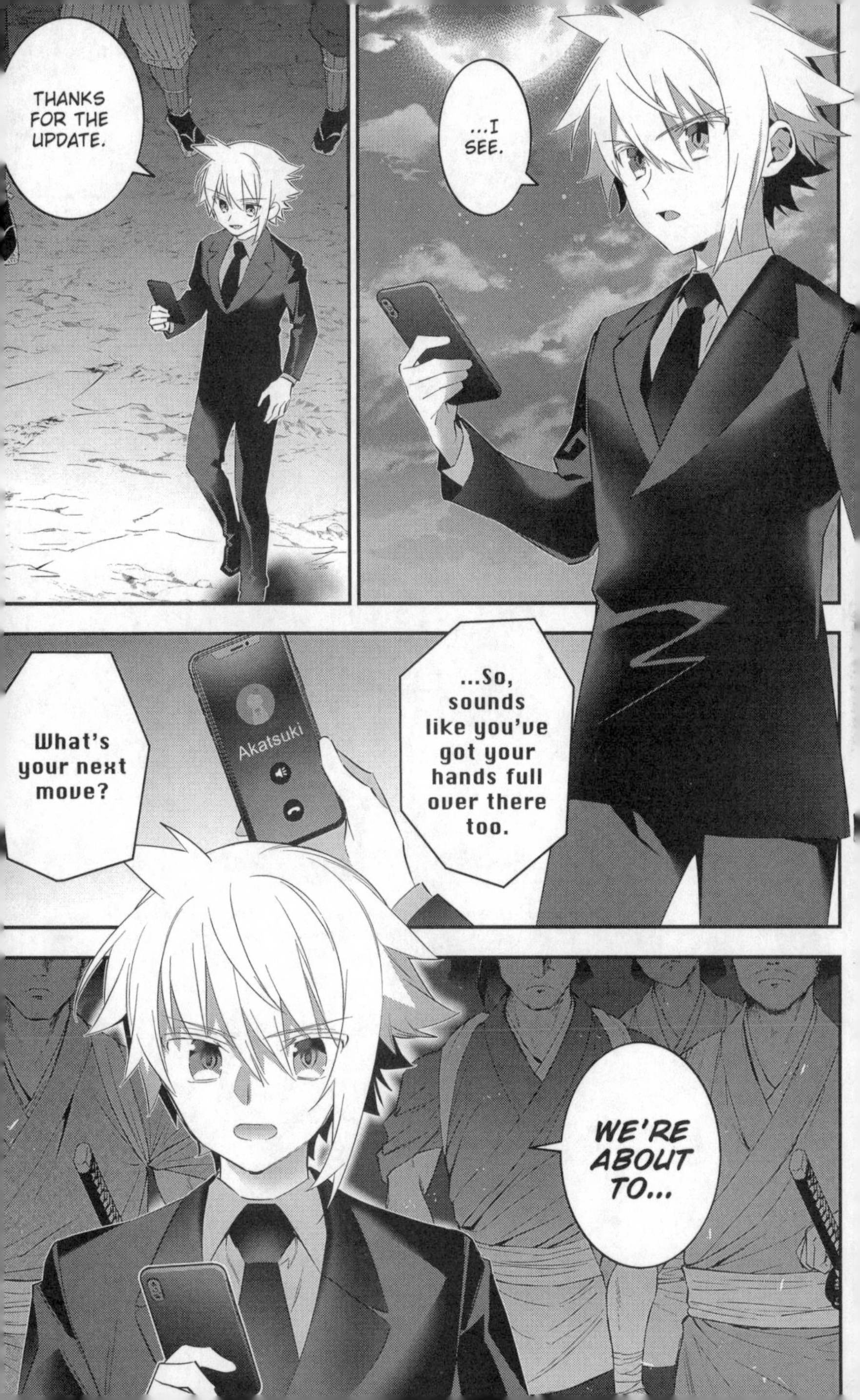
...I SEE.
THANKS FOR THE UPDATE.
...So, sounds like you've got your hands full over there too.
Akatsuki
What's your next move?
WE'RE ABOUT TO...

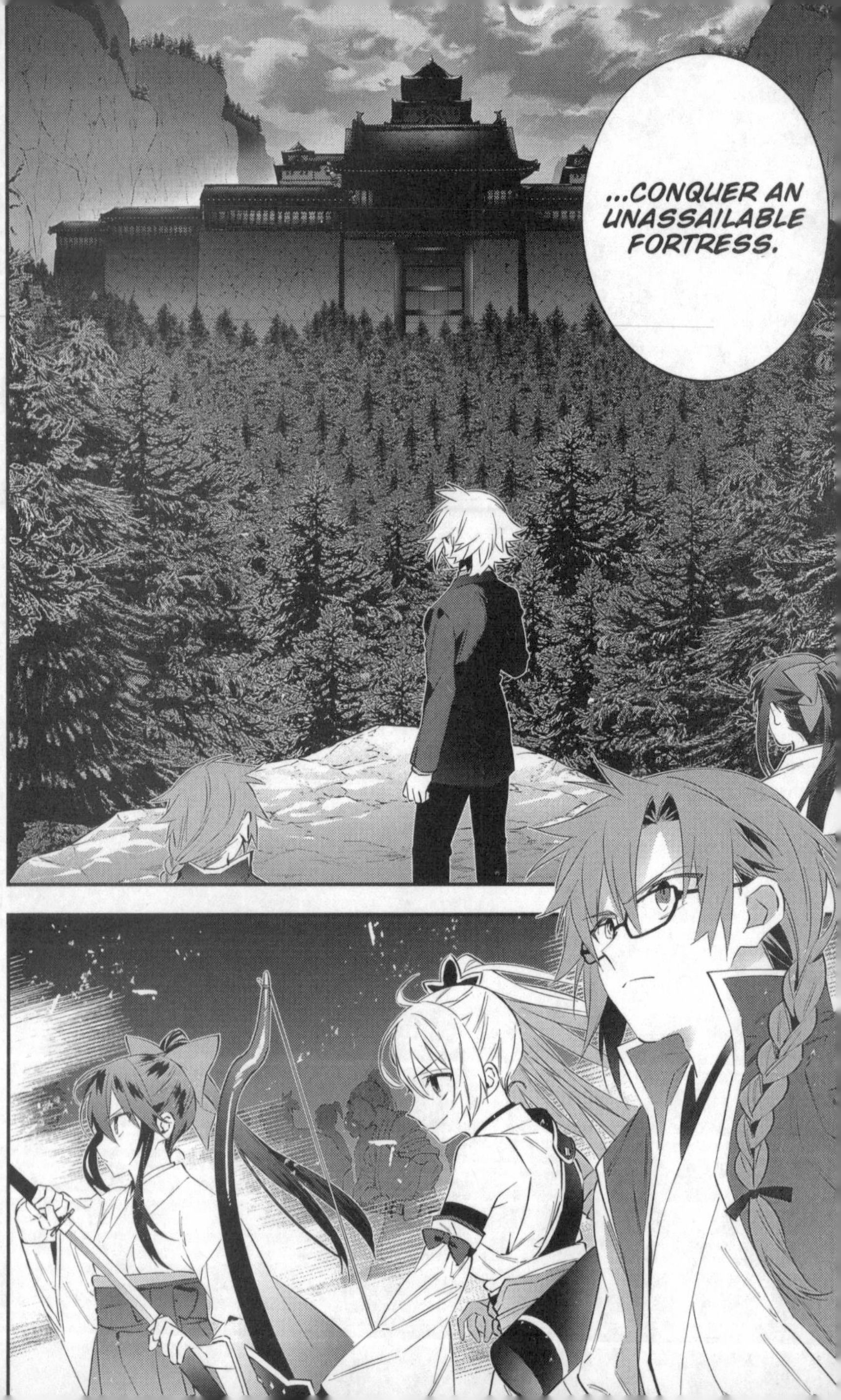
...CONQUER AN UNASSAILABLE FORTRESS.

HIGH SCHOOL PRODIGIES HAVE IT EASY EVEN IN ANOTHER WORLD!

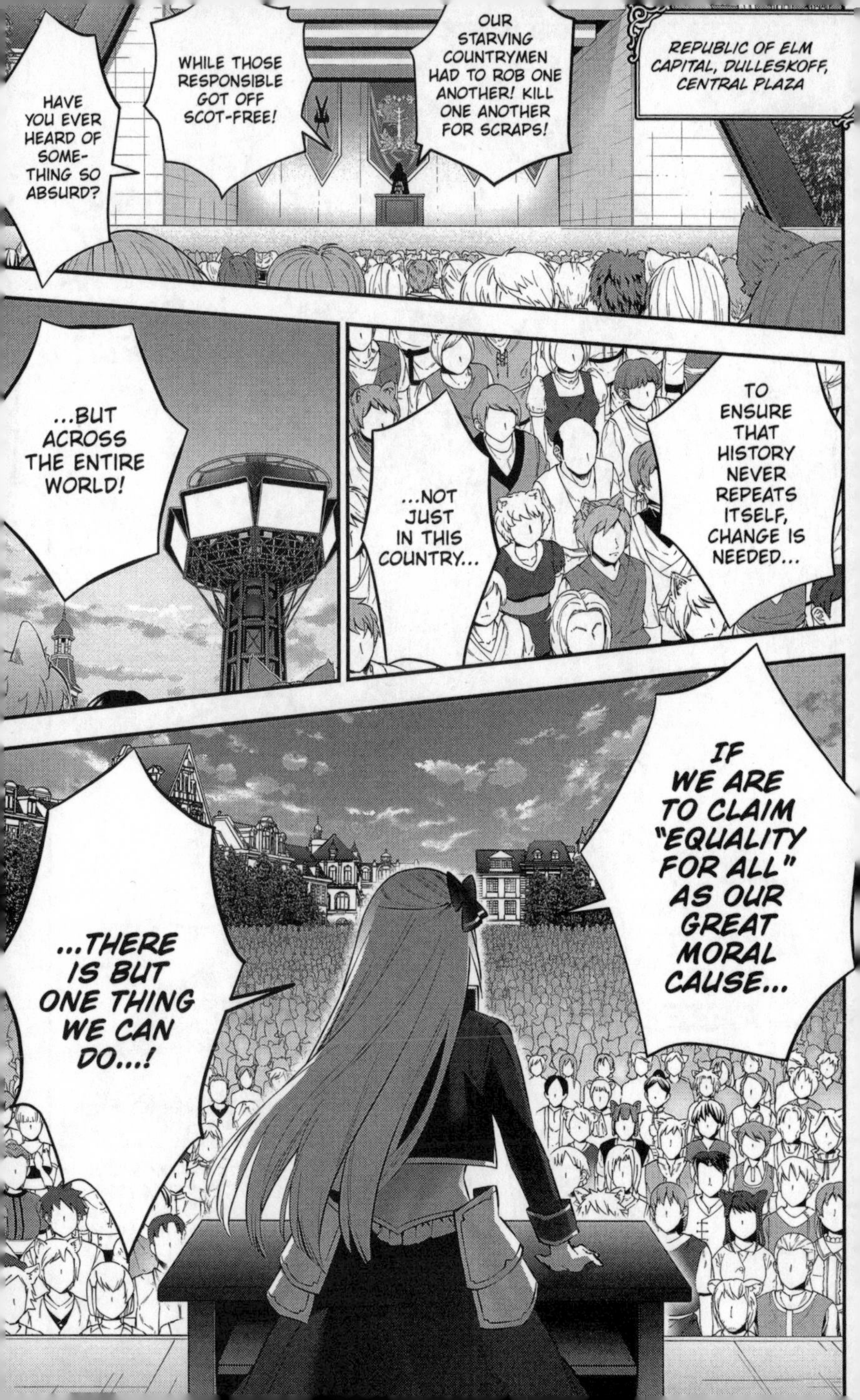
REPUBLIC OF ELM CAPITAL, DULLESKOFF, CENTRAL PLAZA
OUR STARVING COUNTRYMEN HAD TO ROB ONE ANOTHER! KILL ONE ANOTHER FOR SCRAPS!
WHILE THOSE RESPONSIBLE GOT OFF SCOT-FREE!
HAVE YOU EVER HEARD OF SOME-THING SO ABSURD?
TO ENSURE THAT HISTORY NEVER REPEATS ITSELF, CHANGE IS NEEDED...
...NOT JUST IN THIS COUNTRY...
...BUT ACROSS THE ENTIRE WORLD!
IF WE ARE TO CLAIM "EQUALITY FOR ALL" AS OUR GREAT MORAL CAUSE...
...THERE IS BUT ONE THING WE CAN DO...!

CHAPTER 75: WARPED DEMOCRACY

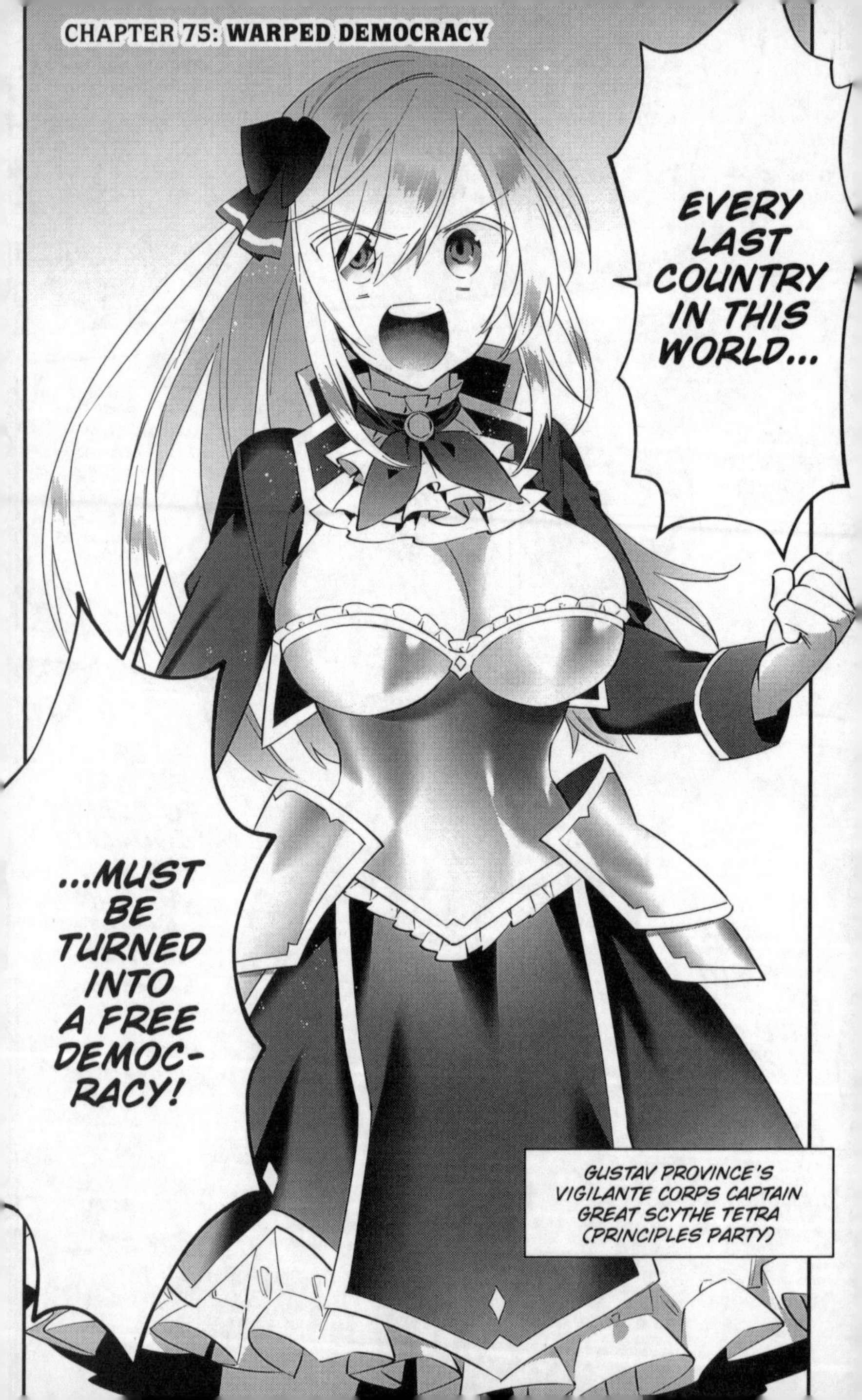
EVERY LAST COUNTRY IN THIS WORLD...
...MUST BE TURNED INTO A FREE DEMOC-RACY!
GUSTAV PROVINCE'S VIGILANTE CORPS CAPTAIN
GREAT SCYTHE TETRA
(PRINCIPLES PARTY)

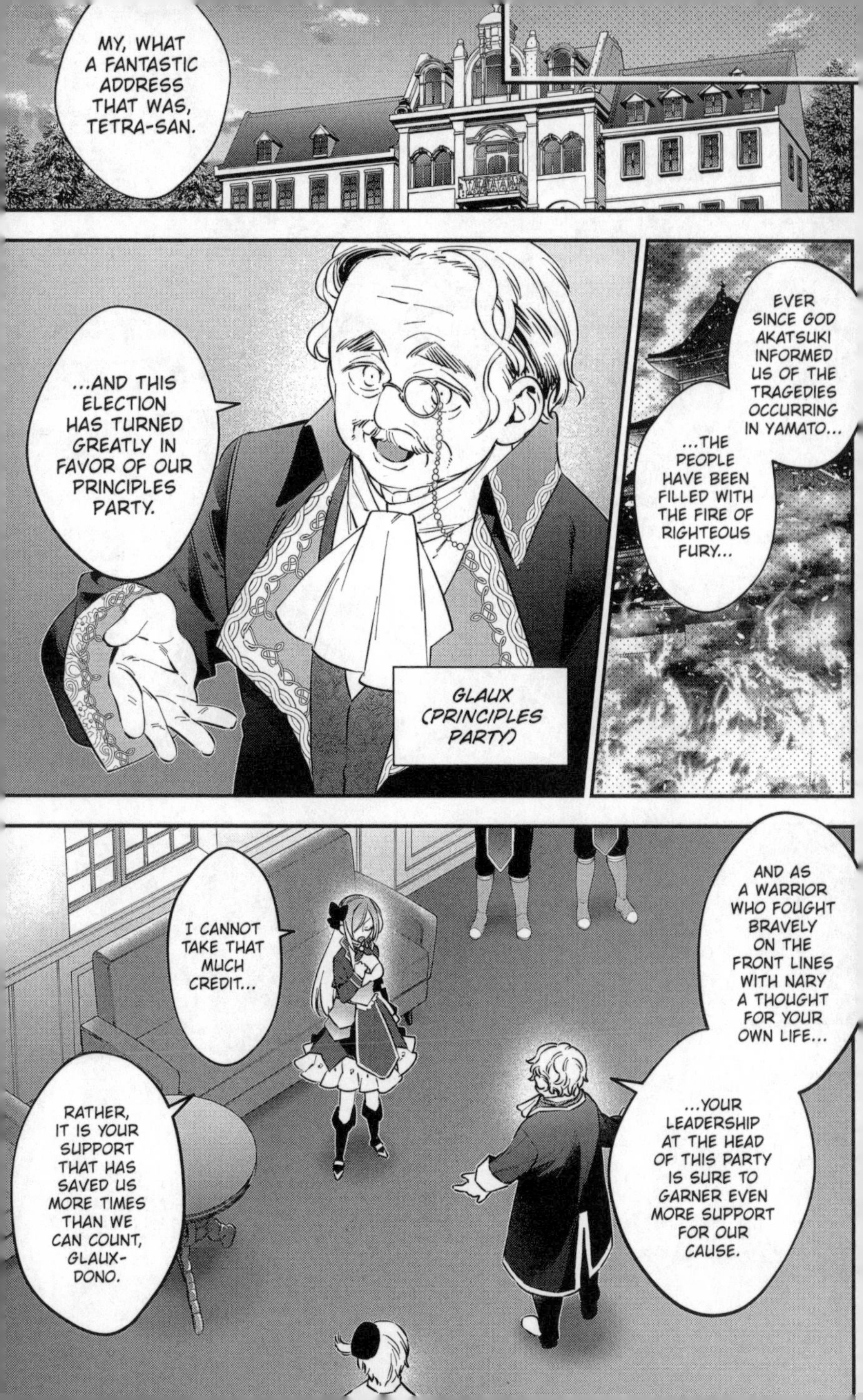
MY, WHAT A FANTASTIC ADDRESS THAT WAS, TETRA-SAN.
EVER SINCE GOD AKATSUKI INFORMED US OF THE TRAGEDIES OCCURRING IN YAMATO...
...THE PEOPLE HAVE BEEN FILLED WITH THE FIRE OF RIGHTEOUS FURY...
...AND THIS ELECTION HAS TURNED GREATLY IN FAVOR OF OUR PRINCIPLES PARTY.
GLAUX (PRINCIPLES PARTY)
AND AS A WARRIOR WHO FOUGHT BRAVELY ON THE FRONT LINES WITH NARY A THOUGHT FOR YOUR OWN LIFE...
...YOUR LEADERSHIP AT THE HEAD OF THIS PARTY IS SURE TO GARNER EVEN MORE SUPPORT FOR OUR CAUSE.
I CANNOT TAKE THAT MUCH CREDIT...
RATHER, IT IS YOUR SUPPORT THAT HAS SAVED US MORE TIMES THAN WE CAN COUNT, GLAUX-DONO.

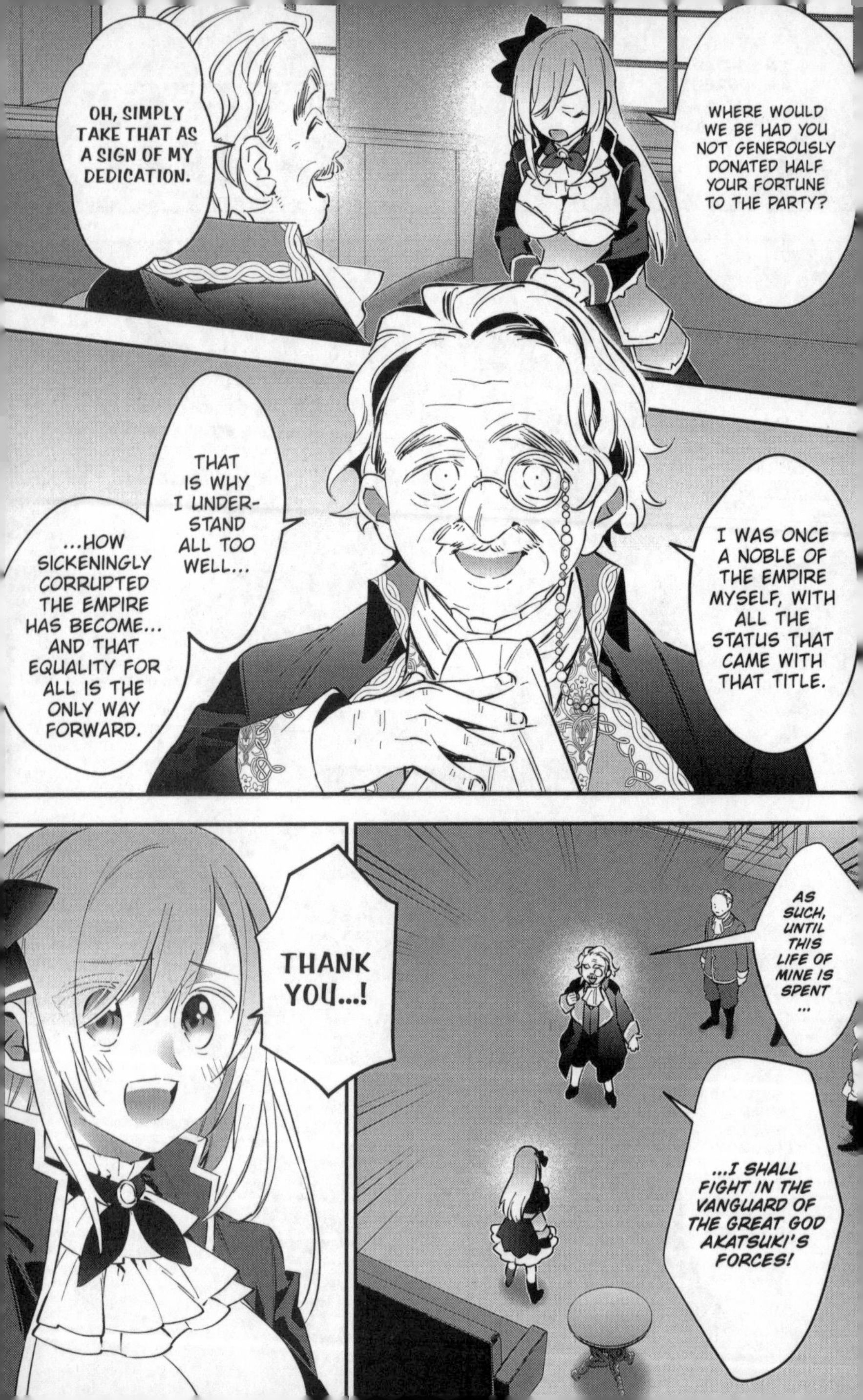
WHERE WOULD WE BE HAD YOU NOT GENEROUSLY DONATED HALF YOUR FORTUNE TO THE PARTY?
OH, SIMPLY TAKE THAT AS A SIGN OF MY DEDICATION.
I WAS ONCE A NOBLE OF THE EMPIRE MYSELF, WITH ALL THE STATUS THAT CAME WITH THAT TITLE.
THAT IS WHY I UNDER-STAND ALL TOO WELL...
...HOW SICKENINGLY CORRUPTED THE EMPIRE HAS BECOME... AND THAT EQUALITY FOR ALL IS THE ONLY WAY FORWARD.
AS SUCH, UNTIL THIS LIFE OF MINE IS SPENT...
...I SHALL FIGHT IN THE VANGUARD OF THE GREAT GOD AKATSUKI'S FORCES!
THANK YOU...!

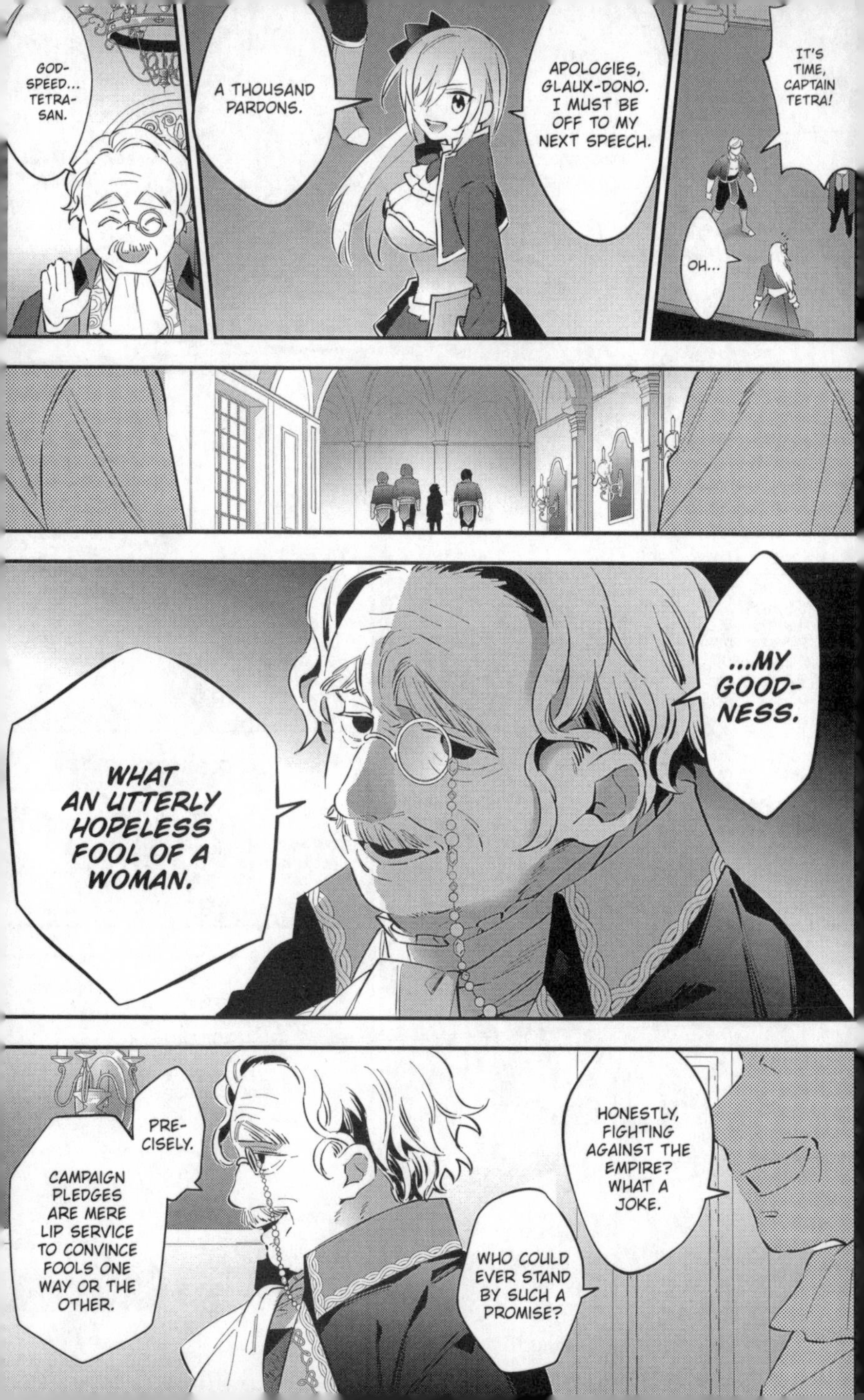
IT'S TIME, CAPTAIN TETRA!
OH...
APOLOGIES, GLAUX-DONO. I MUST BE OFF TO MY NEXT SPEECH.
A THOUSAND PARDONS.
GOD-SPEED... TETRA-SAN.
...MY GOOD-NESS.
WHAT AN UTTERLY HOPELESS FOOL OF A WOMAN.
HONESTLY, FIGHTING AGAINST THE EMPIRE? WHAT A JOKE.
WHO COULD EVER STAND BY SUCH A PROMISE?
PRE-CISELY.
CAMPAIGN PLEDGES ARE MERE LIP SERVICE TO CONVINCE FOOLS ONE WAY OR THE OTHER.

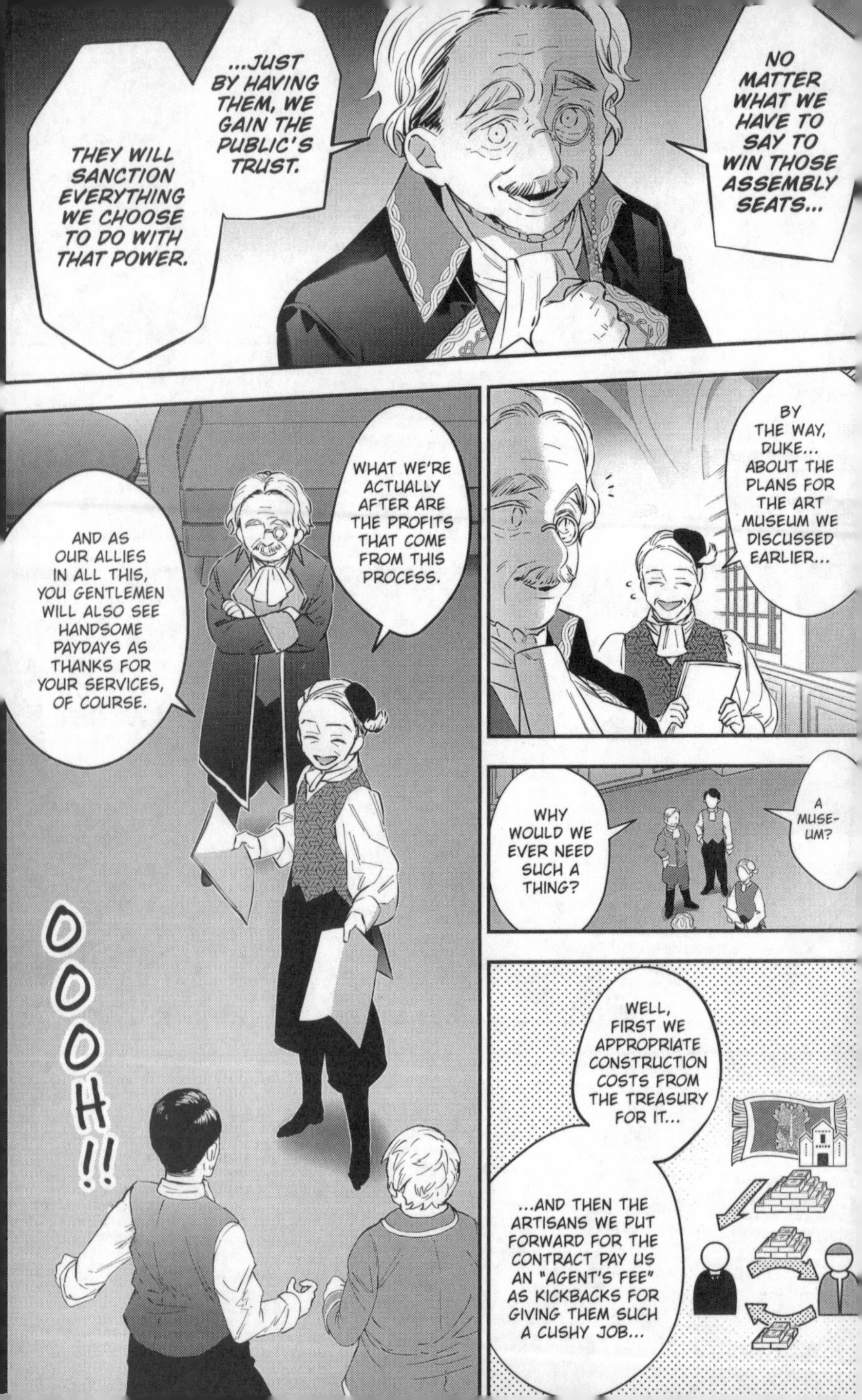
NO MATTER WHAT WE HAVE TO SAY TO WIN THOSE ASSEMBLY SEATS...
...JUST BY HAVING THEM, WE GAIN THE PUBLIC'S TRUST.
THEY WILL SANCTION EVERYTHING WE CHOOSE TO DO WITH THAT POWER.
WHAT WE'RE ACTUALLY AFTER ARE THE PROFITS THAT COME FROM THIS PROCESS.
AND AS OUR ALLIES IN ALL THIS, YOU GENTLEMEN WILL ALSO SEE HANDSOME PAYDAYS AS THANKS FOR YOUR SERVICES, OF COURSE.
OOOH!!
BY THE WAY, DUKE... ABOUT THE PLANS FOR THE ART MUSEUM WE DISCUSSED EARLIER...
A MUSE-UM?
WHY WOULD WE EVER NEED SUCH A THING?
WELL, FIRST WE APPROPRIATE CONSTRUCTION COSTS FROM THE TREASURY FOR IT...
...AND THEN THE ARTISANS WE PUT FORWARD FOR THE CONTRACT PAY US AN "AGENT'S FEE" AS KICKBACKS FOR GIVING THEM SUCH A CUSHY JOB...

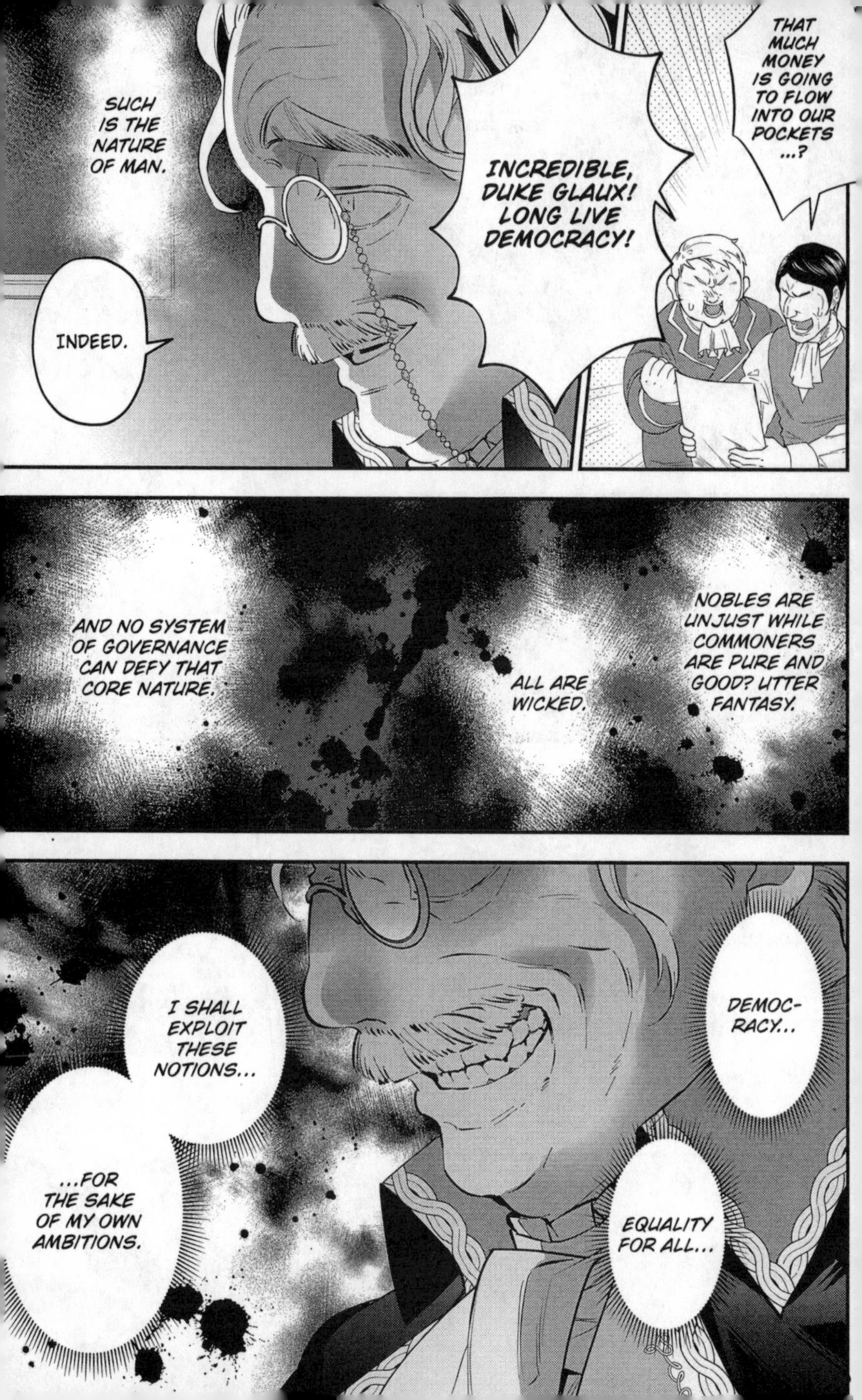
THAT MUCH MONEY IS GOING TO FLOW INTO OUR POCKETS ...?
INCREDIBLE, DUKE GLAUX! LONG LIVE DEMOCRACY!
SUCH IS THE NATURE OF MAN.
INDEED.
NOBLES ARE UNJUST WHILE COMMONERS ARE PURE AND GOOD? UTTER FANTASY.
ALL ARE WICKED.
AND NO SYSTEM OF GOVERNANCE CAN DEFY THAT CORE NATURE.
DEMOC-RACY...
EQUALITY FOR ALL...
I SHALL EXPLOIT THESE NOTIONS...
...FOR THE SAKE OF MY OWN AMBITIONS.

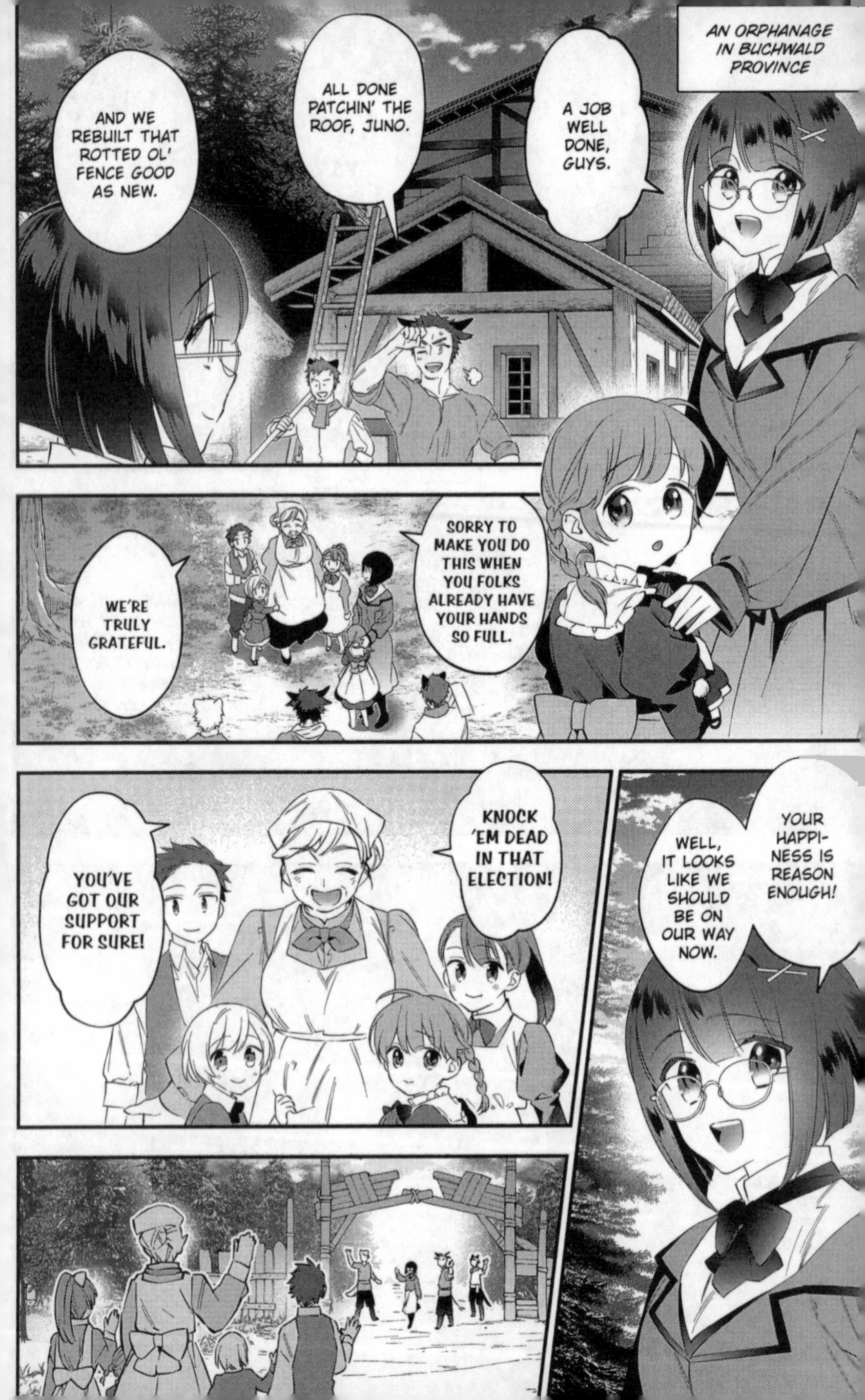
AN ORPHANAGE IN BUCHWALD PROVINCE
A JOB WELL DONE, GUYS.
ALL DONE PATCHIN' THE ROOF, JUNO.
AND WE REBUILT THAT ROTTED OL' FENCE GOOD AS NEW.
SORRY TO MAKE YOU DO THIS WHEN YOU FOLKS ALREADY HAVE YOUR HANDS SO FULL.
WE'RE TRULY GRATEFUL.
YOUR HAPPINESS IS REASON ENOUGH!
WELL, IT LOOKS LIKE WE SHOULD BE ON OUR WAY NOW.
KNOCK 'EM DEAD IN THAT ELECTION!
YOU'VE GOT OUR SUPPORT FOR SURE!

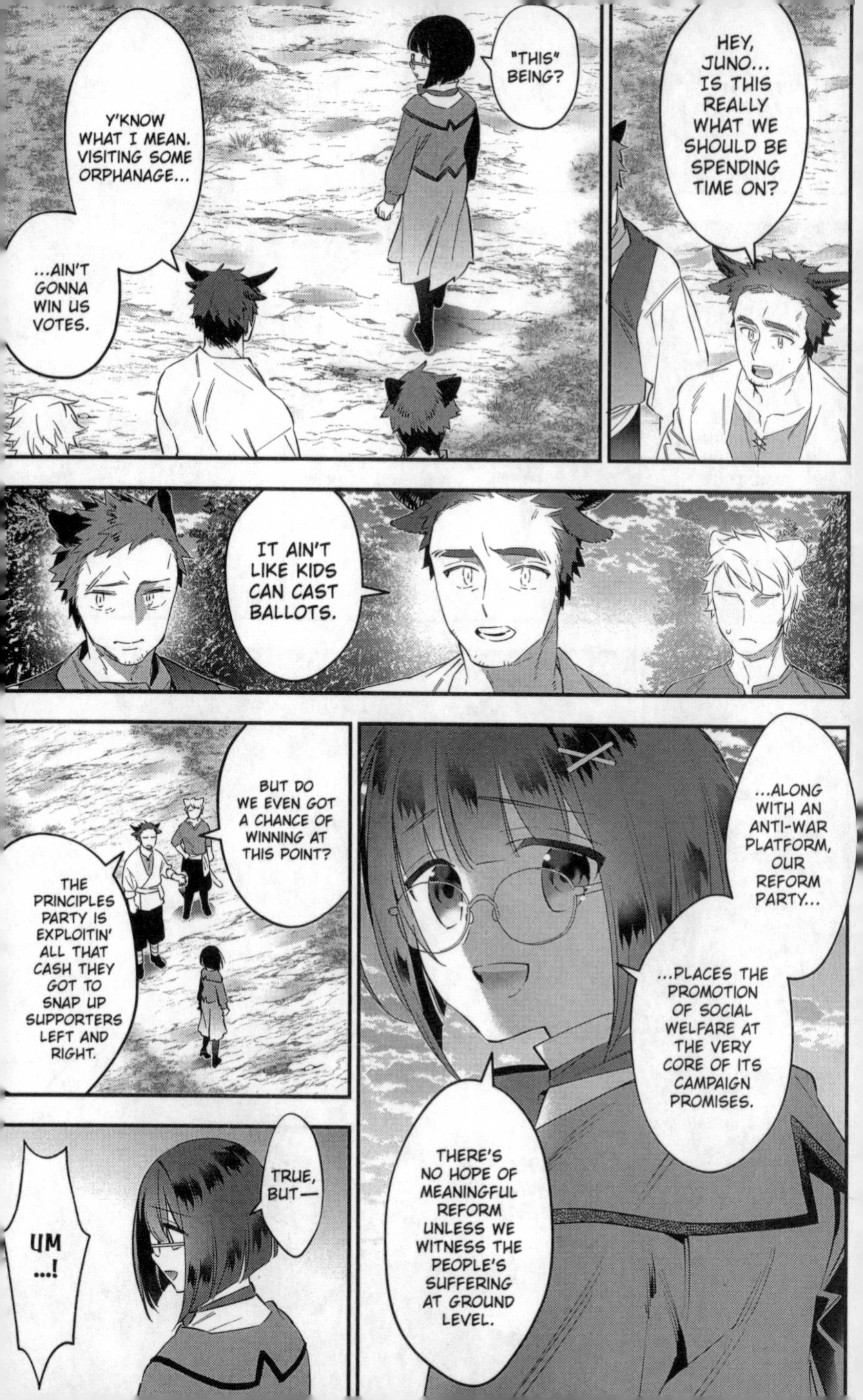
HEY, JUNO... IS THIS REALLY WHAT WE SHOULD BE SPENDING TIME ON?
"THIS" BEING?
Y'KNOW WHAT I MEAN. VISITING SOME ORPHANAGE...
...AIN'T GONNA WIN US VOTES.
IT AIN'T LIKE KIDS CAN CAST BALLOTS.
...ALONG WITH AN ANTI-WAR PLATFORM, OUR REFORM PARTY...
...PLACES THE PROMOTION OF SOCIAL WELFARE AT THE VERY CORE OF ITS CAMPAIGN PROMISES.
THERE'S NO HOPE OF MEANINGFUL REFORM UNLESS WE WITNESS THE PEOPLE'S SUFFERING AT GROUND LEVEL.
BUT DO WE EVEN GOT A CHANCE OF WINNING AT THIS POINT?
THE PRINCIPLES PARTY IS EXPLOITIN' ALL THAT CASH THEY GOT TO SNAP UP SUPPORTERS LEFT AND RIGHT.
TRUE, BUT—
UM ...!

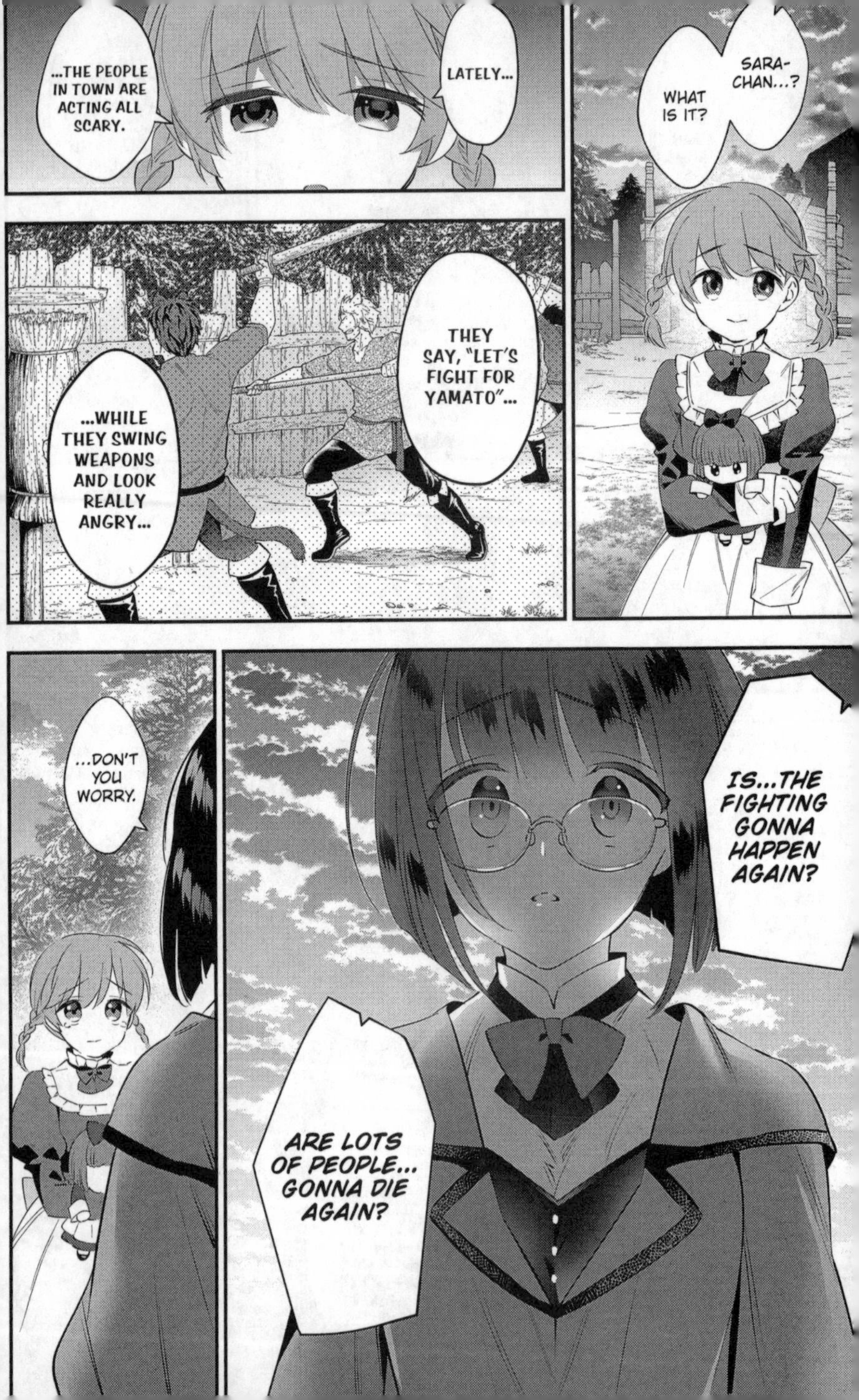
SARA-CHAN...?
WHAT IS IT?
LATELY...
...THE PEOPLE IN TOWN ARE ACTING ALL SCARY.
THEY SAY, "LET'S FIGHT FOR YAMATO"...
...WHILE THEY SWING WEAPONS AND LOOK REALLY ANGRY...
IS...THE FIGHTING GONNA HAPPEN AGAIN?
ARE LOTS OF PEOPLE... GONNA DIE AGAIN?
...DON'T YOU WORRY.

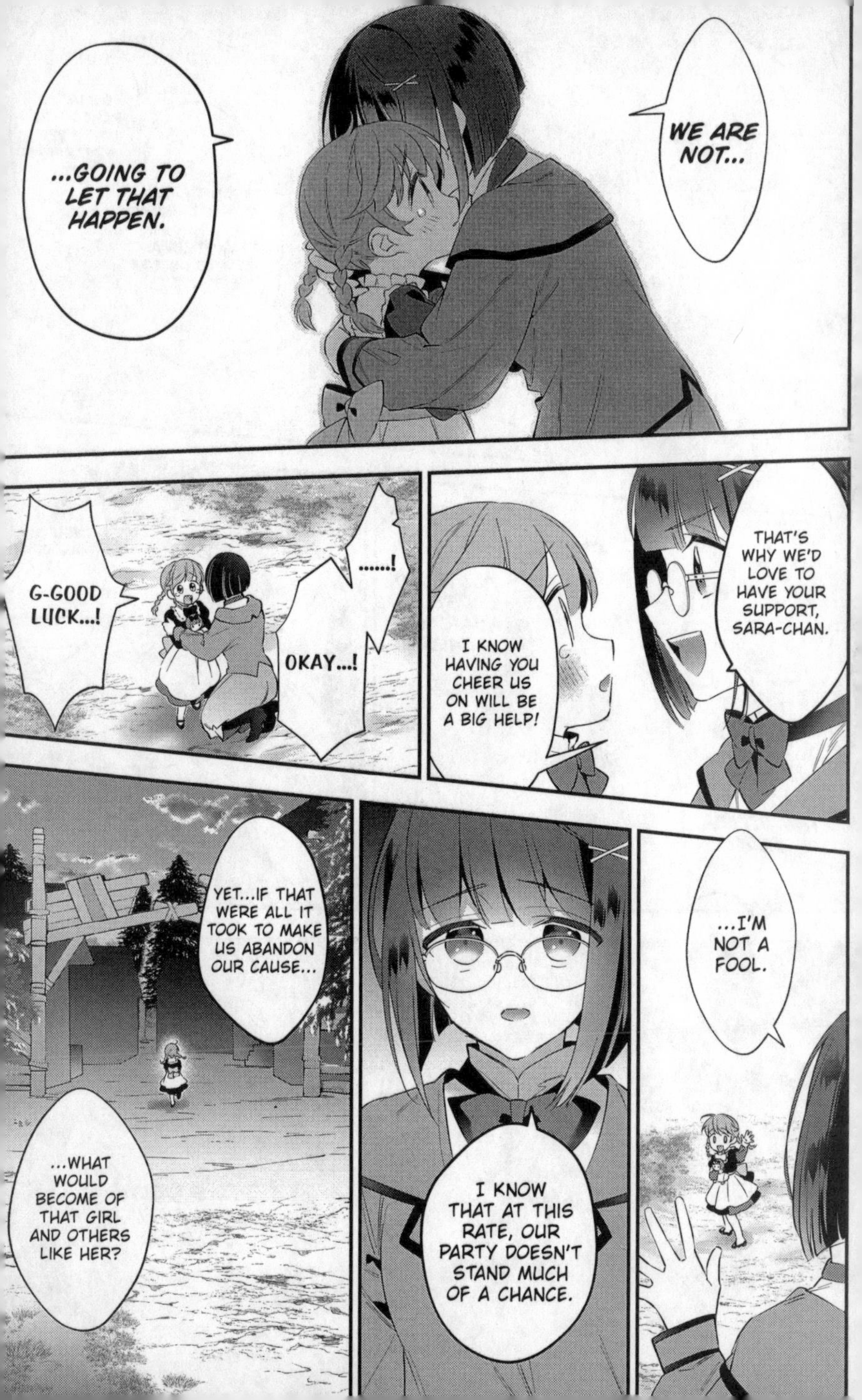
WE ARE NOT...
...GOING TO LET THAT HAPPEN.
THAT'S WHY WE'D LOVE TO HAVE YOUR SUPPORT, SARA-CHAN.
I KNOW HAVING YOU CHEER US ON WILL BE A BIG HELP!
......!
OKAY...!
G-GOOD LUCK...!
...I'M NOT A FOOL.
I KNOW THAT AT THIS RATE, OUR PARTY DOESN'T STAND MUCH OF A CHANCE.
YET...IF THAT WERE ALL IT TOOK TO MAKE US ABANDON OUR CAUSE...
...WHAT WOULD BECOME OF THAT GIRL AND OTHERS LIKE HER?

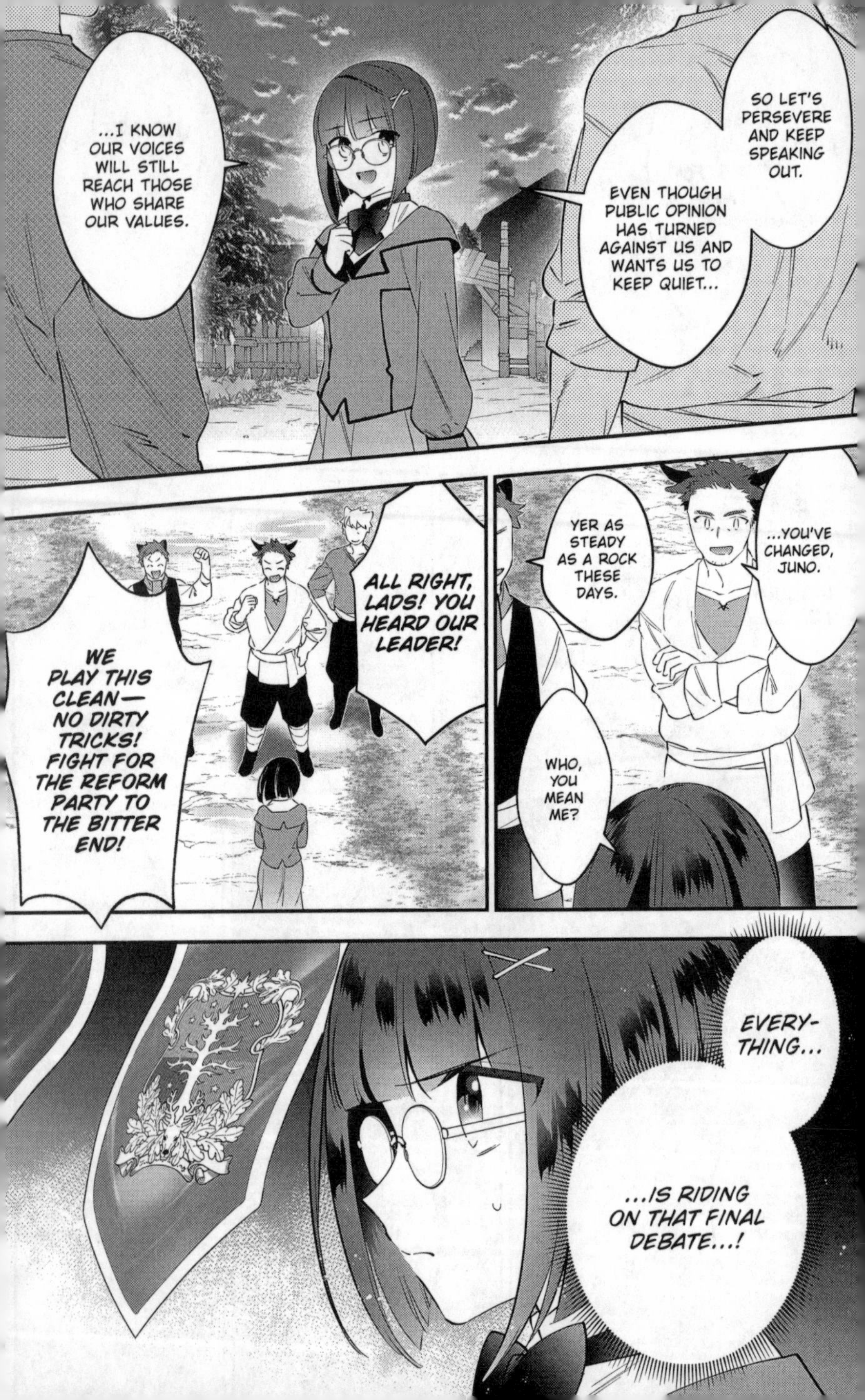
SO LET'S PERSEVERE AND KEEP SPEAKING OUT.
EVEN THOUGH PUBLIC OPINION HAS TURNED AGAINST US AND WANTS US TO KEEP QUIET...
...I KNOW OUR VOICES WILL STILL REACH THOSE WHO SHARE OUR VALUES.
...YOU'VE CHANGED, JUNO.
YER AS STEADY AS A ROCK THESE DAYS.
WHO, YOU MEAN ME?
ALL RIGHT, LADS! YOU HEARD OUR LEADER!
WE PLAY THIS CLEAN—NO DIRTY TRICKS! FIGHT FOR THE REFORM PARTY TO THE BITTER END!
EVERY-THING...
...IS RIDING ON THAT FINAL DEBATE...!

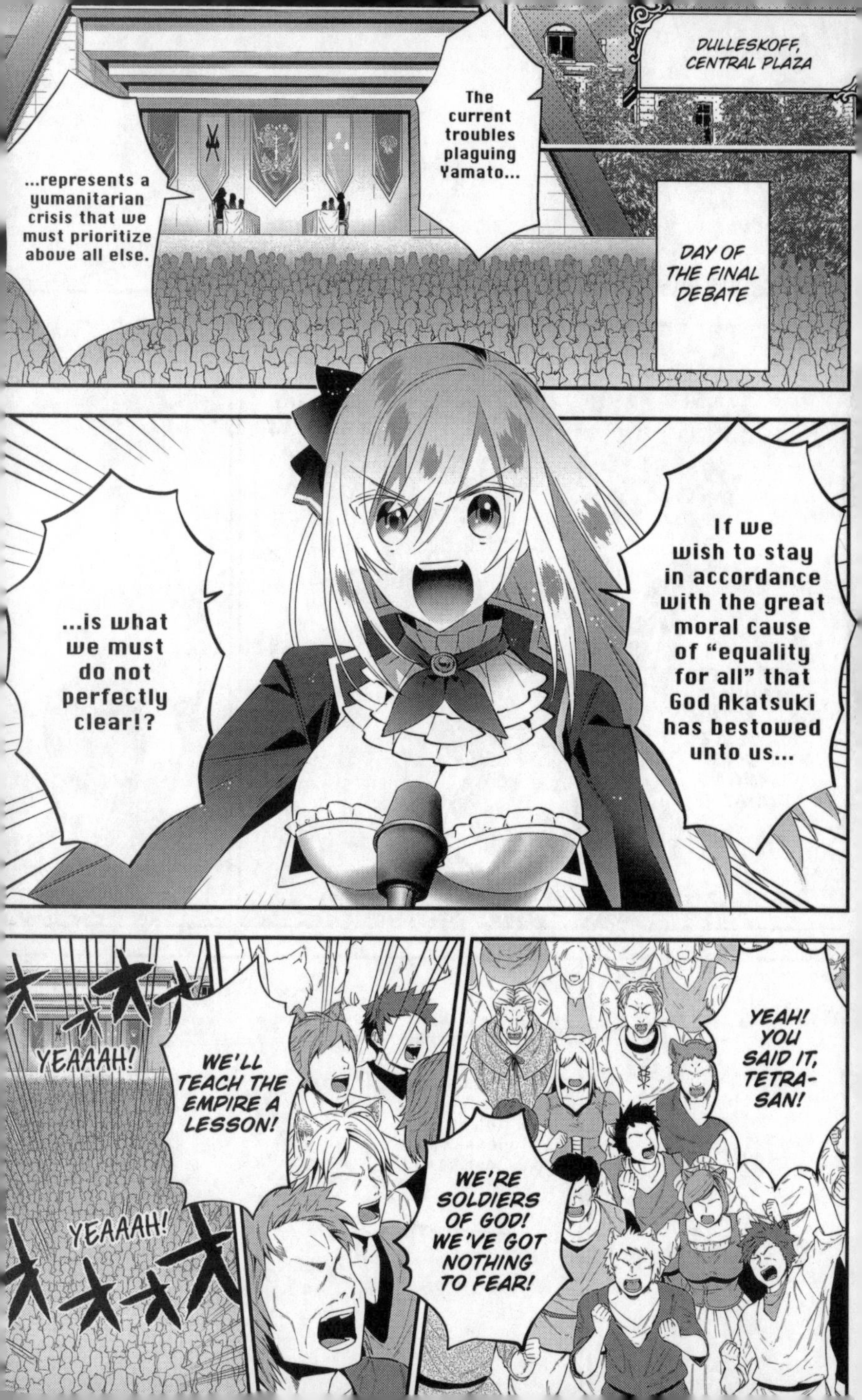
DULLESKOFF, CENTRAL PLAZA
DAY OF THE FINAL DEBATE
The current troubles plaguing Yamato...
...represents a yumanitarian crisis that we must prioritize above all else.
If we wish to stay in accordance with the great moral cause of "equality for all" that God Akatsuki has bestowed unto us...
...is what we must do not perfectly clear!?
YEAH! YOU SAID IT, TETRA-SAN!
WE'RE SOLDIERS OF GOD! WE'VE GOT NOTHING TO FEAR!
WE'LL TEACH THE EMPIRE A LESSON!
YEAAAH!
YEAAAH!

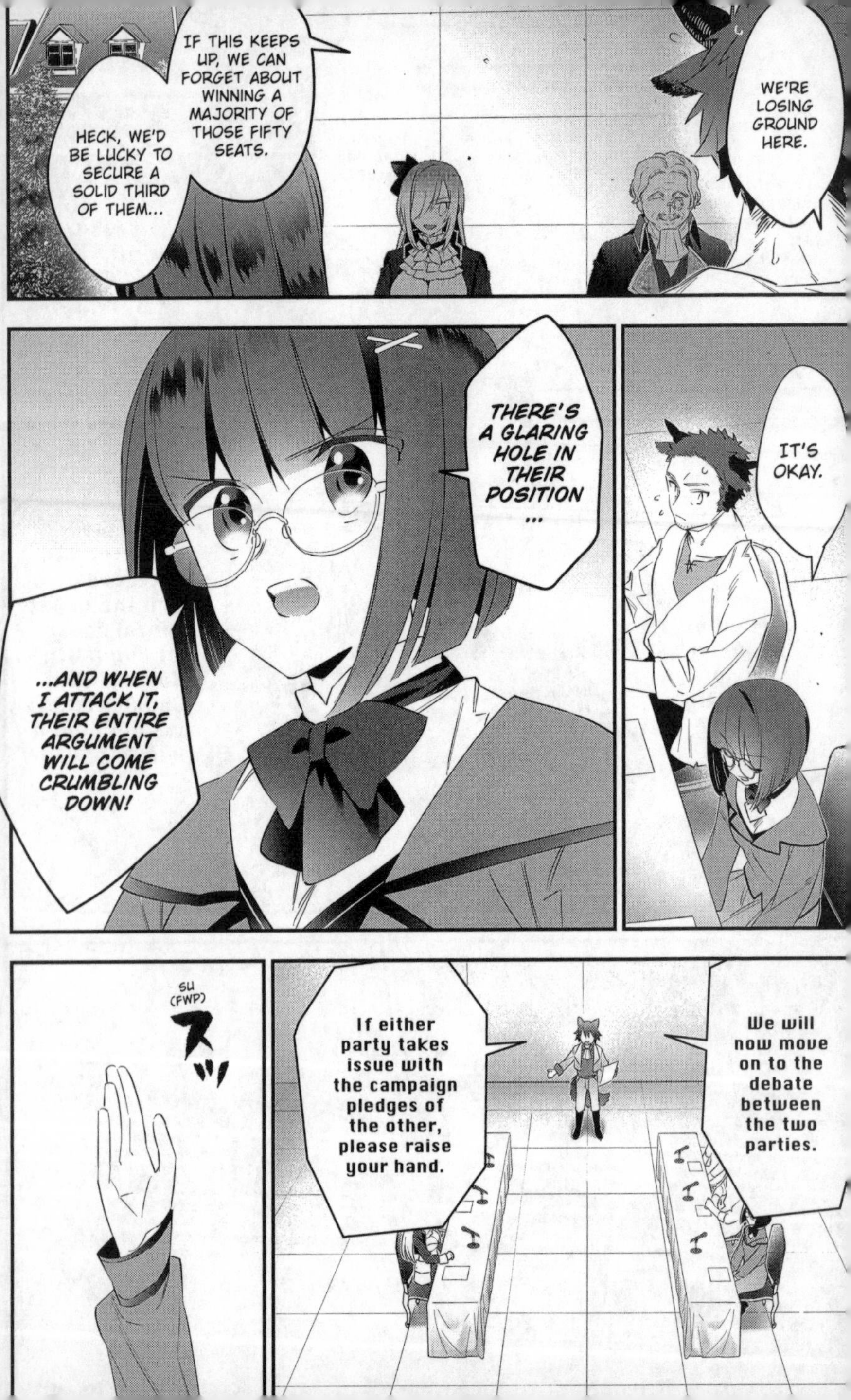
WE'RE LOSING GROUND HERE.
IF THIS KEEPS UP, WE CAN FORGET ABOUT WINNING A MAJORITY OF THOSE FIFTY SEATS.
HECK, WE'D BE LUCKY TO SECURE A SOLID THIRD OF THEM...
IT'S OKAY.
THERE'S A GLARING HOLE IN THEIR POSITION...
...AND WHEN I ATTACK IT, THEIR ENTIRE ARGUMENT WILL COME CRUMBLING DOWN!
We will now move on to the debate between the two parties.
If either party takes issue with the campaign pledges of the other, please raise your hand.
SU (FWP)

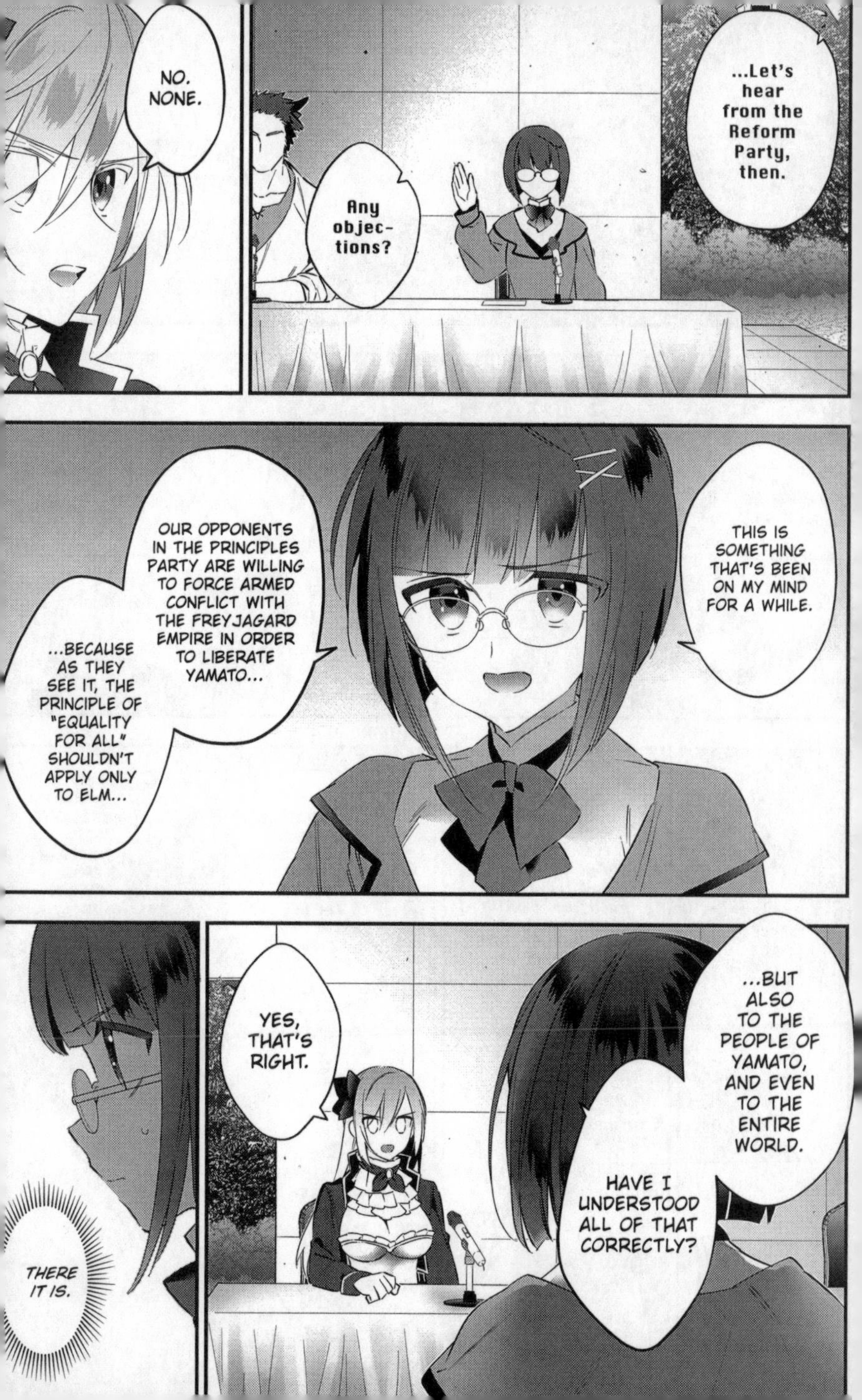
...Let's hear from the Reform Party, then.
Any objections?
NO. NONE.
THIS IS SOMETHING THAT'S BEEN ON MY MIND FOR A WHILE.
OUR OPPONENTS IN THE PRINCIPLES PARTY ARE WILLING TO FORCE ARMED CONFLICT WITH THE FREYJAGARD EMPIRE IN ORDER TO LIBERATE YAMATO...
...BECAUSE AS THEY SEE IT, THE PRINCIPLE OF "EQUALITY FOR ALL" SHOULDN'T APPLY ONLY TO ELM...
...BUT ALSO TO THE PEOPLE OF YAMATO, AND EVEN TO THE ENTIRE WORLD.
HAVE I UNDERSTOOD ALL OF THAT CORRECTLY?
YES, THAT'S RIGHT.
THERE IT IS.

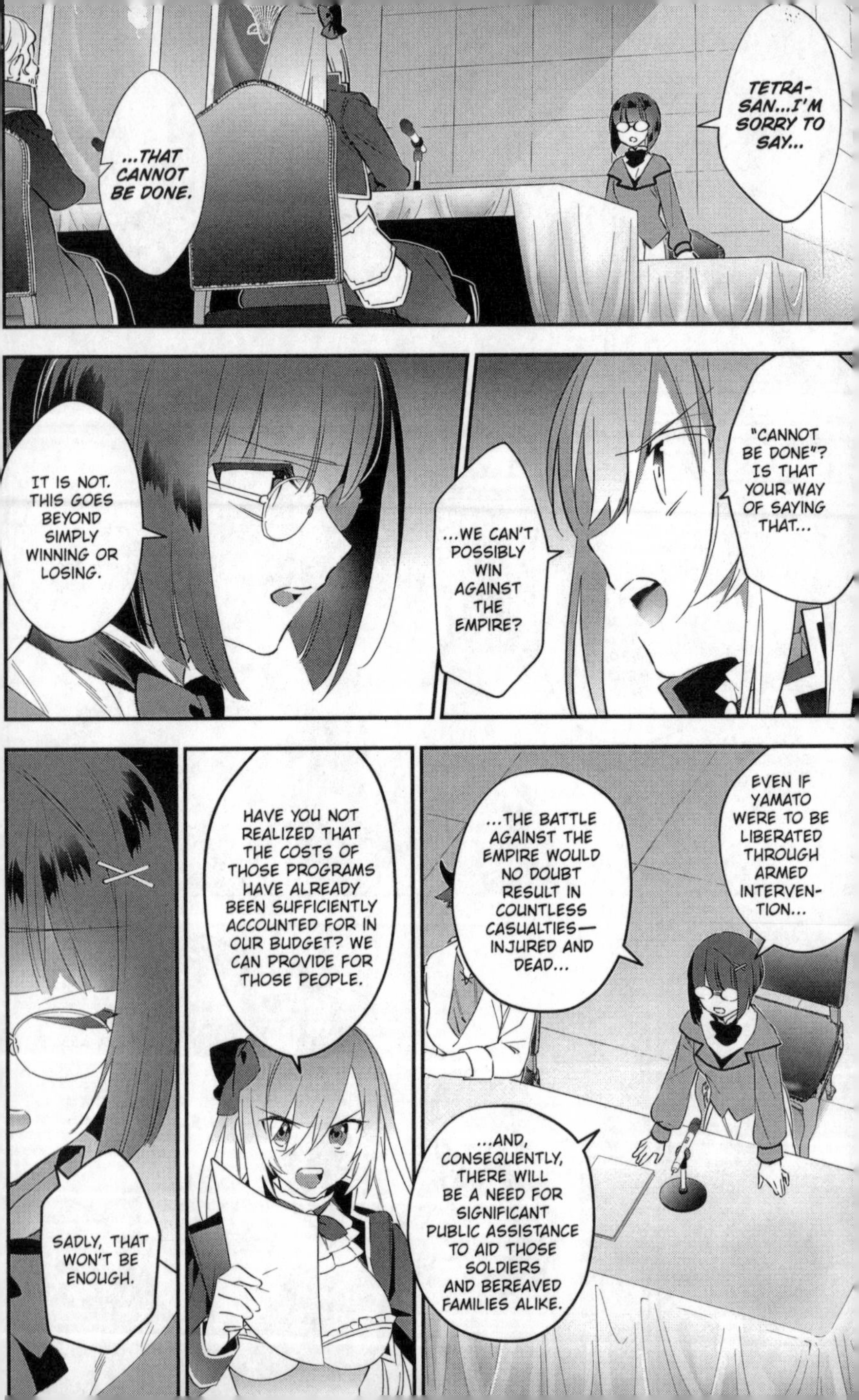
TETRA-SAN...I'M SORRY TO SAY...
...THAT CANNOT BE DONE.
"CANNOT BE DONE"? IS THAT YOUR WAY OF SAYING THAT...
...WE CAN'T POSSIBLY WIN AGAINST THE EMPIRE?
IT IS NOT. THIS GOES BEYOND SIMPLY WINNING OR LOSING.
EVEN IF YAMATO WERE TO BE LIBERATED THROUGH ARMED INTERVEN-TION...
...THE BATTLE AGAINST THE EMPIRE WOULD NO DOUBT RESULT IN COUNTLESS CASUALTIES—INJURED AND DEAD...
...AND, CONSEQUENTLY, THERE WILL BE A NEED FOR SIGNIFICANT PUBLIC ASSISTANCE TO AID THOSE SOLDIERS AND BEREAVED FAMILIES ALIKE.
HAVE YOU NOT REALIZED THAT THE COSTS OF THOSE PROGRAMS HAVE ALREADY BEEN SUFFICIENTLY ACCOUNTED FOR IN OUR BUDGET? WE CAN PROVIDE FOR THOSE PEOPLE.
SADLY, THAT WON'T BE ENOUGH.

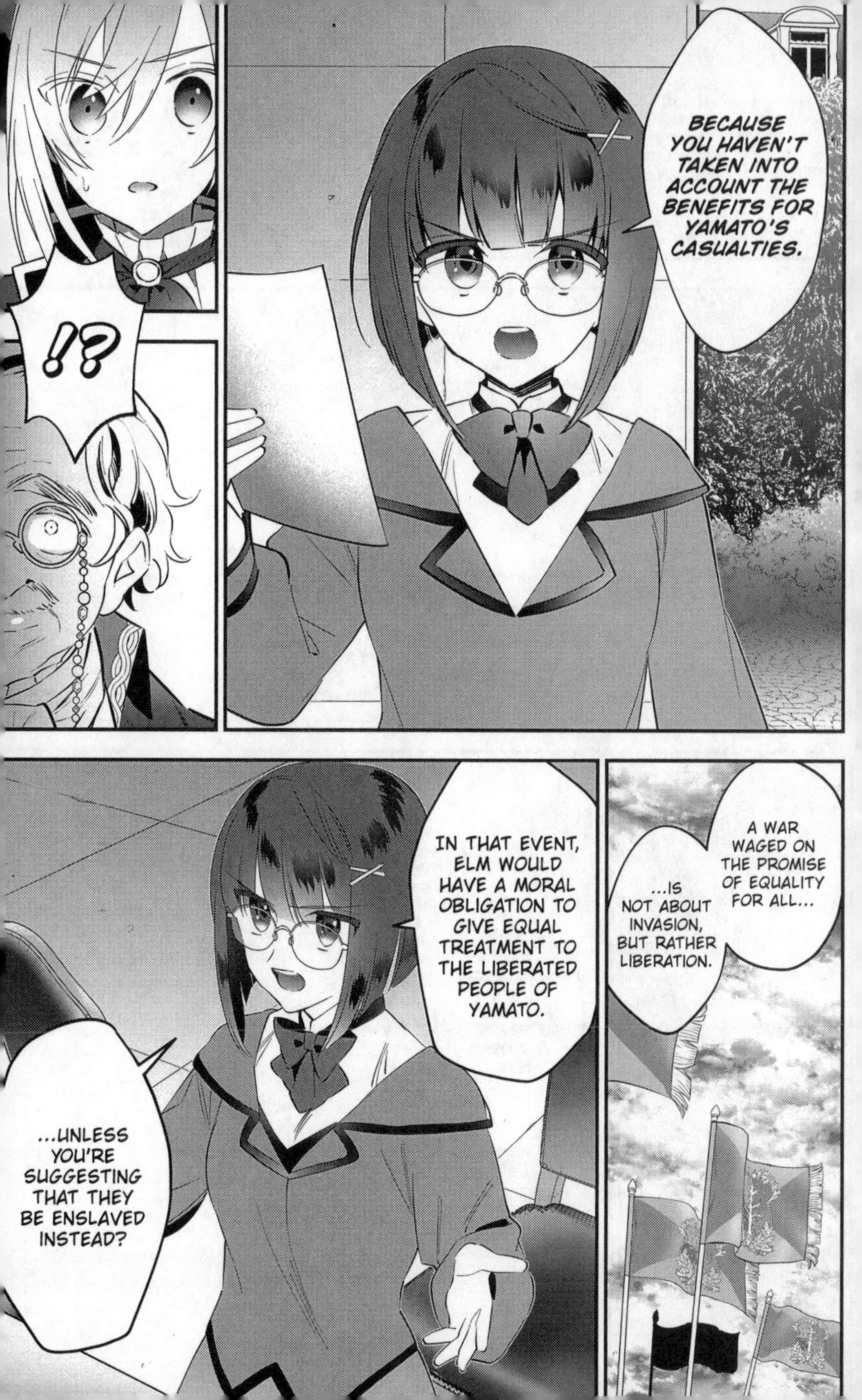
BECAUSE YOU HAVEN'T TAKEN INTO ACCOUNT THE BENEFITS FOR YAMATO'S CASUALTIES.
!?
A WAR WAGED ON THE PROMISE OF EQUALITY FOR ALL...
...IS NOT ABOUT INVASION, BUT RATHER LIBERATION.
IN THAT EVENT, ELM WOULD HAVE A MORAL OBLIGATION TO GIVE EQUAL TREATMENT TO THE LIBERATED PEOPLE OF YAMATO.
...UNLESS YOU'RE SUGGESTING THAT THEY BE ENSLAVED INSTEAD?

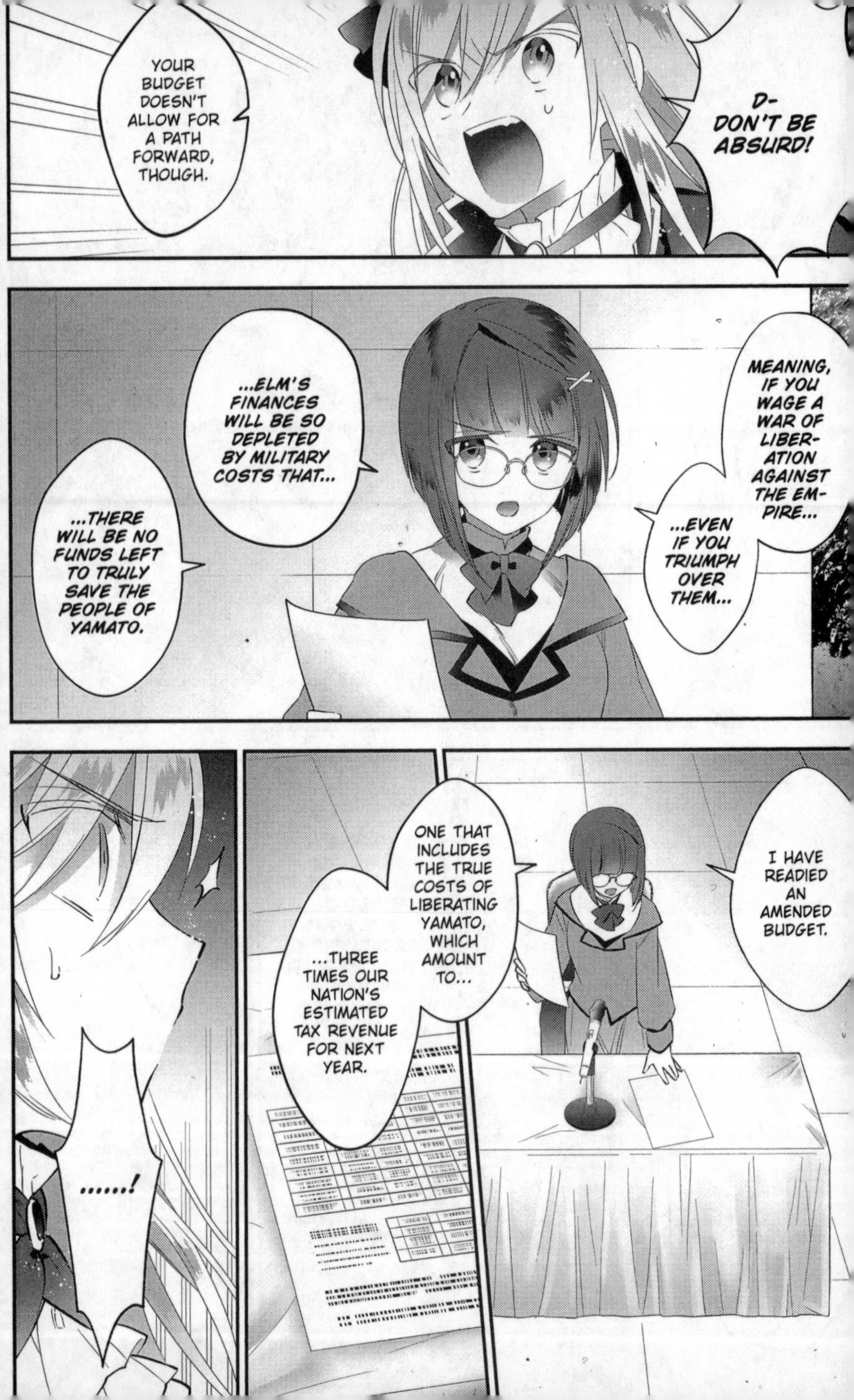
D- DON'T BE ABSURD!
YOUR BUDGET DOESN'T ALLOW FOR A PATH FORWARD, THOUGH.
MEANING, IF YOU WAGE A WAR OF LIBERATION AGAINST THE EMPIRE...
...EVEN IF YOU TRIUMPH OVER THEM...
...ELM'S FINANCES WILL BE SO DEPLETED BY MILITARY COSTS THAT...
...THERE WILL BE NO FUNDS LEFT TO TRULY SAVE THE PEOPLE OF YAMATO.
I HAVE READIED AN AMENDED BUDGET.
ONE THAT INCLUDES THE TRUE COSTS OF LIBERATING YAMATO, WHICH AMOUNT TO...
...THREE TIMES OUR NATION'S ESTIMATED TAX REVENUE FOR NEXT YEAR.
......!

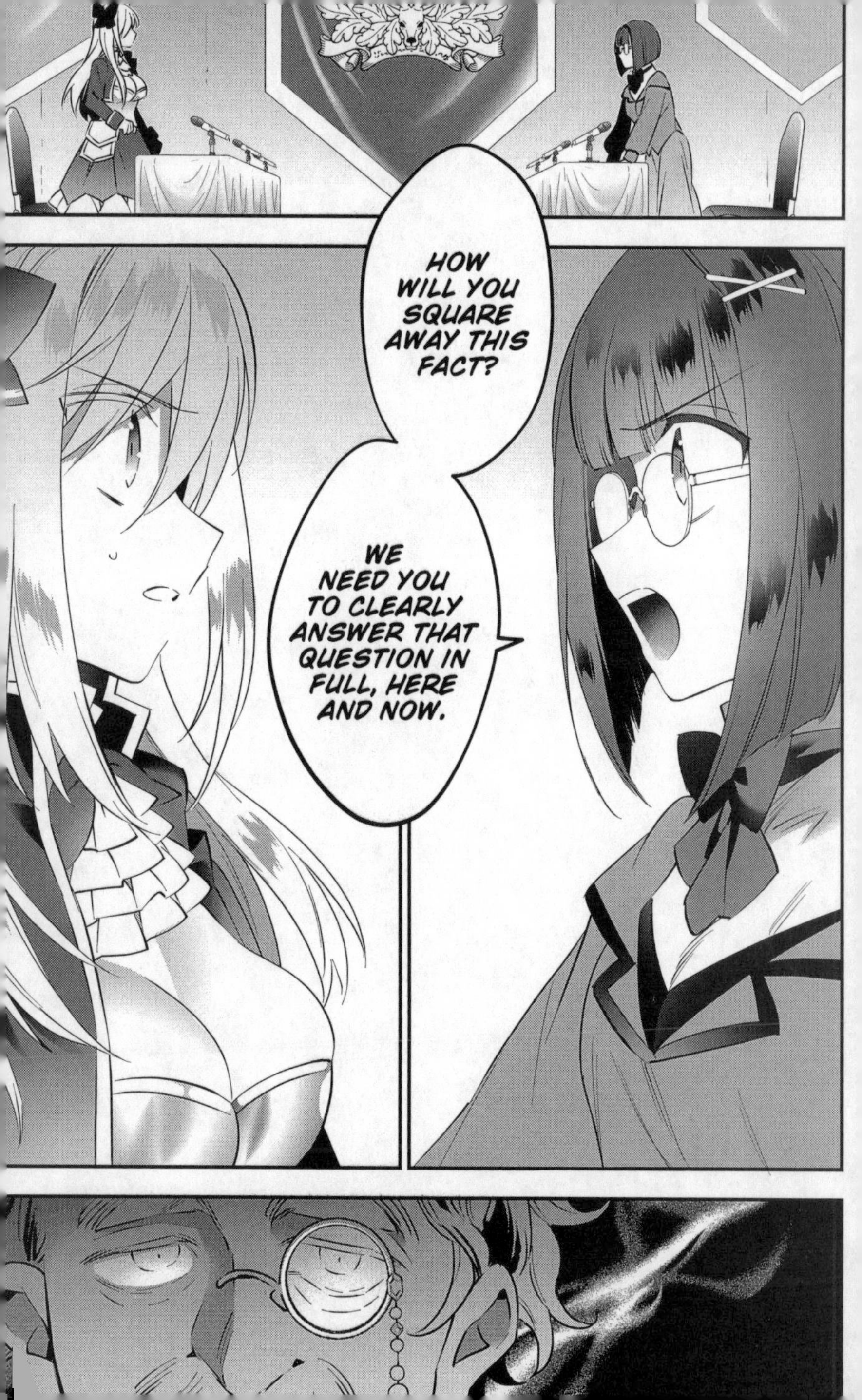
HOW WILL YOU SQUARE AWAY THIS FACT?
WE NEED YOU TO CLEARLY ANSWER THAT QUESTION IN FULL, HERE AND NOW.

HIGH SCHOOL PRODIGIES HAVE IT EASY EVEN IN ANOTHER WORLD!

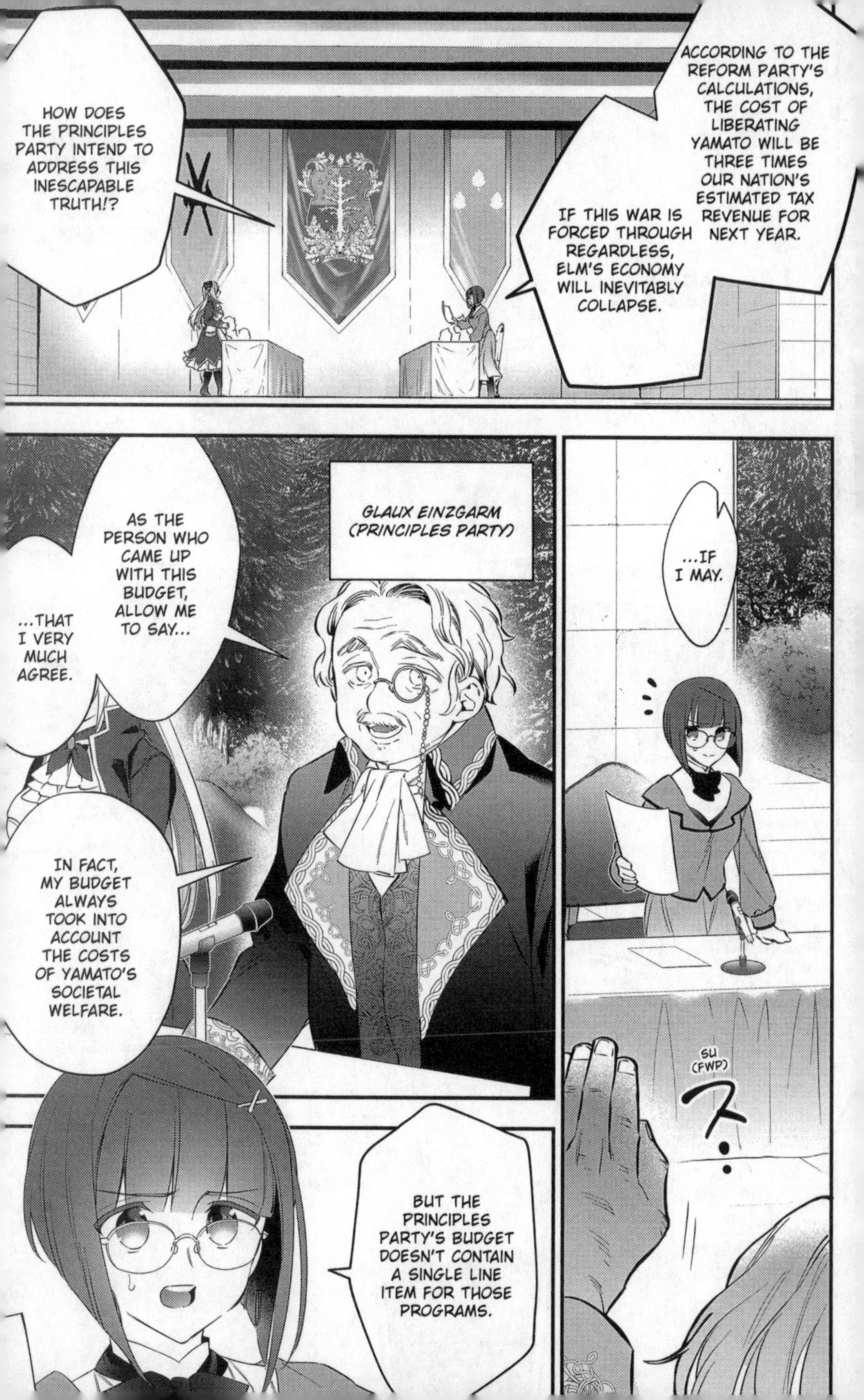
ACCORDING TO THE REFORM PARTY'S CALCULATIONS, THE COST OF LIBERATING YAMATO WILL BE THREE TIMES OUR NATION'S ESTIMATED TAX REVENUE FOR NEXT YEAR.
IF THIS WAR IS FORCED THROUGH REGARDLESS, ELM'S ECONOMY WILL INEVITABLY COLLAPSE.
HOW DOES THE PRINCIPLES PARTY INTEND TO ADDRESS THIS INESCAPABLE TRUTH!?
...IF I MAY.
SU (FWP)
GLAUX EINZGARM (PRINCIPLES PARTY)
AS THE PERSON WHO CAME UP WITH THIS BUDGET, ALLOW ME TO SAY...
...THAT I VERY MUCH AGREE.
IN FACT, MY BUDGET ALWAYS TOOK INTO ACCOUNT THE COSTS OF YAMATO'S SOCIETAL WELFARE.
BUT THE PRINCIPLES PARTY'S BUDGET DOESN'T CONTAIN A SINGLE LINE ITEM FOR THOSE PROGRAMS.

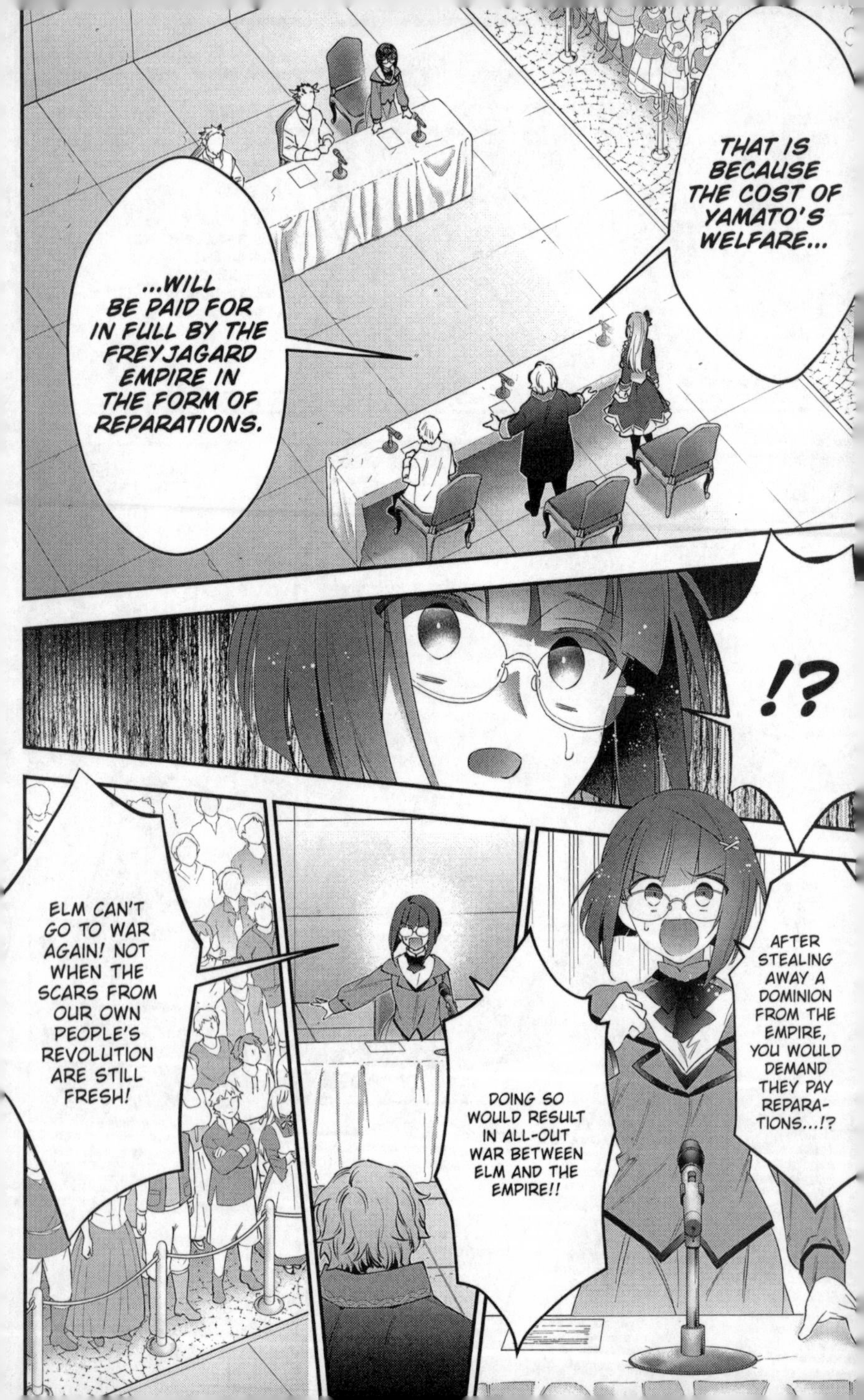
THAT IS BECAUSE THE COST OF YAMATO'S WELFARE...
...WILL BE PAID FOR IN FULL BY THE FREYJAGARD EMPIRE IN THE FORM OF REPARATIONS.
!?
AFTER STEALING AWAY A DOMINION FROM THE EMPIRE, YOU WOULD DEMAND THEY PAY REPARA-TIONS...!?
DOING SO WOULD RESULT IN ALL-OUT WAR BETWEEN ELM AND THE EMPIRE!!
ELM CAN'T GO TO WAR AGAIN! NOT WHEN THE SCARS FROM OUR OWN PEOPLE'S REVOLUTION ARE STILL FRESH!

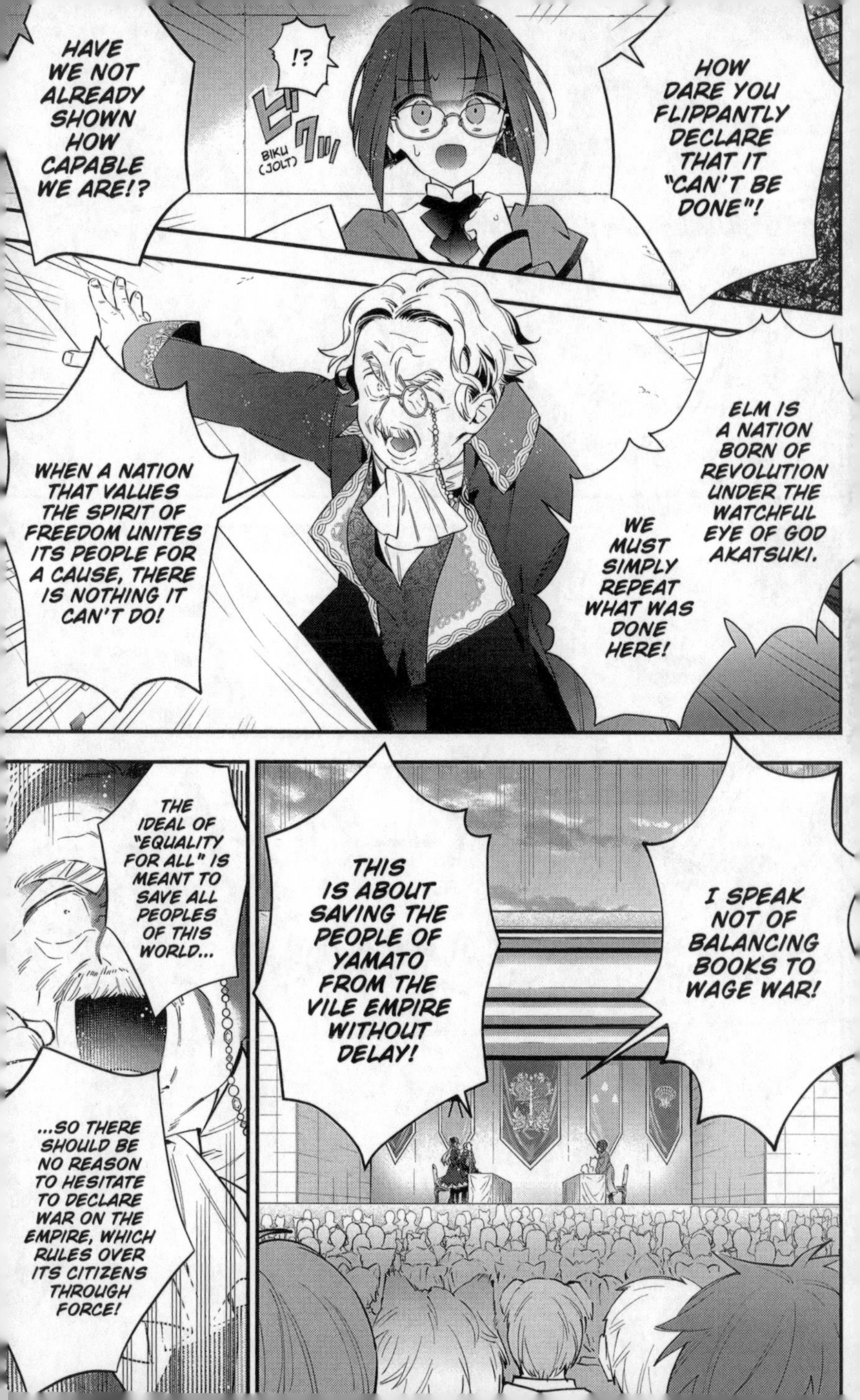
HOW DARE YOU FLIPPANTLY DECLARE THAT IT "CAN'T BE DONE"!
!?
ビクッ
BIKU (JOLT)
HAVE WE NOT ALREADY SHOWN HOW CAPABLE WE ARE!?
ELM IS A NATION BORN OF REVOLUTION UNDER THE WATCHFUL EYE OF GOD AKATSUKI.
WE MUST SIMPLY REPEAT WHAT WAS DONE HERE!
WHEN A NATION THAT VALUES THE SPIRIT OF FREEDOM UNITES ITS PEOPLE FOR A CAUSE, THERE IS NOTHING IT CAN'T DO!
I SPEAK NOT OF BALANCING BOOKS TO WAGE WAR!
THIS IS ABOUT SAVING THE PEOPLE OF YAMATO FROM THE VILE EMPIRE WITHOUT DELAY!
THE IDEAL OF "EQUALITY FOR ALL" IS MEANT TO SAVE ALL PEOPLES OF THIS WORLD...
...SO THERE SHOULD BE NO REASON TO HESITATE TO DECLARE WAR ON THE EMPIRE, WHICH RULES OVER ITS CITIZENS THROUGH FORCE!

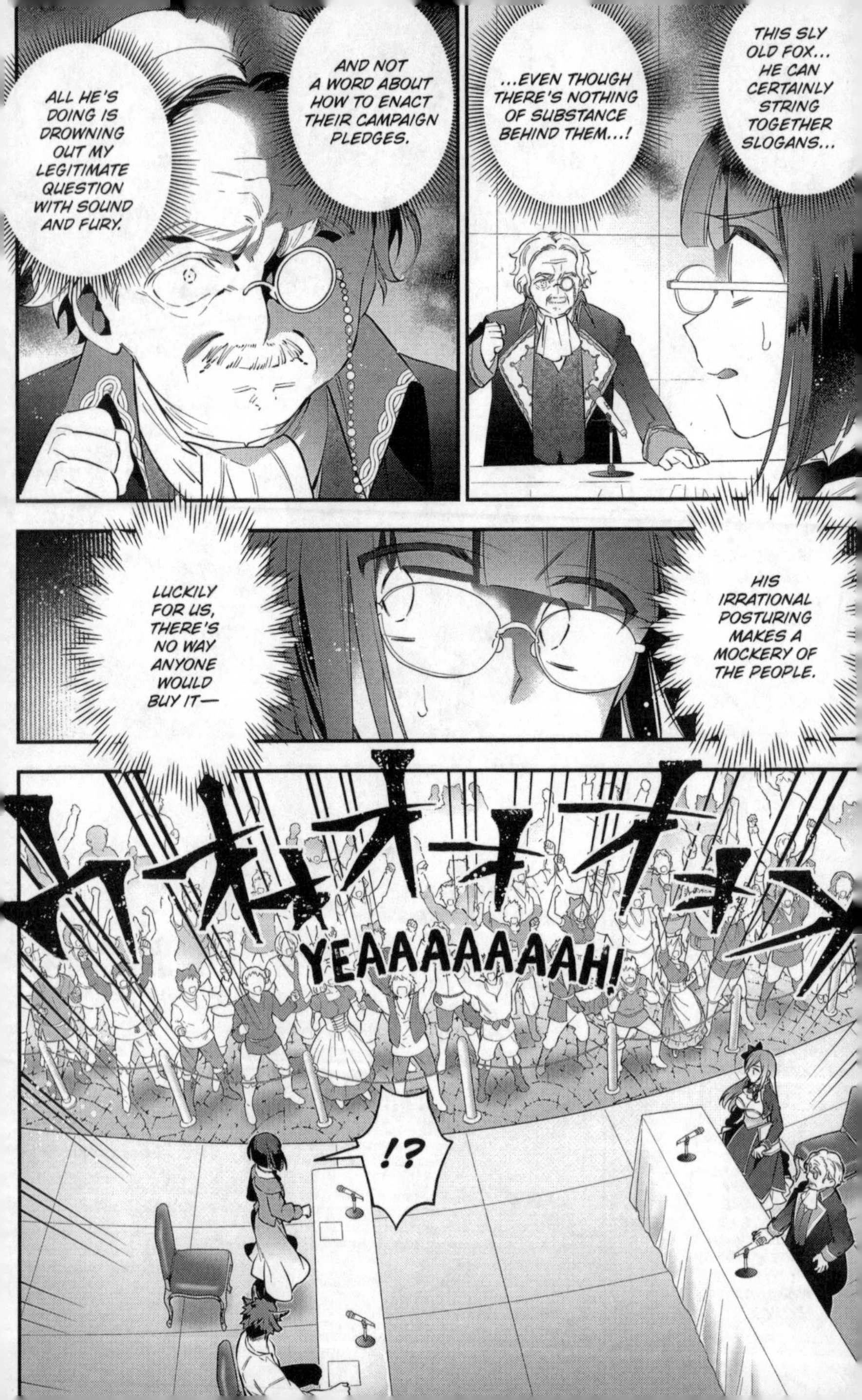
THIS SLY OLD FOX... HE CAN CERTAINLY STRING TOGETHER SLOGANS...
...EVEN THOUGH THERE'S NOTHING OF SUBSTANCE BEHIND THEM...!
AND NOT A WORD ABOUT HOW TO ENACT THEIR CAMPAIGN PLEDGES.
ALL HE'S DOING IS DROWNING OUT MY LEGITIMATE QUESTION WITH SOUND AND FURY.
HIS IRRATIONAL POSTURING MAKES A MOCKERY OF THE PEOPLE.
LUCKILY FOR US, THERE'S NO WAY ANYONE WOULD BUY IT—
YEAAAAAAAH!
!?

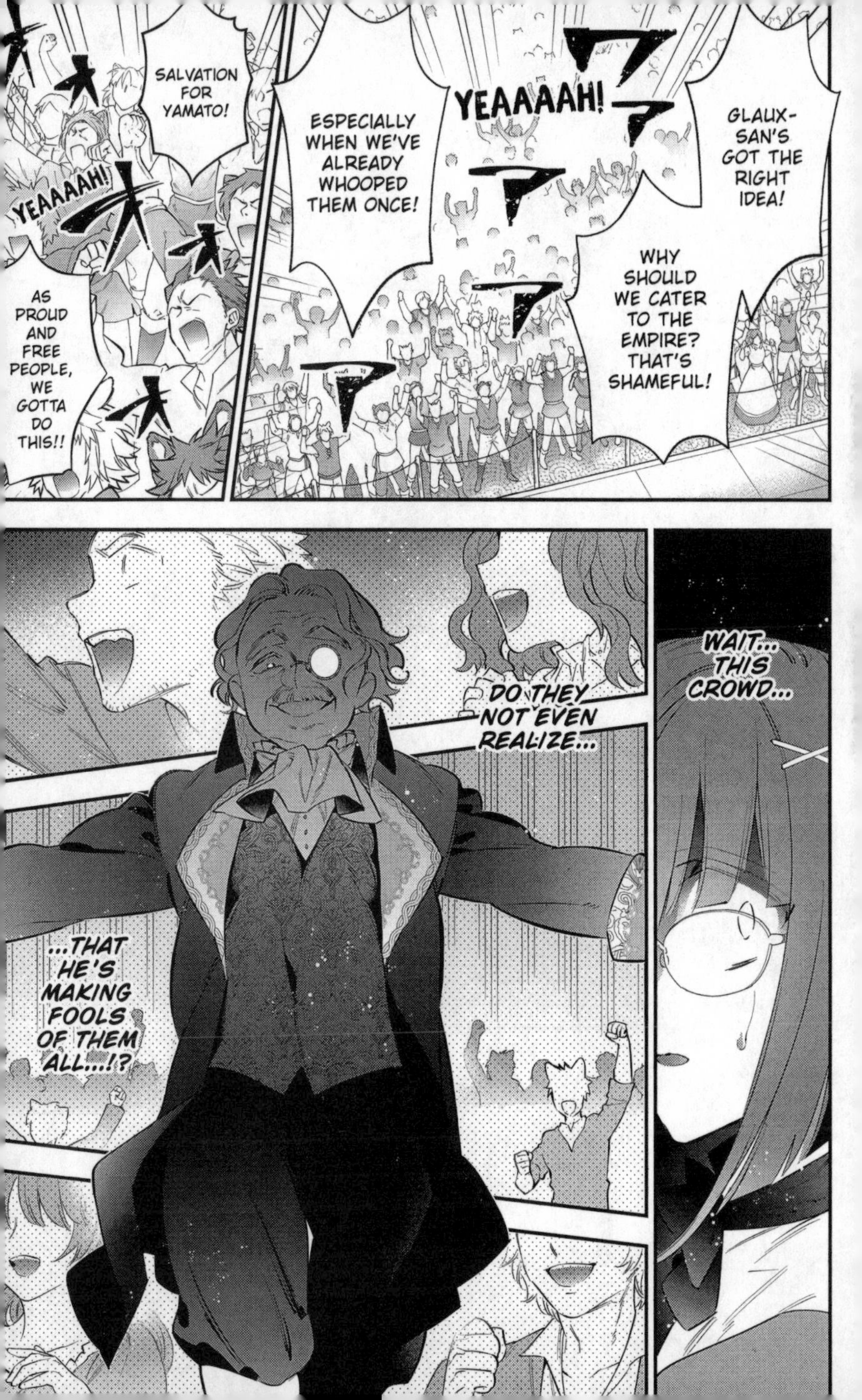
GLAUX-SAN'S GOT THE RIGHT IDEA!
WHY SHOULD WE CATER TO THE EMPIRE? THAT'S SHAMEFUL!
YEAAAAH!
ESPECIALLY WHEN WE'VE ALREADY WHOOPED THEM ONCE!
SALVATION FOR YAMATO!
YEAAAAH!
AS PROUD AND FREE PEOPLE, WE GOTTA DO THIS!!
WAIT... THIS CROWD...
DO THEY NOT EVEN REALIZE...
...THAT HE'S MAKING FOOLS OF THEM ALL...!?

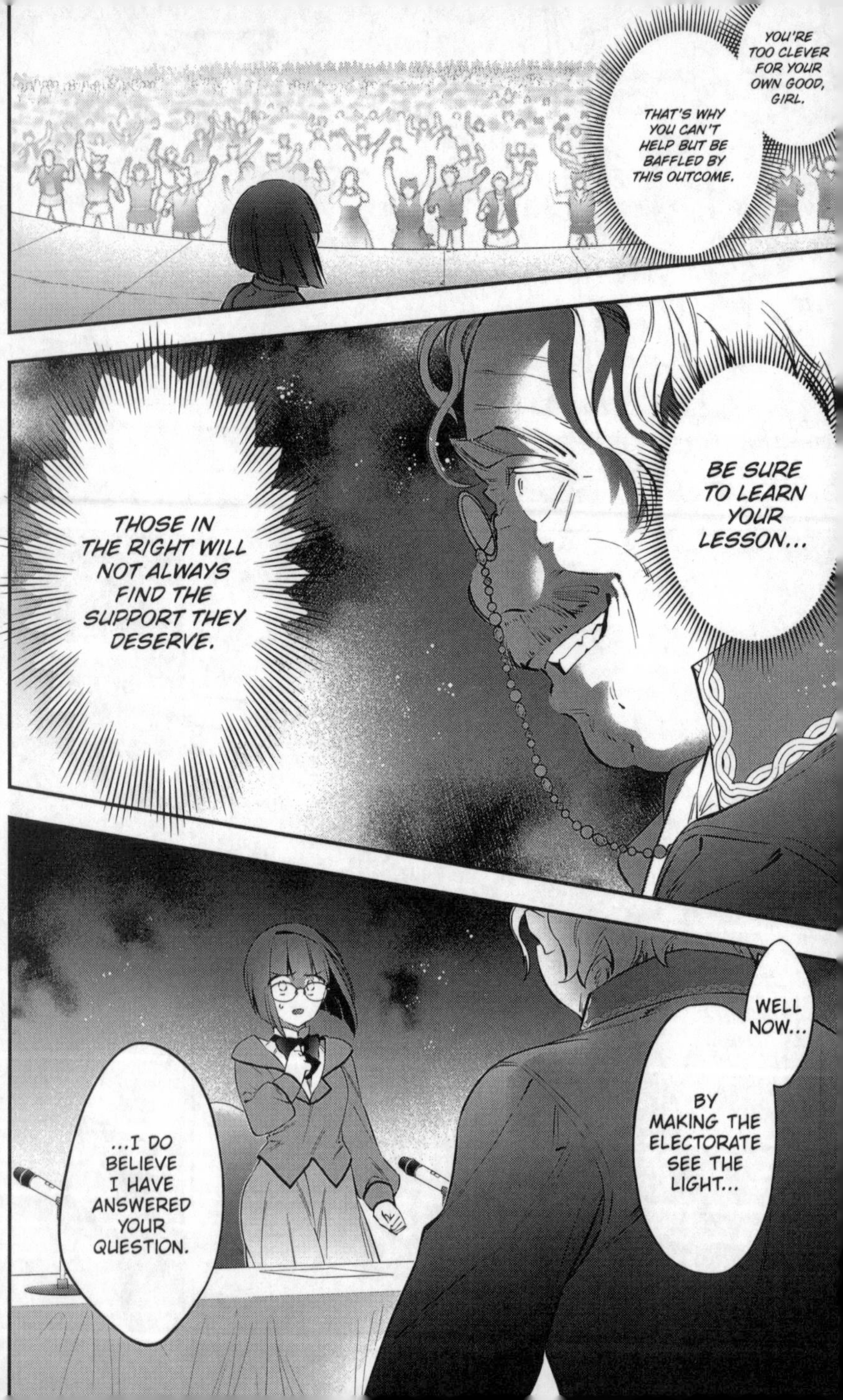
YOU'RE TOO CLEVER FOR YOUR OWN GOOD, GIRL.
THAT'S WHY YOU CAN'T HELP BUT BE BAFFLED BY THIS OUTCOME.
BE SURE TO LEARN YOUR LESSON...
THOSE IN THE RIGHT WILL NOT ALWAYS FIND THE SUPPORT THEY DESERVE.
WELL NOW...
BY MAKING THE ELECTORATE SEE THE LIGHT...
...I DO BELIEVE I HAVE ANSWERED YOUR QUESTION.

CHAPTER 76: **DEBATE'S END**

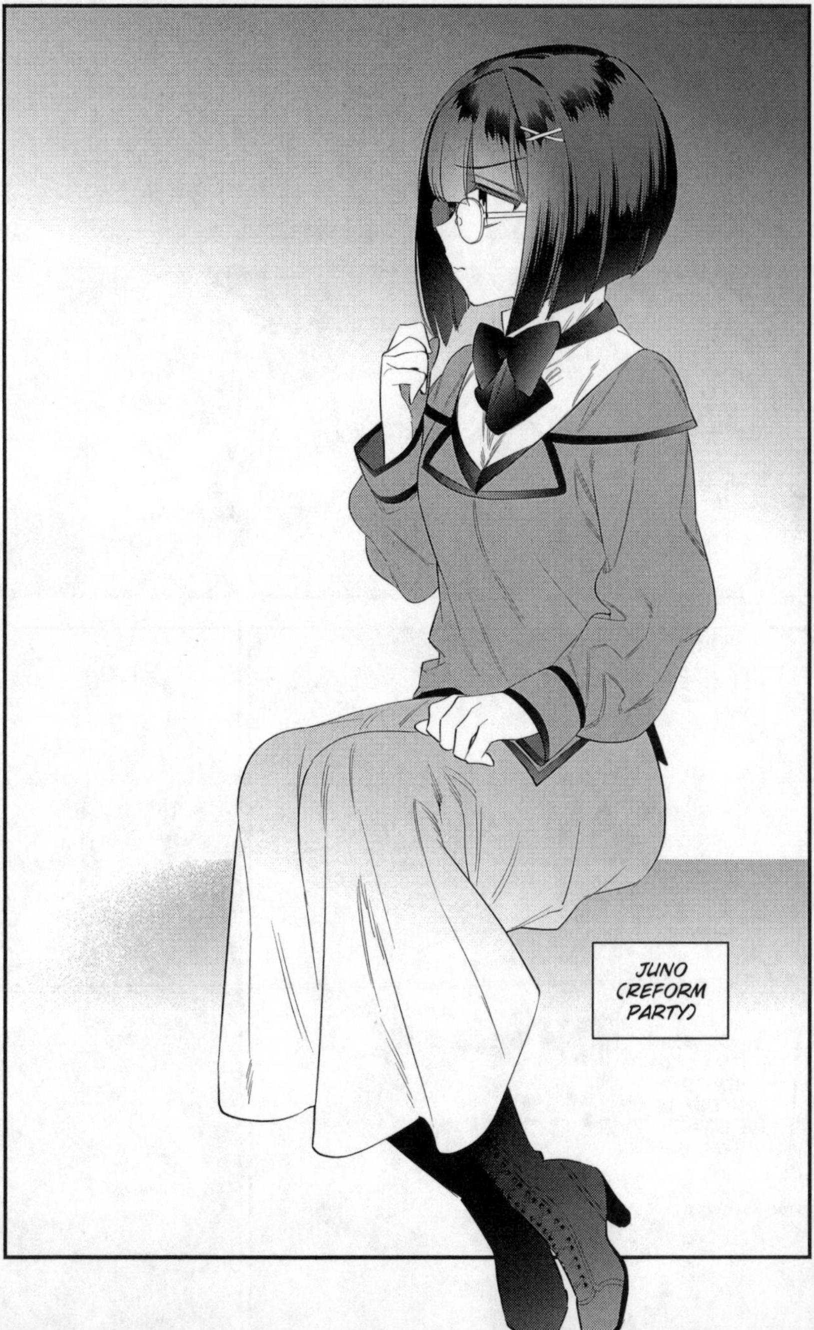
JUNO
(REFORM
PARTY)

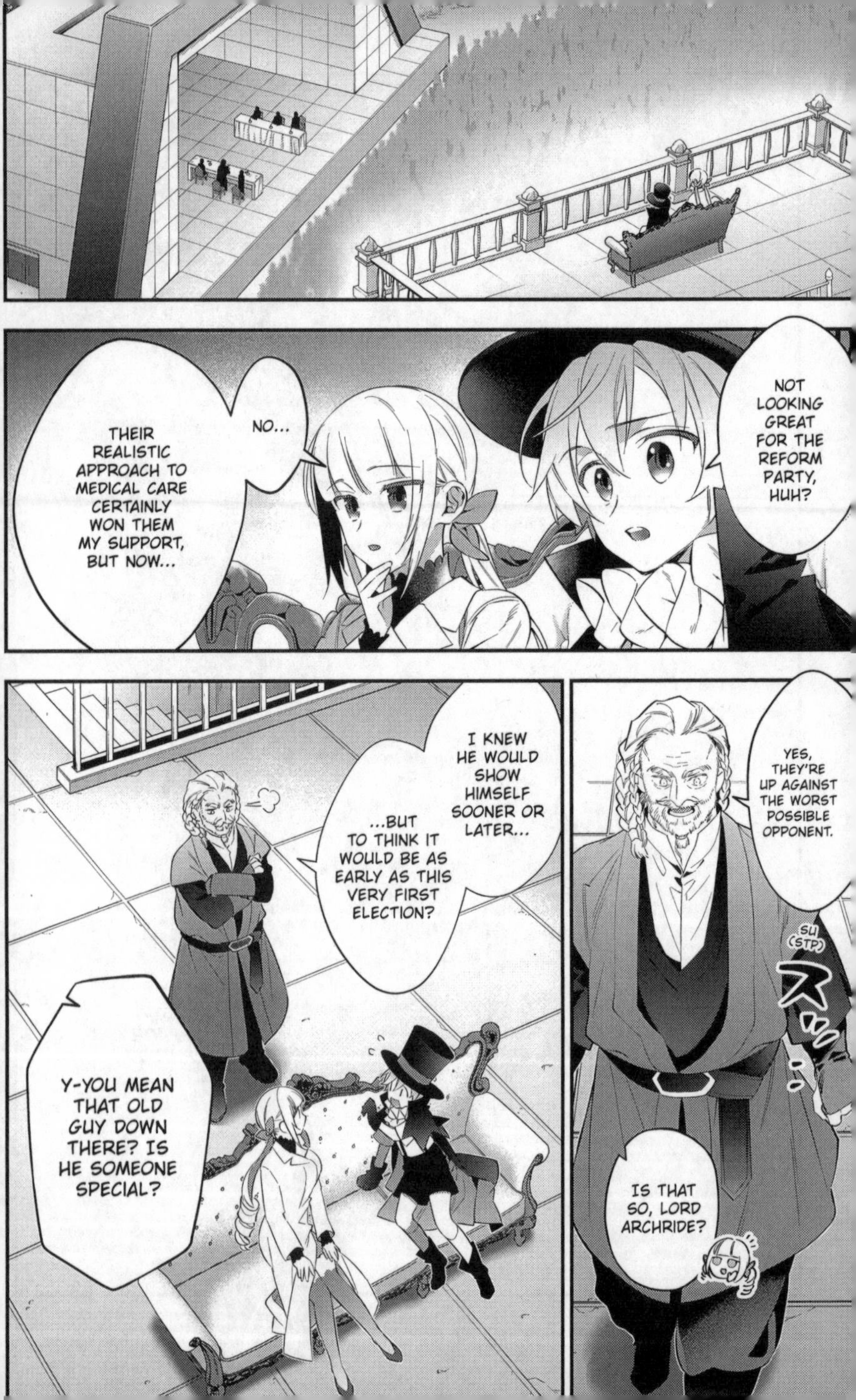
NOT LOOKING GREAT FOR THE REFORM PARTY, HUH?
NO...
THEIR REALISTIC APPROACH TO MEDICAL CARE CERTAINLY WON THEM MY SUPPORT, BUT NOW...
YES, THEY'RE UP AGAINST THE WORST POSSIBLE OPPONENT.
SU (STP)
IS THAT SO, LORD ARCHRIDE?
I KNEW HE WOULD SHOW HIMSELF SOONER OR LATER...
...BUT TO THINK IT WOULD BE AS EARLY AS THIS VERY FIRST ELECTION?
Y-YOU MEAN THAT OLD GUY DOWN THERE? IS HE SOMEONE SPECIAL?

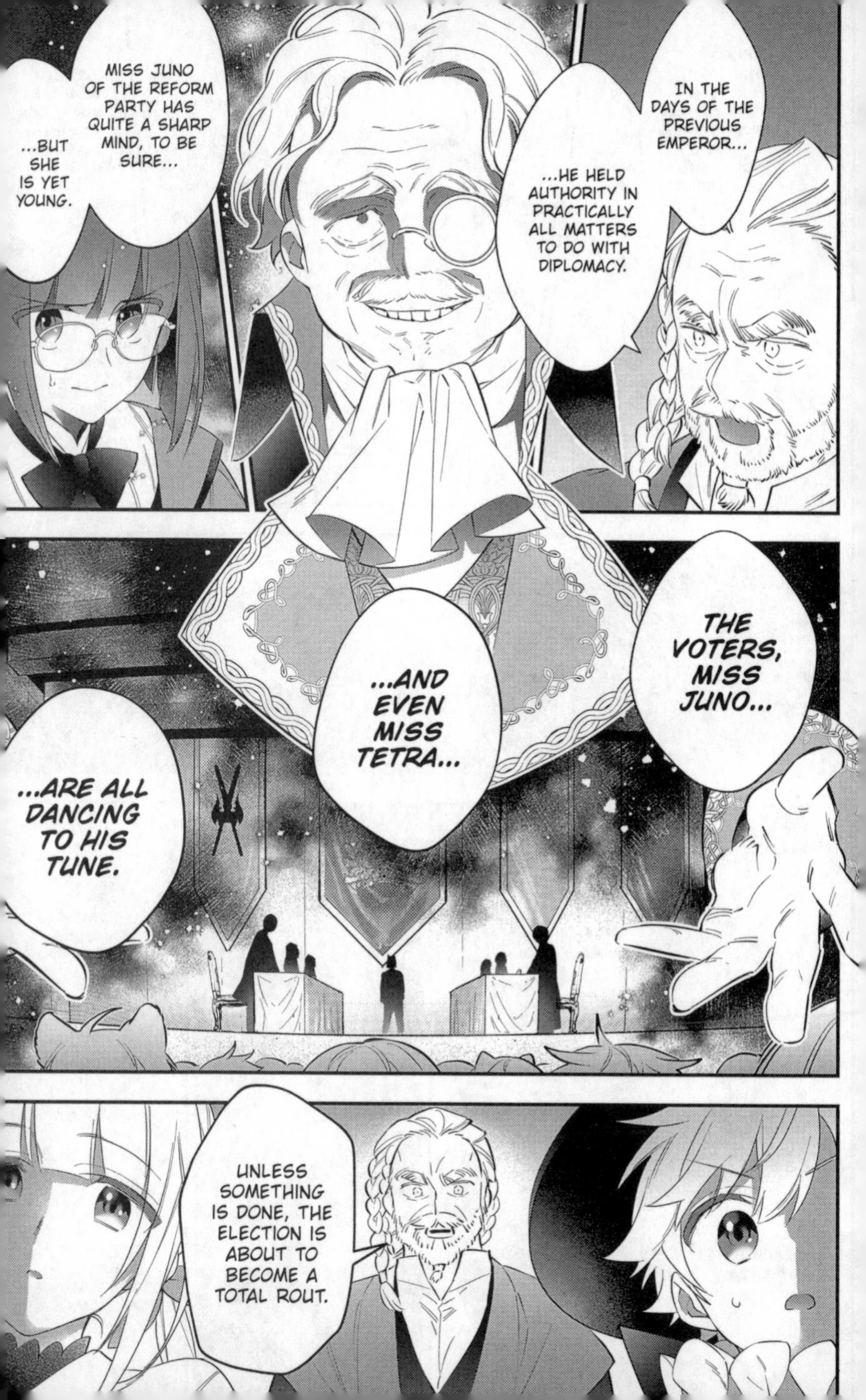
IN THE DAYS OF THE PREVIOUS EMPEROR...
...HE HELD AUTHORITY IN PRACTICALLY ALL MATTERS TO DO WITH DIPLOMACY.
MISS JUNO OF THE REFORM PARTY HAS QUITE A SHARP MIND, TO BE SURE...
...BUT SHE IS YET YOUNG.
THE VOTERS, MISS JUNO...
...AND EVEN MISS TETRA...
...ARE ALL DANCING TO HIS TUNE.
UNLESS SOMETHING IS DONE, THE ELECTION IS ABOUT TO BECOME A TOTAL ROUT.

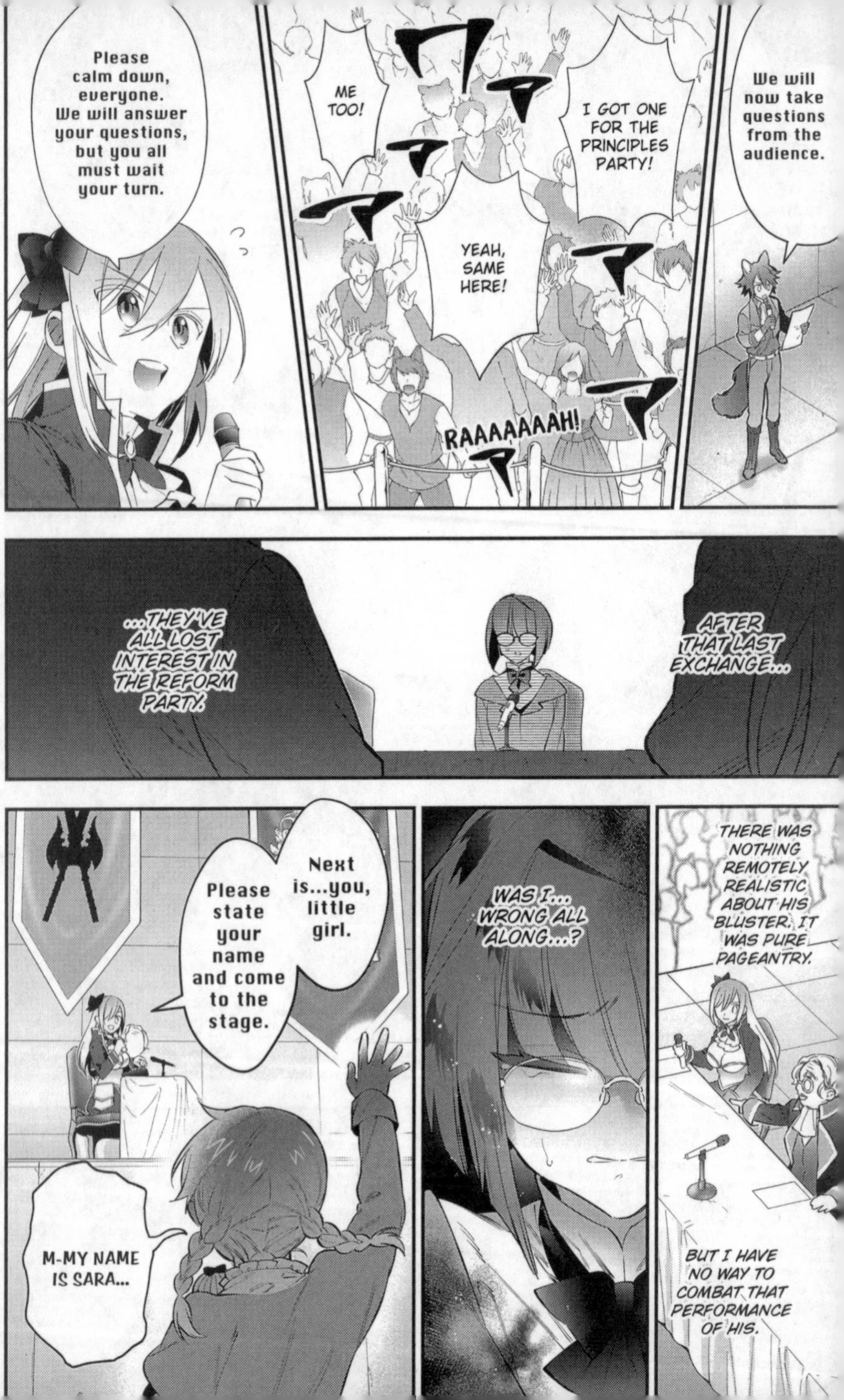
We will now take questions from the audience.
I GOT ONE FOR THE PRINCIPLES PARTY!
ME TOO!
YEAH, SAME HERE!
RAAAAAAAH!
Please calm down, everyone. We will answer your questions, but you all must wait your turn.
AFTER THAT LAST EXCHANGE...
...THEY'VE ALL LOST INTEREST IN THE REFORM PARTY.
THERE WAS NOTHING REMOTELY REALISTIC ABOUT HIS BLUSTER. IT WAS PURE PAGEANTRY.
BUT I HAVE NO WAY TO COMBAT THAT PERFORMANCE OF HIS.
WAS I... WRONG ALL ALONG...?
Next is...you, little girl.
Please state your name and come to the stage.
M-MY NAME IS SARA...

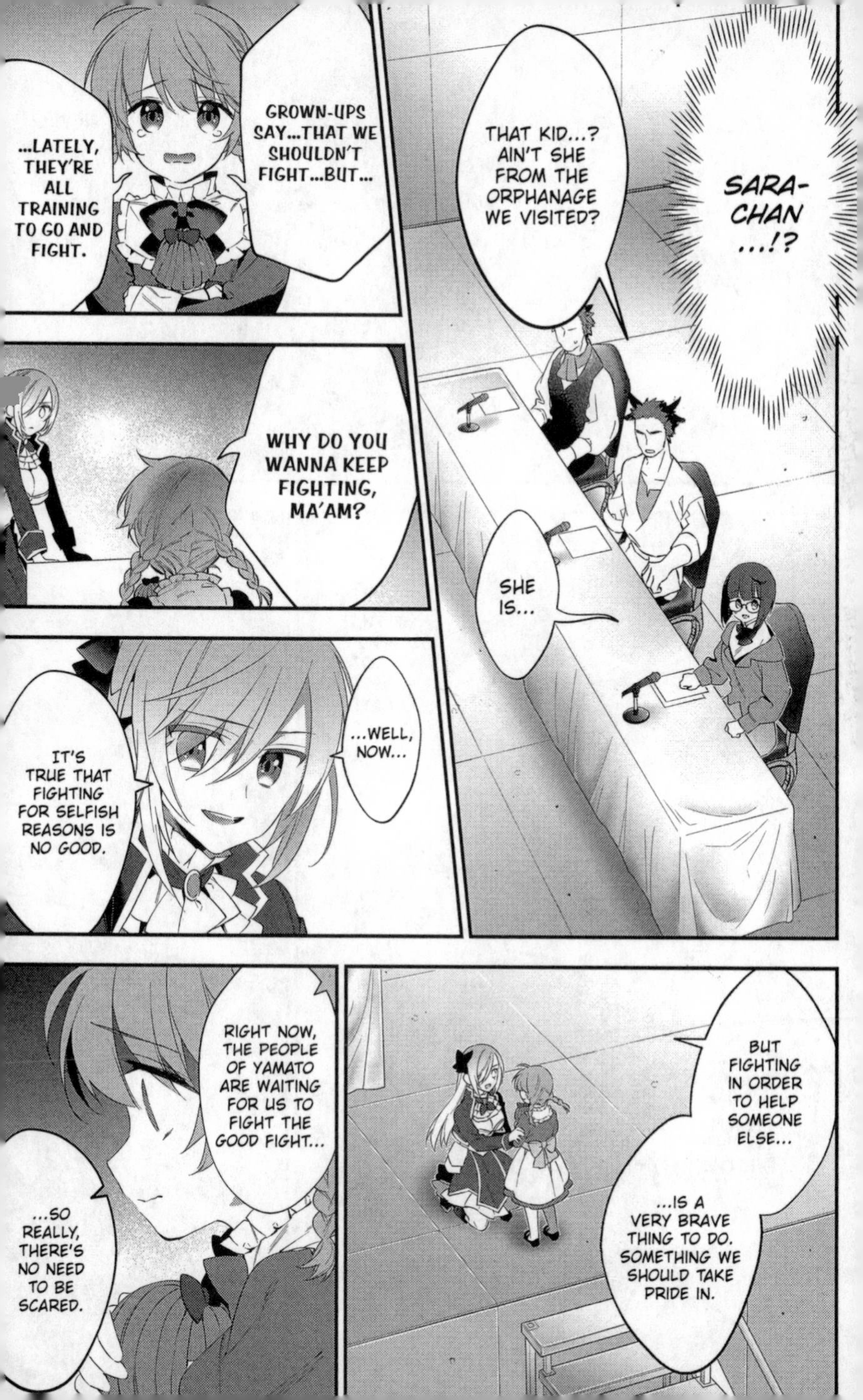
SARA-CHAN...!?
THAT KID...? AIN'T SHE FROM THE ORPHANAGE WE VISITED?
SHE IS...
GROWN-UPS SAY...THAT WE SHOULDN'T FIGHT...BUT...
...LATELY, THEY'RE ALL TRAINING TO GO AND FIGHT.
WHY DO YOU WANNA KEEP FIGHTING, MA'AM?
...WELL, NOW...
IT'S TRUE THAT FIGHTING FOR SELFISH REASONS IS NO GOOD.
BUT FIGHTING IN ORDER TO HELP SOMEONE ELSE...
...IS A VERY BRAVE THING TO DO. SOMETHING WE SHOULD TAKE PRIDE IN.
RIGHT NOW, THE PEOPLE OF YAMATO ARE WAITING FOR US TO FIGHT THE GOOD FIGHT...
...SO REALLY, THERE'S NO NEED TO BE SCARED.

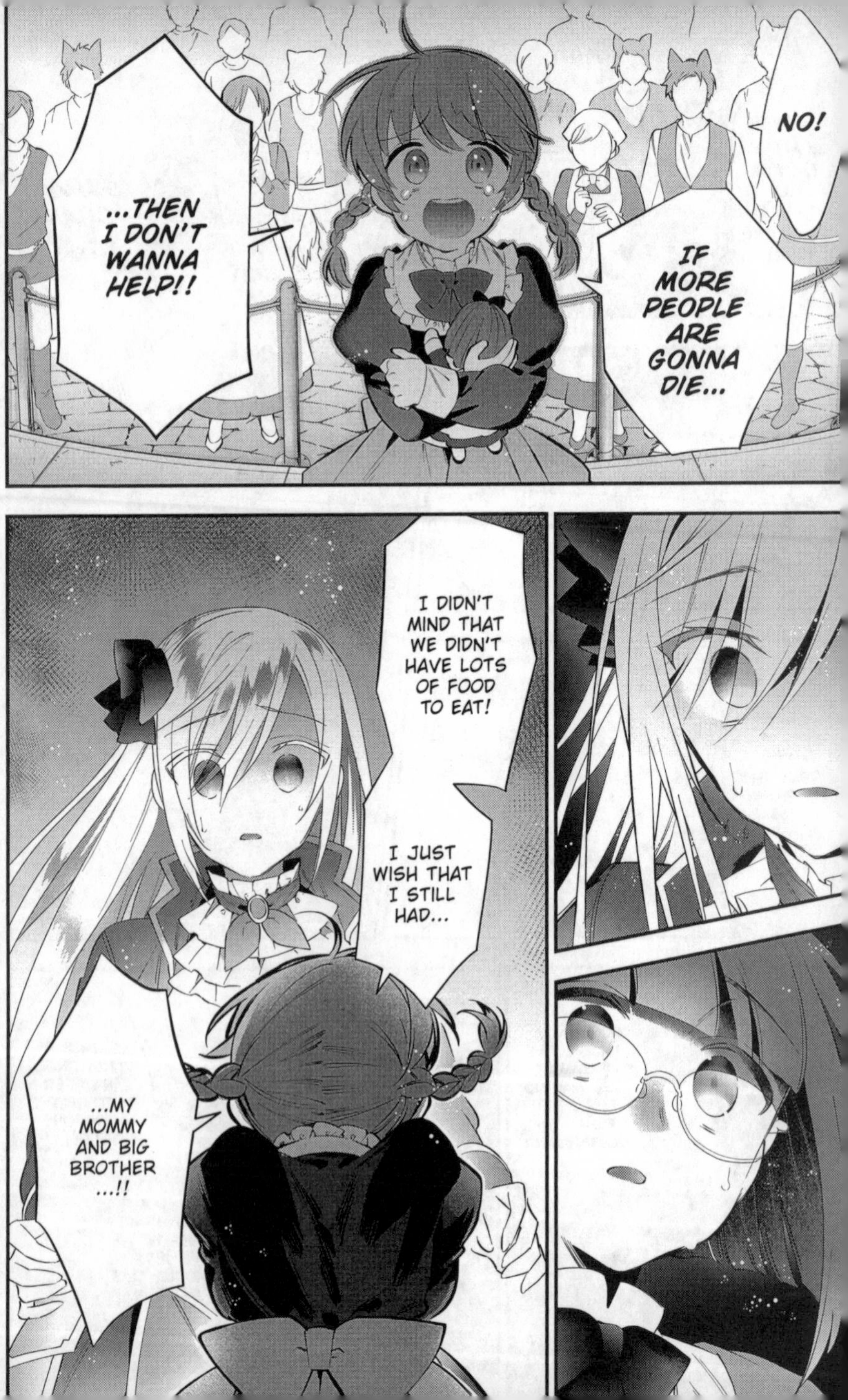
NO!
IF MORE PEOPLE ARE GONNA DIE...
...THEN I DON'T WANNA HELP!!
I DIDN'T MIND THAT WE DIDN'T HAVE LOTS OF FOOD TO EAT!
I JUST WISH THAT I STILL HAD...
...MY MOMMY AND BIG BROTHER ...!!

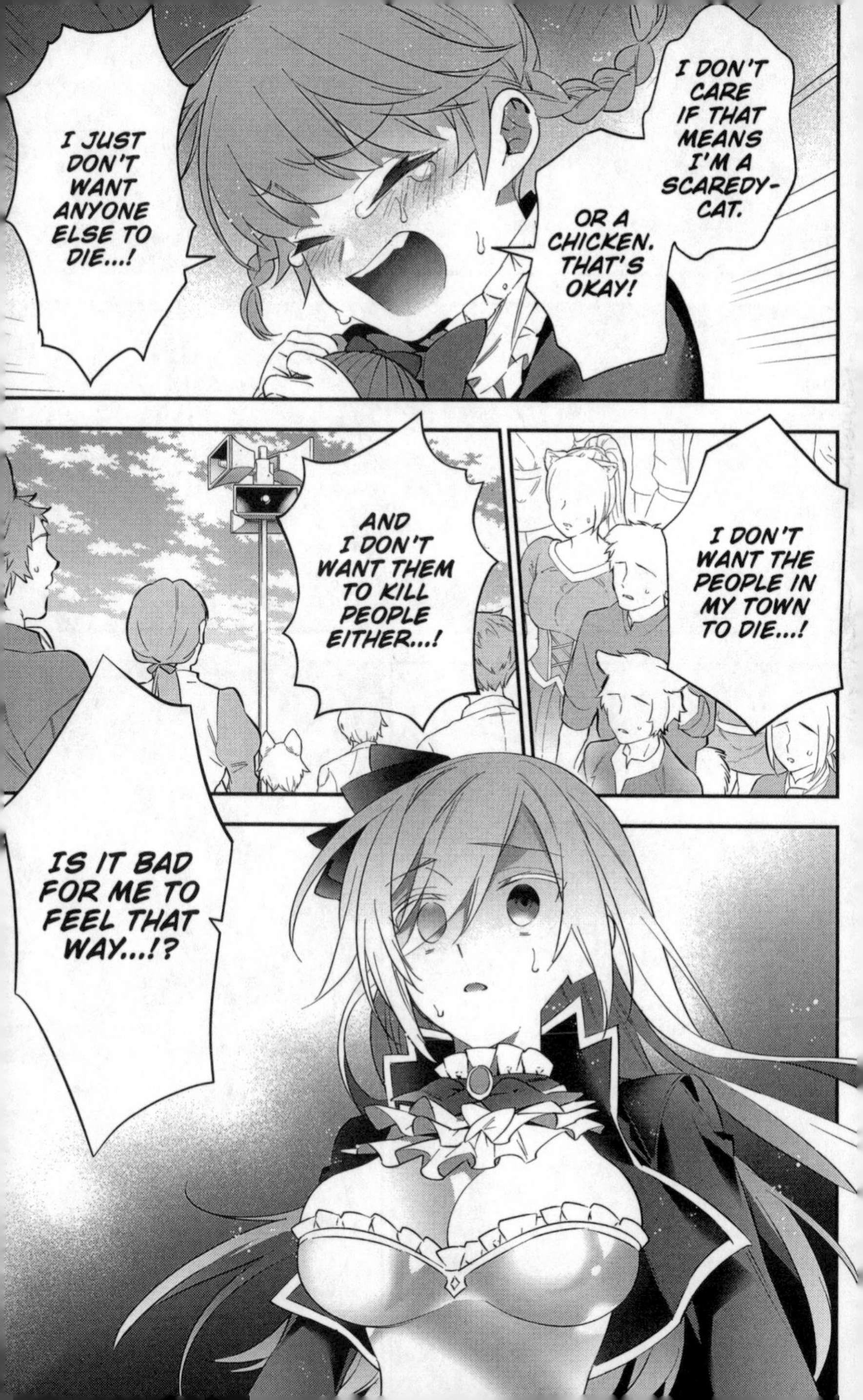
I DON'T CARE IF THAT MEANS I'M A SCAREDY-CAT.
OR A CHICKEN. THAT'S OKAY!
I JUST DON'T WANT ANYONE ELSE TO DIE...!
I DON'T WANT THE PEOPLE IN MY TOWN TO DIE...!
AND I DON'T WANT THEM TO KILL PEOPLE EITHER...!
IS IT BAD FOR ME TO FEEL THAT WAY...!?

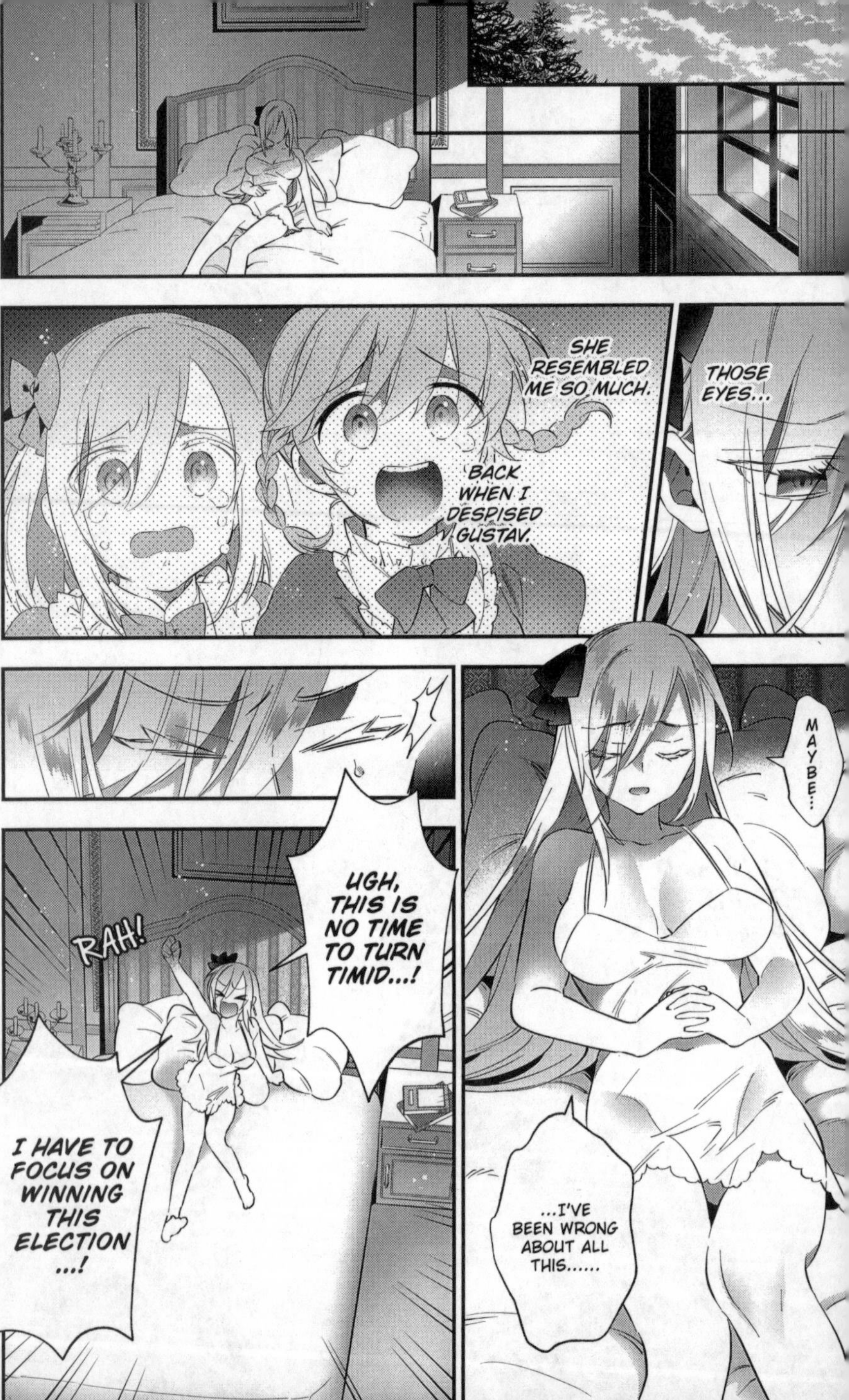
THOSE EYES...
SHE RESEMBLED ME SO MUCH.
BACK WHEN I DESPISED GUSTAV.
MAYBE...
...I'VE BEEN WRONG ABOUT ALL THIS......
UGH, THIS IS NO TIME TO TURN TIMID...!
RAH!
I HAVE TO FOCUS ON WINNING THIS ELECTION...!

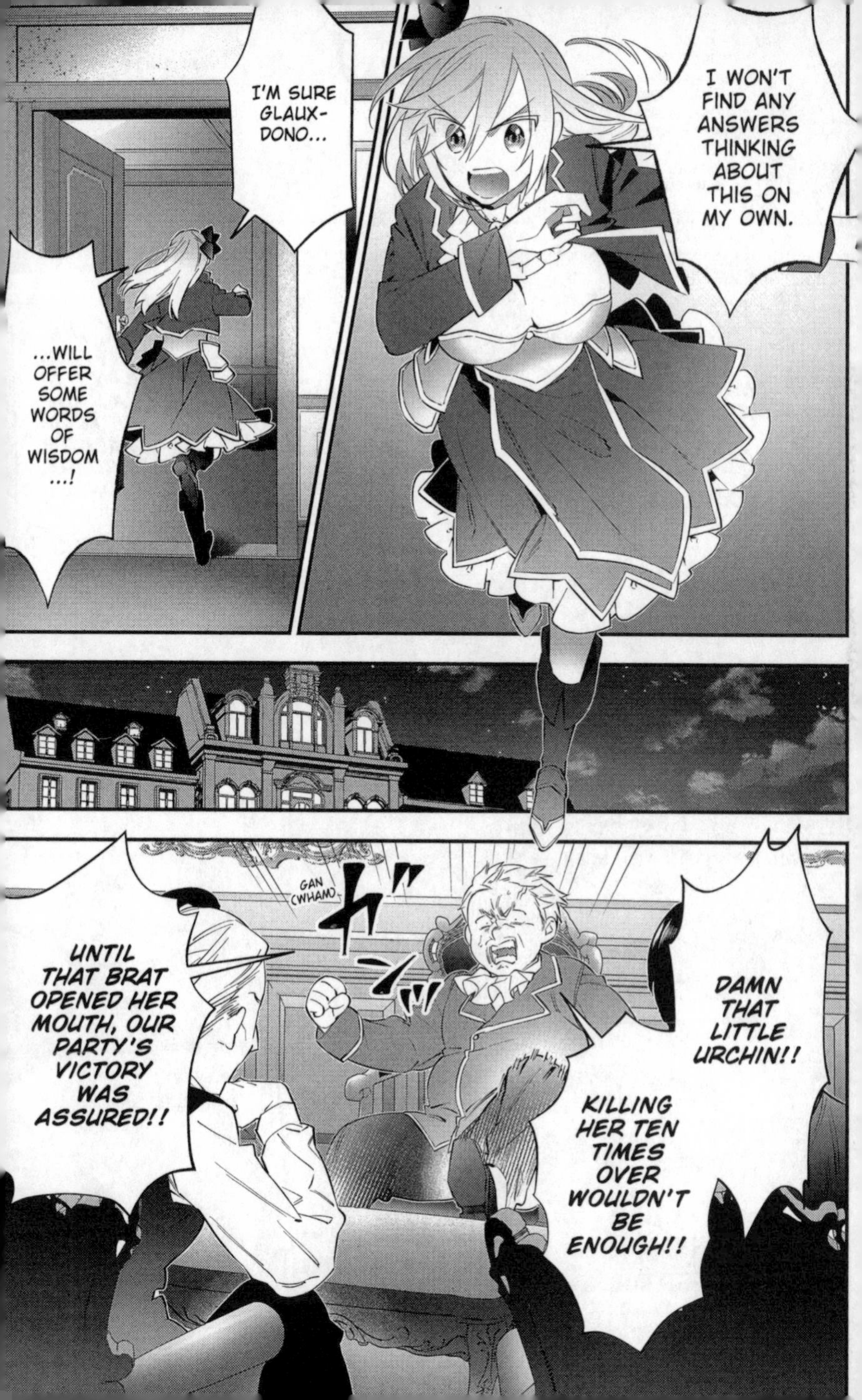
I WON'T FIND ANY ANSWERS THINKING ABOUT THIS ON MY OWN.
I'M SURE GLAUX-DONO...
...WILL OFFER SOME WORDS OF WISDOM...!
DAMN THAT LITTLE URCHIN!!
GAN (WHAM)
KILLING HER TEN TIMES OVER WOULDN'T BE ENOUGH!!
UNTIL THAT BRAT OPENED HER MOUTH, OUR PARTY'S VICTORY WAS ASSURED!!

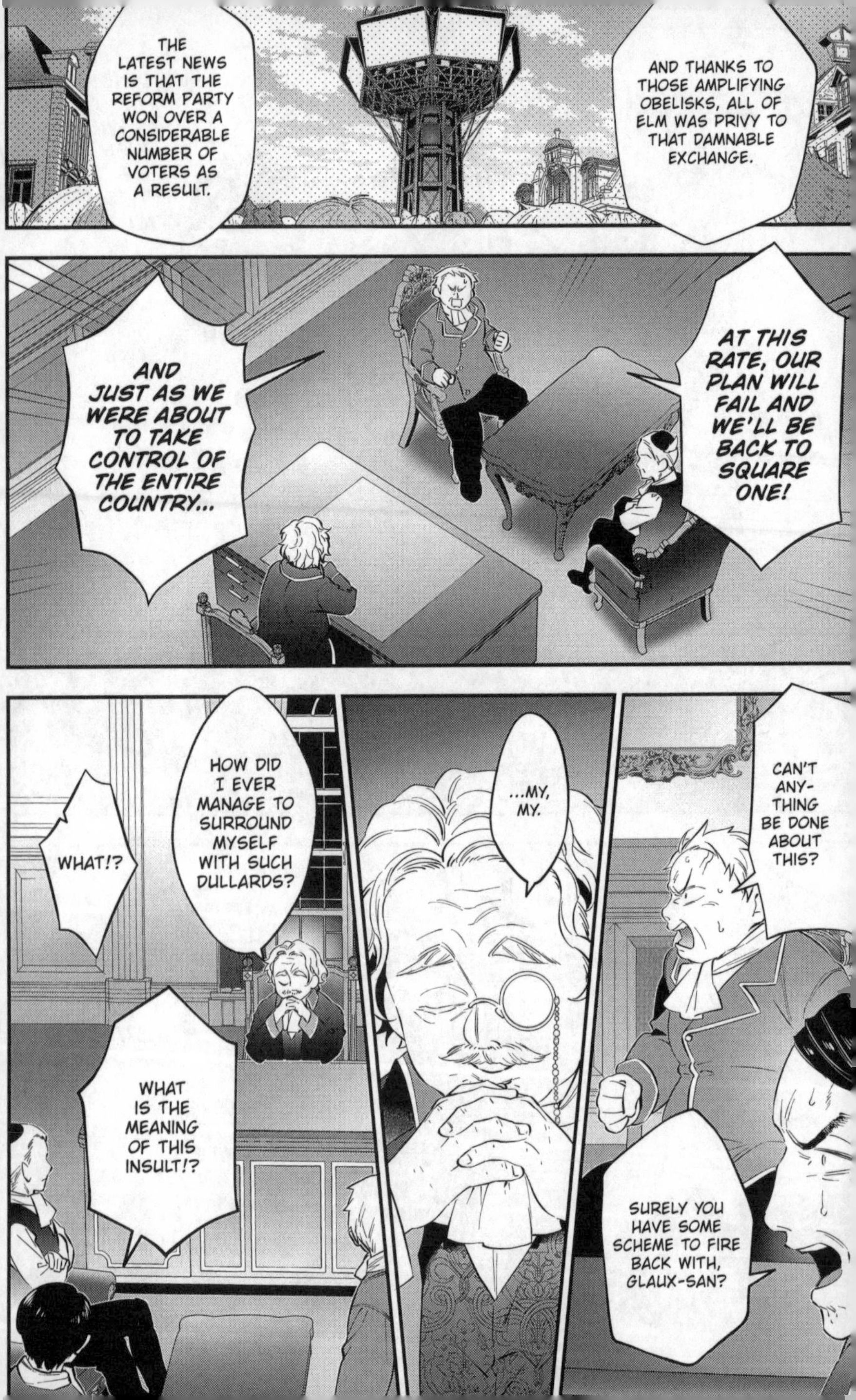
AND THANKS TO THOSE AMPLIFYING OBELISKS, ALL OF ELM WAS PRIVY TO THAT DAMNABLE EXCHANGE.
THE LATEST NEWS IS THAT THE REFORM PARTY WON OVER A CONSIDERABLE NUMBER OF VOTERS AS A RESULT.
AT THIS RATE, OUR PLAN WILL FAIL AND WE'LL BE BACK TO SQUARE ONE!
AND JUST AS WE WERE ABOUT TO TAKE CONTROL OF THE ENTIRE COUNTRY...
CAN'T ANY-THING BE DONE ABOUT THIS?
SURELY YOU HAVE SOME SCHEME TO FIRE BACK WITH, GLAUX-SAN?
...MY, MY.
HOW DID I EVER MANAGE TO SURROUND MYSELF WITH SUCH DULLARDS?
WHAT!?
WHAT IS THE MEANING OF THIS INSULT!?

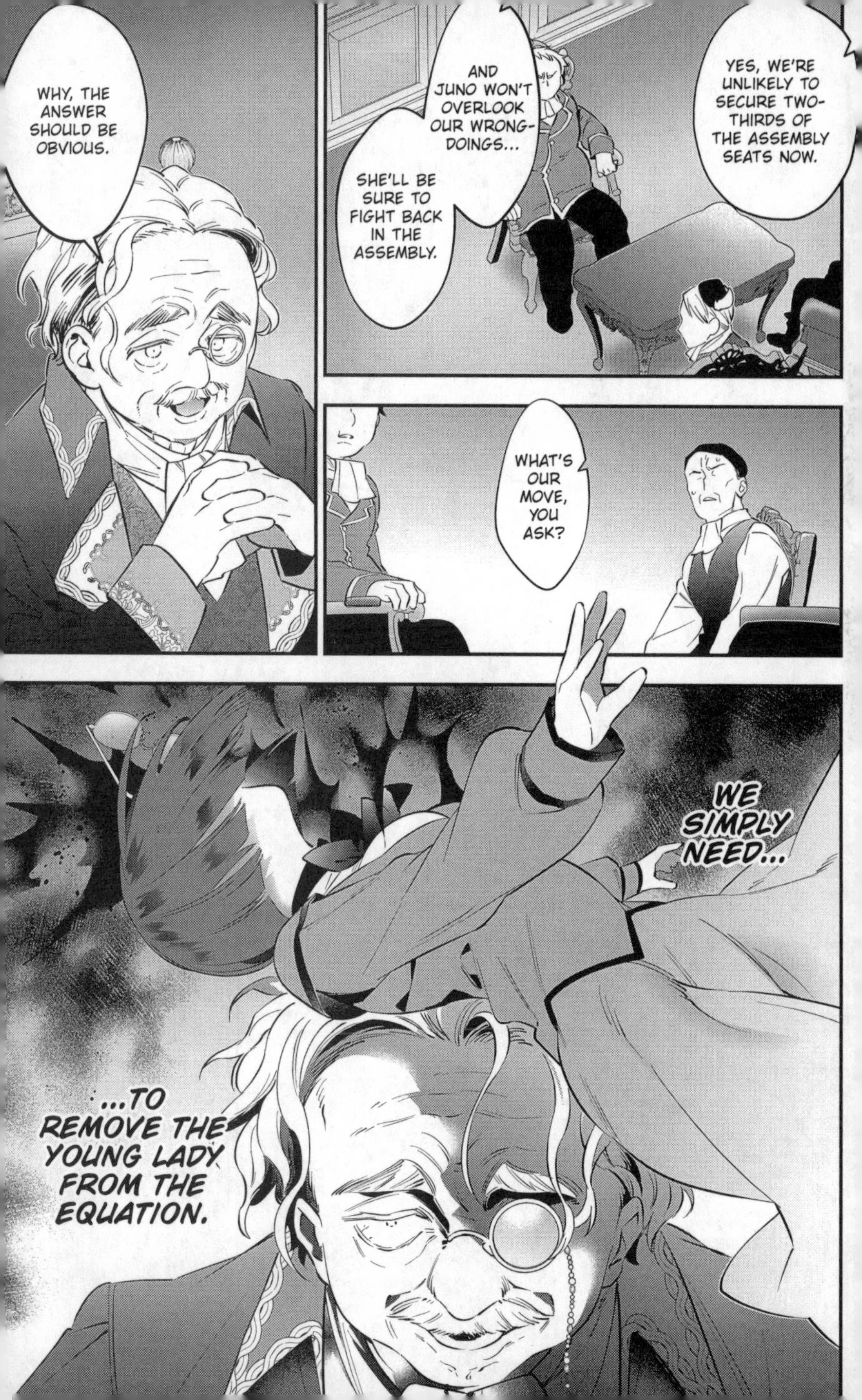
YES, WE'RE UNLIKELY TO SECURE TWO-THIRDS OF THE ASSEMBLY SEATS NOW.
AND JUNO WON'T OVERLOOK OUR WRONG-DOINGS...
SHE'LL BE SURE TO FIGHT BACK IN THE ASSEMBLY.
WHAT'S OUR MOVE, YOU ASK?
WHY, THE ANSWER SHOULD BE OBVIOUS.
WE SIMPLY NEED...
...TO REMOVE THE YOUNG LADY FROM THE EQUATION.

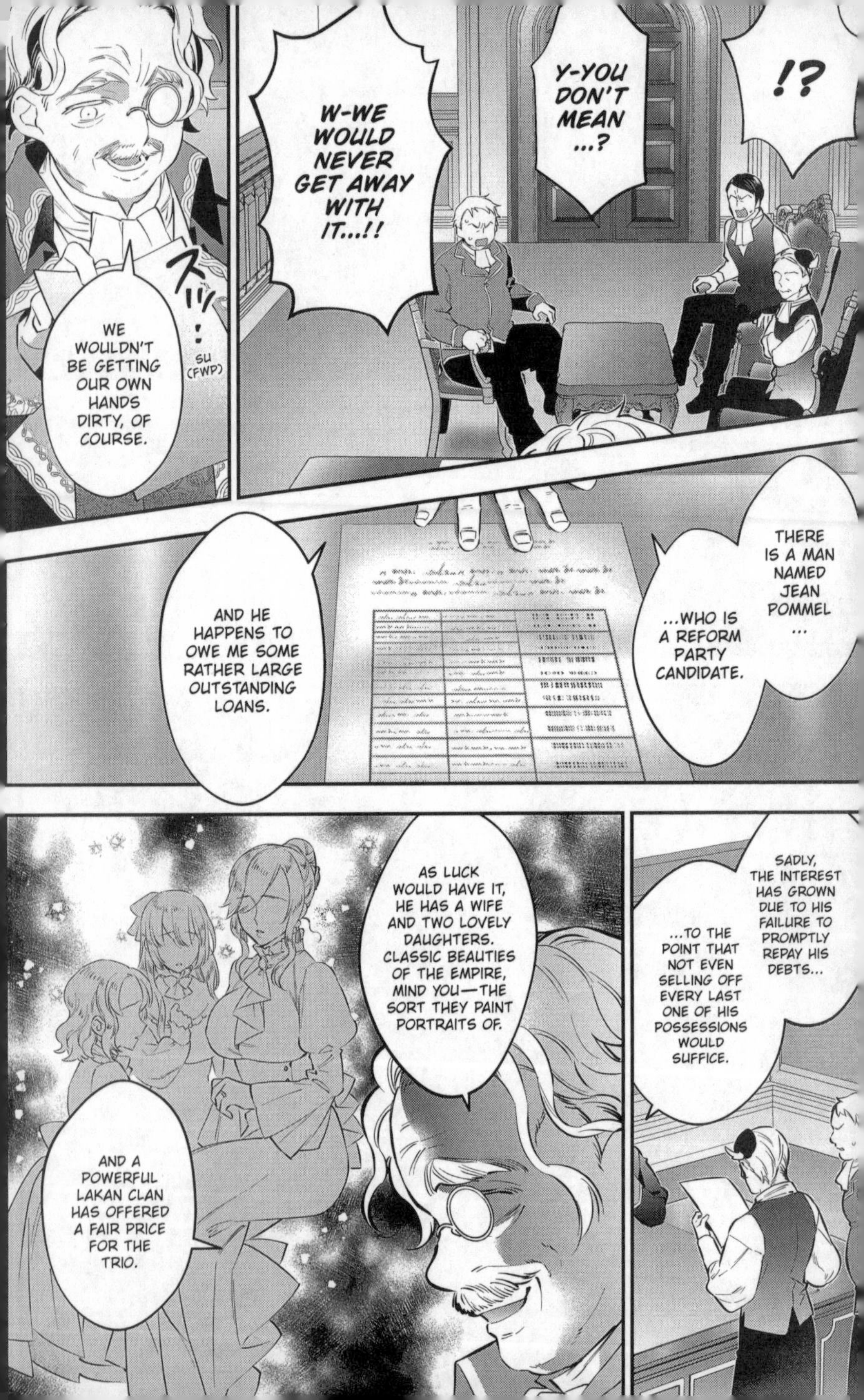
!?
Y-YOU DON'T MEAN ...?
W-WE WOULD NEVER GET AWAY WITH IT...!!
WE WOULDN'T BE GETTING OUR OWN HANDS DIRTY, OF COURSE.
SU (FWP)
THERE IS A MAN NAMED JEAN POMMEL ...
...WHO IS A REFORM PARTY CANDIDATE.
AND HE HAPPENS TO OWE ME SOME RATHER LARGE OUTSTANDING LOANS.
SADLY, THE INTEREST HAS GROWN DUE TO HIS FAILURE TO PROMPTLY REPAY HIS DEBTS...
...TO THE POINT THAT NOT EVEN SELLING OFF EVERY LAST ONE OF HIS POSSESSIONS WOULD SUFFICE.
AS LUCK WOULD HAVE IT, HE HAS A WIFE AND TWO LOVELY DAUGHTERS. CLASSIC BEAUTIES OF THE EMPIRE, MIND YOU—THE SORT THEY PAINT PORTRAITS OF.
AND A POWERFUL LAKAN CLAN HAS OFFERED A FAIR PRICE FOR THE TRIO.

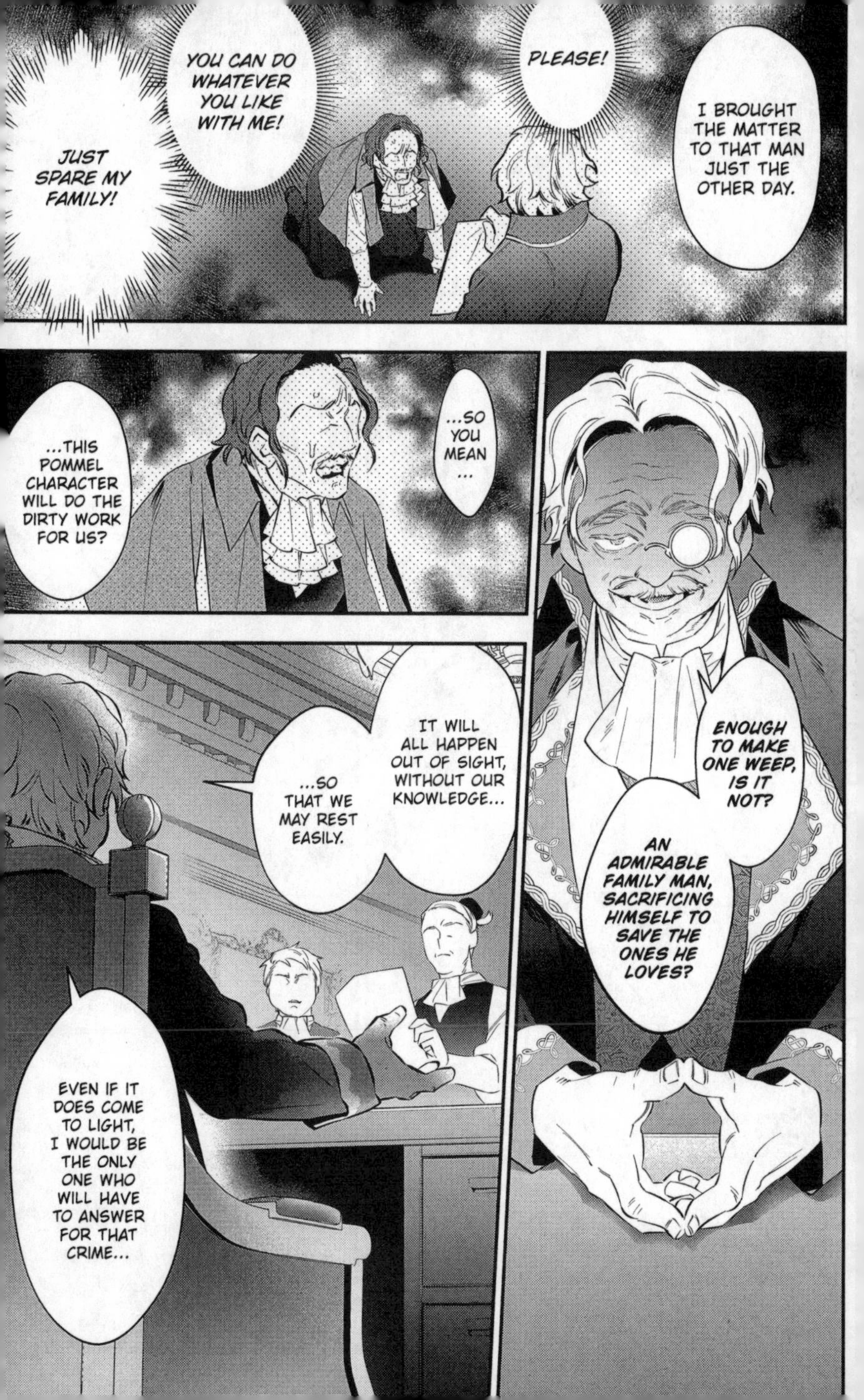
I BROUGHT THE MATTER TO THAT MAN JUST THE OTHER DAY.
PLEASE!
YOU CAN DO WHATEVER YOU LIKE WITH ME!
JUST SPARE MY FAMILY!
ENOUGH TO MAKE ONE WEEP, IS IT NOT?
AN ADMIRABLE FAMILY MAN, SACRIFICING HIMSELF TO SAVE THE ONES HE LOVES?
...SO YOU MEAN...
...THIS POMMEL CHARACTER WILL DO THE DIRTY WORK FOR US?
IT WILL ALL HAPPEN OUT OF SIGHT, WITHOUT OUR KNOWLEDGE...
...SO THAT WE MAY REST EASILY.
EVEN IF IT DOES COME TO LIGHT, I WOULD BE THE ONLY ONE WHO WILL HAVE TO ANSWER FOR THAT CRIME...

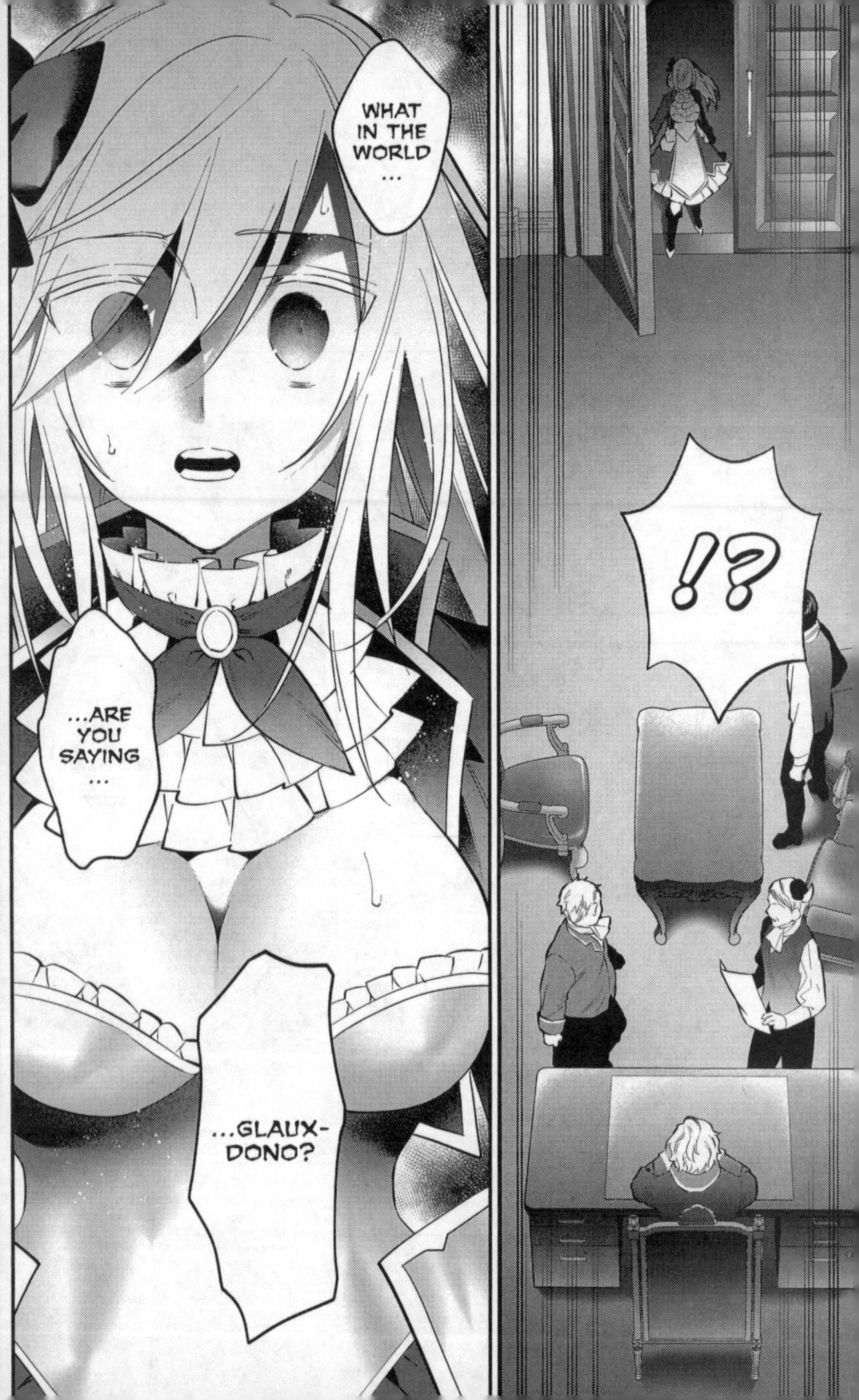
!?
WHAT IN THE WORLD ...
...ARE YOU SAYING ...
...GLAUX-DONO?

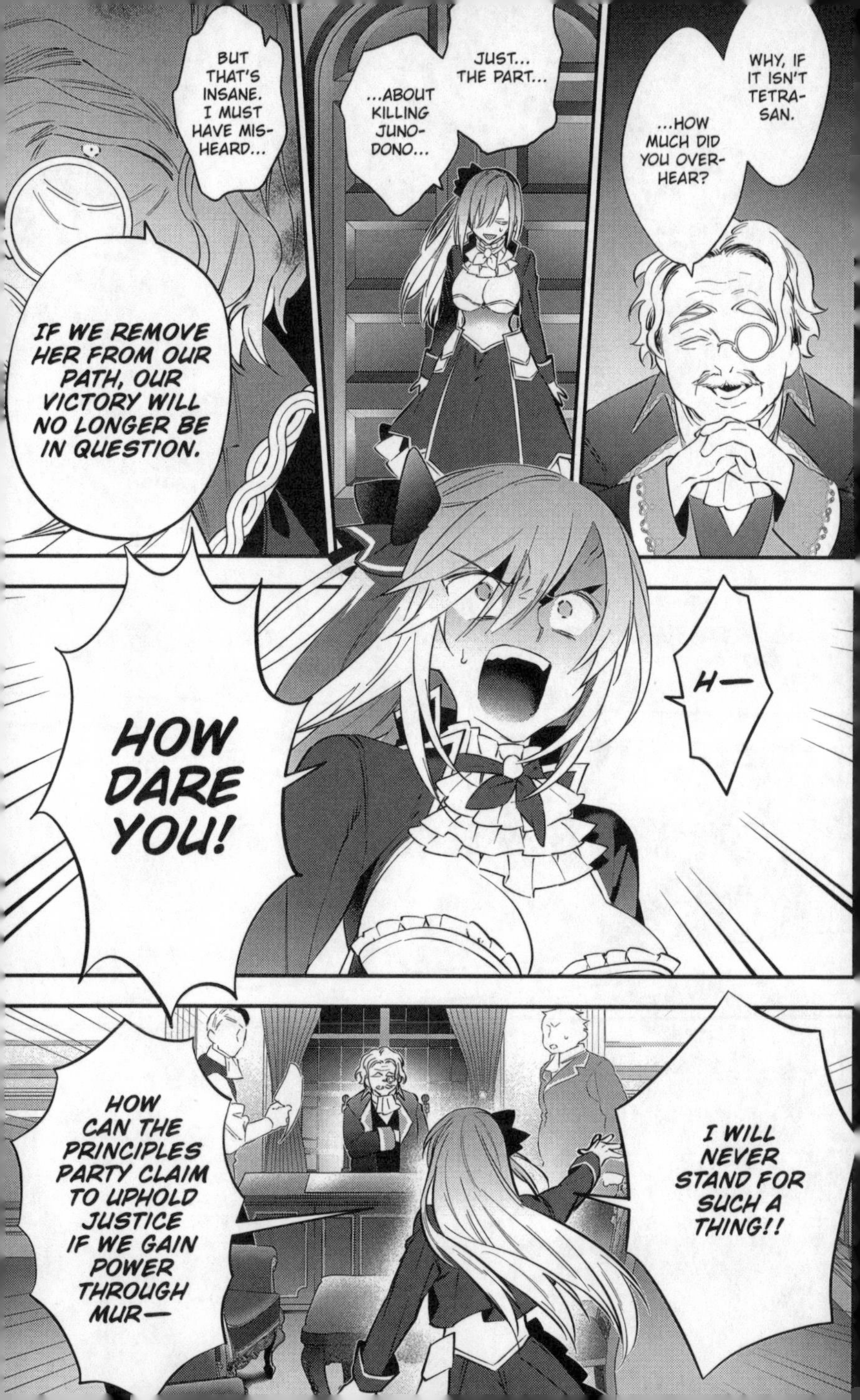
WHY, IF IT ISN'T TETRA-SAN.
...HOW MUCH DID YOU OVER-HEAR?
JUST... THE PART...
...ABOUT KILLING JUNO-DONO...
BUT THAT'S INSANE. I MUST HAVE MIS-HEARD...
IF WE REMOVE HER FROM OUR PATH, OUR VICTORY WILL NO LONGER BE IN QUESTION.
H—
HOW DARE YOU!
I WILL NEVER STAND FOR SUCH A THING!!
HOW CAN THE PRINCIPLES PARTY CLAIM TO UPHOLD JUSTICE IF WE GAIN POWER THROUGH MUR—

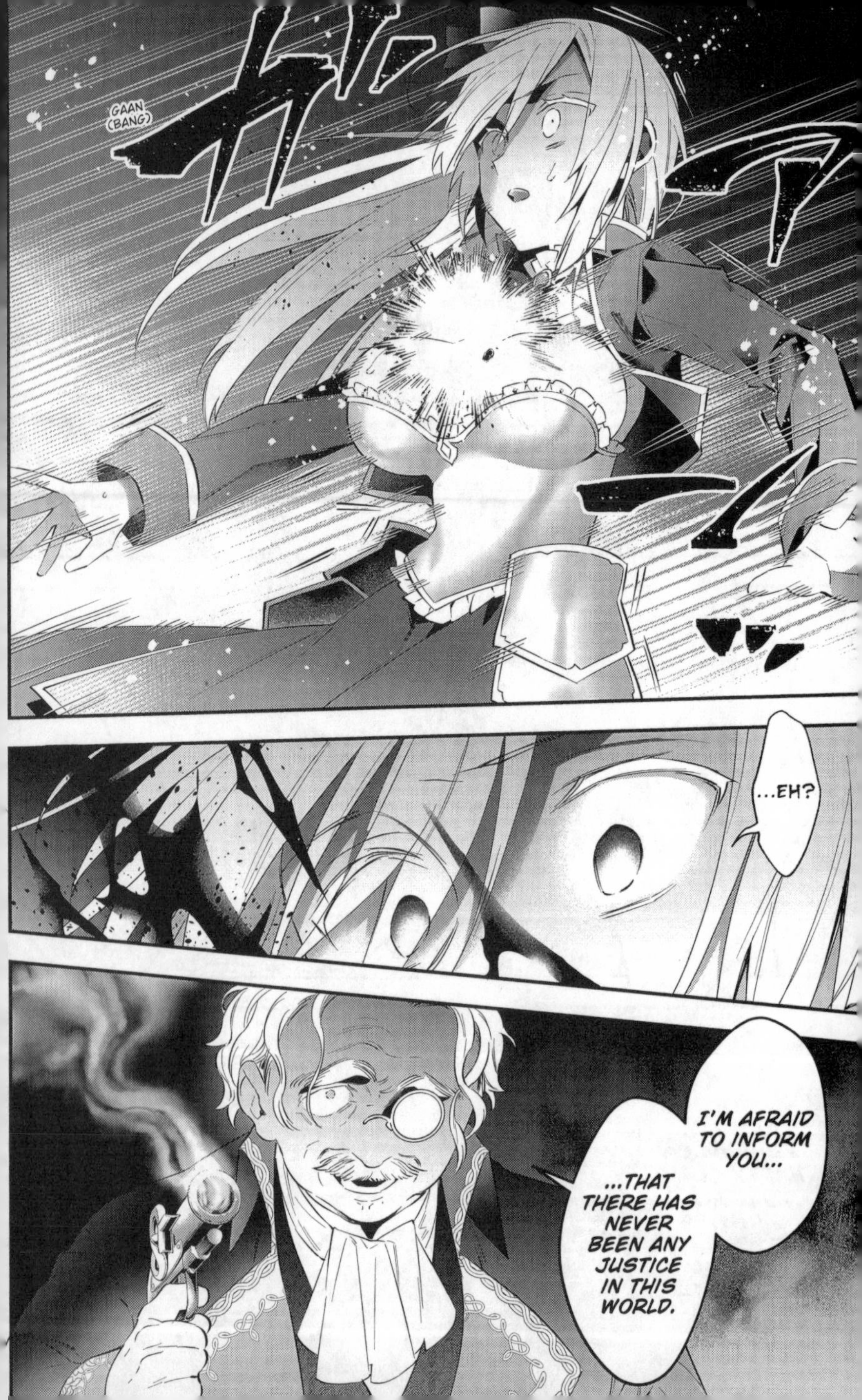
GAAN (BANG)
...EH?
I'M AFRAID TO INFORM YOU...
...THAT THERE HAS NEVER BEEN ANY JUSTICE IN THIS WORLD.

HIGH SCHOOL PRODIGIES HAVE IT EASY EVEN IN ANOTHER WORLD!

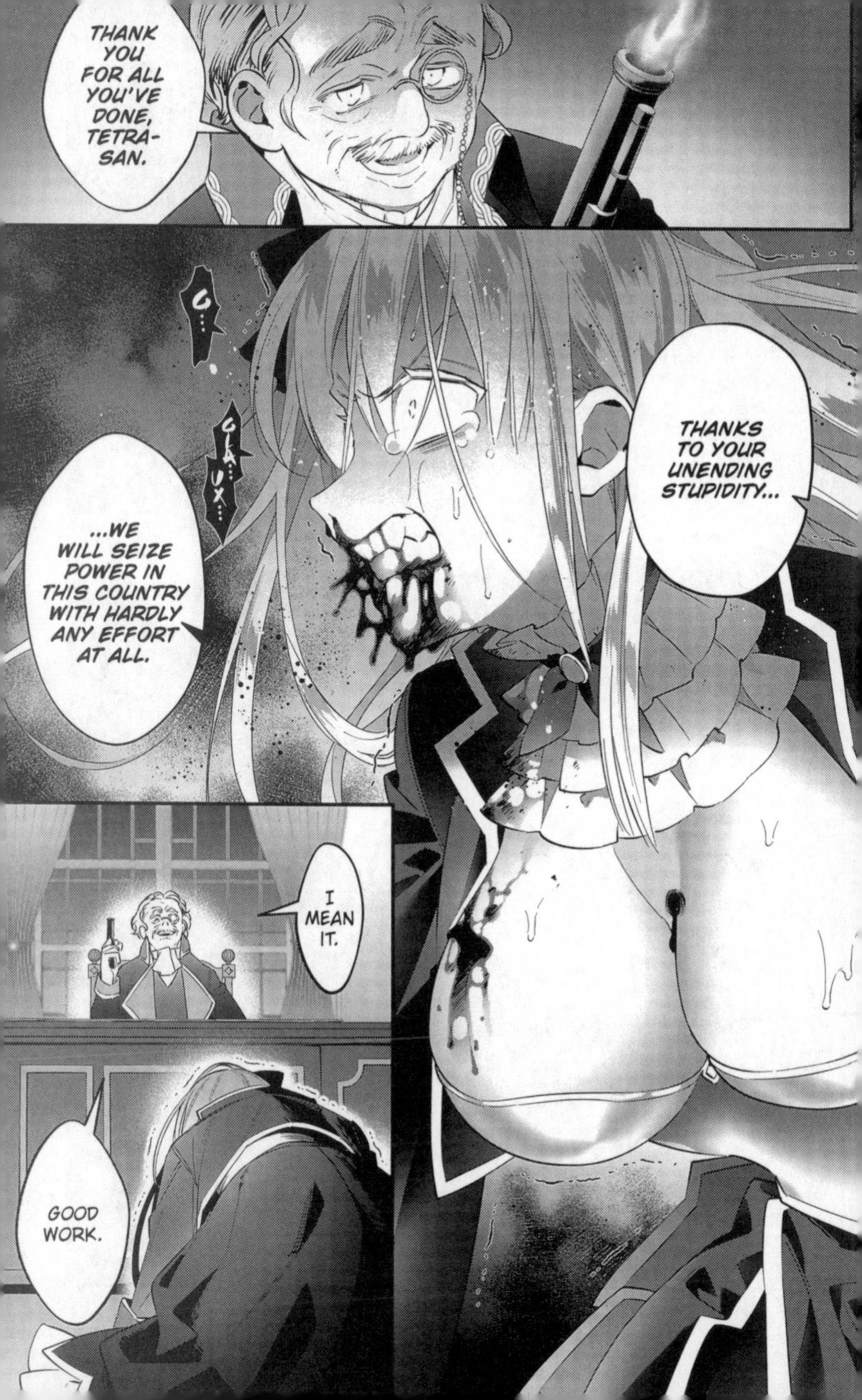
THANK YOU FOR ALL YOU'VE DONE, TETRA-SAN.
THANKS TO YOUR UNENDING STUPIDITY...
G...
GLAUX...
...WE WILL SEIZE POWER IN THIS COUNTRY WITH HARDLY ANY EFFORT AT ALL.
I MEAN IT.
GOOD WORK.

CHAPTER 77: INVIOLABLE RIGHTS

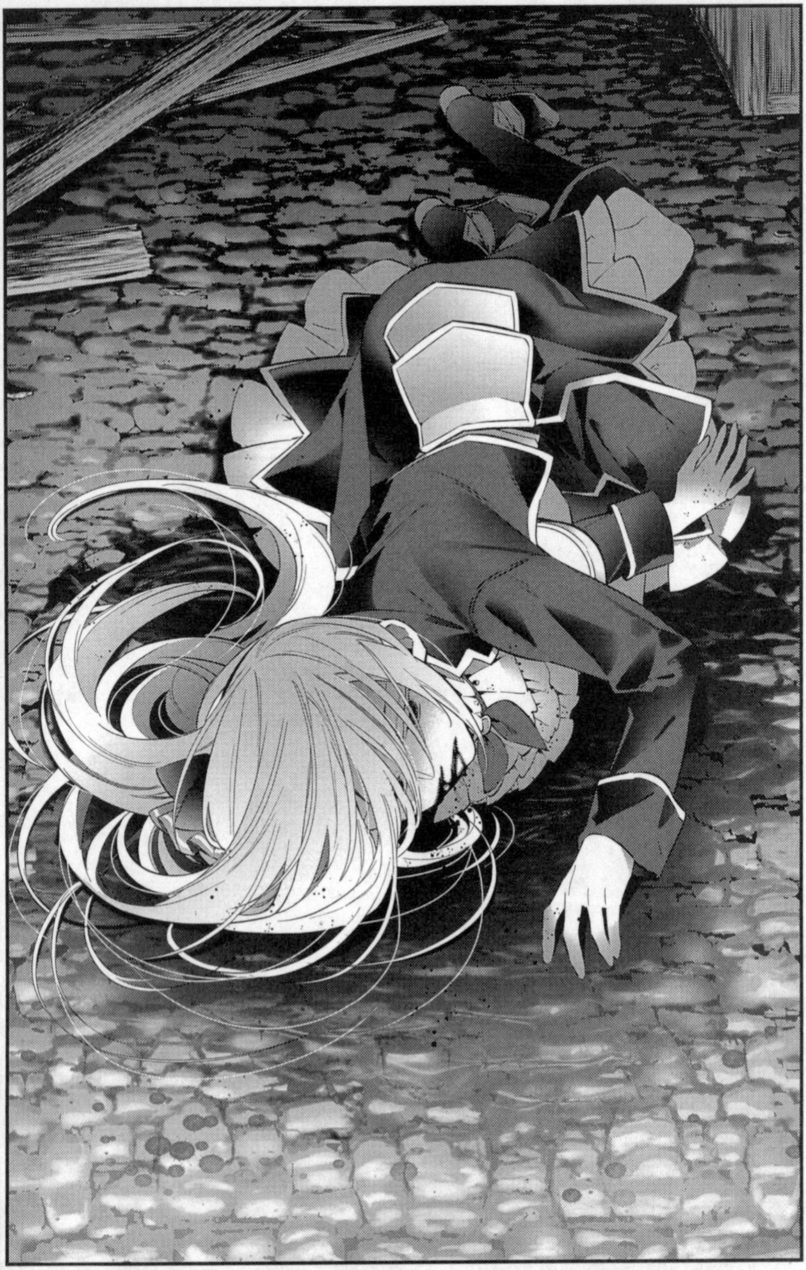

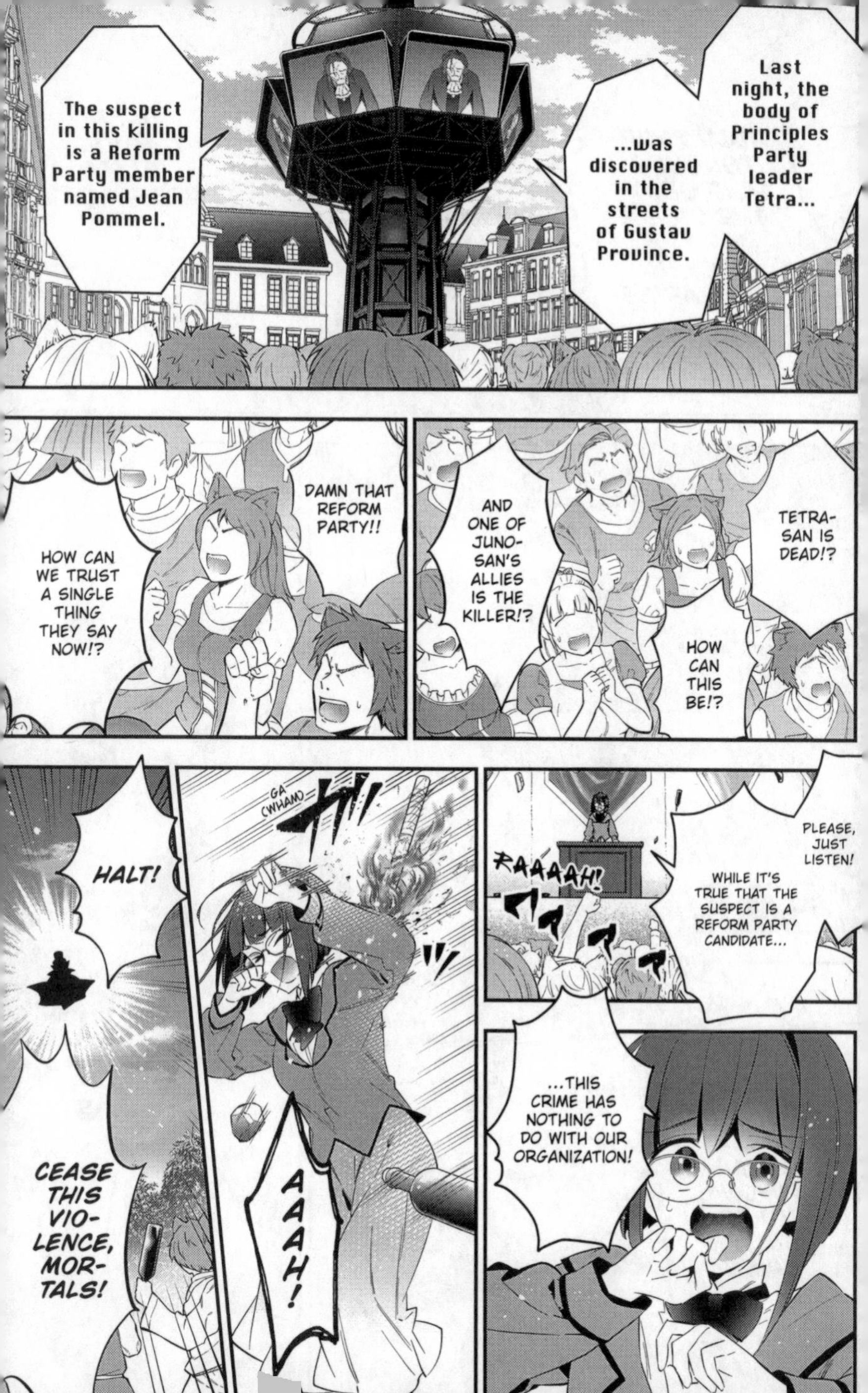
Last night, the body of Principles Party leader Tetra...
...was discovered in the streets of Gustav Province.
The suspect in this killing is a Reform Party member named Jean Pommel.
TETRA-SAN IS DEAD!?
HOW CAN THIS BE!?
AND ONE OF JUNO-SAN'S ALLIES IS THE KILLER!?
DAMN THAT REFORM PARTY!!
HOW CAN WE TRUST A SINGLE THING THEY SAY NOW!?
PLEASE, JUST LISTEN!
RAAAAH!
WHILE IT'S TRUE THAT THE SUSPECT IS A REFORM PARTY CANDIDATE...
...THIS CRIME HAS NOTHING TO DO WITH OUR ORGANIZATION!
GA (WHAM)
AAAAH!
HALT!
CEASE THIS VIO-LENCE, MOR-TALS!

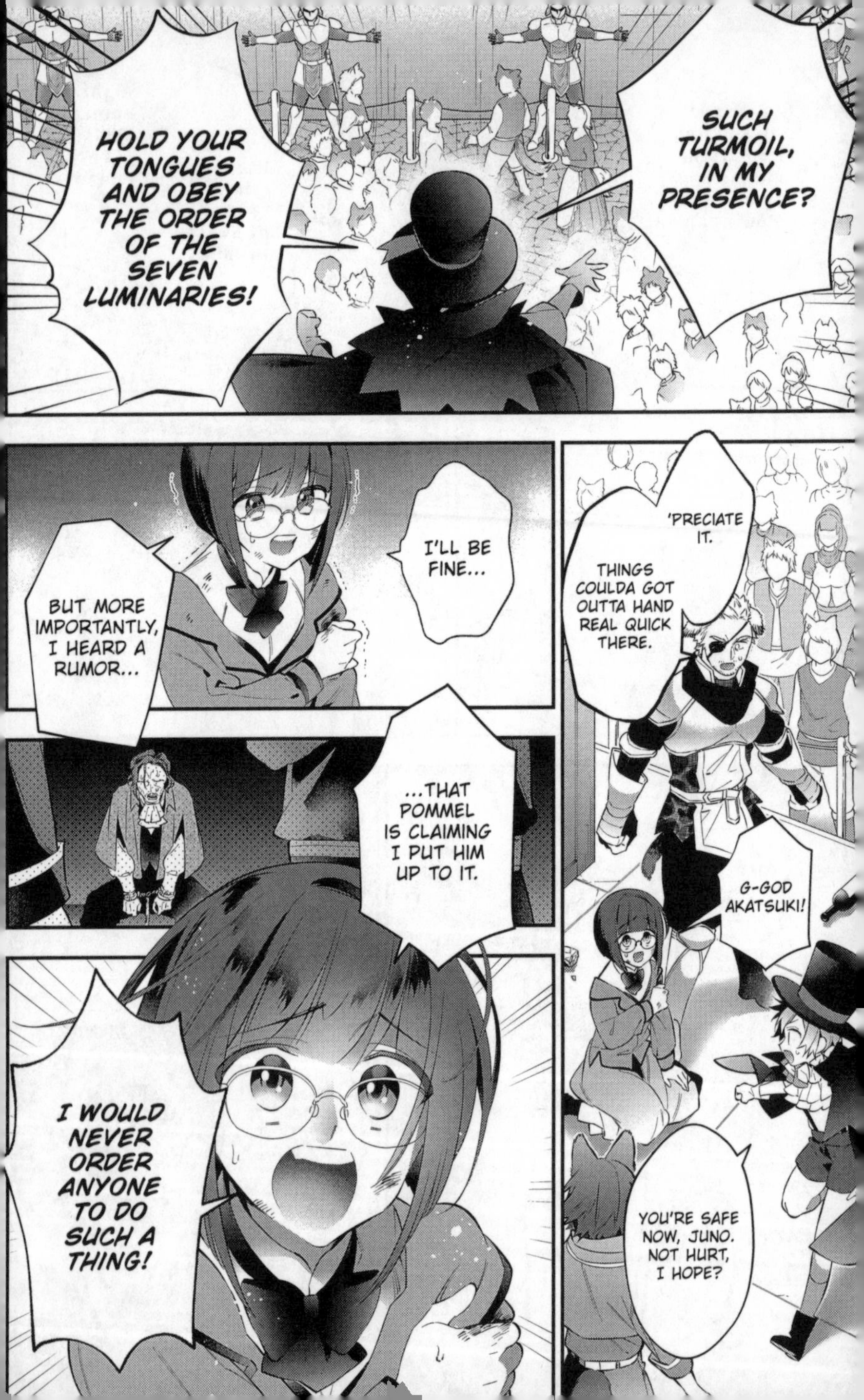
SUCH TURMOIL, IN MY PRESENCE?
HOLD YOUR TONGUES AND OBEY THE ORDER OF THE SEVEN LUMINARIES!
'PRECIATE IT.
THINGS COULDA GOT OUTTA HAND REAL QUICK THERE.
G-GOD AKATSUKI!
YOU'RE SAFE NOW, JUNO. NOT HURT, I HOPE?
I'LL BE FINE...
BUT MORE IMPORTANTLY, I HEARD A RUMOR...
...THAT POMMEL IS CLAIMING I PUT HIM UP TO IT.
I WOULD NEVER ORDER ANYONE TO DO SUCH A THING!

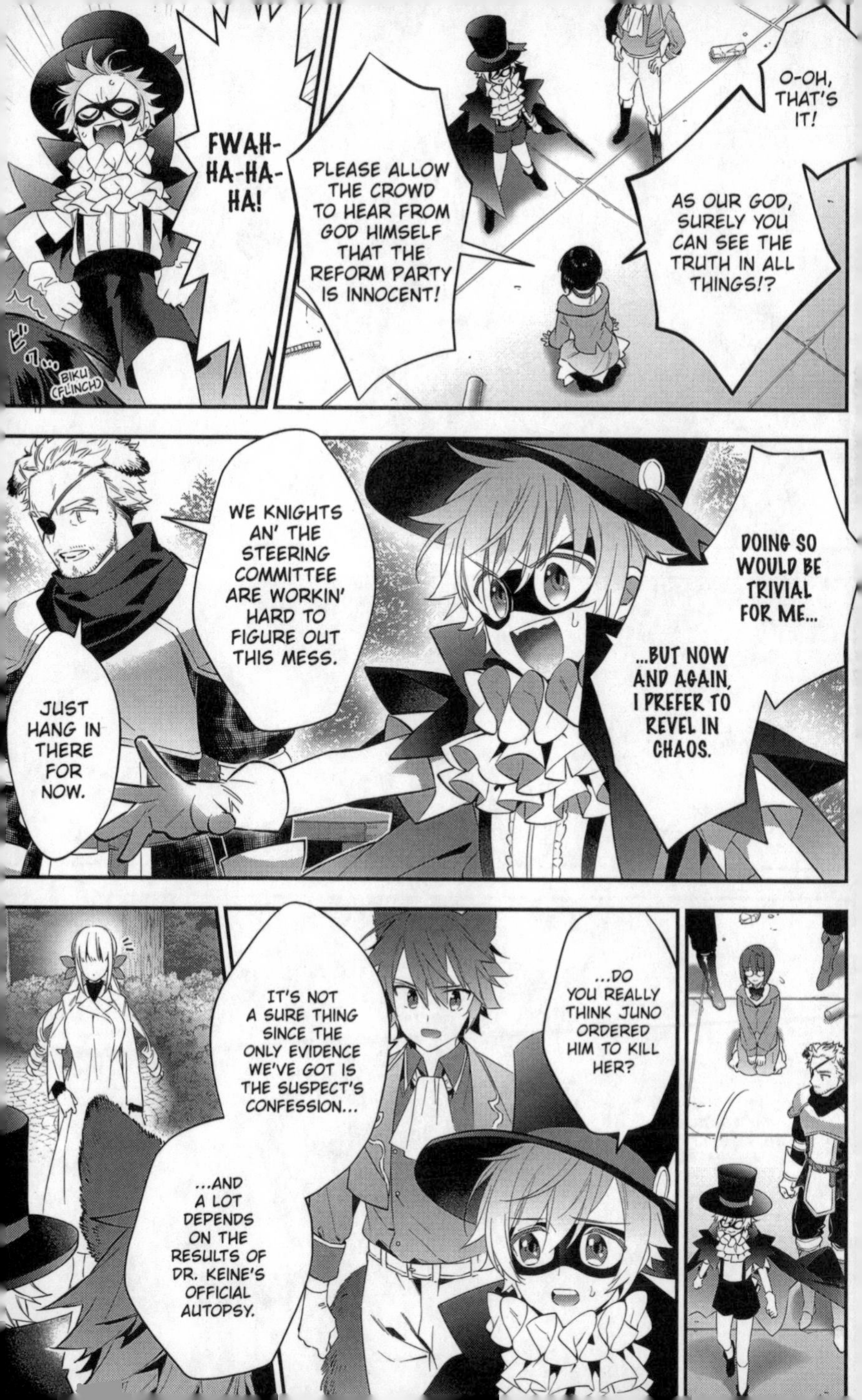

O-OH, THAT'S IT!
AS OUR GOD, SURELY YOU CAN SEE THE TRUTH IN ALL THINGS!?
PLEASE ALLOW THE CROWD TO HEAR FROM GOD HIMSELF THAT THE REFORM PARTY IS INNOCENT!
FWAH-HA-HA-HA!
BIKU (FLINCH)
DOING SO WOULD BE TRIVIAL FOR ME...
...BUT NOW AND AGAIN, I PREFER TO REVEL IN CHAOS.
WE KNIGHTS AN' THE STEERING COMMITTEE ARE WORKIN' HARD TO FIGURE OUT THIS MESS.
JUST HANG IN THERE FOR NOW.
...DO YOU REALLY THINK JUNO ORDERED HIM TO KILL HER?
IT'S NOT A SURE THING SINCE THE ONLY EVIDENCE WE'VE GOT IS THE SUSPECT'S CONFESSION...
...AND A LOT DEPENDS ON THE RESULTS OF DR. KEINE'S OFFICIAL AUTOPSY.

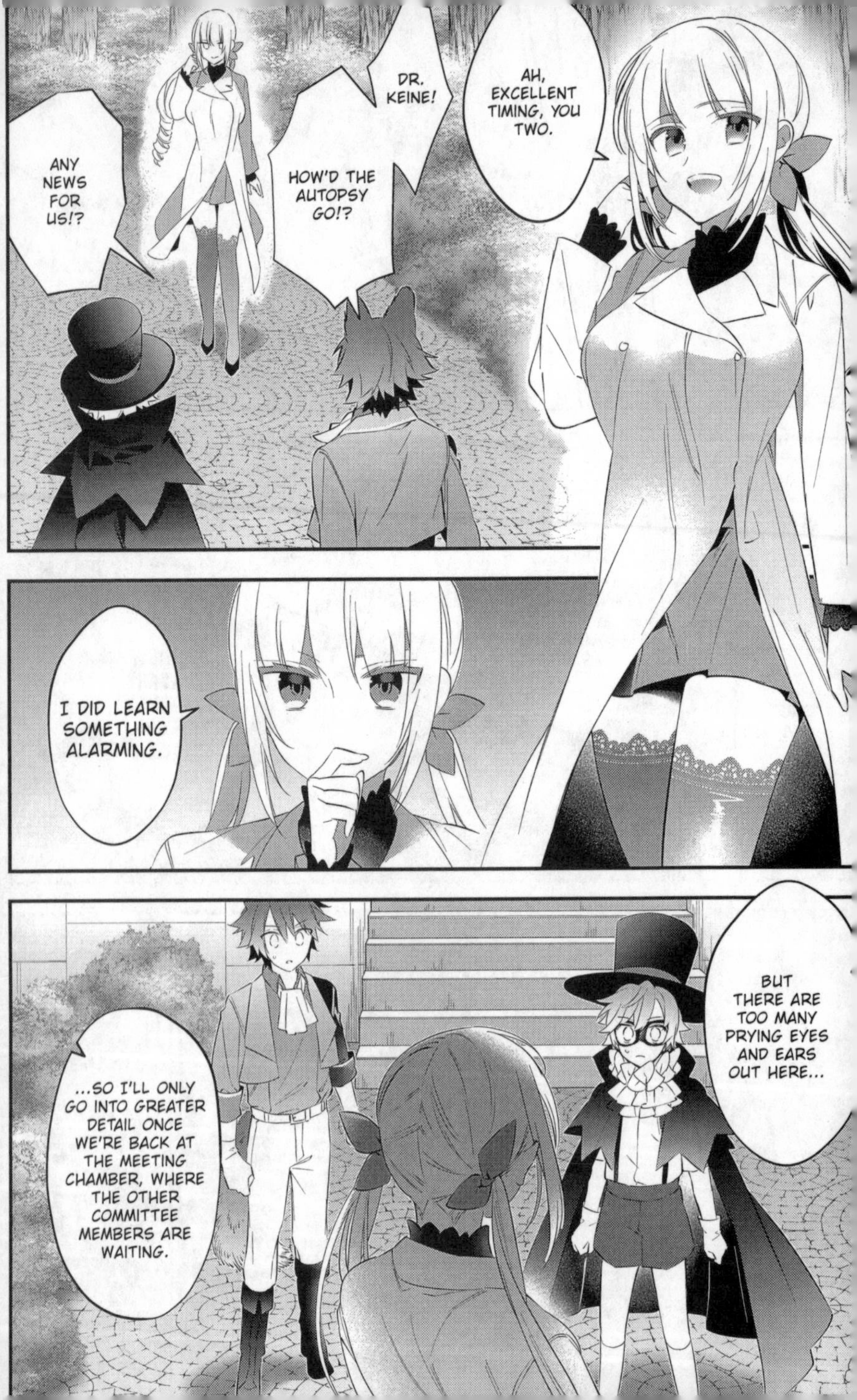

AH, EXCELLENT TIMING, YOU TWO.
DR. KEINE!
HOW'D THE AUTOPSY GO!?
ANY NEWS FOR US!?
I DID LEARN SOMETHING ALARMING.
BUT THERE ARE TOO MANY PRYING EYES AND EARS OUT HERE...
...SO I'LL ONLY GO INTO GREATER DETAIL ONCE WE'RE BACK AT THE MEETING CHAMBER, WHERE THE OTHER COMMITTEE MEMBERS ARE WAITING.

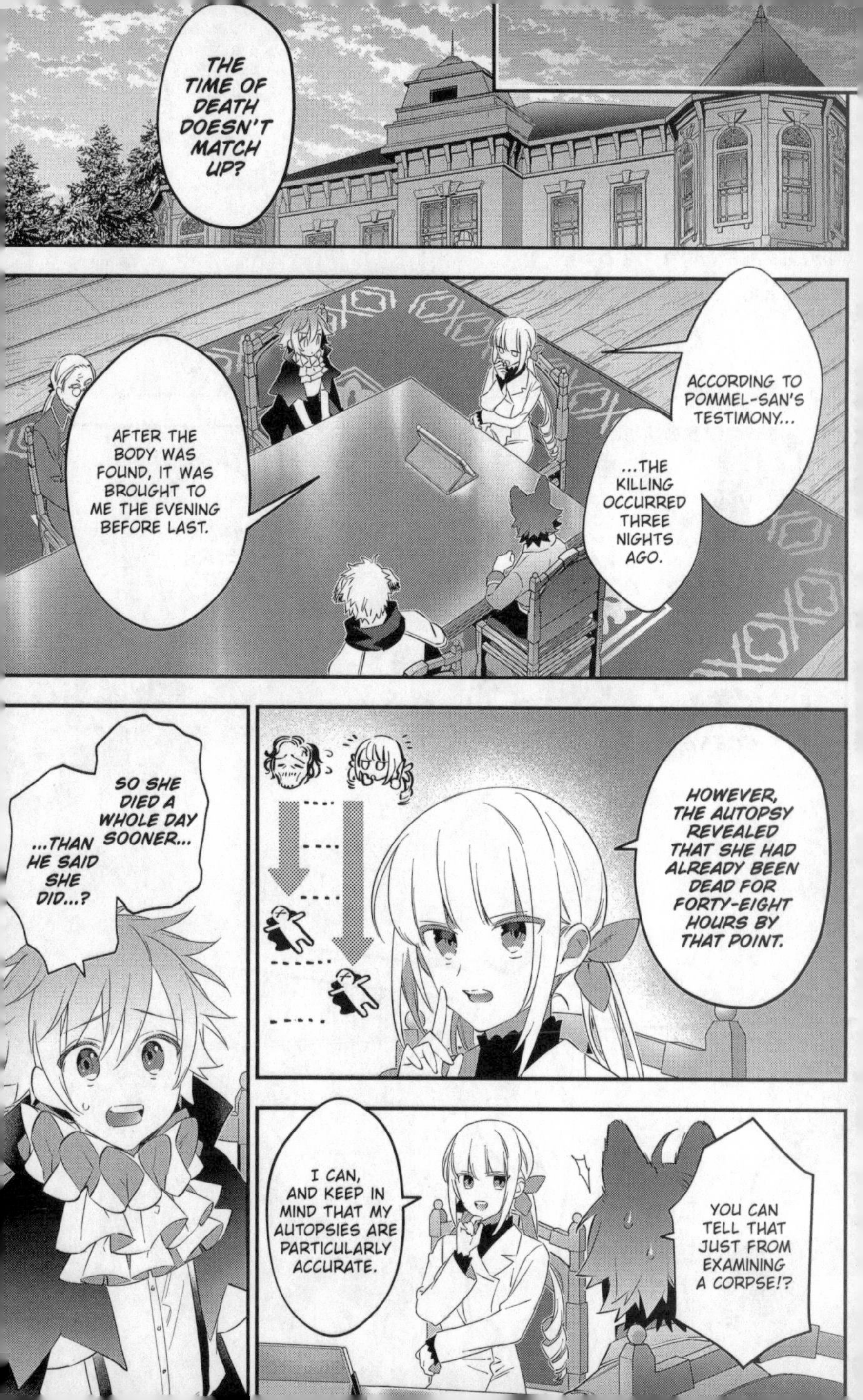
THE TIME OF DEATH DOESN'T MATCH UP?
ACCORDING TO POMMEL-SAN'S TESTIMONY...
...THE KILLING OCCURRED THREE NIGHTS AGO.
AFTER THE BODY WAS FOUND, IT WAS BROUGHT TO ME THE EVENING BEFORE LAST.
HOWEVER, THE AUTOPSY REVEALED THAT SHE HAD ALREADY BEEN DEAD FOR FORTY-EIGHT HOURS BY THAT POINT.
YOU CAN TELL THAT JUST FROM EXAMINING A CORPSE!?
I CAN, AND KEEP IN MIND THAT MY AUTOPSIES ARE PARTICULARLY ACCURATE.
SO SHE DIED A WHOLE DAY SOONER...
...THAN HE SAID SHE DID...?

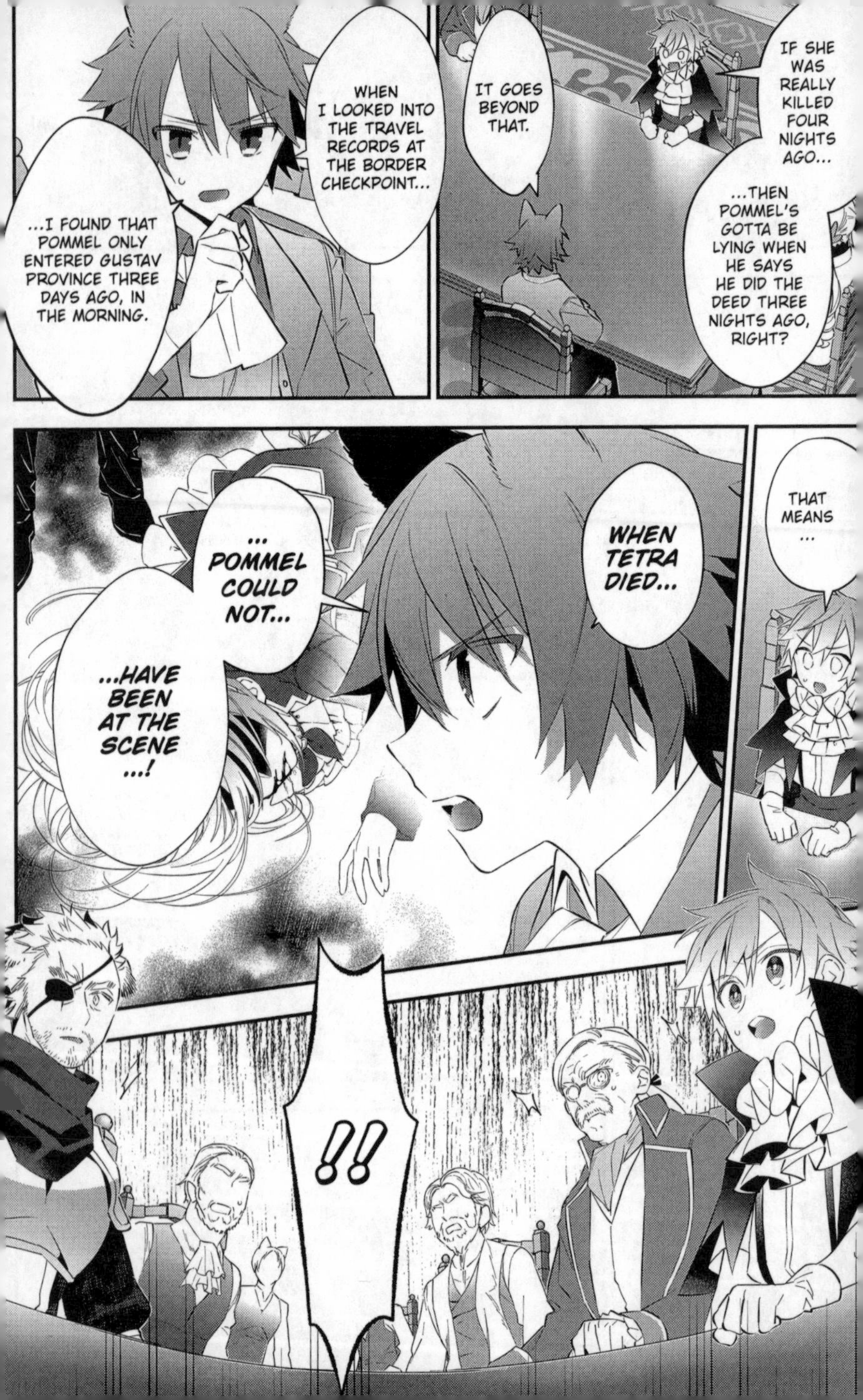
IF SHE WAS REALLY KILLED FOUR NIGHTS AGO...
...THEN POMMEL'S GOTTA BE LYING WHEN HE SAYS HE DID THE DEED THREE NIGHTS AGO, RIGHT?
IT GOES BEYOND THAT.
WHEN I LOOKED INTO THE TRAVEL RECORDS AT THE BORDER CHECKPOINT...
...I FOUND THAT POMMEL ONLY ENTERED GUSTAV PROVINCE THREE DAYS AGO, IN THE MORNING.
THAT MEANS...
WHEN TETRA DIED...
...POMMEL COULD NOT...
...HAVE BEEN AT THE SCENE...!
!!

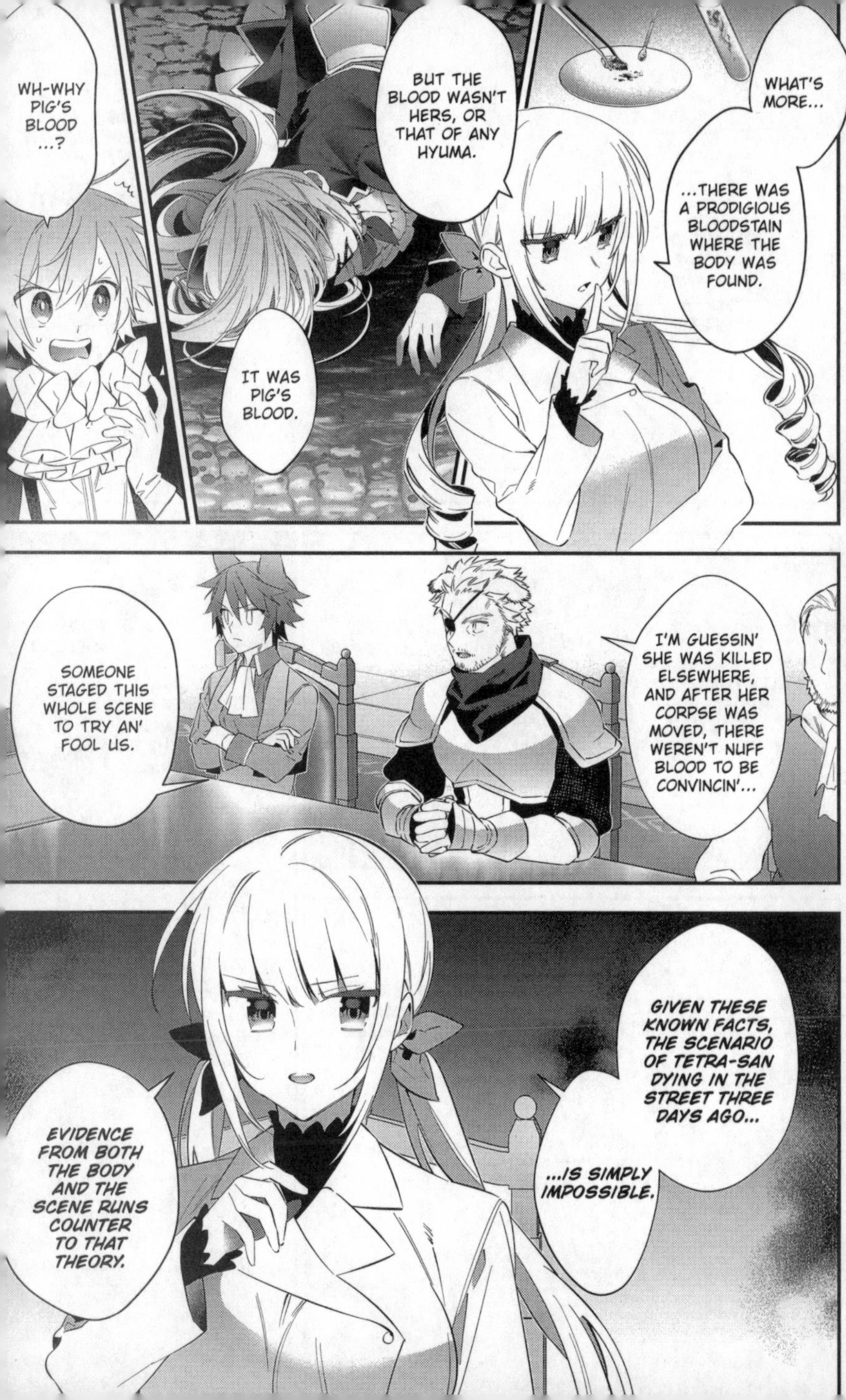
WHAT'S MORE...
...THERE WAS A PRODIGIOUS BLOODSTAIN WHERE THE BODY WAS FOUND.
BUT THE BLOOD WASN'T HERS, OR THAT OF ANY HYUMA.
IT WAS PIG'S BLOOD.
WH-WHY PIG'S BLOOD ...?
I'M GUESSIN' SHE WAS KILLED ELSEWHERE, AND AFTER HER CORPSE WAS MOVED, THERE WEREN'T NUFF BLOOD TO BE CONVINCIN'...
SOMEONE STAGED THIS WHOLE SCENE TO TRY AN' FOOL US.
GIVEN THESE KNOWN FACTS, THE SCENARIO OF TETRA-SAN DYING IN THE STREET THREE DAYS AGO...
...IS SIMPLY IMPOSSIBLE.
EVIDENCE FROM BOTH THE BODY AND THE SCENE RUNS COUNTER TO THAT THEORY.

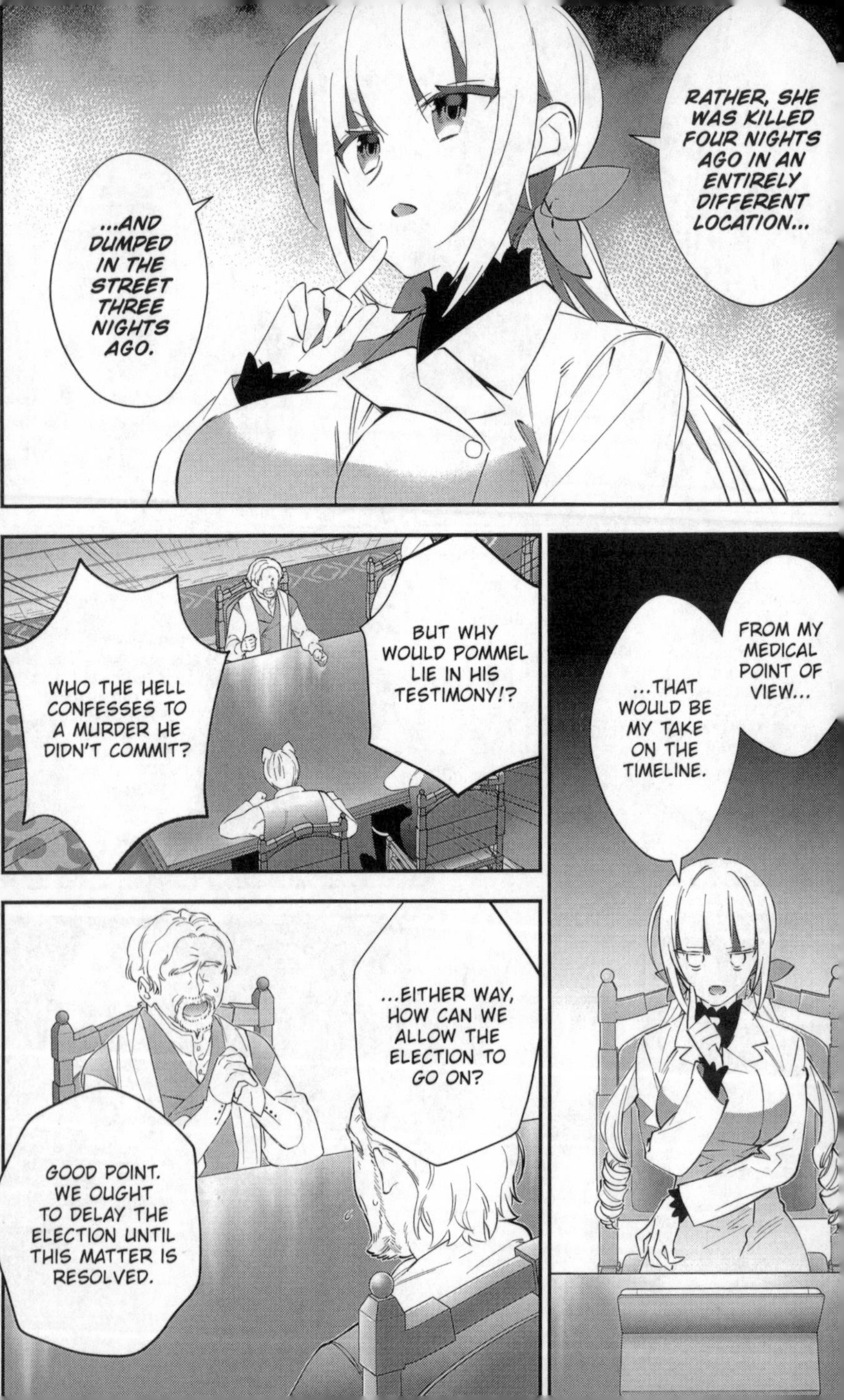
RATHER, SHE WAS KILLED FOUR NIGHTS AGO IN AN ENTIRELY DIFFERENT LOCATION...
...AND DUMPED IN THE STREET THREE NIGHTS AGO.
FROM MY MEDICAL POINT OF VIEW...
...THAT WOULD BE MY TAKE ON THE TIMELINE.
BUT WHY WOULD POMMEL LIE IN HIS TESTIMONY!?
WHO THE HELL CONFESSES TO A MURDER HE DIDN'T COMMIT?
...EITHER WAY, HOW CAN WE ALLOW THE ELECTION TO GO ON?
GOOD POINT. WE OUGHT TO DELAY THE ELECTION UNTIL THIS MATTER IS RESOLVED.

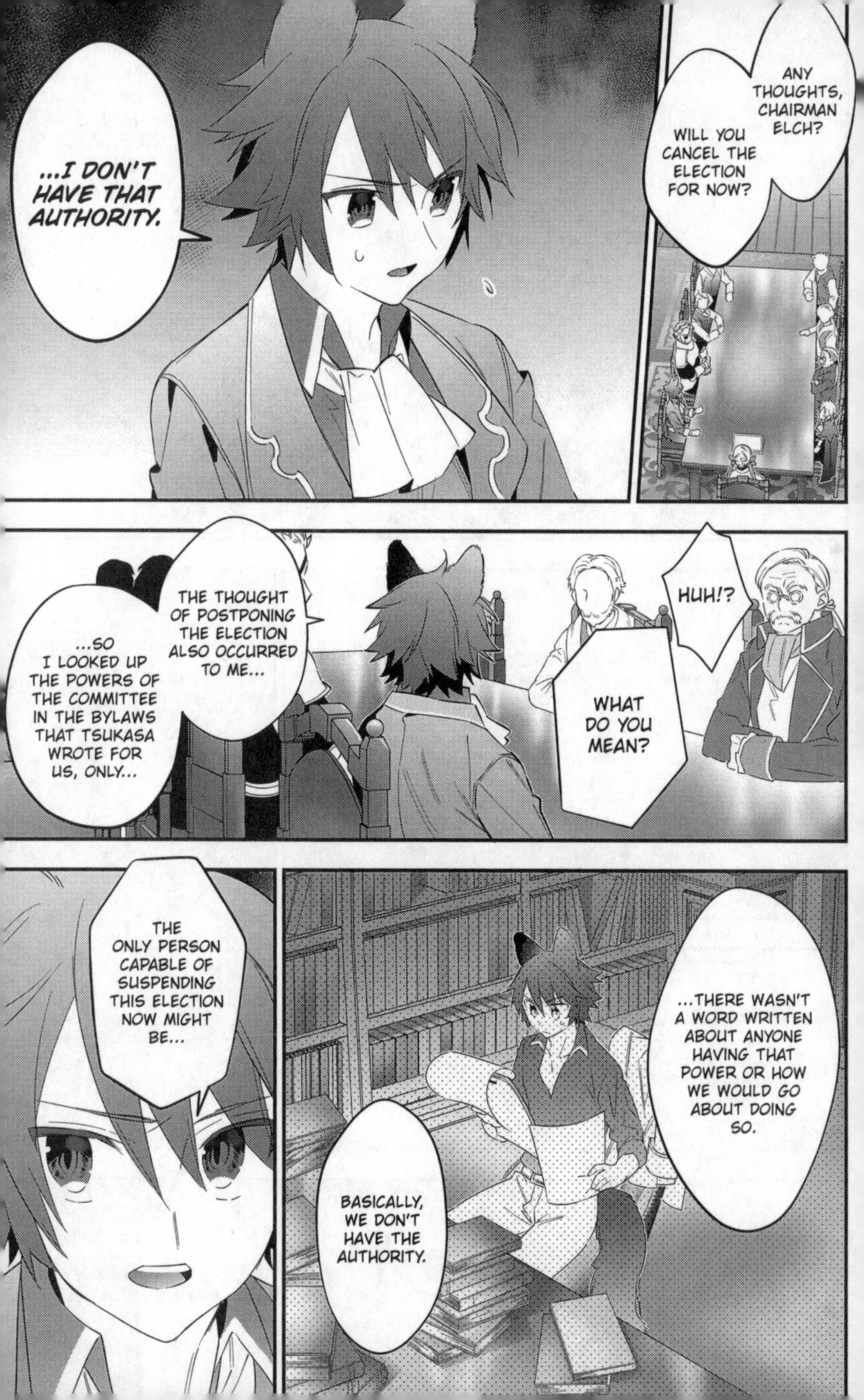
ANY THOUGHTS, CHAIRMAN ELCH?
WILL YOU CANCEL THE ELECTION FOR NOW?
...I DON'T HAVE THAT AUTHORITY.
HUH!?
WHAT DO YOU MEAN?
THE THOUGHT OF POSTPONING THE ELECTION ALSO OCCURRED TO ME...
...SO I LOOKED UP THE POWERS OF THE COMMITTEE IN THE BYLAWS THAT TSUKASA WROTE FOR US, ONLY...
...THERE WASN'T A WORD WRITTEN ABOUT ANYONE HAVING THAT POWER OR HOW WE WOULD GO ABOUT DOING SO.
BASICALLY, WE DON'T HAVE THE AUTHORITY.
THE ONLY PERSON CAPABLE OF SUSPENDING THIS ELECTION NOW MIGHT BE...

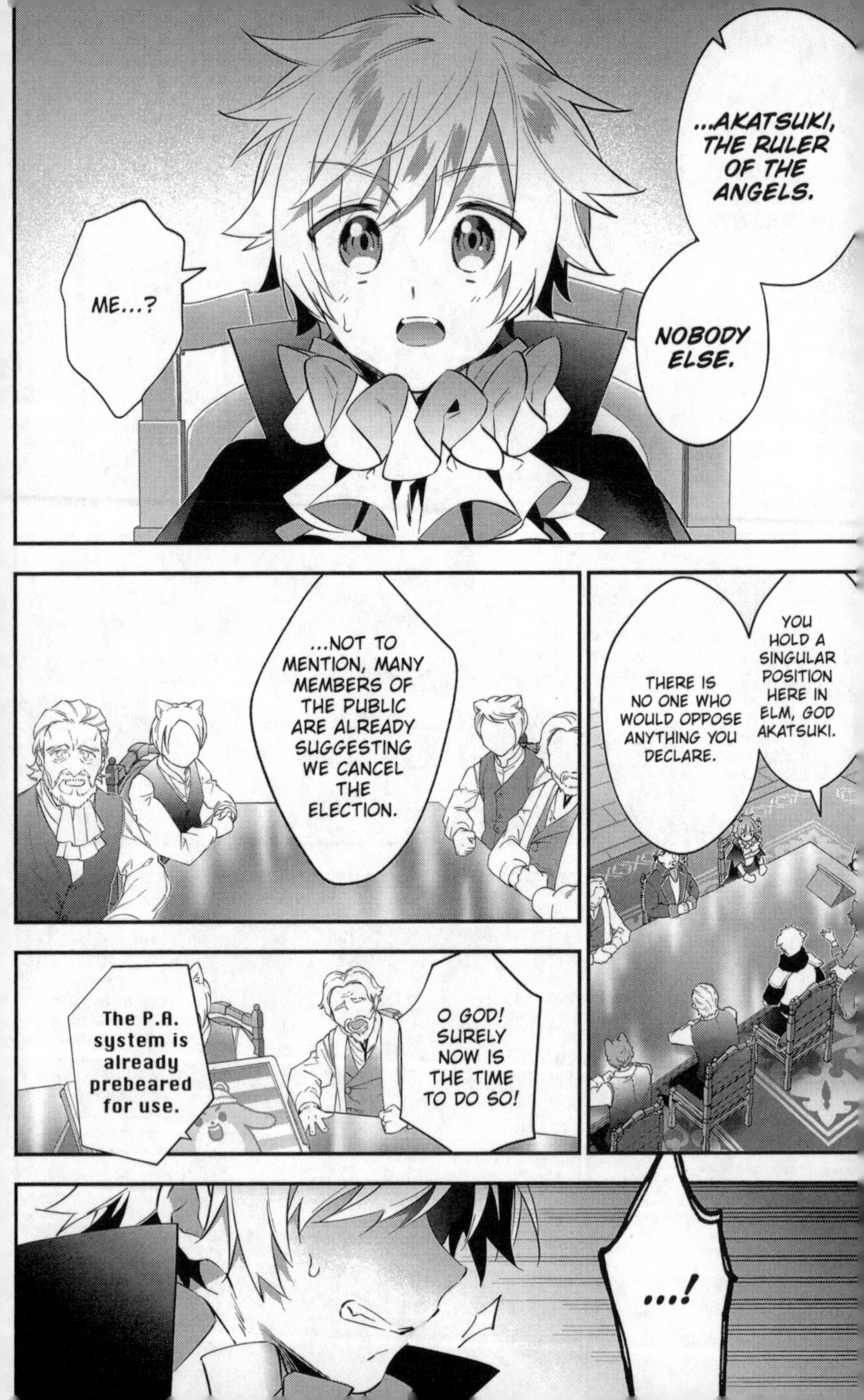
...AKATSUKI, THE RULER OF THE ANGELS.
NOBODY ELSE.
ME...?
YOU HOLD A SINGULAR POSITION HERE IN ELM, GOD AKATSUKI.
THERE IS NO ONE WHO WOULD OPPOSE ANYTHING YOU DECLARE.
...NOT TO MENTION, MANY MEMBERS OF THE PUBLIC ARE ALREADY SUGGESTING WE CANCEL THE ELECTION.
O GOD! SURELY NOW IS THE TIME TO DO SO!
The P.A. system is already prebeared for use.
...!

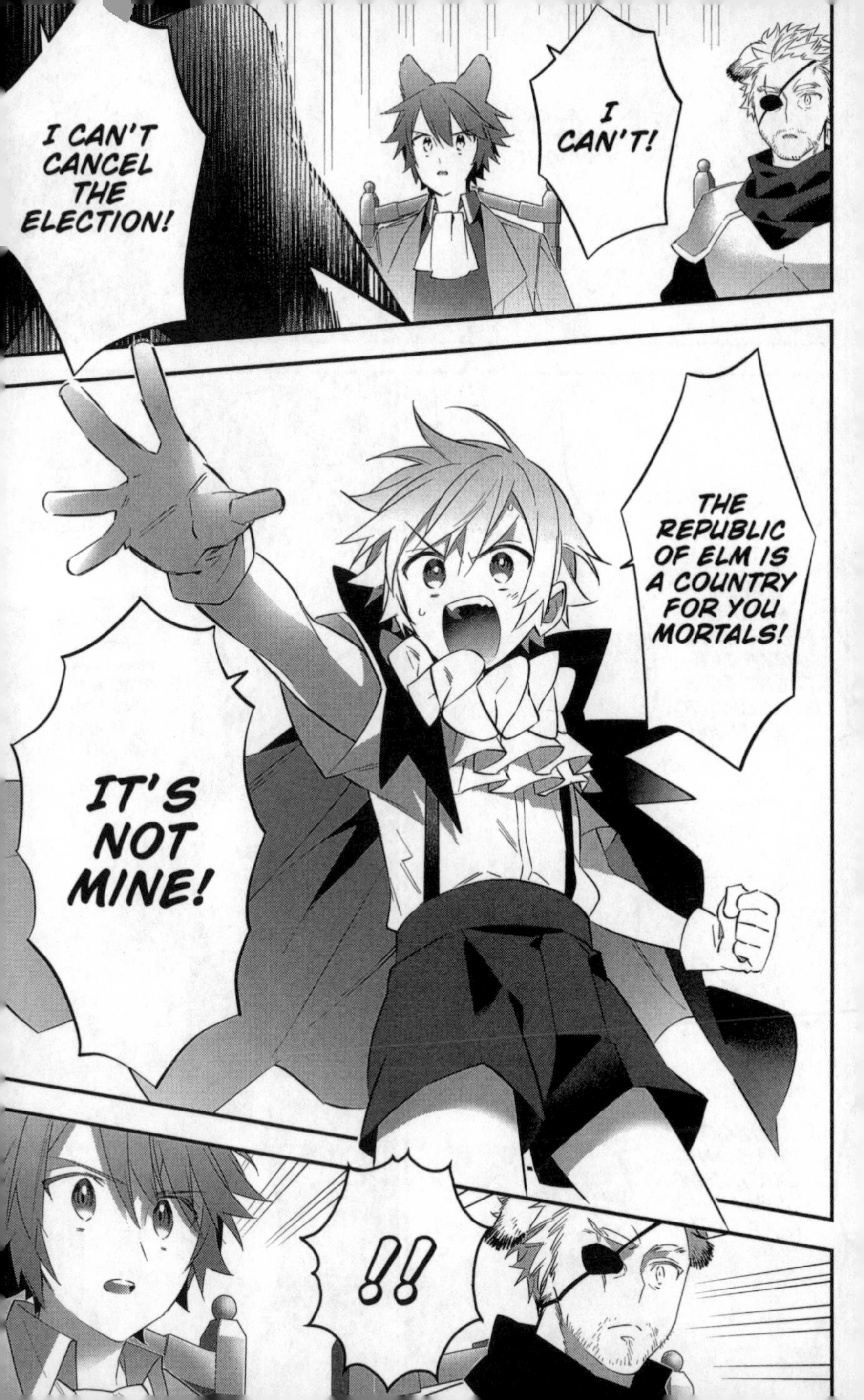
I CAN'T!
I CAN'T CANCEL THE ELECTION!
THE REPUBLIC OF ELM IS A COUNTRY FOR YOU MORTALS!
IT'S NOT MINE!
!!

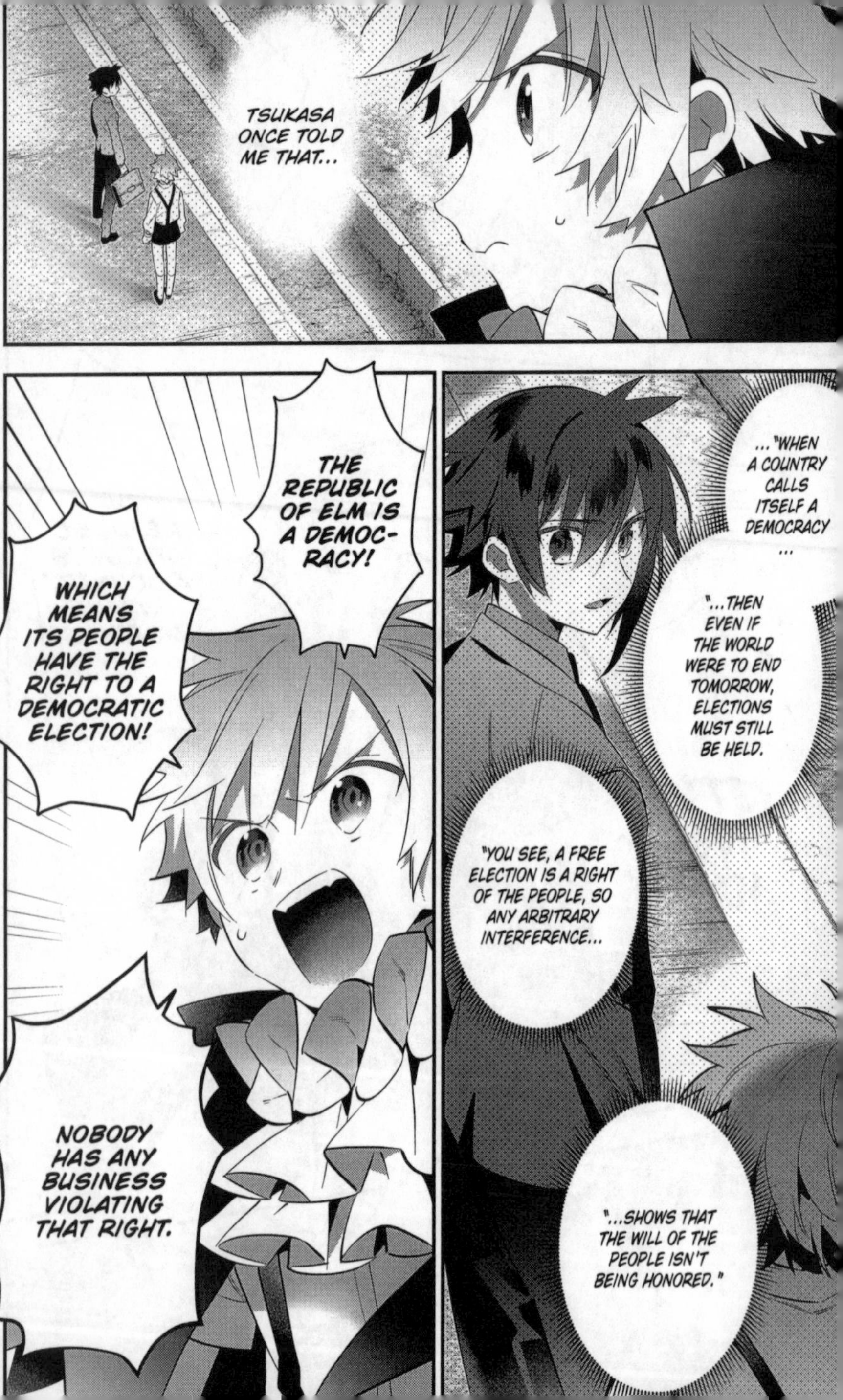
TSUKASA ONCE TOLD ME THAT...
..."WHEN A COUNTRY CALLS ITSELF A DEMOCRACY ...
"...THEN EVEN IF THE WORLD WERE TO END TOMORROW, ELECTIONS MUST STILL BE HELD.
"YOU SEE, A FREE ELECTION IS A RIGHT OF THE PEOPLE, SO ANY ARBITRARY INTERFERENCE...
"...SHOWS THAT THE WILL OF THE PEOPLE ISN'T BEING HONORED."
THE REPUBLIC OF ELM IS A DEMOC-RACY!
WHICH MEANS ITS PEOPLE HAVE THE RIGHT TO A DEMOCRATIC ELECTION!
NOBODY HAS ANY BUSINESS VIOLATING THAT RIGHT.

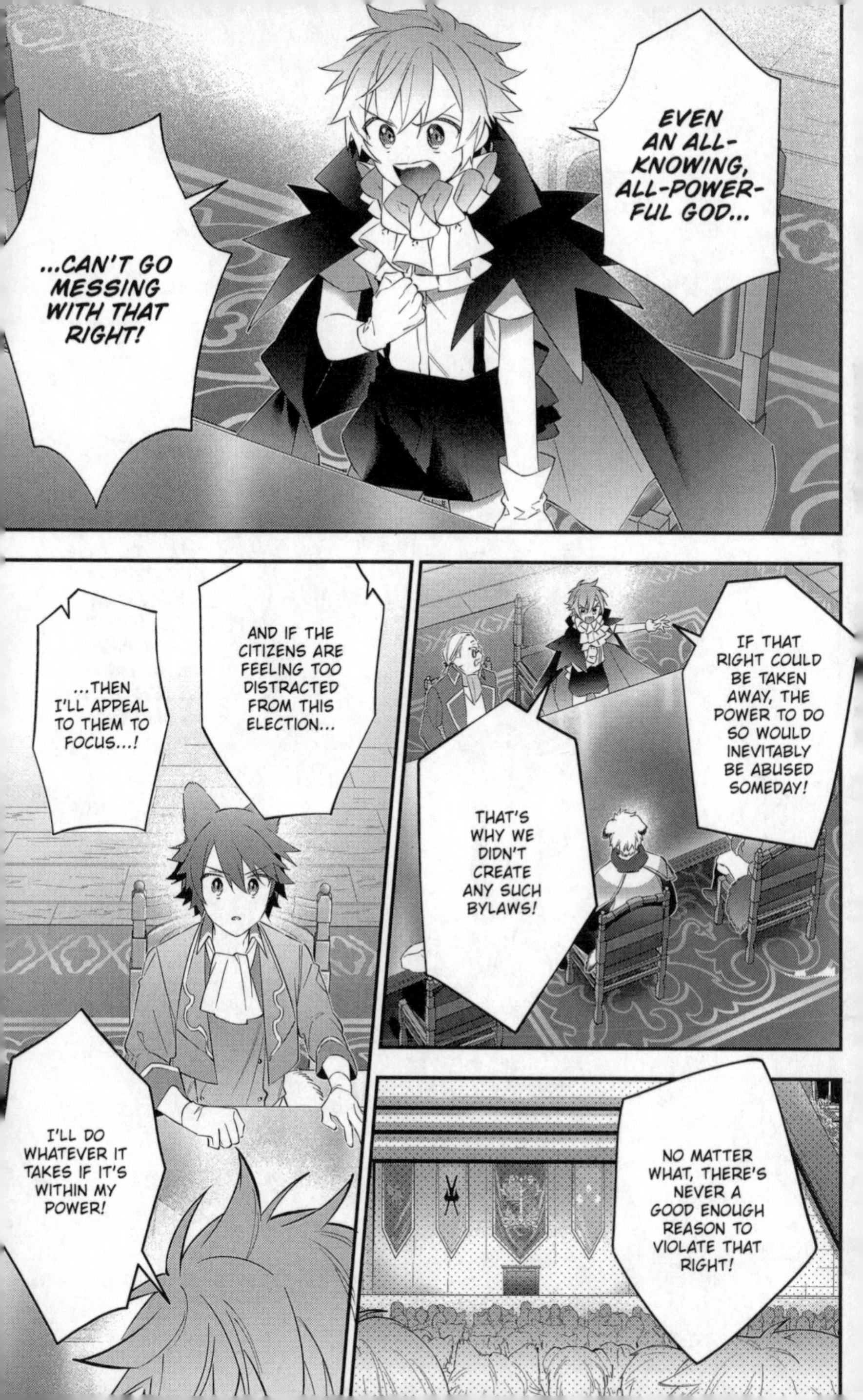
EVEN AN ALL-KNOWING, ALL-POWERFUL GOD...
...CAN'T GO MESSING WITH THAT RIGHT!
IF THAT RIGHT COULD BE TAKEN AWAY, THE POWER TO DO SO WOULD INEVITABLY BE ABUSED SOMEDAY!
THAT'S WHY WE DIDN'T CREATE ANY SUCH BYLAWS!
NO MATTER WHAT, THERE'S NEVER A GOOD ENOUGH REASON TO VIOLATE THAT RIGHT!
AND IF THE CITIZENS ARE FEELING TOO DISTRACTED FROM THIS ELECTION...
...THEN I'LL APPEAL TO THEM TO FOCUS...!
I'LL DO WHATEVER IT TAKES IF IT'S WITHIN MY POWER!

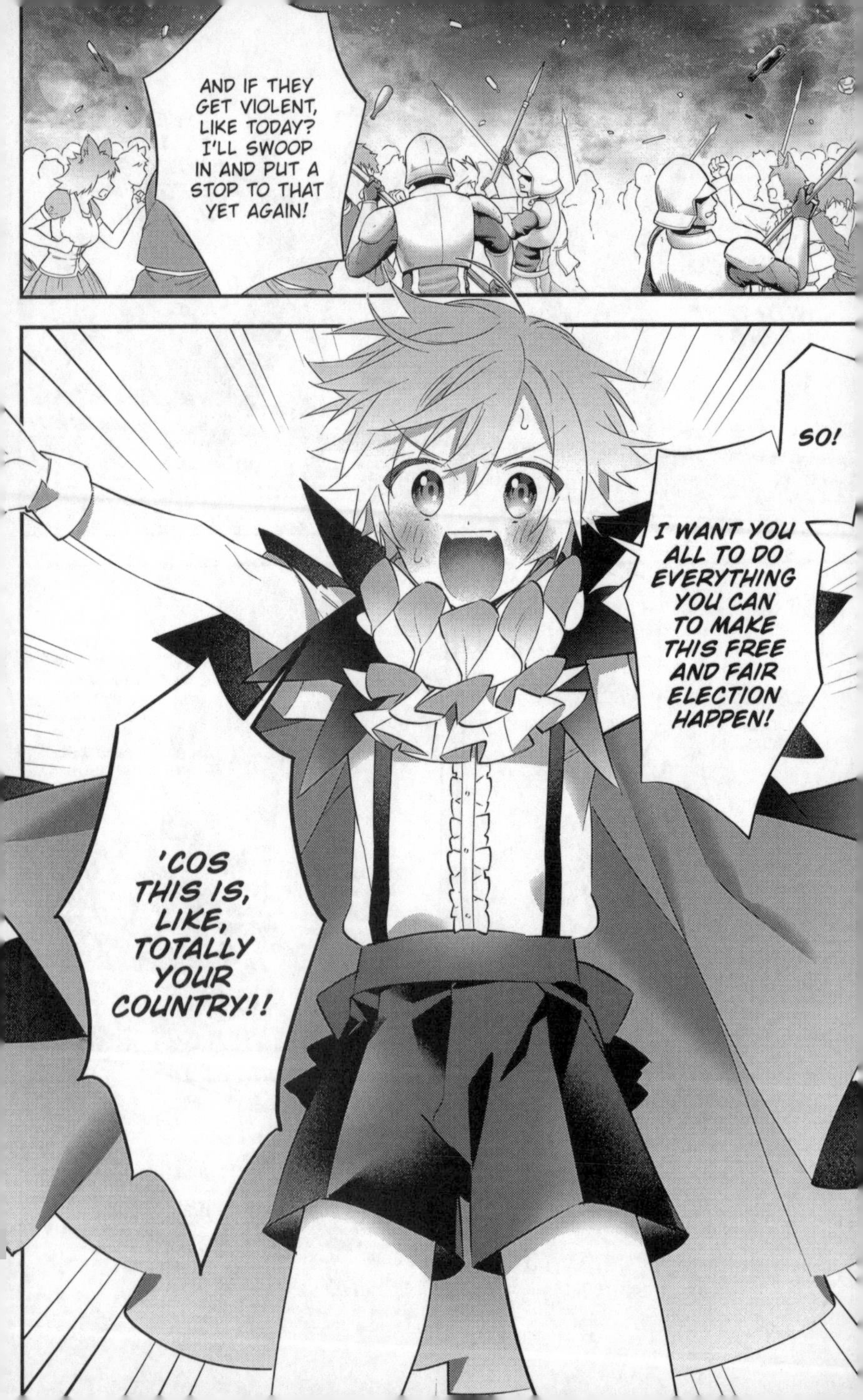
AND IF THEY GET VIOLENT, LIKE TODAY? I'LL SWOOP IN AND PUT A STOP TO THAT YET AGAIN!
SO!
I WANT YOU ALL TO DO EVERYTHING YOU CAN TO MAKE THIS FREE AND FAIR ELECTION HAPPEN!
'COS THIS IS, LIKE, TOTALLY YOUR COUNTRY!!

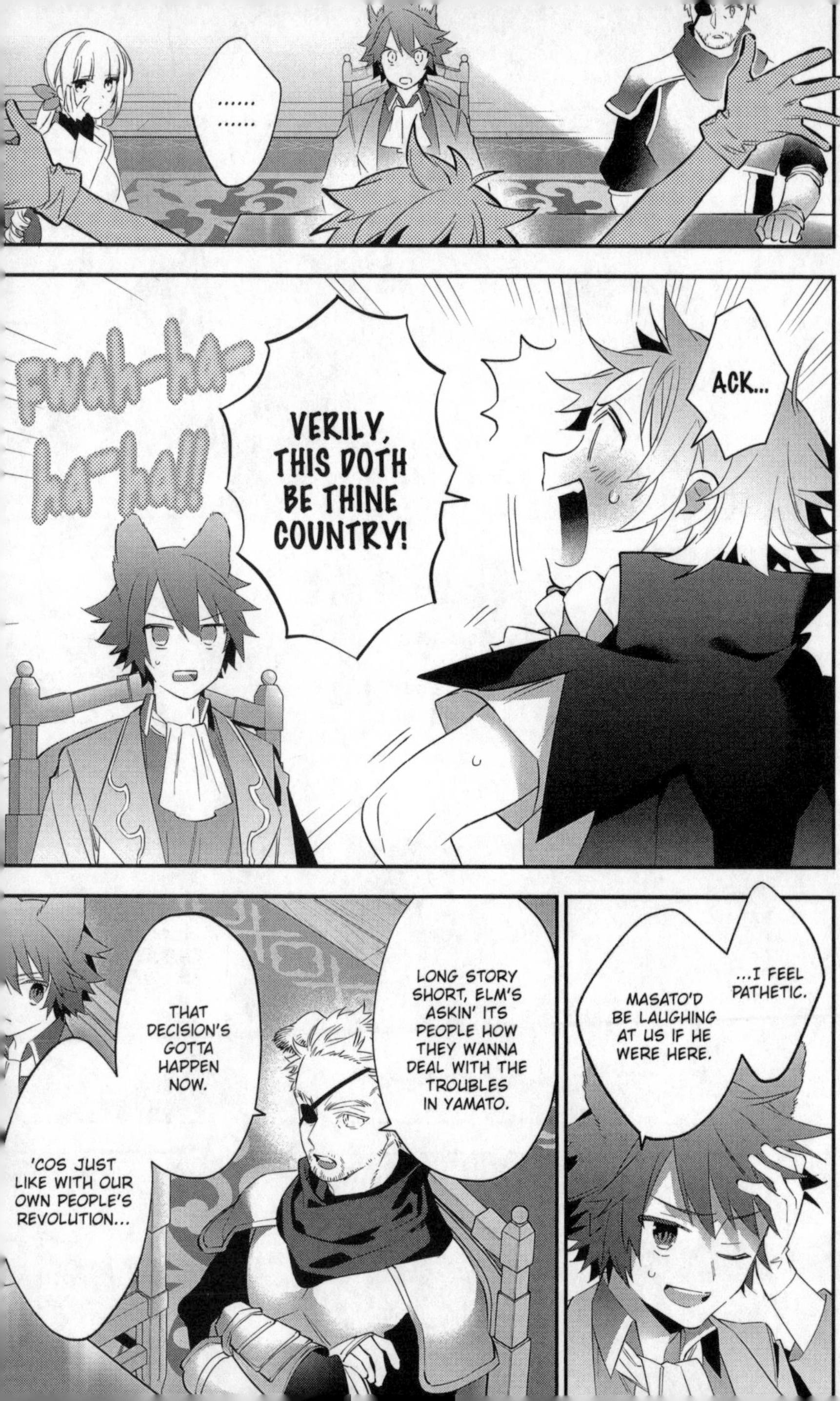
......
......
ACK...
VERILY, THIS DOTH BE THINE COUNTRY!
...I FEEL PATHETIC.
MASATO'D BE LAUGHING AT US IF HE WERE HERE.
LONG STORY SHORT, ELM'S ASKIN' ITS PEOPLE HOW THEY WANNA DEAL WITH THE TROUBLES IN YAMATO.
THAT DECISION'S GOTTA HAPPEN NOW.
'COS JUST LIKE WITH OUR OWN PEOPLE'S REVOLUTION...

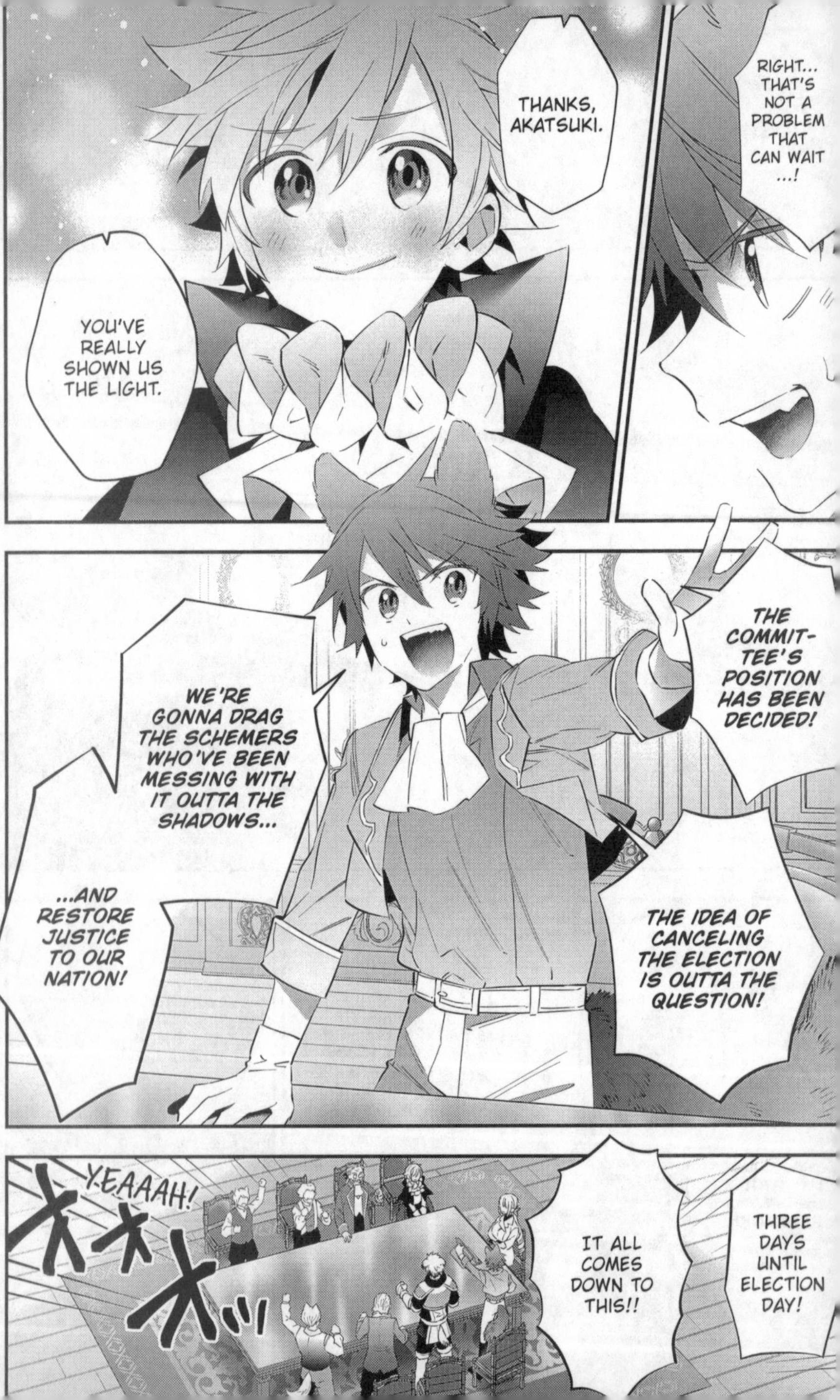
RIGHT... THAT'S NOT A PROBLEM THAT CAN WAIT ...!
THANKS, AKATSUKI.
YOU'VE REALLY SHOWN US THE LIGHT.
THE COMMIT-TEE'S POSITION HAS BEEN DECIDED!
THE IDEA OF CANCELING THE ELECTION IS OUTTA THE QUESTION!
WE'RE GONNA DRAG THE SCHEMERS WHO'VE BEEN MESSING WITH IT OUTTA THE SHADOWS...
...AND RESTORE JUSTICE TO OUR NATION!
THREE DAYS UNTIL ELECTION DAY!
IT ALL COMES DOWN TO THIS!!
YEAAAH!

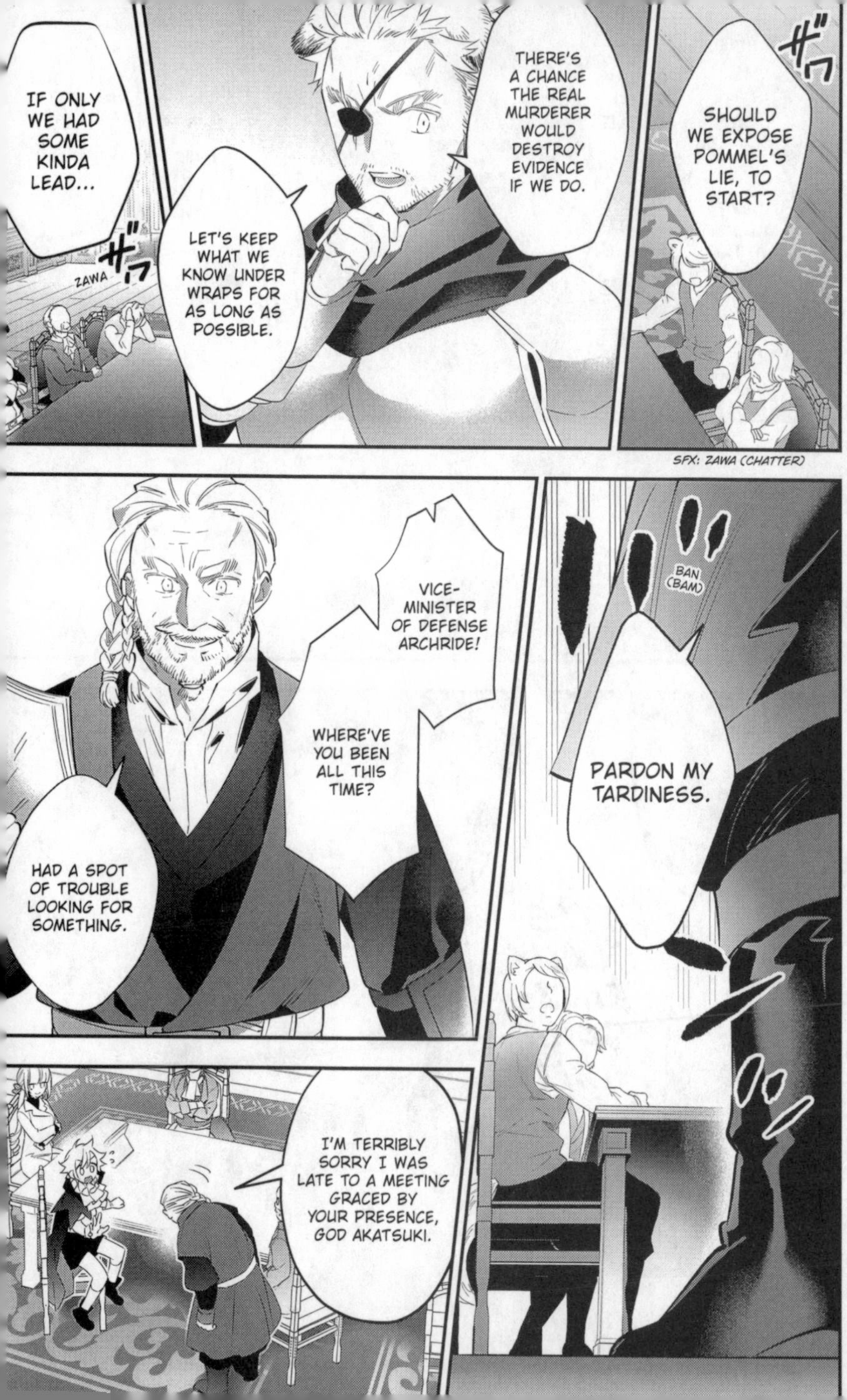
SHOULD WE EXPOSE POMMEL'S LIE, TO START?
THERE'S A CHANCE THE REAL MURDERER WOULD DESTROY EVIDENCE IF WE DO.
LET'S KEEP WHAT WE KNOW UNDER WRAPS FOR AS LONG AS POSSIBLE.
IF ONLY WE HAD SOME KINDA LEAD...
ZAWA
SFX: ZAWA (CHATTER)
BAN (BAM)
PARDON MY TARDINESS.
VICE-MINISTER OF DEFENSE ARCHRIDE!
WHERE'VE YOU BEEN ALL THIS TIME?
HAD A SPOT OF TROUBLE LOOKING FOR SOMETHING.
I'M TERRIBLY SORRY I WAS LATE TO A MEETING GRACED BY YOUR PRESENCE, GOD AKATSUKI.

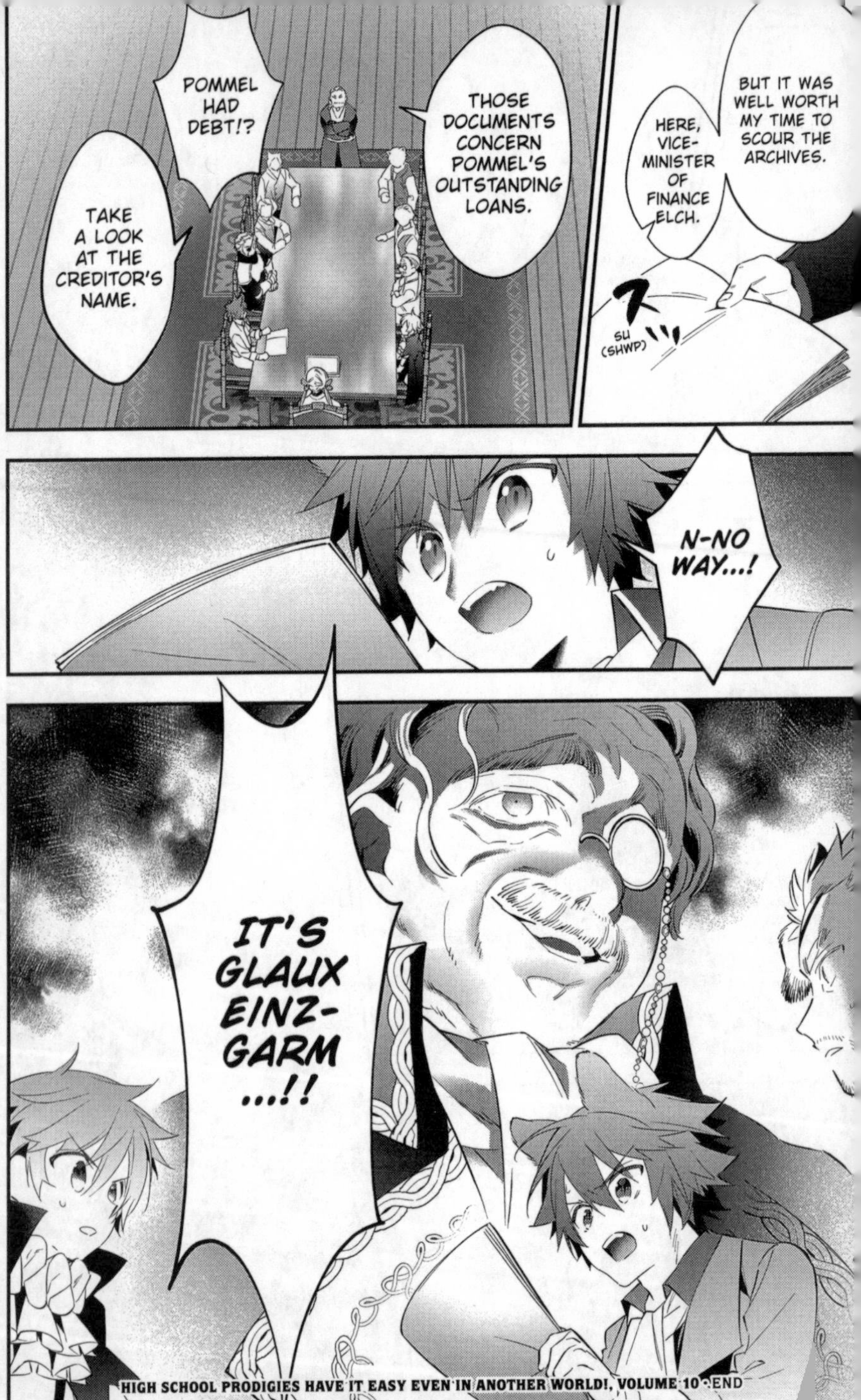
BUT IT WAS WELL WORTH MY TIME TO SCOUR THE ARCHIVES.
HERE, VICE-MINISTER OF FINANCE ELCH.
SU (SHWP)
THOSE DOCUMENTS CONCERN POMMEL'S OUTSTANDING LOANS.
POMMEL HAD DEBT!?
TAKE A LOOK AT THE CREDITOR'S NAME.
N-NO WAY...!
IT'S GLAUX EINZ-GARM...!!
HIGH SCHOOL PRODIGIES HAVE IT EASY EVEN IN ANOTHER WORLD!, VOLUME 10 • END

TRANSLATION NOTES

COMMON HONORIFICS

no honorific: Indicates familiarity or closeness; if used without permission or reason, addressing someone in this manner would constitute an insult.

-san: The Japanese equivalent of Mr./Mrs./Miss. If a situation calls for politeness, this is the fail-safe honorific.

-sama: Conveys great respect; may also indicate that the social status of the speaker is lower than the addressee's.

-kun: Used most often when referring to boys, this indicates affection or familiarity. Occasionally used by older men among their peers, but it may also be used by anyone referring to a person of lower standing.

-sensei: A respectful term for teachers, artists, or high-level professionals.

-dono: A respectful term typically equated with "lord" or "master," this honorific has an archaic spin to it when used in colloquial parlance.

Page 31
Aoi's technique is named after the **dragon robe**, an everyday garment worn by emperors and kings in China, Korea, and other parts of Asia. A similar robe was worn among nobility and the imperial court in Japan.

Page 35
While the actual name of this gate is Rashomon, this soldier is referring to a common architectural motif used in it when he calls it a **guardian gate**. Known as *nioumon* ("two kings gate" or "two devas gate") in Japanese, these gates have a statue of a mighty bodhisattva on either side, standing guard with the same ferocity that they use to protect the Buddha. The one on the right is known as Misshaku Kongou, whose mouth is shaped forming the sound *a*, the pronunciation of the first letter in the Sanskrit alphabet; the one on the left, Naraen Kongou, is making the sound *un*, which is the last letter. Together, they make *aun*, which symbolizes the birth and death of all things and all of creation, reinforcing the sense of strength and solidity of the gates they are part of.

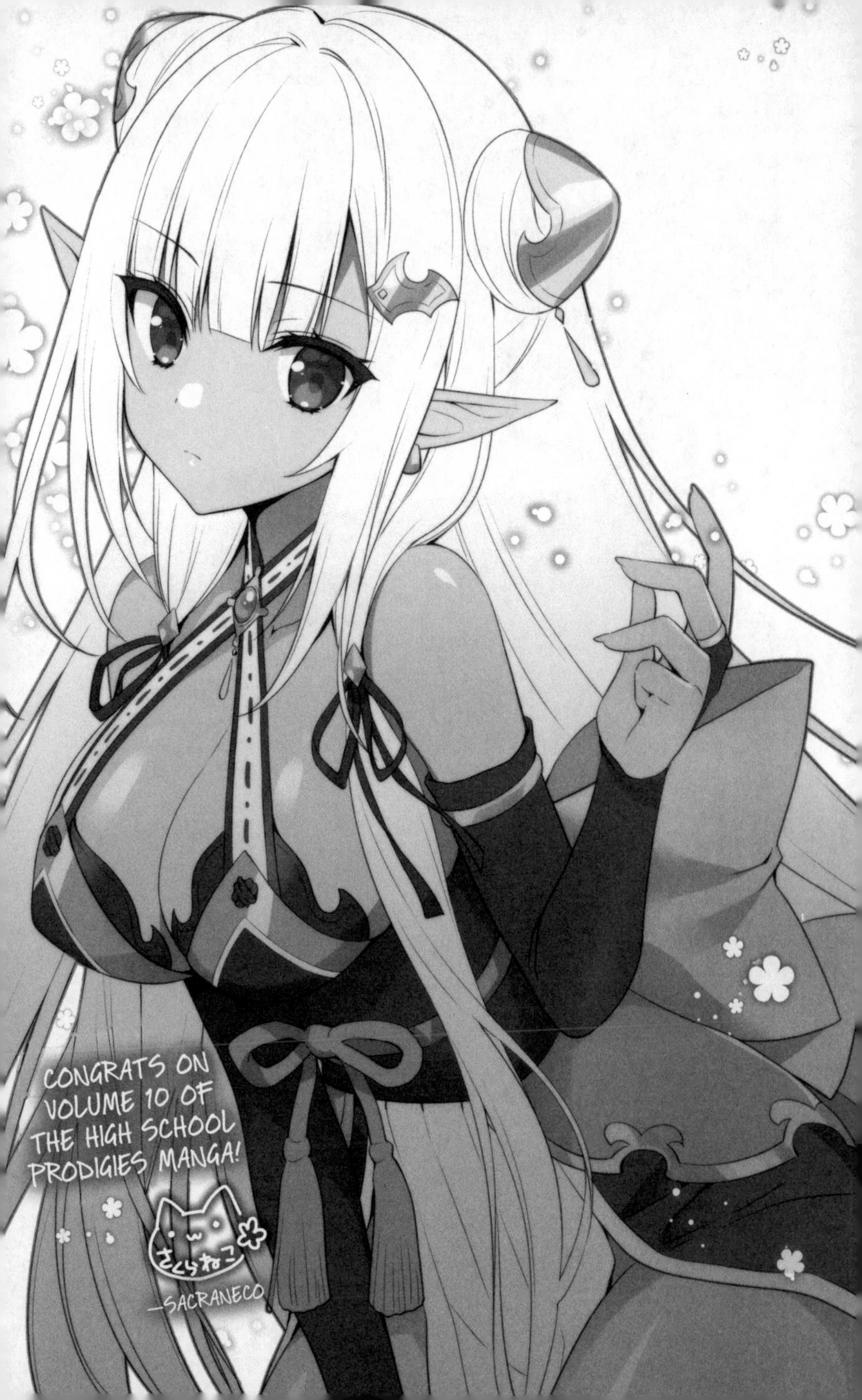
CONGRATS ON VOLUME 10 OF THE HIGH SCHOOL PRODIGIES MANGA!
さくらねこ
—SACRANECO

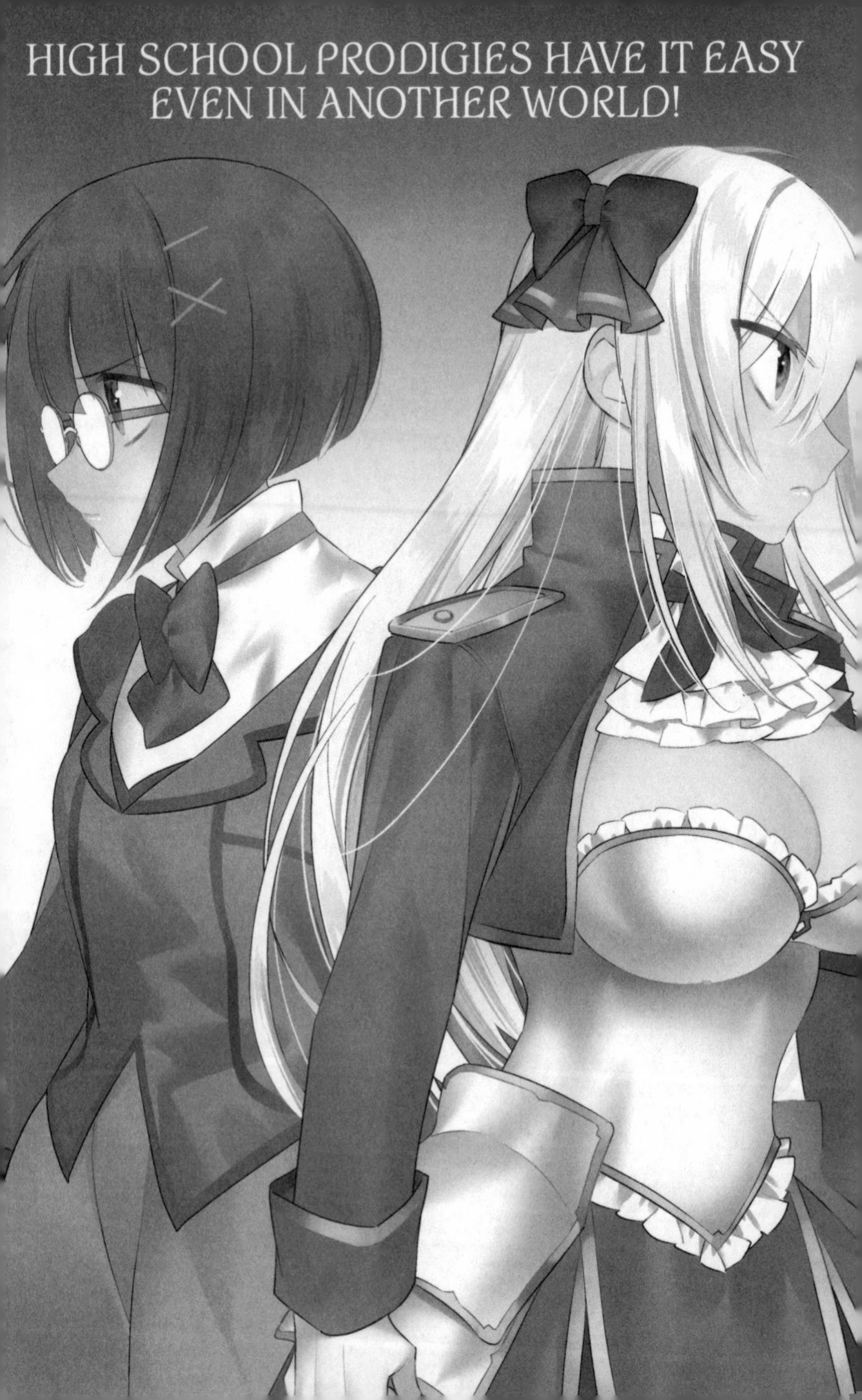
HIGH SCHOOL PRODIGIES HAVE IT EASY
EVEN IN ANOTHER WORLD!

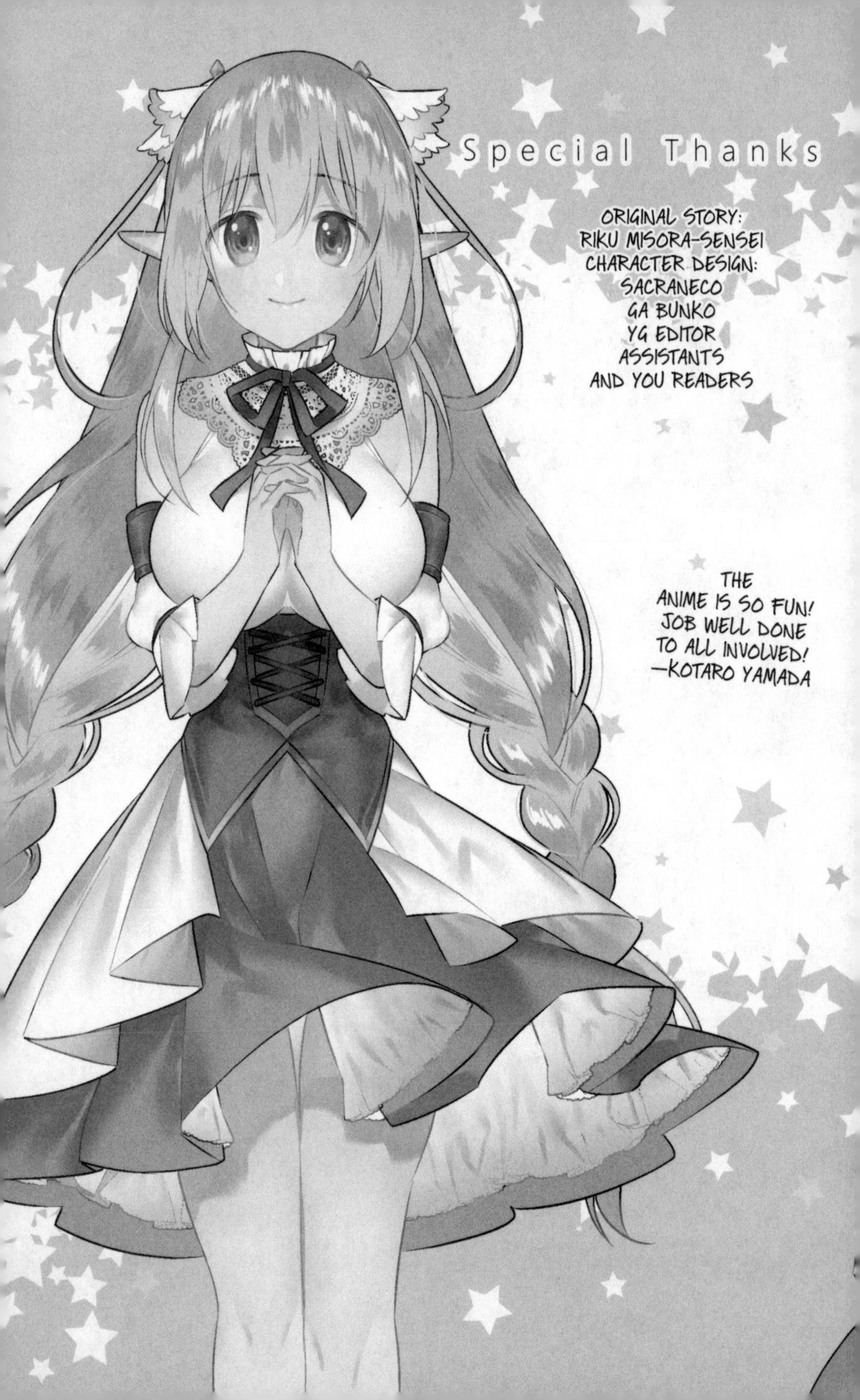
Special Thanks
ORIGINAL STORY:
RIKU MISORA-SENSEI
CHARACTER DESIGN:
SACRANECO
GA BUNKO
YG EDITOR
ASSISTANTS
AND YOU READERS
THE
ANIME IS SO FUN!
JOB WELL DONE
TO ALL INVOLVED!
—KOTARO YAMADA

NEXT VOLUME PREVIEW!

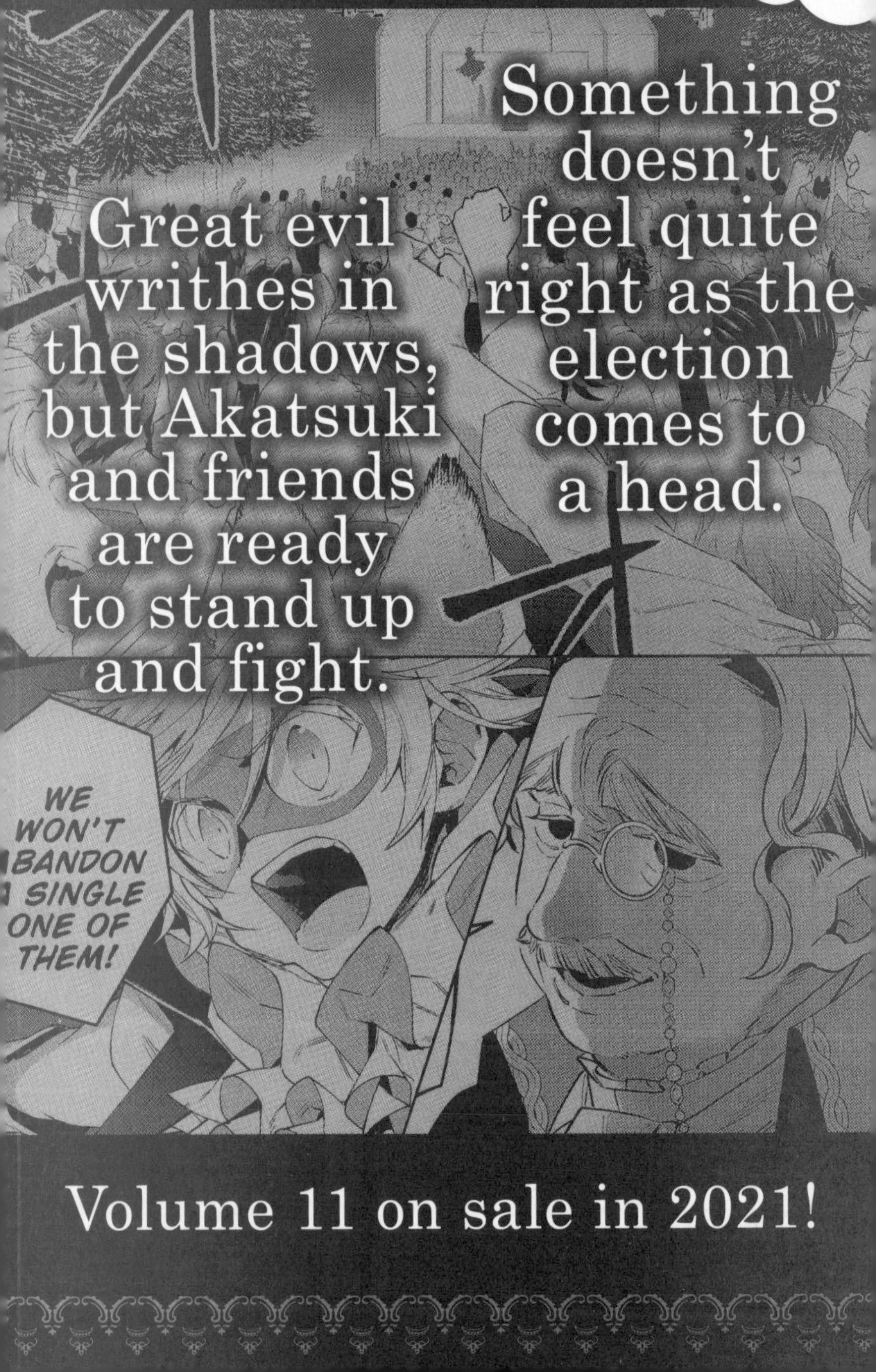
Something doesn't feel quite right as the election comes to a head.
Great evil writhes in the shadows, but Akatsuki and friends are ready to stand up and fight.
WE WON'T BANDON SINGLE ONE OF THEM!

Volume 11 on sale in 2021!